select material from

SURVEY OF
ACCOUNTING

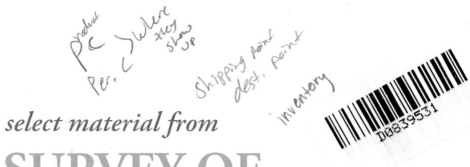

THIRD EDITION

Thomas P. Edmonds
University of Alabama–Birmingham

Frances M. McNair
Mississippi State University

Philip R. Olds
Virginia Commonwealth University

Bor-Yi Tsay
University of Alabama at Birmingham

A200: FOUNDATIONS OF ACCOUNTING

Mr. Rick Schrimper
Kelley School of Business
Indiana University

 Learning Solutions

Boston Burr Ridge, IL Dubuque, IA New York San Francisco St. Louis
Bangkok Bogotá Caracas Lisbon London Madrid
Mexico City Milan New Delhi Seoul Singapore Sydney Taipei Toronto

Select Material from
Survey of Accounting, Third Edition
A200: Foundations of Accounting
Mr. Rick Schrimper
Kelley School of Business
Indiana University

Copyright © 2012 by The McGraw-Hill Companies, Inc. All rights reserved. Printed in the United States of America. Except as permitted under the United States Copyright Act of 1976, no part of this publication may be reproduced or distributed in any form or by any means, or stored in a data base retrieval system, without prior written permission of the publisher.

This book is a McGraw-Hill Learning Solutions textbook and contains select material from *Survey of Accounting*, Third Edition by Thomas P. Edmonds, Frances M. McNair, Philip R. Olds, and Bor-Yi Tsay. Copyright © 2012 by The McGraw-Hill Companies, Inc. Reprinted with permission of the publisher. Many custom published texts are modified versions or adaptations of our best-selling textbooks. Some adaptations are printed in black and white to keep prices at a minimum, while others are in color.

1 2 3 4 5 6 7 8 9 0 QDB QDB 13 12 11

ISBN-13: 978-0-07-754697-7
ISBN-10: 0-07-754697-0

Learning Solutions Representative: Ann Hayes
Production Editor: Nichole Birkenholz
Printer/Binder: Quad/Graphics

Contents

Chapter 1   An Introduction to Accounting   2

Chapter 2   Understanding the Accounting Cycle   44

Chapter 3   Accounting for Merchandising Businesses   86

Chapter 4   Internal Controls, Accounting for Cash, and Ethics   124

Chapter 8 Proprietorships, Partnerships, and Corporations 286

Chapter 10 An Introduction to Managerial Accounting 358

Chapter 11 Cost Behavior, Operating Leverage, and Profitability Analysis 396

CHAPTER 1

An Introduction to Accounting

LEARNING OBJECTIVES

After you have mastered the material in this chapter, you will be able to:

1 Explain the role of accounting in society.

2 Construct an accounting equation using elements of financial statements terminology.

3 Record business events in general ledger accounts organized under an accounting equation.

4 Classify business events as asset source, use, or exchange transactions.

5 Use general ledger account information to prepare four financial statements.

6 Record business events using a horizontal financial statements model.

CHAPTER OPENING

Why should you study accounting? You should study accounting because it can help you succeed in business. Businesses use accounting to keep score. Imagine trying to play football without knowing how many points a touchdown is worth. Like sports, business is competitive. If you do not know how to keep score, you are not likely to succeed.

Accounting is an information system that reports on the economic activities and financial condition of a business or other organization. Do not underestimate the importance of accounting information. If you had information that enabled you to predict business success, you could become a very wealthy Wall Street investor. Communicating economic information is so important that accounting is frequently called the *language of business*.

The Curious Accountant

Who owns **Starbucks**? Who owns the **American Cancer Society** (ACS)? Many people and organizations other than owners are interested in the operations of Starbucks and the ACS. These parties are called *stakeholders*. Among others, they include lenders, employees, suppliers, customers, benefactors, research institutions, local governments, cancer patients, lawyers, bankers, financial analysts, and government agencies such as the Internal Revenue Service and the Securities and Exchange Commission. Organizations communicate information to stakeholders through *financial reports*.

How do you think the financial reports of Starbucks differ from those of the ACS? (Answer on page 11.)

ROLE OF ACCOUNTING IN SOCIETY

Explain the role of accounting in society.

How should society allocate its resources? Should we spend more to harvest food or cure disease? Should we build computers or cars? Should we invest money in IBM or General Motors? Accounting provides information that helps answer such questions.

Using Free Markets to Set Resource Priorities

Suppose you want to start a business. You may have heard "you have to have money to make money." In fact, you will need more than just money to start and operate a business. You will likely need such resources as equipment, land, materials, and employees. If you do not have these resources, how can you get them? In the United States, you compete for resources in open markets.

A **market** is a group of people or entities organized to exchange items of value. The market for business resources involves three distinct participants: consumers, conversion agents, and resource owners. *Consumers* use resources. Resources are frequently not in a form consumers want. For example, nature provides trees but consumers want furniture. *Conversion agents* (businesses) transform resources such as trees into desirable products such as furniture. *Resource owners* control the distribution of resources to conversion agents. Thus resource owners provide resources (inputs) to conversion agents who provide goods and services (outputs) to consumers.

For example, a home builder (conversion agent) transforms labor and materials (inputs) into houses (output) that consumers use. The transformation adds value to the inputs, creating outputs worth more than the sum of the inputs. A house that required

$220,000 of materials and labor to build could have a market value of $250,000.

Common terms for the added value created in the transformation process include **profit, income,** or **earnings.** Accountants measure the added value as the difference between the cost of a product or service and the selling price of that product or service. The profit on the house described above is $30,000, the difference between its $220,000 cost and $250,000 market value.

Conversion agents who successfully and efficiently (at low cost) satisfy consumer preferences are rewarded with high earnings. These earnings are shared with resource owners, so conversion agents who exhibit high earnings potential are more likely to compete successfully for resources.

Return to the original question. How can you get the resources you need to start a business? You must go to open markets and convince resource owners that you can produce profits. Exhibit 1.1 illustrates the market trilogy involved in resource allocation.

The specific resources businesses commonly use to satisfy consumer demand are financial resources, physical resources, and labor resources.

Financial Resources

Businesses (conversion agents) need **financial resources** (money) to get started and to operate. *Investors* and *creditors* provide financial resources.

■ **Investors** provide financial resources in exchange for ownership interests in businesses. Owners expect businesses to return to them a share of the business income earned.

■ **Creditors** lend financial resources to businesses. Instead of a share of business income, creditors expect businesses to repay borrowed resources at a future date.

The resources controlled by a business are called **assets.** If a business ceases to operate, its remaining assets are sold and the sale proceeds are returned to the investors and creditors through a process called business **liquidation.** Creditors have a priority claim on assets in business liquidations. After creditor claims are satisfied, any remaining assets are distributed to investors (owners).

EXHIBIT 1.1

Market Trilogy in Resource Allocation

To illustrate, suppose a business acquired $100 cash from investors and $200 cash from creditors. Assume the business lost $75 and returned the remaining $225 ($300 − $75) to the resource providers. The creditors would receive $200; the owners would receive only $25. If the business lost $120, the creditors would receive only $180 ($300 − $120); the investors would receive nothing.

As this illustration suggests, both creditors and investors can lose resources when businesses fail. Creditors, however, are in a more secure position because of their priority claim on resources. In exchange for their more secure position, creditors normally do not share business profits. Instead, they receive a fixed amount of money called **interest.**

Investors and creditors prefer to provide financial resources to businesses with high earnings potential because such companies are better able to share profits and make interest payments. Profitable businesses are also less likely to experience bankruptcy and liquidation.

Physical Resources

In their most primitive form, **physical resources** are natural resources. Physical resources often move through numerous stages of transformation. For example, standing timber may be successively transformed into harvested logs, raw lumber, and finished furniture. Owners of physical resources seek to sell those resources to businesses with high earnings potential because profitable businesses are able to pay higher prices and make repeat purchases.

Labor Resources

Labor resources include both intellectual and physical labor. Like other resource providers, workers prefer businesses that have high income potential because these businesses are able to pay higher wages and offer continued employment.

Accounting Provides Information

How do providers of financial, physical, and labor resources identify conversion agents (businesses) with high profit potential? Investors, creditors, and workers rely heavily on accounting information to evaluate which businesses are worthy of receiving resources. In addition, other people and organizations have an interest in accounting information about businesses. The many **users** of accounting information are commonly called **stakeholders.** Stakeholders include resource providers, financial analysts, brokers, attorneys, government regulators, and news reporters.

The link between conversion agents (businesses) and those stakeholders who provide resources is direct: businesses pay resource providers. Resource providers use accounting information to identify companies with high earnings potential because those companies are more likely to return higher profits, make interest payments, repay debt, pay higher prices, and provide stable employment.

The link between conversion agents and other stakeholders is indirect. Financial analysts, brokers, and attorneys may use accounting information when advising their clients. Government agencies may use accounting information to assess companies' compliance with income tax laws and other regulations. Reporters may use accounting information in news reports.

Types of Accounting Information

Stakeholders such as investors, creditors, lawyers, and financial analysts exist outside of and separate from the businesses in which they are interested. The accounting information these *external users* need is provided by **financial accounting.** In contrast, the accounting information needed by *internal users,* stakeholders such as managers and employees who work within a business, is provided by **managerial accounting.**

The information needs of external and internal users frequently overlap. For example, external and internal users are both interested in the amount of income a business earns. Managerial accounting information, however, is usually more detailed than financial accounting reports. Investors are concerned about the overall profitability of Wendy's versus Burger King; a Wendy's regional manager is interested in the profits of individual Wendy's restaurants. In fact, a regional manager is also interested in nonfinancial measures, such as the number of employees needed to operate a restaurant, the times at which customer demand is high versus low, and measures of cleanliness and customer satisfaction.

Nonbusiness Resource Usage

The U.S. economy is not *purely* market based. Factors other than profitability often influence resource allocation priorities. For example, governments allocate resources to national defense, to redistribute wealth, or to protect the environment. Foundations, religious groups, the Peace Corps, and other benevolent organizations prioritize resource usage based on humanitarian concerns.

Like profit-oriented businesses, civic or humanitarian organizations add value through resource transformation. For example, a soup kitchen adds value to uncooked meats and vegetables by converting them into prepared meals. The individuals who consume the meals, however, are unable to pay for the kitchen's operating costs, much less for the added value. The soup kitchen's motivation is to meet humanitarian needs, not to earn profits. Organizations that are not motivated by profit are called **not-for-profit entities** (also called *nonprofit* or *nonbusiness organizations*).

Stakeholders interested in nonprofit organizations also need accounting information. Accounting systems measure the cost of the goods and services not-for-profit organizations provide, the efficiency and effectiveness of the organizations' operations, and the ability of the organizations to continue to provide goods and services. This information serves a host of stakeholders, including taxpayers, contributors, lenders, suppliers, employees, managers, financial analysts, attorneys, and beneficiaries.

The focus of accounting, therefore, is to provide information useful to making decisions for a variety of business and nonbusiness user groups. The different types of accounting information and the stakeholders that commonly use the information are summarized in Exhibit 1.2.

EXHIBIT 1.2

Accounting as Information Provider

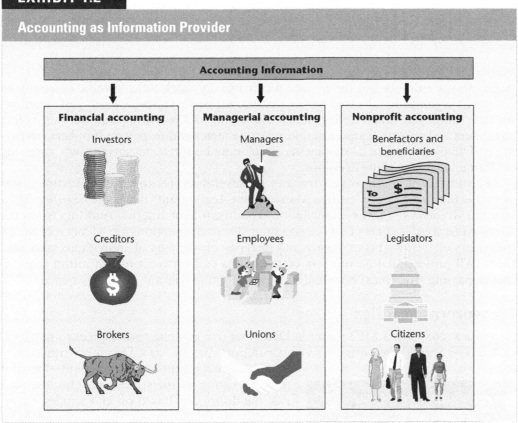

Careers in Accounting

An accounting career can take you to the top of the business world. *BusinessWeek* studied the backgrounds of the chief executive officers (CEOs) of the 1,000 largest public corporations. More CEOs had backgrounds in finance and accounting than any other field. Exhibit 1.3 provides additional detail regarding the career paths followed by these executives.

What do accountants do? Accountants identify, record, analyze, and communicate information about the economic events that affect organizations. They may work in either public accounting or private accounting.

Public Accounting

You are probably familiar with the acronym CPA. CPA stands for certified *public* accountant. Public accountants provide services to various clients. They are usually paid a fee that varies depending on the service provided. Services typically offered by public accountants include (1) audit services, (2) tax services, and (3) consulting services.

- *Audit services* involve examining a company's accounting records in order to issue an opinion about whether the company's financial statements conform to generally accepted accounting principles. The auditor's opinion adds credibility to the statements, which are prepared by the company's management.

- *Tax services* include both determining the amount of tax due and tax planning to help companies minimize tax expense.

- *Consulting services* cover a wide range of activities that includes everything from installing sophisticated computerized accounting systems to providing personal financial advice.

EXHIBIT 1.3

Career Paths of Chief Executive Officers

Finance and accounting
31%

Engineering and technical
22%

Other
20%

Marketing
27%

All public accountants are not certified. Each state government establishes certification requirements applicable in that state. Although the requirements vary from state to state, CPA candidates normally must have a college education, pass a demanding technical examination, and obtain work experience relevant to practicing public accounting.

Private Accounting

Accountants employed in the private sector usually work for a specific company or nonprofit organization. Private sector accountants perform a wide variety of functions for their employers. Their duties include classifying and recording transactions, billing customers and collecting amounts due, ordering merchandise, paying suppliers, preparing and analyzing financial statements, developing budgets, measuring costs, assessing performance, and making decisions.

Private accountants may earn any of several professional certifications. For example, the Institute of Certified Management Accountants issues the *Certified Management Accounting (CMA)* designation. The Institute of Internal Auditors issues the *Certified Internal Auditor (CIA)* designation. These designations are widely recognized indicators of technical competence and integrity on the part of individuals who hold them. All professional accounting certifications call for meeting education requirements, passing a technical examination, and obtaining relevant work experience.

Measurement Rules

Suppose a store sells a MP3 player in December to a customer who agrees to pay for it in January. Should the business *recognize* (report) the sale as a December transaction

or as a January transaction? It really does not matter as long as the storeowner discloses the rule the decision is based on and applies it consistently to other transactions. Because businesses may use different reporting rules, however, clear communication also requires full and fair disclosure of the accounting rules chosen.

Communicating business results would be simpler if each type of business activity were reported using only one measurement method. World economies and financial reporting practices, however, have not evolved uniformly. Even in highly sophisticated countries such as the United States, companies exhibit significant diversity in reporting methods. Providers of accounting reports assume that users are educated about accounting practices.

The **Financial Accounting Standards Board (FASB)**[1] is a privately funded organization with the primary authority for establishing accounting standards in the United States. The measurement rules established by the FASB are called **generally accepted accounting principles (GAAP).** Financial reports issued to the public must follow GAAP. This textbook introduces these principles so you will be able to understand business activity reported by companies in the USA.

Companies are not required to follow GAAP when preparing *management accounting* reports. Although there is considerable overlap between financial and managerial accounting, managers are free to construct internal reports in whatever fashion best suits the effective operation of their companies.

[1]The FASB consists of seven full-time members appointed by the supporting organization, the Financial Accounting Foundation (FAF). The FAF membership is intended to represent the broad spectrum of individuals and institutions that have an interest in accounting and financial reporting. FAF members include representatives of the accounting profession, industry, financial institutions, the government, and the investing public.

FOCUS ON **INTERNATIONAL ISSUES**

IS THERE GLOBAL GAAP?

As explained in this chapter, accounting is a measurement and communication discipline based on rules referred to as *generally accepted accounting principles (GAAP)*. The rules described in this text are based on GAAP used in the United States, but what rules do the rest of the world use? Is there a global GAAP, or does each country establish its own unique GAAP?

Not long ago each country developed its own unique GAAP. Global companies were required to prepare multiple sets of financial statements to satisfy each country's GAAP. The use of multiple accounting standards across the globe made comparing company performance difficult and expensive. To address the need for a common set of financial standards, the International Accounting Standards Committee was formed in 1973. The committee was reorganized as the **International Accounting Standards Board (IASB)** in 2001. The IASB issues **International Financial Reporting Standards (IFRS),** which are rapidly gaining support worldwide. In 2005, companies in the countries who were members of the European Union were required to use the IFRS as established by the IASB, which is headquartered in London. Today, over 100 countries require or permit companies to prepare their financial statements using IFRS.

As of 2009 most of the major economic countries had either switched from their local GAAP to IFRS, or had rules in place to make the switch by 2012. One notable exception is the United States, but even here, the Securities and Exchange Commission announced in 2008 that it was seriously considering adopting rules that would allow U.S. companies to use either GAAP or IFRS. Although not finalized when this book was being prepared, many accountants in the United States believe this will occur. Additionally, there is an active process in place to reduce the differences between IFRS and U.S. GAAP.

There are many similarities between the IASB and the FASB. Both the FASB and the IASB are required to include members with a variety of backgrounds, including auditors, users of financial information, academics, and so forth. Also, both groups primarily require that their members work full-time for their respective boards; they cannot serve on the board while being compensated by another organization. (The IASB does allow up to three of its members to be part-time.) Members of each board serve five-year terms, and can be reappointed once. The funds to support both boards, and the large organizations that support them are obtained from a variety of sources, including selling publications and private contributions. To help maintain independence of the boards' members, fundraising is performed by separate sets of trustees.

There are significant differences between the IASB and the FASB, and one of these relates to size and geographic diversity. The FASB has only seven members, all from the United States. The IASB has fourteen members, and these must include at least four from Asia, four from Europe, four from North America, one from Africa, and one from South America.

Not only is the structure of the standards-setting boards different but the standards and principles they establish may also differ significantly. In this chapter, you will learn that GAAP employs the *historical cost concept*. This means that the assets of most U.S. companies are shown on the balance sheet at the amount for which they were purchased. For example, land owned by U.S. Steel, Inc., that has a market value of millions of dollars may be shown on US Steel's financial statements with a value of only a few hundred thousand dollars. This occurs because GAAP requires US Steel to show the land at its cost rather than its market value. In contrast, IFRS permits companies to show market values on their financial statements. This means that the exact same assets may show radically different values if the statements are prepared under IFRS rather than GAAP.

Throughout this text, where appropriate, we will note the differences between U.S. GAAP and IFRS. However, by the time you graduate, it is likely that among the major industrialized nations, there will be a global GAAP.

Reporting Entities

Think of accountants as you would of news reporters. A news reporter gathers and discloses information about some person, place, or thing. Likewise, an accountant gathers and discloses financial information about specific people or businesses. The people or businesses accountants report on are called **reporting entities.** When studying accounting you should think of yourself as an accountant. Your first step is to identify the person or business on which you are reporting. This is not always as easy as it may seem. To illustrate, consider the following scenario.

Jason Winston recently started a business. During the first few days of operation, Mr. Winston transferred cash from his personal account into a business account for a company he named Winston Enterprises. Mr. Winston's brother, George, invested cash in Winston Enterprises for which he received an ownership interest in the company. Winston Enterprises borrowed cash from First Federal Bank. Winston Enterprises paid cash to purchase a building from Commercial Properties, Inc. Winston Enterprises earned cash revenues from its customers and paid its employees cash for salaries expense.

How many reporting entities are described in this scenario? Assuming all of the customers are counted as a single entity and all of the employees are counted as a single entity, there are a total of seven entities named in the scenario. These entities include: (1) Jason Winston, (2) Winston Enterprises (3) George Winston, (4) First Federal Bank, (5) Commercial Properties, Inc., (6) the customers, and (7) the employees. A separate set of accounting records would be maintained for each entity.

Your ability to learn accounting will be greatly influenced by how you approach the entity concept. Based on your everyday experiences you likely think from the perspective of a customer. In contrast, this text is written from the perspective of a business entity. These opposing perspectives dramatically affect how you view business events. For example, as a customer you consider a sales discount a great bargain. The view is different from the perspective of the business granting the discount. A sales discount means an item did not sell at the expected price. To move the item, the business had to accept less money than it originally planned to receive. From this perspective, a sales discount is not a good thing. To understand accounting, train yourself to interpret transactions from the perspective of a business rather than a consumer. Each time you encounter an accounting event ask yourself, how does this affect the business?

✓ CHECK YOURSELF 1.1

In a recent business transaction, land was exchanged for cash. Did the amount of cash increase or decrease?

Answer The answer depends on the reporting entity to which the question pertains. One entity sold land. The other entity bought land. For the entity that sold land, cash increased. For the entity that bought land, cash decreased.

ELEMENTS OF FINANCIAL STATEMENTS

LO 2

Construct an accounting equation using elements of financial statements terminology.

The individuals and organizations that need information about a business are called *stakeholders.* Stakeholders include owners, lenders, government agencies, employees, news reporters, and others. Businesses communicate information to stakeholders through four financial statements:[2] (1) an income statement, (2) a statement of changes in equity, (3) a balance sheet, and (4) a statement of cash flows.

The information reported in **financial statements** is organized into ten categories known as **elements.** Eight financial statement elements are discussed in this chapter: assets, liabilities, equity, contributed capital, revenue, expenses, distributions, and net income. The other two elements, gains and losses, are discussed in a later chapter. In practice, the business world uses various titles to identify several of the financial statement elements. For example, business people use net income, net *earnings,* and net *profit* interchangeably to describe the same element. Contributed capital may be called *common stock* and equity

[2]In practice these statements have alternate names. For example, the income statement may be called *results of operations* or *statement of earnings.* The balance sheet is sometimes called the *statement of financial position.* The statement of changes in equity might be called *statement of capital* or *statement of stockholders' equity.* Since the Financial Accounting Standards Board (FASB) called for the title *statement of cash flows,* companies do not use alternate names for that statement.

Answers to The Curious Accountant

Anyone who owns stock in Starbucks owns a part of the company. Starbucks has many owners. In contrast, nobody actually owns the American Cancer Society (ACS). The ACS has a board of directors that is responsible for overseeing its operations, but the board is not its owner.

Ultimately, the purpose of a business entity is to increase the wealth of its owners. To this end, it "spends money to make money." The expense that Starbucks incurs for advertising is a cost incurred in the hope that it will generate revenues when it sells coffee. The financial statements of a business show, among other things, whether and how the company made a profit during the current year. For example, Starbucks' income statements show how much revenue was generated from "company-owned retail" operations versus from "licensing operations."

The ACS is a not-for-profit entity. It operates to provide services to society at large, not to make a profit. It cannot increase the wealth of its owners, because it has no owners. When the ACS spends money to assist cancer patients, it does not spend this money in the expectation that it will generate revenues. The revenues of the ACS come from contributors who wish to support efforts related to fighting cancer. Because the ACS does not spend money to make money, it has no reason to prepare an *income statement* like that of Starbucks. The ACS's statement of activities shows how much revenue was received from "contributions" versus from "special events."

Not-for-profit entities do prepare financial statements that are similar in appearance to those of commercial enterprises. The financial statements of not-for-profit entities are called the *statement of financial position,* the *statement of activities,* and the *cash flow statement.*

may be called *stockholders' equity, owner's capital,* and *partners' equity.* Furthermore, the transfer of assets from a business to its owners may be called *distributions, withdrawals,* or *dividends.* Think of accounting as a language. Different terms can describe the same business event. Detailed definitions of the elements and their placement on financial statements will be discussed in the following sections of the chapter.

Using Accounts to Gather Information

Detailed information about the elements is maintained in records commonly called **accounts.** For example, information regarding the element *assets* may be organized in separate accounts for cash, equipment, buildings, land, and so forth. The types and number of accounts used by a business depends on the information needs of its stakeholders. Some businesses provide very detailed information; others report highly summarized information. The more detail desired, the greater number of accounts needed. Think of accounts like the notebooks students keep for their classes. Some students keep detailed notes about every class they take in a separate notebook. Other students keep only the key points for all of their classes in a single notebook. Similarly, some businesses use more accounts than other businesses.

Diversity also exists regarding the names used for various accounts. For example, employee pay may be called salaries, wages, commissions, and so forth. Do not become frustrated with the diversity of terms used in accounting. Remember, accounting is a language. The same word can have different meanings. Similarly, different words can be used to describe the same phenomenon. The more you study and use accounting, the more familiar it will become to you.

Accounting Equation

The resources that a business uses to produce earnings are called *assets.* Examples of assets include land, buildings, equipment, materials, and supplies. Assets result from historical events. For example, if a business owns a truck that it purchased in a past transaction, the truck is an asset of the business. A truck that a business *plans* to purchase in the future, however, is not an asset of that business, no matter how certain the future purchase might be.

The resource providers (creditors and investors) have potential **claims**[3] on the assets owned by a business. The relationship between the assets and the providers' claims is described by the **accounting equation:**

$$\text{Assets} = \text{Claims}$$

Creditor claims are called **liabilities** and investor claims are called **equity.** Substituting these terms into the accounting equation produces the following expanded form:

$$\overbrace{\text{Assets} = \text{Liabilities} + \text{Equity}}^{\text{Claims}}$$

Liabilities can also be viewed as future *obligations of the enterprise.* To settle the obligations, the business will probably either relinquish some of its assets (e.g., pay off its debts with cash), provide services to its creditors (e.g., work off its debts), or accept other obligations (e.g., trade short-term debt for long-term debt).

As indicated by the accounting equation, the amount of total assets is equal to the total of the liabilities plus the equity. To illustrate, assume that Hagan Company has assets of $500, liabilities of $200, and equity of $300. These amounts appear in the accounting equation as follows:

$$\overbrace{\text{Assets} = \text{Liabilities} + \text{Equity}}^{\text{Claims}}$$
$$\$500 = \$200 + \$300$$

The claims side of the accounting equation (liabilities plus equity) may also be viewed as listing the sources of the assets. For example, when a bank loans assets (money) to a business, it establishes a claim to have those assets returned at some future date. Liabilities can therefore be viewed as sources of assets.

Equity can also be viewed as a source of assets. In fact, equity represents two distinct sources of assets. First, businesses typically acquire assets from their owners (investors). Many businesses issue **common stock**[4] certificates as receipts to acknowledge assets received from owners. The owners of such businesses are often called **stockholders,** and the ownership interest in the business is called **stockholders' equity.**

Second, businesses usually obtain assets through their earnings activities (the business acquires assets by working for them). Assets a business has earned can either be distributed to the owners or kept in the business. The portion of assets that has been provided by earnings activities and not returned as dividends is called **retained earnings.** Since stockholders own the business, they are entitled to assets acquired through its earnings activities. Retained earnings is therefore a component of stockholders' equity. Further

---

[3]A claim is a legal action to obtain money, property, or the enforcement of a right against another party.

[4]This presentation assumes the business is organized as a corporation. Other forms of business organization include proprietorships and partnerships. The treatment of equity for these types of businesses is slightly different from that of corporations. A detailed discussion of the differences is included in a later chapter of the text.

expansion of the accounting equation can show the three sources of assets (liabilities, common stock, and retained earnings):

$$\text{Assets} = \text{Liabilities} + \underbrace{\text{Common stock} + \text{Retained earnings}}_{\text{Stockholders' equity}}$$

✓ CHECK YOURSELF 1.2

Gupta Company has $250,000 of assets, $60,000 of liabilities, and $90,000 of common stock. What percentage of the assets was provided by retained earnings?

Answer First, using algebra, determine the dollar amount of retained earnings:

Assets = Liabilities + Common stock + Retained earnings
Retained earnings = Assets − Liabilities − Common stock
Retained earnings = $250,000 − $60,000 − $90,000
Retained earnings = $100,000

Second, determine the percentage:

Percentage of assets provided by retained earnings = Retained earnings/Total assets
Percentage of assets provided by retained earnings = $100,000/$250,000 = 40%

RECORDING BUSINESS EVENTS UNDER THE ACCOUNTING EQUATION

An **accounting event** is an economic occurrence that changes an enterprise's assets, liabilities, or stockholders' equity. A **transaction** is a particular kind of event that involves transferring something of value between two entities. Examples of transactions include acquiring assets from owners, borrowing money from creditors, and purchasing or selling goods and services. The following section of the text explains how several different types of accounting events affect a company's accounting equation.

Record business events in general ledger accounts organized under an accounting equation.

Asset Source Transactions

As previously mentioned, businesses obtain assets (resources) from three sources. They acquire assets from owners (stockholders); they borrow assets from creditors; and they earn assets through profitable operations. Asset source transactions increase total assets and total claims. A more detailed discussion of the effects of asset source transactions is provided below:

EVENT 1 **Rustic Camp Sites (RCS) was formed on January 1, 2012, when it acquired $120,000 cash from issuing common stock.**

When RCS issued stock, it received cash and gave each investor (owner) a stock certificate as a receipt. Since this transaction provided $120,000 of assets (cash) to the business, it is an **asset source transaction.** It increases the business's assets (cash) and its stockholders' equity (common stock).

	Assets		=	Liab.	+	Stockholders' Equity	
	Cash	+ Land	=	N. Pay.	+	Com. Stk.	+ Ret. Earn.
Acquired cash through stock issue	120,000	+ NA	=	NA	+	120,000	+ NA

Notice the elements have been divided into accounts. For example, the element *assets* is divided into a Cash account and a Land account. Do not be concerned if some of these account titles are unfamiliar. They will be explained as new transactions are presented. Recall that the number of accounts a company uses depends on the nature of its business and the level of detail management needs to operate the business. For example, Sears would have an account called Cost of Goods Sold although GEICO Insurance would not. Why? Because Sears sells goods (merchandise) but GEICO does not.

Also, notice that a stock issue transaction affects the accounting equation in two places, both under an asset (cash) and also under the source of that asset (common stock). All transactions affect the accounting equation in at least two places. It is from this practice that the **double-entry bookkeeping** system derives its name.

EVENT 2   RCS acquired an additional $400,000 of cash by borrowing from a creditor.

This transaction is also an asset source transaction. It increases assets (cash) and liability claims (notes payable). The account title Notes Payable is used because the borrower (RCS) is required to issue a promissory note to the creditor (a bank). A promissory note describes, among other things, the amount of interest RCS will pay and for how long it will borrow the money.[5] The effect of the borrowing transaction on the accounting equation is indicated below.

	Assets			=	Liab.	+	Stockholders' Equity		
	Cash	+	Land	=	N. Pay.	+	Com. Stk.	+	Ret. Earn.
Beginning balances	120,000	+	NA	=	NA	+	120,000	+	NA
Acquired cash by issuing note	400,000	+	NA	=	400,000	+	NA	+	NA
Ending balances	520,000	+	NA	=	400,000	+	120,000	+	NA

The beginning balances above came from the ending balances produced by the prior transaction. This practice is followed throughout the illustration.

Asset Exchange Transactions

Businesses frequently trade one asset for another asset. In such cases, the amount of one asset decreases and the amount of the other asset increases. Total assets are unaffected by asset exchange transactions. Event 3 is an asset exchange transaction.

EVENT 3   RCS paid $500,000 cash to purchase land.

This asset exchange transaction reduces the asset account Cash and increases the asset account Land. The amount of total assets is not affected. An **asset exchange transaction** simply reflects changes in the composition of assets. In this case, the company traded cash for land. The amount of cash decreased by $500,000 and the amount of land increased by the same amount.

	Assets			=	Liab.	+	Stockholders' Equity		
	Cash	+	Land	=	N. Pay.	+	Com. Stk.	+	Ret. Earn.
Beginning balances	520,000	+	NA	=	400,000	+	120,000	+	NA
Paid cash to buy land	(500,000)	+	500,000	=	NA	+	NA	+	NA
Ending balances	20,000	+	500,000	=	400,000	+	120,000	+	NA

[5]For simplicity, the effects of interest are ignored in this chapter. We discuss accounting for interest in future chapters.

Another Asset Source Transaction

EVENT 4 RCS obtained $85,000 cash by leasing camp sites to customers.

Revenue represents an economic benefit a company obtains by providing customers with goods and services. In this example the economic benefit is an increase in the asset cash. Revenue transactions can therefore be viewed as *asset source transactions*. The asset increase is balanced by an increase in the retained earnings section of stockholders' equity because producing revenue increases the amount of earnings that can be retained in the business.

	Assets			=	Liab.	+	Stockholders' Equity			
	Cash	+	Land	=	N. Pay.	+	Com. Stk.	+	Ret. Earn.	Acct. Title
Beginning balances	20,000	+	500,000	=	400,000	+	120,000	+	NA	
Acquired cash by earning revenue	85,000	+	NA	=	NA	+	NA	+	85,000	Revenue
Ending balances	105,000	+	500,000	=	400,000	+	120,000	+	85,000	

Note carefully that the $85,000 ending balance in the retained earnings column is *not* in the Retained Earnings account. It is in the Revenue account. It will be transferred to the Retained Earnings account at the end of the accounting period. Transferring the Revenue account balance to the Retained Earnings account is part of a process called *closing the accounts*.

Asset Use Transactions

Businesses use assets for a variety of purposes. For example, assets may be used to pay off liabilities or they may be transferred to owners. Assets may also be used in the process of generating earnings. All **asset use transactions** decrease the total amount of assets and the total amount of claims on assets (liabilities or stockholders' equity).

EVENT 5 RCS paid $50,000 cash for operating expenses such as salaries, rent, and interest. (RCS could establish a separate account for each type of expense. However, the management team does not currently desire this level of detail. Remember, the number of accounts a business uses depends on the level of information managers need to make decisions.)

In the normal course of generating revenue, a business consumes various assets and services. The assets and services consumed to generate revenue are called **expenses.** Revenue results from providing goods and services to customers. In exchange, the business acquires assets from its customers. Since the owners bear the ultimate risk and reap the rewards of operating the business, revenues increase stockholders' equity (retained earnings), and expenses decrease retained earnings. In this case, the asset account, Cash, decreased. This decrease is balanced by a decrease in the retained earnings section of stockholders' equity because expenses decrease the amount of earnings retained in the business.

	Assets			=	Liab.	+	Stockholders' Equity			
	Cash	+	Land	=	N. Pay.	+	Com. Stk.	+	Ret. Earn.	Acct. Title
Beginning balances	105,000	+	500,000	=	400,000	+	120,000	+	85,000	
Used cash to pay expenses	(50,000)	+	NA	=	NA	+	NA	+	(50,000)	Expense
Ending balances	55,000	+	500,000	=	400,000	+	120,000	+	35,000	

Like revenues, expenses are not recorded directly into the Retained Earnings account. The $50,000 of expense is recorded in the Expense account. It will be transferred to the Retained Earnings account at the end of the accounting period as part of the closing process. The $35,000 ending balance in the retained earnings column shows what would be in the Retained Earnings account after the balances in the Revenue and Expense accounts have been closed. The current balance in the Retained Earnings account is zero.

EVENT 6   RCS paid $4,000 in cash dividends to its owners.

To this point the enterprise's total assets and equity have increased by $35,000 ($85,000 of revenue − $50,000 of expense) as a result of its earnings activities. RCS can keep the additional assets in the business or transfer them to the owners. If a business transfers some or all of its earned assets to owners, the transfer is frequently called a **dividend.** Since assets distributed to stockholders are not used for the purpose of generating revenue, *dividends are not expenses.* Furthermore, dividends are a transfer of *earnings,* not a return of the assets acquired from the issue of common stock.

	Assets			=	Liab.	+			Stockholders' Equity			
	Cash	+	Land	=	N. Pay.	+	Com. Stk.	+	Ret. Earn.		Acct. Title
Beginning balances	55,000	+	500,000	=	400,000	+	120,000	+	35,000		
Used cash to pay dividends	(4,000)	+	NA	=	NA	+	NA	+	(4,000)		Dividends
Ending balances	51,000	+	500,000	=	400,000	+	120,000	+	31,000		

Like revenues and expenses, dividends are not recorded directly into the Retained Earnings account. The $4,000 dividend is recorded in the Dividends account. It will be transferred to retained earnings at the end of the accounting period as part of the closing process. The $31,000 ending balance in the retained earnings column shows what would be in the Retained Earnings account after the balances in the Revenue, Expense, and Dividend accounts have been closed. The current balance in the Retained Earnings account is zero.

EVENT 7   The land that RCS paid $500,000 to purchase had an appraised market value of $525,000 on December 31, 2012.

Although the appraised value of the land is higher than the original cost, RCS will not increase the amount recorded in its accounting records above the land's $500,000 historical cost. In general, accountants do not recognize changes in market value. The **historical cost concept** requires that most assets be reported at the amount paid for them (their historical cost) regardless of increases in market value.

Surely investors would rather know what an asset is worth instead of how much it originally cost. So why do accountants maintain records and report financial information based on historical cost? Accountants rely heavily on the **reliability concept.** Information is reliable if it can be independently verified. For example, two people looking at the legal documents associated with RCS's land purchase will both conclude that RCS paid $500,000 for the land. That historical cost is a verifiable fact. The appraised value, in contrast, is an opinion. Even two persons who are experienced appraisers are not likely to come up with the same amount for the land's market value. Accountants do not report market values in financial statements because such values are not reliable.

Accountants recognize the conflict between *relevance* and *reliability.* As a result, there are exceptions to the application of the historical cost rule. When market value can be clearly established, GAAP not only permits but requires its use. For example, securities that are traded on the New York Stock Exchange must be shown at market value rather than historical cost. We will discuss other notable exceptions to the historical cost principle later in the text. However, as a general rule you should assume that assets shown in a company's financial statements are valued at historical cost.

EXHIBIT 1.4

Accounting Events

1.	RCS issued common stock, acquiring $120,000 cash from its owners.
2.	RCS borrowed $400,000 cash.
3.	RCS paid $500,000 cash to purchase land.
4.	RCS received $85,000 cash from earning revenue.
5.	RCS paid $50,000 cash for expenses.
6.	RCS paid dividends of $4,000 cash to the owners.
7.	The land that RCS paid $500,000 to purchase had an appraised market value of $525,000 on December 31, 2012.

General Ledger Accounts Organized Under the Accounting Equation

Event No.	Assets			=	Liabilities	+	Stockholders' Equity			Other Account Titles
	Cash	+	Land	=	Not es Payable	+	Common Stock	+	Retained Earnings	
Beg. bal.	0		0		0		0		0	
1.	120,000						120,000			
2.	400,000				400,000					
3.	(500,000)		500,000							
4.	85,000								85,000	Revenue
5.	(50,000)								(50,000)	Expense
6.	(4,000)								(4,000)	Dividend
7.	NA		NA		NA		NA		NA	
	51,000	+	500,000	=	400,000	+	120,000	+	31,000	

Summary of Transactions

The complete collection of a company's accounts is called the **general ledger.** A summary of the accounting events and the general ledger account information for RCS's 2012 accounting period is shown in Exhibit 1.4. The revenue, expense, and dividend account data appear in the retained earnings column. These account titles are shown immediately to the right of the dollar amounts listed in the retained earnings column.

RECAP: TYPES OF TRANSACTIONS

The transactions described above have each been classified into one of three categories: (1) asset source transactions; (2) asset exchange transactions; and (3) asset use transactions. A fourth category, claims exchange transactions, is introduced in a later chapter. In summary

Classify business events as asset source, use, or exchange transactions.

■ *Asset source transactions* increase the total amount of assets and increase the total amount of claims. In its first year of operation, RCS acquired assets from three sources: first, from owners (Event 1); next, by borrowing (Event 2); and finally, through earnings activities (Event 4).

■ *Asset exchange transactions* decrease one asset and increase another asset. The total amount of assets is unchanged by asset exchange transactions. RCS experienced one asset exchange transaction; it used cash to purchase land (Event 3).

■ *Asset use transactions* decrease the total amount of assets and the total amount of claims. RCS used assets to pay expenses (Event 5) and to pay dividends (Event 6).

As you proceed through this text, practice classifying transactions into one of the four categories. Businesses engage in thousands of transactions every day. It is far more effective to learn how to classify the transactions into meaningful categories than to attempt to memorize the effects of thousands of transactions.

PREPARING FINANCIAL STATEMENTS

LO 5

Use general ledger account information to prepare four financial statements.

As indicated earlier, accounting information is normally presented to external users in four general-purpose financial statements. The information in the ledger accounts is used to prepare these financial statements. The data in the ledger accounts in Exhibit 1.4 are color coded to help you understand the source of information in the financial statements. The numbers in *green* are used in the *statement of cash flows.* The numbers in *red* are used to prepare the *balance sheet.* Finally, the numbers in *blue* are used to prepare the *income statement.* The numbers reported in the statement of changes in stockholders' equity have not been color coded because they appear in more than one statement. The next section explains how the information in the accounts is presented in financial statements.

The financial statements for RCS are shown in Exhibit 1.5. The information used to prepare these statements was drawn from the ledger accounts. Information in one statement may relate to information in another statement. For example, the amount of net income reported on the income statement also appears on the statement of changes in stockholders' equity. Accountants use the term **articulation** to describe the interrelationships among the various elements of the financial statements. The key articulated relationships in RCS's financial statements are highlighted with arrows (Exhibit 1.5). A description of each statement follows.

Income Statement and the Matching Concept

A business must make sacrifices in order to obtain benefits. For example, RCS must sacrifice cash to pay for employee salaries, rent, and interest. In turn, RCS receives a benefit when it collects cash from its customers. As this example implies, sacrifices are defined as decreases in assets; and benefits are increases in assets. In accounting terms sacrifices are called expenses; and benefits are called revenues. *Therefore, expenses are decreases in assets; and revenues are increases in assets.*[6]

The **income statement** matches the expenses with the revenues that occur when operating a business. If revenues exceed expenses, the difference is called **net income.** If expenses are greater than revenues, the difference is called **net loss.** The practice of pairing revenues with expenses on the income statement is called the **matching concept.**

The income statement in Exhibit 1.5 indicates that RCS has earned more assets than it has used. The statement shows that RCS has increased its assets by $35,000 (net income) as a result of operating its business. Observe the phrase *For the Year Ended December 31, 2012,* in the heading of the income statement. Income is measured for a span of time called the **accounting period.** While accounting periods of one year are normal for external financial reporting, income can be measured weekly, monthly, quarterly, semiannually, or over any other desired time period. Notice that the cash RCS paid to its stockholders (dividends) is not reported as expense. The decrease in assets for dividend payments is not incurred for the purpose of generating revenue. Instead, dividends are transfers of wealth to the owners of the business. Dividend payments are not reported on the income statement.

---

[6]The definitions for revenue and expense is expanded in subsequent chapters as additional relationships among the elements of financial statements are introduced.

EXHIBIT 1.5	Financial Statements

RUSTIC CAMP SITES
Income Statement
For the Year Ended December 31, 2012

Rental revenue (*asset increases*)	$ 85,000
Operating expenses (*asset decreases*)	(50,000)
Net income	$ 35,000

RUSTIC CAMP SITES
Statement of Changes in Stockholders' Equity
For the Year Ended December 31, 2012

Beginning common stock	$ 0	
Plus: common stock issued	120,000	
Ending common stock		$120,000
Beginning retained earnings	0	
Plus: Net income	35,000	
Less: Dividends	(4,000)	
Ending retained earnings		31,000
Total stockholders' equity		$151,000

RUSTIC CAMP SITES
Balance Sheet
As of December 31, 2012

Assets		
Cash	$ 51,000	
Land	500,000	
Total assets		$551,000
Liabilities		
Notes payable		$400,000
Stockholders' equity		
Common stock	$120,000	
Retained earnings	31,000	
Total stockholders' equity		151,000
Total liabilities and stockholders' equity		$551,000

RUSTIC CAMP SITES
Statement of Cash Flows
For the Year Ended December 31, 2012

Cash flows from operating activities:		
Cash receipts from revenue	$ 85,000	
Cash payments for expenses	(50,000)	
Net cash flow from operating activities		$ 35,000
Cash flows for investing activities:		
Cash payments to purchase land		(500,000)
Cash flows from financing activities:		
Cash receipts from borrowing funds	400,000	
Cash receipts from issuing common stock	120,000	
Cash payments for dividends	(4,000)	
Net cash flow from financing activities		516,000
Net increase in cash		51,000
Plus: beginning cash balance		0
Ending cash balance		$ 51,000

✓ CHECK YOURSELF 1.3

Mahoney, Inc., was started when it issued common stock to its owners for $300,000. During its first year of operation Mahoney received $523,000 cash for services provided to customers. Mahoney paid employees $233,000 cash. Advertising costs paid in cash amounted to $102,000. Other cash operating expenses amounted to $124,000. Finally, Mahoney paid a $25,000 cash dividend to its stockholders. What amount of net income would Mahoney's report on its earnings statement?

Answer   The amount of net income is $64,000 ($523,000 Revenue − $233,000 Salary Expense − $102,000 Advertising Expense − $124,000 Other Operating Expenses). The cash received from issuing stock is not revenue because it was not acquired from earnings activities. In other words, Mahoney did not work (perform services) for this money; it was contributed by owners of the business. The dividends are not expenses because the decrease in cash was not incurred for the purpose of generating revenue. Instead, the dividends represent a transfer of wealth to the owners.

Statement of Changes in Stockholders' Equity

The **statement of changes in stockholders' equity** explains the effects of transactions on stockholders' equity during the accounting period. It starts with the beginning balance in the common stock account. In the case of RCS, the beginning balance in the common stock account is zero because the company did not exist before the 2012 accounting period. The $120,000 of stock issued during the accounting period is added to the beginning balance to determine the ending balance in the common stock account.

In addition to reporting the changes in common stock, the statement describes the changes in retained earnings for the accounting period. RCS had no beginning balance in retained earnings. During the period, the company earned $35,000 and paid $4,000 in dividends to the stockholders, producing an ending retained earnings balance of $31,000 ($0 + $35,000 − $4,000). Since equity consists of common stock and retained earnings, the ending total equity balance is $151,000 ($120,000 + $31,000). This statement is also dated with the phrase *For the Year Ended December 31, 2012,* because it describes what happened to stockholders' equity during 2012.

Balance Sheet

The **balance sheet** draws its name from the accounting equation. Total assets balances with (equals) claims (liabilities and stockholders' equity) on those assets. The balance sheet for RCS is shown in Exhibit 1.5. Note that total claims (liabilities plus stockholders' equity) are equal to total assets ($551,000 = $551,000).

At this point we take a closer look at the term *assets*. Previously, we have defined assets as the resources a company uses to produce revenues. More precisely, the assets shown on a balance sheet represent the resources that a company plans to use *in the future* to generate revenues. In contrast, expenses represent the assets that have been used in the current period to generate revenues in the current period. In summary, businesses use resources to produce revenue. The resources that *have been sacrificed* to produce revenues in the current period are expenses. The resources that *will be sacrificed* in the future to produce future revenues are called assets.

Note the order of the assets in the balance sheet. Cash appears first, followed by land. Assets are displayed in the balance sheet based on their level of **liquidity.** This means that assets are listed in order of how rapidly they will be converted to cash. Finally, note that the balance sheet is dated with the phrase *As of December 31, 2012,* indicating that it describes the company's financial condition on the last day of the accounting period.

✓ CHECK YOURSELF 1.4

To gain a clear understanding of the balance sheet, try to create one that describes your personal financial condition. First list your assets, then your liabilities. Determine the amount of your equity by subtracting your liabilities from your assets.

Answer Answers for this exercise will vary depending on the particular assets and liabilities each student identifies. Common student assets include automobiles, computers, stereos, TVs, phones, MP3 players, clothes, and textbooks. Common student liabilities include car loans, mortgages, student loans, and credit card debt. The difference between the assets and the liabilities is the equity.

Statement of Cash Flows

The **statement of cash flows** explains how a company obtained and used *cash* during the accounting period. Receipts of cash are called *cash inflows,* and payments are *cash outflows.* The statement classifies cash receipts (inflows) and payments (outflows) into three categories: financing activities, investing activities, and operating activities.

Businesses normally start with an idea. Implementing the idea usually requires cash. For example, suppose you decide to start an apartment rental business. First, you would need cash to buy the apartments. Acquiring cash to start a business is a financing activity. **Financing activities** include obtaining cash (inflow) from owners or paying cash (outflow) to owners (dividends). Financing activities also include borrowing cash (inflow) from creditors and repaying the principal (outflow) to creditors. Because interest on borrowed money is an expense, however, cash paid to creditors for interest is reported in the operating activities section of the statement of cash flows.

After obtaining cash from financing activities, you would invest the money by building or buying apartments. **Investing activities** involve paying cash (outflow) to purchase long-term assets or receiving cash (inflow) from selling long-term assets. Long-term assets are normally used for more than one year. Cash outflows to purchase land or cash inflows from selling a building are examples of investing activities.

After investing in the productive assets (apartments), you would engage in operating activities. **Operating activities** involve receiving cash (inflow) from revenue and paying cash (outflow) for expenses. Note that cash spent to purchase short-term assets such as office supplies is reported in the operating activities section because the office supplies would likely be used (expensed) within a single accounting period.

The primary cash inflows and outflows related to the types of business activity introduced in this chapter are summarized in Exhibit 1.6. The exhibit will be expanded as additional types of events are introduced in subsequent chapters.

The statement of cash flows for Rustic Camp Sites in Exhibit 1.5 shows that the amount of cash increased by $51,000 during the year. The beginning balance in the Cash account was zero; adding the $51,000 increase to the beginning balance results in a $51,000 ending balance. Notice that the $51,000 ending cash balance on the statement of cash flows is the same as the amount of cash reported in the asset section on the December 31 year-end balance sheet. Also, note that the statement of cash flows is dated with the phrase *For the Year Ended December 31, 2012,* because it describes what happened to cash over the span of the year.

EXHIBIT 1.6

Classification Scheme for Statement of Cash Flows

Cash flows from operating activities:
Cash receipts (inflows) from customers
Cash payments (outflows) to suppliers

Cash flows from investing activities:
Cash receipts (inflows) from the sale of long-term assets
Cash payments (outflows) for the purchase of long-term assets

Cash flows from financing activities:
Cash receipts (inflows) from borrowing funds
Cash receipts (inflows) from issuing common stock
Cash payments (outflows) to repay borrowed funds
Cash payments (outflows) for dividends

✓ CHECK YOURSELF 1.5

Classify each of the following cash flows as an operating activity, investing activity, or financing activity.

1. Acquired cash from owners.
2. Borrowed cash from creditors.
3. Paid cash to purchase land.
4. Earned cash revenue.
5. Paid cash for salary expenses.
6. Paid cash dividend.
7. Paid cash for interest.

Answer   (1) financing activity; (2) financing activity; (3) investing activity; (4) operating activity; (5) operating activity; (6) financing activity; (7) operating activity.

The Closing Process

As previously indicated transaction data are recorded in the Revenue, Expense, and Dividend accounts during the accounting period. At the end of the accounting period the data in theses accounts is transferred to the Retained Earnings account. The process of transferring the balances is called **closing.** Since the Revenue, Expense, and Dividend accounts are closed each period, they are called **temporary accounts.** At the beginning of each new accounting period, the temporary accounts have zero balances. The Retained Earnings account carries forward from one accounting period to the next. Since this account is not closed, it is called a **permanent account.**

Since RCS started operations on January 1, 2012, the beginning Retained Earnings account balance was zero. In other words, there were no previous earnings available to be retained by the business. During 2012, amounts were recorded in the Revenue, Expense, and Dividend accounts. Since the Retained Earnings account is separate from the Revenue, Expense, and Dividend accounts, the entries in these temporary accounts did not affect the Retained Earnings balance. Specifically, the *before closing* balance in the Retained Earnings account on December 31, 2012, is still zero. In contrast, the Revenue account has a balance of $85,000; the Expense account has a balance of $50,000; and the Dividends account has a balance of $4,000. The closing process transfers the balances in the Revenue, Expense, and Dividend accounts to the Retained Earnings account. Therefore, *after closing* the balance in the Retained Earnings account is $31,000 ($85,000 − $50,000 − $4,000) and the Revenue, Expense, and Dividend accounts have zero balances.

Since the asset, liability, common stock, and retained earnings accounts are permanent accounts, they are not closed at the end of the accounting period. After the closing account process, RCS's general ledger will contain the following account balances as of December 31, 2012.

Cash	+	Land	=	Notes Payable	+	Common Stock	+	Retained Earnings
51,000	+	500,000	=	400,000	+	120,000	+	31,000

Take note that the December 31, 2012, ending account balances become the January 1, 2013, beginning account balances. So, RCS will start the 2013 accounting period with these same accounts balances. In other words, the current period's after closing ending balances become the next period's beginning balances.

✓ CHECK YOURSELF 1.6

After closing on December 31, 2012, Walston Company had $4,600 of assets, $2,000 of liabilities, and $700 of common stock. During January of 2013, Walston earned $750 of revenue and incurred $300 of expense. Walston closes it books each year on December 31.

1. Determine the balance in the Retained Earnings account as of December 31, 2012.
2. Determine the balance in the Retained Earnings account as of January 1, 2013.
3. Determine the balance in the Retained Earnings account as of January 31, 2013.

Answer

1. Assets = Liabilities + Common Stock + Retained Earnings

   $4,600 = $2,000 + $700 + Retained Earnings

   Retained Earnings = $1,900

2. The balance in the Retained Earnings account on January 1, 2013, is the same as it was on December 31, 2012. This year's ending balance becomes next year's beginning balance. Therefore, the balance in the Retained Earnings account on January 1, 2013, is $1,900.

3. The balance in the Retained Earnings account on January 31, 2013, is still $1,900. The revenue earned and expenses incurred during January are not recorded in the Retained Earnings account. Revenue is recorded in a Revenue account and expenses are recorded in an Expense account during the accounting period. The balances in the Revenue and Expense accounts are transferred to the Retained Earnings account during the closing process at the end of the accounting period (December 31, 2013).

THE HORIZONTAL FINANCIAL STATEMENTS MODEL

Financial statements are the scorecard for business activity. If you want to succeed in business, you must know how your business decisions affect your company's financial statements. This text uses a **horizontal statements model** to help you understand how business events affect financial statements. This model shows a set of financial statements horizontally across a single page of paper. The balance sheet is displayed first, adjacent to the income statement, and then the statement of cash flows. Because the effects of equity transactions can be analyzed by referring to certain balance sheet columns, and because of limited space, the statement of changes in stockholders' equity is not shown in the horizontal statements model.

Record business events using a horizontal financial statements model.

The model frequently uses abbreviations. For example, activity classifications in the statement of cash flows are identified using OA for operating activities, IA for investing activities, and FA for financing activities. NC designates the net change in cash. The statements model uses "NA" when an account is not affected by an event. The background of the *balance sheet* is red, the *income statement* is blue, and the *statement of cash flows* is green. To demonstrate the usefulness of the horizontal statements model, we use it to display the seven accounting events that RCS experienced during its first year of operation (2012).

1. RCS acquired $120,000 cash from the issuance of common stock.
2. RCS borrowed $400,000 cash.
3. RCS paid $500,000 cash to purchase land.
4. RCS received $85,000 cash from earning revenue.
5. RCS paid $50,000 cash for expenses.
6. RCS paid $4,000 of cash dividends to the owners.
7. The market value of the land owned by RCS was appraised at $525,000 on December 31, 2012.

Event No.	Balance Sheet										Income Statement					Statement of Cash Flows	
	Assets			=	Liab.	+	Stockholders' Equity										
	Cash	+	Land	=	N. Pay.	+	Com. Stk.	+	Ret. Earn.		Rev.	−	Exp.	=	Net Inc.		
Beg. bal.	0	+	0	=	0	+	0	+	0		0	−	0	=	0	NA	
1.	120,000	+	NA	=	NA	+	120,000	+	NA		NA	−	NA	=	NA	120,000	FA
2.	400,000	+	NA	=	400,000	+	NA	+	NA		NA	−	NA	=	NA	400,000	FA
3.	(500,000)	+	500,000	=	NA	+	NA	+	NA		NA	−	NA	=	NA	(500,000)	IA
4.	85,000	+	NA	=	NA	+	NA	+	85,000		85,000	−	NA	=	85,000	85,000	OA
5.	(50,000)	+	NA	=	NA	+	NA	+	(50,000)		NA	−	50,000	=	(50,000)	(50,000)	OA
6.	(4,000)	+	NA	=	NA	+	NA	+	(4,000)		NA	−	NA	=	NA	(4,000)	FA
7.	NA	+	NA	=	NA	+	NA	+	NA		NA	−	NA	=	NA	NA	
Totals	51,000	+	500,000	=	400,000	+	120,000	+	31,000		85,000	−	50,000	=	35,000	51,000	NC

Recognize that statements models are learning tools. Because they are helpful in understanding how accounting events affect financial statements, they are used extensively in this book. However, the models omit many of the details used in published financial statements. For example, the horizontal model shows only a partial set of statements. Also, since the statements are presented in aggregate, the description of dates (i.e., "as of" versus "for the period ended") does not distinguish periodic from cumulative data.

REAL-WORLD FINANCIAL REPORTS

As previously indicated, organizations exist in many different forms, including *business* entities and *not-for-profit* entities. Business entities are typically service, merchandising, or manufacturing companies. **Service businesses,** which include doctors, attorneys, accountants, dry cleaners, and maids, provide services to their customers. **Merchandising businesses,** sometimes called *retail* or *wholesale companies,* sell goods to customers that other entities make. **Manufacturing businesses** make the goods that they sell to their customers.

Some business operations include combinations of these three categories. For example, an automotive repair shop might change oil (service function), sell parts such as oil filters (retail function), and rebuild engines (manufacturing function). The nature of the reporting entity affects the form and content of the information reported in an entity's financial statements. For example, governmental entities provide statements of revenues, expenditures, and changes in fund equity while business entities provide income statements. Similarly, income statements of retail companies show an expense

Service

Merchandising

Manufacturing

REALITY BYTES

On April 19, 2010, the stock of BP, Plc. (formally known as British Petroleum) was trading at $59.48 per share. On that same day, the stock of Chevron Corp. was trading at $81.32 and the stock of Exxon Mobil Corp. was trading at $68.23. About six weeks later, on June 4, 2010, these companies' stocks had fallen to $37.16, $71.28, and $59.53 per share, respectively. Why did this happen? Did the companies report a large drop in their net earnings during these six weeks? No. What happened was that on April 20, 2010, the Deepwater Horizon oil well, owned by BP, failed and began discharging 60,000 barrels of oil daily into the Gulf of Mexico.

While it is easy to see why this event could cause BP's stock to lose 38 percent of its value, why would this cause Chevron's stock to fall 12 percent and Exxon's stock to fall 13 percent? These two companies did not have any oil spills during this time. One reason that the stock price of most oil companies declined significantly after BP's problems was that investors were concerned the failure would result in tighter regulation of all oil companies. Additionally, there was the concern that the government would ban, or seriously reduce, all future deepwater drilling. More regulations, and certainly a ban on future drilling, could drastically reduce the future earnings potential of all oil companies, not just BP.

As this situation illustrates, investors frequently use information not yet reported in a company's annual report. The annual report focuses on historical data, but investors are more concerned about the future. The historical information contained in the annual report is important because the past is frequently a strong predictor of the future. However, current negative news, such as an oil spill, may give investors more information about a company's furture than last year's annual report. For example, while the oil spill was bad news for the oil companies, it was, in financial terms, good news for companies that manufacture the oil-booms used to prevent oil from reaching the beaches. Similarly, a new company, that has never earned a profit, may have an idea that is so innovative investors rush to buy it stock, even though they expect it to be a few years to have positive earnings. Also, investors and creditors may be motivated by nonfinancial considerations such as social consciousness, humanitarian concerns, or personal preferences. While accounting information is critically important, it is only one dimension of the information pool that investors and creditors use to make decisions.

item called *cost of goods sold,* but service companies that do not sell goods have no such item in their income statements. You should expect some diversity when reviewing real-world financial statements.

Annual Report for Target Corporation

Organizations normally provide information, including financial statements, to *stakeholders* yearly in a document known as an **annual report.** The annual report for Target Corporation is reproduced in Appendix B of this text. This report includes the company's financial statements. Immediately following the statements are footnotes that provide additional details about the items described in the statements. The annual report contains commentary describing management's assessment of significant events that affected the company during the reporting period. This commentary is called *management's discussion and analysis* (MD&A).

The U.S. Securities and Exchange Commission (SEC) requires public companies to file an annual report in a document known as a 10-K. Even though the annual report is usually flashier (contains more color and pictures) than the 10-K, the 10-K is normally more comprehensive with respect to content. As a result, the 10-K report frequently substitutes for the annual report, but the annual report cannot substitute for the 10-K. In an effort to reduce costs, many companies now use the 10-K report as their annual report.

Special Terms in Real-World Reports

The financial statements of real-world companies include numerous items relating to advanced topics that are not covered in survey accounting textbooks, especially the first chapter of a survey accounting textbook. Do not, however, be discouraged from browsing through real-world annual reports. You will significantly enhance your learning if you look at many annual reports and attempt to identify as many items as you can. As your accounting knowledge grows, you will likely experience increased interest in real-world financial reports and the businesses they describe.

We encourage you to look for annual reports in the library or ask your employer for a copy of your company's report. The Internet is another excellent source for obtaining annual reports. Most companies provide links to their annual reports on their home pages. Look for links labeled "about the company" or "investor relations" or other phrases that logically lead to the company's financial reports. The best way to learn accounting is to use it. Accounting is the language of business. Learning the language will serve you well in almost any area of business that you pursue.

 ## A Look Back

This chapter introduced the role of accounting in society and business: to provide information helpful in operating and evaluating the performance of organizations. Accounting is a measurement discipline. To communicate effectively, users of accounting must agree on the rules of measurement. *Generally accepted accounting principles (GAAP)* constitute the rules used by the accounting profession in the United States to govern financial reporting. GAAP is a work in progress that continues to evolve.

This chapter has discussed eight elements of financial statements: *assets, liabilities, equity, common stock (contributed capital), revenue, expenses, dividends (distributions),* and *net income.* The elements represent broad classifications reported on financial statements. Four basic financial statements appear in the reports of public companies: the *balance sheet,* the *income statement,* the *statement of changes in stockholders' equity,* and the *statement of cash flows.* The chapter discussed the form and content of each statement as well as the interrelationships among the statements.

This chapter introduced a *horizontal financial statements model* as a tool to help you understand how business events affect a set of financial statements. This model is used throughout the text. You should carefully study this model before proceeding to Chapter 2.

 ## A Look Forward

To keep matters as simple as possible and to focus on the interrelationships among financial statements, this chapter considered only cash events. Obviously, many real-world events do not involve an immediate exchange of cash. For example, customers use telephone service throughout the month without paying for it until the next month. Such phone usage represents an expense in one month with a cash exchange in the following month. Events such as this are called *accruals.* Understanding the effects that accrual events have on the financial statements is included in Chapter 2.

A step-by-step audio-narrated series of slides is provided on the text website at www.mhhe.com/edmondssurvey3e.

SELF-STUDY REVIEW PROBLEM

During 2013 Rustic Camp Sites experienced the following transactions.

1. RCS acquired $32,000 cash by issuing common stock.
2. RCS received $116,000 cash for providing services to customers (leasing camp sites).
3. RCS paid $13,000 cash for salaries expense.
4. RCS paid a $9,000 cash dividend to the owners.

5. RCS sold land that had cost $100,000 for $100,000 cash.
6. RCS paid $47,000 cash for other operating expenses.

Required

a. Record the transaction data in a horizontal financial statements model like the following one. In the Cash Flow column, classify the cash flows as operating activities (OA), investing activities (IA), or financing activities (FA). The beginning balances have been recorded as an example. They are the ending balances shown on RCS's December 31, 2012, financial statements illustrated in the chapter. Note that the revenue and expense accounts have a zero beginning balance. Amounts in these accounts apply only to a single accounting period. Revenue and expense account balances are not carried forward from one accounting period to the next.

Event No.	Balance Sheet									Income Statement						Statement of Cash Flows
	Assets			=	Liab.	+	Stockholders' Equity									
	Cash	+	Land	=	N. Pay.	+	Com. Stk.	+	Ret. Earn.	Rev.	−	Exp.	=	Net Inc.		
Beg. bal.	51,000	+	500,000	=	400,000	+	120,000	+	31,000	NA	−	NA	=	NA		NA

b. Explain why there are no beginning balances in the Income Statement columns.
c. What amount of net income will RCS report on the 2013 income statement?
d. What amount of total assets will RCS report on the December 31, 2013, balance sheet?
e. What amount of retained earnings will RCS report on the December 31, 2013, balance sheet?
f. What amount of net cash flow from operating activities will RCS report on the 2013 statement of cash flows?

Solution

a.

Event No.	Balance Sheet									Income Statement						Statement of Cash Flows
	Assets			=	Liab.	+	Stockholders' Equity									
	Cash	+	Land	=	N. Pay.	+	Com. Stk.	+	Ret. Earn.	Rev.	−	Exp.	=	Net Inc.		
Beg. bal.	51,000	+	500,000	=	400,000	+	120,000	+	31,000	NA	−	NA	=	NA		NA
1.	32,000	+	NA	=	NA	+	32,000	+	NA	NA	−	NA	=	NA		32,000 FA
2.	116,000	+	NA	=	NA	+	NA	+	116,000	116,000	−	NA	=	116,000		116,000 OA
3.	(13,000)	+	NA	=	NA	+	NA	+	(13,000)	NA	−	13,000	=	(13,000)		(13,000) OA
4.	(9,000)	+	NA	=	NA	+	NA	+	(9,000)	NA	−	NA	=	NA		(9,000) FA
5.	100,000	+	(100,000)	=	NA	+	NA	+	NA	NA	−	NA	=	NA		100,000 IA
6.	(47,000)	+	NA	=	NA	+	NA	+	(47,000)	NA	−	47,000	=	(47,000)		(47,000) OA
Totals	230,000	+	400,000	=	400,000	+	152,000	+	78,000	116,000	−	60,000	=	56,000		179,000 NC*

*The letters NC on the last line of the column designate the net change in cash.

b. The revenue and expense accounts are temporary accounts used to capture data for a single accounting period. They are closed (amounts removed from the accounts) to retained earnings at the end of the accounting period and therefore always have zero balances at the beginning of the accounting cycle.

c. RCS will report net income of $56,000 on the 2013 income statement. Compute this amount by subtracting the expenses from the revenue ($116,000 Revenue − $13,000 Salaries expense − $47,000 Other operating expense).

d. RCS will report total assets of $630,000 on the December 31, 2013, balance sheet. Compute total assets by adding the cash amount to the land amount ($230,000 Cash + $400,000 Land).

e. RCS will report retained earnings of $78,000 on the December 31, 2013, balance sheet. Compute this amount using the following formula: Beginning retained earnings + Net income − Dividends = Ending retained earnings. In this case, $31,000 + $56,000 − $9,000 = $78,000.

f. Net cash flow from operating activities is the difference between the amount of cash collected from revenue and the amount of cash spent for expenses. In this case, $116,000 cash inflow from revenue − $13,000 cash outflow for salaries expense − $47,000 cash outflow for other operating expenses = $56,000 net cash inflow from operating activities.

KEY TERMS

accounting 2
accounting equation 12
accounting event 13
accounting period 15
accounts 11
annual report 25
articulation 18
asset exchange transaction 14
asset source transaction 13
asset use transaction 15
assets 4
balance sheet 9
claims 4
closing 22
common stock 12
creditors 4
dividend 16
double-entry bookkeeping 14
earnings 4
elements 10
equity 12
expenses 15
financial accounting 6
Financial Accounting Standards
    Board (FASB) 8

financial resources 4
financial statements 10
financing activities 21
general ledger 17
generally accepted accounting
    principles (GAAP) 8
historical cost concept 16
horizontal statements
    model 23
income 4
income statement 18
International Accounting
    Standards Board (IASB) 9
International Financial
    Reporting Standards
    (IFRS) 9
interest 5
investing activities 21
investors 4
labor resources 4
liabilities 10
liquidation 4
liquidity 20
managerial accounting 6
manufacturing businesses 24

market 4
matching concept 18
merchandising
    businesses 24
net income 18
net loss 18
not-for-profit entities 6
operating activities 21
permanent accounts 22
physical resources 5
profit 4
reliability concept 16
reporting entities 9
retained earnings 12
revenue 10
service businesses 24
stakeholders 6
statement of cash flows 10
statement of changes in
    stockholders' equity 10
stockholders 12
stockholders' equity 12
temporary accounts 22
transaction 12
users 6

QUESTIONS

1. Explain the term *stakeholder*. Distinguish between stakeholders with a direct versus an indirect interest in the companies that issue accounting reports.

2. Why is accounting called the *language of business?*

3. What is the primary mechanism used to allocate resources in the United States?

4. In a business context, what does the term *market* mean?

5. What market trilogy components are involved in the process of transforming resources into finished products?

6. Give an example of a financial resource, a physical resource, and a labor resource.

7. What type of return does an investor expect to receive in exchange for providing financial resources to a business? What type of return does a creditor expect from

providing financial resources to an organization or business?

8. How do financial and managerial accounting differ?

9. Describe a not-for-profit or nonprofit enterprise. What is the motivation for this type of entity?

10. What are the U.S. rules of accounting information measurement called?

11. Explain how a career in public accounting differs from a career in private accounting.

12. Distinguish between elements of financial statements and accounts.

13. What role do assets play in business profitability?

14. To whom do the assets of a business belong?

15. What is the nature of creditors' claims on assets?

16. What term describes creditors' claims on the assets of a business?

17. What is the accounting equation? Describe each of its three components.

18. Who ultimately bears the risk and collects the rewards associated with operating a business?

19. What does a *double-entry bookkeeping system* mean?

20. How does acquiring capital from owners affect the accounting equation?

21. What is the difference between assets that are acquired by issuing common stock and those that are acquired using retained earnings?

22. How does earning revenue affect the accounting equation?

23. What are the three primary sources of assets?

24. What is the source of retained earnings?

25. How does distributing assets (paying dividends) to owners affect the accounting equation?

26. What are the similarities and differences between dividends and expenses?

27. What four general-purpose financial statements do business enterprises use?

28. Which of the general-purpose financial statements provides information about the enterprise at a specific designated date?

29. What causes a net loss?

30. What three categories of cash receipts and cash payments do businesses report on the statement of cash flows? Explain the types of cash flows reported in each category.

31. How are asset accounts usually arranged in the balance sheet?

32. Discuss the term *articulation* as it relates to financial statements.

33. How do temporary accounts differ from permanent accounts? Name three temporary accounts. Is retained earnings a temporary or a permanent account?

34. What is the historical cost concept and how does it relate to the reliability concept?

35. Identify the three types of accounting transactions discussed in this chapter. Provide an example of each type of transaction, and explain how it affects the accounting equation.

36. What type of information does a business typically include in its annual report?

37. What is U.S. GAAP? What is IFRS?

 ## MULTIPLE-CHOICE QUESTIONS

Multiple-choice questions are provided on the text website at www.mhhe.com/edmondssurvey3e.

EXERCISES

All applicable Exercises are available with McGraw-Hill's *Connect Accounting*.

Exercise 1-1   *The role of accounting in society*

Free economies use open markets to allocate resources.

Required

Identify the three participants in a free business market. Write a brief memo explaining how these participants interact to ensure that goods and services are distributed in a manner that satisfies consumers. Your memo should include answers to the following questions: If you work as a public accountant, what role would you play in the allocation of resources? Which professional certification would be most appropriate to your career?

LO 1

Exercise 1-2   *Distributions in a business liquidation*

Assume that Kennedy Company acquires $1,600 cash from creditors and $1,800 cash from investors.

Required

a. Explain the primary differences between investors and creditors.

b. If Kennedy has a net loss of $1,600 cash and then liquidates, what amount of cash will the creditors receive? What amount of cash will the investors receive?

c. If Kennedy has net income of $1,600 and then liquidates, what amount of cash will the creditors receive? What amount of cash will the investors receive?

LO 1

LO 1

Exercise 1-3 *Careers in accounting*

Accounting is commonly divided into two sectors. One sector is called public accounting. The other sector is called private accounting.

Required

a. Identify three areas of service provided by public accountants.
b. Describe the common duties performed by private accountants.

LO 1

Exercise 1-4 *Identifying the reporting entities*

Kenneth Chang recently started a business. During the first few days of operation, Mr. Chang transferred $30,000 from his personal account into a business account for a company he named Chang Enterprises. Chang Enterprises borrowed $40,000 from First Bank. Mr. Chang's father-in-law, Jim Harwood, invested $64,000 into the business for which he received a 25 percent ownership interest. Chang Enterprises purchased a building from Morton Realty Company. The building cost $120,000 cash. Chang Enterprises earned $28,000 in revenue from the company's customers and paid its employees $25,000 for salaries expense.

Required

Identify the entities that were mentioned in the scenario and explain what happened to the cash accounts of each entity that you identify.

LO 2

Exercise 1-5 *Titles and accounts appearing on financial statements*

Annual reports normally include an income statement, a statement of changes in stockholders' equity, a balance sheet, and a statement of cash flows.

Required

Identify the financial statements on which each of the following titles or accounts would appear. If a title or an account appears on more than one statement, list all statements that would include it.

a. Common Stock
b. Land
c. Ending Cash Balance
d. Beginning Cash Balance
e. Notes Payable
f. Retained Earnings
g. Revenue
h. Cash Dividends
i. Financing Activities
j. Salaries Expense

LO 2

Exercise 1-6 *Components of the accounting equation*

Required

The following three requirements are independent of each other.

a. Craig's Cars has assets of $4,550 and stockholders' equity of $3,200. What is the amount of liabilities? What is the amount of claims?
b. Heavenly Bakery has liabilities of $4,800 and stockholders' equity of $5,400. What is the amount of assets?
c. Bell's Candy Co. has assets of $49,200 and liabilities of $28,200. What is the amount of stockholders' equity?

LO 2

Exercise 1-7 *Missing information in the accounting equation*

Required

Calculate the missing amounts in the following table.

Company	Assets	=	Liabilities	+	Stockholders' Equity Common Stock	+	Retained Earnings
A	$?		$25,000		$48,000		$50,000
B	40,000		?		7,000		30,000
C	75,000		15,000		?		42,000
D	125,000		45,000		60,000		?

Exercise 1-8   *Missing information in the accounting equation*

LO 2

As of December 31, 2012, Eber Company had total assets of $156,000, total liabilities of $85,600, and common stock of $52,400. During 2013 Eber earned $36,000 of cash revenue, paid $20,000 for cash expenses, and paid a $2,000 cash dividend to the stockholders.

Required

a. Determine the amount of retained earnings as of December 31, 2012, after closing.
b. Determine the amount of net income earned in 2013.
c. Determine the amount of retained earnings as of December 31, 2013, after closing.
d. Determine the amount of cash that is in the retained earnings account as of December 31, 2013.

Exercise 1-9   *Missing information for determining net income*

LO 2

The December 31, 2012, balance sheet for Classic Company showed total stockholders' equity of $82,500. Total stockholders' equity increased by $53,400 between December 31, 2012, and December 31, 2013. During 2013 Classic Company acquired $13,000 cash from the issue of common stock. Classic Company paid an $8,000 cash dividend to the stockholders during 2013.

Required

Determine the amount of net income or loss Classic reported on its 2013 income statement. (*Hint:* Remember that stock issues, net income, and dividends all change total stockholders' equity.)

Exercise 1-10   *Effect of events on the accounting equation*

LO 2, 3

Olive Enterprises experienced the following events during 2012.

1. Acquired cash from the issue of common stock.
2. Paid cash to reduce the principal on a bank note.
3. Sold land for cash at an amount equal to its cost.
4. Provided services to clients for cash.
5. Paid utilities expenses with cash.
6. Paid a cash dividend to the stockholders.

Required

Explain how each of the events would affect the accounting equation by writing the letter I for increase, the letter D for decrease, and NA for does not affect under each of the components of the accounting equation. The first event is shown as an example.

Event Number	Assets	= Liabilities	+	Stockholders' Equity Common Stock	+ Retained Earnings
1	I	NA		I	NA

LO 2, 3

Exercise 1-11   *Effects of issuing stock*

Shiloh Company was started in 2012 when it acquired $15,000 cash by issuing common stock. The cash acquisition was the only event that affected the business in 2012.

Required

Write an accounting equation, and record the effects of the stock issue under the appropriate general ledger account headings.

LO 2, 3

Exercise 1-12   *Effects of borrowing*

Marcum Company was started in 2012 when it issued a note to borrow $6,200 cash.

Required

Write an accounting equation, and record the effects of the borrowing transaction under the appropriate general ledger account headings.

LO 2, 3

Exercise 1-13   *Effects of revenue, expense, dividend, and the closing process*

Rhodes Company was started on January 1, 2011. During 2012, the company experienced the following three accounting events: (1) earned cash revenues of $13,500, (2) paid cash expenses of $9,200, and (3) paid a $500 cash dividend to its stockholders. These were the only events that affected the company during 2012.

Required

a. Write an accounting equation, and record the effects of each accounting event under the appropriate general ledger account headings.

b. Prepare an income statement for the 2012 accounting period and a balance sheet at the end of 2012 for Rhodes Company.

c. What is the balance in the Retained Earnings account immediately after the cash revenue is recognized?

d. What is the balance in the Retained Earnings account after the closing process is complete?

LO 2, 3

Exercise 1-14   *Effect of transactions on general ledger accounts*

At the beginning of 2012, J & J Corp.'s accounting records had the following general ledger accounts and balances.

J & J CORP.								
Accounting Equation								
Event	Assets		=	Liabilities	+	Stockholders' Equity		Acct. Titles for RE
	Cash	Land		Notes Payable		Common Stock	Retained Earnings	
Balance 1/1/2012	10,000	20,000		12,000		7,000	11,000	

J & J Corp. completed the following transactions during 2012.

1. Purchased land for $5,000 cash.
2. Acquired $25,000 cash from the issue of common stock.
3. Received $75,000 cash for providing services to customers.
4. Paid cash operating expenses of $42,000.
5. Borrowed $10,000 cash from the bank.
6. Paid a $5,000 cash dividend to the stockholders.
7. Determined that the market value of the land is $35,000.

Required

a. Record the transactions in the appropriate general ledger accounts. Record the amounts of revenue, expense, and dividends in the Retained Earnings column. Provide the appropriate titles for these accounts in the last column of the table.

b. Determine the net cash flow from financing activities.

c. What is the balance in the Retained Earnings account as of January 1, 2013?

Exercise 1-15   *Classifying events as asset source, use, or exchange*   **LO 4**

BJ's Business Services experienced the following events during its first year of operations.

1. Acquired $10,000 cash from the issue of common stock.
2. Borrowed $8,000 cash from First Bank.
3. Paid $4,000 cash to purchase land.
4. Received $5,000 cash for providing boarding services.
5. Acquired an additional $2,000 cash from the issue of common stock.
6. Purchased additional land for $3,500 cash.
7. Paid $2,500 cash for salary expense.
8. Signed a contract to provide additional services in the future.
9. Paid $1,000 cash for rent expense.
10. Paid a $1,000 cash dividend to the stockholders.
11. Determined the market value of the land to be $8,000 at the end of the accounting period.

Required

Classify each event as an asset source, use, or exchange transaction or as not applicable (NA).

Exercise 1-16   *Classifying items for the statement of cash flows*   **LO 5**

Required

Indicate how each of the following would be classified on the statement of cash flows as operating activities (OA), investing activities (IA), financing activities (FA), or not applicable (NA).

a. Paid $4,000 cash for salary expense.
b. Borrowed $8,000 cash from State Bank.
c. Received $30,000 cash from the issue of common stock.
d. Purchased land for $8,000 cash.
e. Performed services for $14,000 cash.
f. Paid $4,200 cash for utilities expense.
g. Sold land for $7,000 cash.
h. Paid a cash dividend of $1,000 to the stockholders.
i. Hired an accountant to keep the books.
j. Paid $3,000 cash on the loan from State Bank.

Exercise 1-17   *Preparing financial statements*   **LO 2, 3, 5**

Montana Company experienced the following events during 2012.

1. Acquired $30,000 cash from the issue of common stock.
2. Paid $12,000 cash to purchase land.
3. Borrowed $10,000 cash.
4. Provided services for $20,000 cash.
5. Paid $1,000 cash for rent expense.
6. Paid $15,000 cash for other operating expenses.
7. Paid a $2,000 cash dividend to the stockholders.
8. Determined that the market value of the land purchased in Event 2 is now $12,700.

Required

a. The January 1, 2012, general ledger account balances are shown in the following account-ing equation. Record the eight events in the appropriate general ledger accounts. Record the amounts of revenue, expense, and dividends in the Retained Earnings column. Provide the appropriate titles for these accounts in the last column of the table. The first event is shown as an example.

MONTANA COMPANY
Accounting Equation

Event	Assets		=	Liabilities	+	Stockholders' Equity		Acct. Titles for RE
	Cash	Land		Notes Payable		Common Stock	Retained Earnings	
Balance 1/1/2012	2,000	12,000		0		6,000	8,000	
1.	30,000					30,000		

b. Prepare an income statement, statement of changes in equity, year-end balance sheet, and statement of cash flows for the 2012 accounting period.

c. Determine the percentage of assets that were provided by retained earnings. How much cash is in the retained earnings account?

LO 5

Exercise 1-18   *Retained earnings and the closing process*

Davis Company was started on January 1, 2012. During the month of January, Davis earned $4,600 of revenue and incurred $3,000 of expense. Davis closes its books on December 31 of each year.

Required

a. Determine the balance in the Retained Earnings account as of January 31, 2012.
b. Comment on whether retained earnings is an element of financial statements or an account.
c. What happens to the Retained Earnings account at the time expenses are recognized?

LO 5

Exercise 1-19   *Relationship between assets and retained earnings*

Washington Company was organized when it acquired $2,000 cash from the issue of common stock. During its first accounting period the company earned $800 of cash revenue and incurred $500 of cash expenses. Also, during the accounting period the company paid its owners a $200 cash dividend.

Required

a. Determine the balance in the Retained Earnings account before and after the temporary accounts are closed.
b. As of the end of the accounting period, determine what percentage of total assets were provided by retained earnings.

LO 5

Exercise 1-20   *Historical cost versus market value*

Hilltop, Inc., purchased land in January 2009 at a cost of $270,000. The estimated market value of the land is $350,000 as of December 31, 2012.

Required

a. Name the December 31, 2012, financial statement(s) on which the land will be shown.
b. At what dollar amount will the land be shown in the financial statement(s)?
c. Name the key concept that will be used in determining the dollar amount that will be reported for land that is shown in the financial statement(s).

Exercise 1-21   *Relating accounting events to entities*   **LO 1, 4, 5**

Wright Company was started in 2012 when it acquired $25,000 cash by issuing common stock to Cal Wright.

Required

a. Was this event an asset source, use, or exchange transaction for Wright Company?
b. Was this event an asset source, use, or exchange transaction for Cal Wright?
c. Was the cash flow an operating, investing, or a financing activity on Wright Company's 2012 statement of cash flows?
d. Was the cash flow an operating, investing, or a financing activity on Cal Wright's 2012 statement of cash flows?

Exercise 1-22   *Effect of events on a horizontal financial statements model*   **LO 6**

City Consulting Services experienced the following events during 2012.

1. Acquired cash by issuing common stock.
2. Collected cash for providing tutoring services to clients.
3. Borrowed cash from a local government small business foundation.
4. Purchased land for cash.
5. Paid cash for operating expenses.
6. Paid a cash dividend to the stockholders.
7. Determined that the market value of the land is higher than its historical cost.

Required

Use a horizontal statements model to show how each event affects the balance sheet, income statement, and statement of cash flows. Indicate whether the event increases (I), decreases (D), or does not affect (NA) each element of the financial statements. Also, in the Cash Flows column, classify the cash flows as operating activities (OA), investing activities (IA), or financing activities (FA). The first transaction is shown as an example.

Event No.	Cash	+	Land	=	N. Pay	+	C. Stock.	+	Ret. Ear.	Rev.	−	Exp.	=	Net Inc.	Statement of Cash Flows
1.	I	+	NA	=	NA	+	I	+	NA	NA	−	NA	=	NA	I FA

Exercise 1-23   *Record events in the horizontal statements model*   **LO 6**

Expo Co. was started in 2012. During 2012, the company (1) acquired $11,000 cash from the issue of common stock, (2) earned cash revenue of $18,000, (3) paid cash expenses of $10,500, and (4) paid a $1,000 cash dividend to the stockholders.

Required

a. Record these four events in a horizontal statements model. Also, in the Cash Flows column, classify the cash flows as operating activities (OA), investing activities (IA), or financing activities (FA). The first event is shown as an example.

Event No.	Cash	=	N. Pay	+	C. Stock.	+	Ret. Ear.	Rev.	−	Exp.	=	Net Inc.	Statement of Cash Flows
1.	11,000	=	NA	+	11,000	+	NA	NA	−	NA	=	NA	11,000 FA

b. What does the income statement tell you about the assets of this business?

LO 6

Exercise 1-24 *Effect of events on a horizontal statements model*

Solito, Inc., was started on January 1, 2012. The company experienced the following events during its first year of operation.

1. Acquired $50,000 cash from the issue of common stock.
2. Paid $12,000 cash to purchase land.
3. Received $50,000 cash for providing tax services to customers.
4. Paid $9,500 cash for salary expense.
5. Acquired $5,000 cash from the issue of additional common stock.
6. Borrowed $10,000 cash from the bank.
7. Purchased additional land for $10,000 cash.
8. Paid $8,000 cash for other operating expenses.
9. Paid a $2,800 cash dividend to the stockholders.
10. Determined that the market value of the land is $25,000.

Required

a. Record these events in a horizontal statements model. Also, in the Cash Flows column, classify the cash flows as operating activities (OA), investing activities (IA), or financing activities (FA). The first event is shown as an example.

Event No.	Balance Sheet										Income Statement						Statement of Cash Flows
	Cash	+	Land	=	N. Pay	+	C. Stock.	+	Ret. Ear.		Rev.	−	Exp.	=	Net Inc.		
1.	50,000	+	NA	=	NA	+	50,000	+	NA		NA	−	NA	=	NA		50,000 FA

b. What is the net income earned in 2012?
c. What is the amount of total assets at the end of 2012?
d. What is the net cash flow from operating activities for 2012?
e. What is the net cash flow from investing activities for 2012?
f. What is the net cash flow from financing activities for 2012?
g. What is the cash balance at the end of 2012?
h. As of the end of the year 2012, what percentage of total assets were provided by creditors, investors, and retained earnings?
i. What is the balance in the Retained Earnings account immediately after Event 4 is recorded?

LO 4, 6

Exercise 1-25 *Types of transactions and the horizontal statements model*

Partner's Pet Store experienced the following events during its first year of operations, 2012.

1. Acquired cash by issuing common stock.
2. Purchased land with cash.
3. Borrowed cash from a bank.
4. Signed a contract to provide services in the future.
5. Paid a cash dividend to the stockholders.
6. Paid cash for operating expenses.
7. Determined that the market value of the land is higher than the historical cost.

Required

a. Indicate whether each event is an asset source, use, or exchange transaction.
b. Use a horizontal statements model to show how each event affects the balance sheet, income statement, and statement of cash flows. Indicate whether the event increases (I), decreases (D), or does not affect (NA) each element of the financial statements. Also, in the Cash

Flows column, classify the cash flows as operating activities (OA), investing activities (IA), or financing activities (FA). The first transaction is shown as an example.

Event No.	Balance Sheet							Income Statement				Statement of Cash Flows
	Cash	+	Land	=	N. Pay	+	C. Stock.	+	Ret. Ear.	Rev.	−	Exp.	=	Net Inc.	
1.	I	+	NA	=	NA	+	I	+	NA	NA	−	NA	=	NA	I FA

Exercise 1-26   *International Financial Reporting Standards*   **IFRS**

Seacrest Company is a U.S.–based company that develops its financial statements under GAAP. The total amount of the company's assets shown on its December 31, 2012, balance sheet was approximately $225 million. The president of Seacrest is considering the possibility of relocating the company to a country that practices accounting under IFRS. The president has hired an international accounting firm to determine what the company's statements would look like if they were prepared under IFRS. One striking difference is that under IFRS the assets shown on the balance sheet would be valued at approximately $275 million.

Required

a. Would Seacrest's assets really be worth $50 million more if it moves its headquarters?
b. Discuss the underlying conceptual differences between U.S. GAAP and IFRS that cause the difference in the reported asset values.

PROBLEMS

All applicable Problems are available with McGraw-Hill's *Connect Accounting*.

🔳 connect
|ACCOUNTING

Problem 1-27   *Accounting's role in not-for-profits*   **LO 1**

Teresa Hill is struggling to pass her introductory accounting course. Teresa is intelligent but she likes to party. Studying is a low priority for Teresa. When one of her friends tells her that she is going to have trouble in business if she doesn't learn accounting, Teresa responds that she doesn't plan to go into business. She says that she is arts oriented and plans someday to be a director of a museum. She is in the school of business to develop her social skills, not her quantitative skills. Teresa says she won't have to worry about accounting, since museums are not intended to make a profit.

Required

a. Write a brief memo explaining whether you agree or disagree with Teresa's position regarding accounting and not-for-profit organizations.
b. Distinguish between financial accounting and managerial accounting.
c. Identify some of the stakeholders of not-for-profit institutions that would expect to receive financial accounting reports.
d. Identify some of the stakeholders of not-for-profit institutions that would expect to receive managerial accounting reports.

Problem 1-28   *Accounting entities*   **LO 1**

The following business scenarios are independent from one another.

1. Beth Mays purchased an automobile from Mills Bros. Auto Sales for $9,000.
2. Bill Becham loaned $15,000 to the business in which he is a stockholder.
3. First State Bank paid interest to Levi Co. on a certificate of deposit that Levi Co. has invested at First State Bank.
4. Southside Restaurant paid the current utility bill of $128 to Midwest Utilities.
5. Filmore, Inc., borrowed $50,000 from City National Bank and used the funds to purchase land from Tuchols Realty.

CHECK FIGURE
1. Entities mentioned:
Beth Mays and Mills Bros.
Auto Sales

6. Jing Chu purchased $10,000 of common stock of International Sales Corporation from the corporation.

7. Bill Mann loaned $4,000 cash to his daughter.

8. Research Service Co. earned $5,000 in cash revenue.

9. Yang Imports paid $1,500 for salaries to each of its four employees.

10. Meyers Inc. paid a cash dividend of $3,000 to its sole shareholder, Mark Meyers.

Required

a. For each scenario, create a list of all of the entities that are mentioned in the description.

b. Describe what happens to the cash account of each entity that you identified in Requirement *a*.

LO 2, 5

Problem 1-29 *Relating titles and accounts to financial statements*

Required

Identify the financial statements on which each of the following items (titles, date descriptions, and accounts) appears by placing a check mark in the appropriate column. If an item appears on more than one statement, place a check mark in every applicable column.

Item	Income Statement	Statement of Changes in Stockholders' Equity	Balance Sheet	Statement of Cash Flows
Notes payable				
Beginning common stock				
Service revenue				
Utility expense				
Cash from stock issue				
Operating activities				
For the period ended (date)				
Net income				
Investing activities				
Net loss				
Ending cash balance				
Salary expense				
Consulting revenue				
Dividends				
Financing activities				
Ending common stock				
Interest expense				
As of (date)				
Land				
Beginning cash balance				

LO 2, 3, 5, 6

e**X**cel

Problem 1-30 *Preparing financial statements for two complete accounting cycles*

Webster Consulting experienced the following transactions for 2012, its first year of operations, and 2013. *Assume that all transactions involve the receipt or payment of cash.*

Transactions for 2012

1. Acquired $20,000 by issuing common stock.
2. Received $35,000 cash for providing services to customers.
3. Borrowed $25,000 cash from creditors.
4. Paid expenses amounting to $22,000.
5. Purchased land for $30,000 cash.

Transactions for 2013

Beginning account balances for 2013 are:

Cash	$28,000
Land	30,000
Notes payable	25,000
Common stock	20,000
Retained earnings	13,000

1. Acquired an additional $24,000 from the issue of common stock.
2. Received $95,000 for providing services.
3. Paid $15,000 to creditors to reduce loan.
4. Paid expenses amounting to $71,500.
5. Paid a $3,000 dividend to the stockholders.
6. Determined that the market value of the land is $47,000.

Required

a. Write an accounting equation, and record the effects of each accounting event under the appropriate headings for each year. Record the amounts of revenue, expense, and dividends in the Retained Earnings column. Provide appropriate titles for these accounts in the last column of the table.

b. Prepare an income statement, statement of changes in stockholders' equity, year-end balance sheet, and statement of cash flows for each year.

c. Determine the amount of cash that is in the retained earnings account at the end of 2012 and 2013.

d. Examine the balance sheets for the two years. How did assets change from 2012 to 2013?

e. Determine the balance in the Retained Earnings account immediately after Event 2 in 2012 and in 2013 are recorded.

Problem 1-31   *Interrelationships among financial statements*

Gofish Enterprises started the 2012 accounting period with $50,000 of assets (all cash), $18,000 of liabilities, and $4,000 of common stock. During the year, Gofish earned cash revenues of $38,000, paid cash expenses of $32,000, and paid a cash dividend to stockholders of $2,000. Gofish also acquired $15,000 of additional cash from the sale of common stock and paid $10,000 cash to reduce the liability owed to a bank.

Required

a. Prepare an income statement, statement of changes in stockholders' equity, period-end balance sheet, and statement of cash flows for the 2012 accounting period. (*Hint:* Determine the amount of beginning retained earnings before considering the effects of the current period events. It also might help to record all events under an accounting equation before preparing the statements.)

b. Determine the percentage of total assets that were provided by creditors, investors, and retained earnings.

LO 4

Problem 1-32   *Classifying events as asset source, use, or exchange*

The following unrelated events are typical of those experienced by business entities.

1. Acquire cash by issuing common stock.
2. Purchase land with cash.
3. Purchase equipment with cash.
4. Pay monthly rent on an office building.
5. Hire a new office manager.
6. Borrow cash from a bank.
7. Pay a cash dividend to stockholders.
8. Pay cash for operating expenses.
9. Pay an office manager's salary with cash.
10. Receive cash for services that have been performed.
11. Pay cash for utilities expense.
12. Acquire land by accepting a liability (financing the purchase).
13. Pay cash to purchase a new office building.
14. Discuss plans for a new office building with an architect.
15. Repay part of a bank loan.

Required

Identify each of the events as an asset source, use, or exchange transaction. If an event would not be recorded under generally accepted accounting principles, identify it as not applicable (NA). Also indicate for each event whether total assets would increase, decrease, or remain unchanged. Organize your answer according to the following table. The first event is shown in the table as an example.

Event No.	Type of Event	Effect on Total Assets
1	Asset source	Increase

LO 6

Problem 1-33   *Recording the effect of events in a horizontal statements model*

Texas Corporation experienced the following transactions during 2012.

1. Paid a cash dividend to the stockholders.
2. Acquired cash by issuing additional common stock.
3. Signed a contract to perform services in the future.
4. Performed services for cash.
5. Paid cash expenses.
6. Sold land for cash at an amount equal to its cost.
7. Borrowed cash from a bank.
8. Determined that the market value of the land is higher than its historical cost.

Required

Use a horizontal statements model to show how each event affects the balance sheet, income statement, and statement of cash flows. Indicate whether the event increases (I), decreases (D), or does not affect (NA) each element of the financial statements. Also, in the Cash Flows column, classify the cash flows as operating activities (OA), investing activities (IA), or financing activities (FA). The first transaction is shown as an example.

Event No.	Cash	+	Land	=	N. Pay	+	C. Stock.	+	Ret. Ear.	Rev.	−	Exp.	=	Net Inc.	Statement of Cash Flows
				Balance Sheet								**Income Statement**			
1.	D	+	NA	=	NA	+	NA	+	D	NA	−	NA	=	NA	D FA

Problem 1-34 *Recording events in a horizontal statements model*

Cooley Company was started on January 1, 2012, and experienced the following events during its first year of operation.

1. Acquired $30,000 cash from the issue of common stock.
2. Borrowed $40,000 cash from National Bank.
3. Earned cash revenues of $48,000 for performing services.
4. Paid cash expenses of $45,000.
5. Paid a $1,000 cash dividend to the stockholders.
6. Acquired an additional $20,000 cash from the issue of common stock.
7. Paid $10,000 cash to reduce the principal balance of the bank note.
8. Paid $53,000 cash to purchase land.
9. Determined that the market value of the land is $75,000.

CHECK FIGURES
a. Net Income: $3,000
e. Net Cash Flow from
    Operating Activities: $3,000

Required

a. Record the preceding transactions in the horizontal statements model. Also, in the Cash Flows column, classify the cash flows as operating activities (OA), investing activities (IA), or financing activities (FA). The first event is shown as an example.

Event No.	Balance Sheet									Income Statement				Statement of Cash Flows
	Cash	+	Land	=	N. Pay	+	C. Stock.	+	Ret. Ear.	Rev.	−	Exp.	= Net Inc.	
1.	30,000	+	NA	=	NA	+	30,000	+	NA	NA	−	NA	= NA	30,000 FA

b. Determine the amount of total assets that Cooley would report on the December 31, 2012, balance sheet.
c. Identify the asset source transactions and related amounts for 2012.
d. Determine the net income that Cooley would report on the 2012 income statement. Explain why dividends do not appear on the income statement.
e. Determine the net cash flows from operating activities, financing activities, and investing activities that Cooley would report on the 2012 statement of cash flows.
f. Determine the percentage of assets that were provided by investors, creditors, and retained earnings.
g. What is the balance in the Retained Earnings account immediately after Event 3 is recorded?

ANALYZE, THINK, COMMUNICATE

ATC 1-1 **Business Applications Case** *Understanding real-world annual reports*

Required

Use the Target Corporation's annual report in Appendix B to answer the following questions. Note that net income and net earnings are synonymous terms.

Target Corporation

a. What was Target's net income for 2009?
b. Did Target's net income increase or decrease from 2008 to 2009, and by how much?
c. What was Target's accounting equation for 2009?
d. Which of the following had the largest percentage change from 2008 to 2009: net sales, cost of sales, or selling, general, and administrative expenses? Show all computations.

ATC 1-2   Group Assignment   *Missing information*

The following selected financial information is available for HAS, Inc. Amounts are in millions of dollars.

Income Statements	2014	2013	2012	2011
Revenue	$ 860	$1,520	$ (a)	$1,200
Cost and expenses	(a)	(a)	(2,400)	(860)
Income from continuing operations	(b)	450	320	(a)
Unusual items	-0-	175	(b)	(b)
Net income	$ 20	$ (b)	$ 175	$ 300

Balance Sheets				
Assets				
Cash and marketable securities	$ 350	$1,720	$ (c)	$ 940
Other assets	1,900	(c)	2,500	(c)
Total assets	2,250	$2,900	$ (d)	$3,500
Liabilities	$ (c)	$ (d)	$1,001	$ (d)
Stockholders' equity				
Common stock	880	720	(e)	800
Retained earnings	(d)	(e)	800	(e)
Total stockholders' equity	1,520	1,345	(f)	2,200
Total liabilities and stockholders' equity	$2,250	$ (f)	$3,250	$3,500

Required

a. Divide the class into groups of four or five students each. Organize the groups into four sections. Assign Task 1 to the first section of groups, Task 2 to the second section, Task 3 to the third section, and Task 4 to the fourth section.

Group Tasks

   (1) Fill in the missing information for 2011.

   (2) Fill in the missing information for 2012.

   (3) Fill in the missing information for 2013.

   (4) Fill in the missing information for 2014.

b. Each section should select two representatives. One representative is to put the financial statements assigned to that section on the board, underlining the missing amounts. The second representative is to explain to the class how the missing amounts were determined.

c. Each section should list events that could have caused the unusual items category on the income statement.

ATC 1-3   Research Assignment   *Finding real-world accounting information*

This chapter introduced the basic four financial statements companies use annually to keep their stakeholders informed of their accomplishments and financial situation. Complete the requirements below using the most recent (20xx) financial statements available on the McDonald Corporation's website. Obtain the statements on the Internet by following the steps below. (The formatting of the company's website may have changed since these instructions were written.)

1. Go to www.mcdonalds.com.
2. Click on the "Corporate" link at the bottom of the page. (Most companies have a link titled "investors relations" that leads to their financial statements; McDonald's uses "corporate" instead.)
3. Click on the "INVESTORS" link at the top of the page.

4. Click on *"McDonald's 20xx Annual Report"* and then on *"20xx Financial Report."*
5. Go to the company's financial statements that begin on page 45 of the annual report.

Required

a. What was the company's net income in each of the last 3 years?
b. What amount of total assets did the company have at the end of the most recent year?
c. How much retained earnings did the company have at the end of the most recent year?
d. For the most recent year, what was the company's cash flow from operating activities, cash flow from investing activities, and cash flow from financing activities?

ATC 1-4   Writing Assignment   *Elements of financial statements defined*

Sam and his sister Blair both attend the state university. As a reward for their successful completion of the past year (Sam had a 3.2 GPA in business, and Blair had a 3.7 GPA in art), their father gave each of them 100 shares of The Walt Disney Company stock. They have just received their first annual report. Blair does not understand what the information means and has asked Sam to explain it to her. Sam is currently taking an accounting course, and she knows he will understand the financial statements.

Required

Assume that you are Sam. Write Blair a memo explaining the following financial statement items to her. In your explanation, describe each of the two financial statements and explain the financial information each contains. Also define each of the elements listed for each financial statement and explain what it means.

Balance Sheet
Assets
Liabilities
Stockholders' equity
Income Statement
Revenue
Expense
Net income

CHAPTER 2

Understanding the Accounting Cycle

LEARNING OBJECTIVES

After you have mastered the material in this chapter, you will be able to:

1 Record basic accrual and deferral events in a horizontal financial statements model.

2 Organize general ledger accounts under an accounting equation.

3 Prepare financial statements based on accrual accounting.

4 Describe the closing process, the accounting cycle, and the matching concept.

5 Explain how business events affect financial statements over multiple accounting cycles.

6 Classify accounting events into one of four categories:

a. asset source transactions.

b. asset use transactions.

c. asset exchange transactions.

d. claims exchange transactions.

CHAPTER OPENING

Users of financial statements must distinguish between the terms *recognition* and *realization*. **Recognition** means formally *reporting* an economic item or event in the financial statements. **Realization** refers to collecting money, generally from the sale of products or services. Companies may recognize (report) revenue in the income statement in a different accounting period from the period in which they collect the cash related to the revenue. Furthermore, companies frequently make cash payments for expenses in accounting periods other than the periods in which the expenses are recognized in the income statement.

To illustrate assume Johnson Company provides services to customers in 2012 but collects cash for those services in 2013. In this case, realization occurs in 2013. When should Johnson recognize the services revenue?

Users of *cash basis* accounting recognize (report) revenues and expenses in the period in which cash is collected or paid. Under cash basis accounting Johnson would recognize the revenue in 2013. When it collects the cash. In contrast, users of **accrual accounting** recognize revenues and expenses in the period in which they occur, regardless of when cash is collected or paid. Under accrual accounting Johnson would recognize the revenue in 2012 (the period in which it performed the services) even though it does not collect (realize) the cash until 2013.

Accrual accounting is required by generally accepted accounting principles. Virtually all major companies operating in the United States use it. Its two distinguishing features are called *accruals* and *deferrals*

- The term **accrual** describes a revenue or an expense event that is recognized ***before*** cash is exchanged. Johnson's recognition of revenue in 2012 related to cash realized in 2013 is an example of an accrual.
- The term **deferral** describes a revenue or an expense event that is recognized ***after*** cash has been exchanged. Suppose Johnson pays cash in 2012 to purchase office supplies it uses in 2013. In this case the cash payment occurs in 2012 although supplies expense is recognized in 2013. This example is a deferral.

The Curious Accountant

Suppose Arno Forst wishes to purchase a subscription to *Fitness magazine* for his sister for her birthday. He pays $12 for a one-year subscription to the Meredith Corporation, the company that publishes *Fitness, American Baby, Better Homes and Gardens, The Ladies Home Journal,* and several other magazines. It also owns 12 television stations. His sister will receive her first issue of the magazine in October.

How should Meredith Corporation account for the receipt of this cash? How would this event be reported on its December 31, 2012, financial statements? (Answer on page 60.)

ACCRUAL ACCOUNTING

Record basic accrual and deferral events in a horizontal financial statements model.

The next section of the text describes seven events experienced by Cato Consultants, a training services company that uses accrual accounting.

EVENT 1   Cato Consultants was started on January 1, 2012, when it acquired $5,000 cash by issuing common stock.

The issue of stock for cash is an **asset source transaction.** It increases the company's assets (cash) and its equity (common stock). The transaction does not affect the income statement. The cash inflow is classified as a financing activity (acquisition from owners). These effects are shown in the following financial statements model:

Assets	=	Liab.	+	Stockholders' Equity						
Cash	=			Com. Stk.	+	Ret. Earn.	Rev. − Exp. = Net Inc.			Cash Flow
5,000	=	NA	+	5,000	+	NA	NA − NA = NA			5,000 FA

Accounting for Accounts Receivable

EVENT 2   During 2012 Cato Consultants provided $84,000 of consulting services to its clients. The business has completed the work and sent bills to the clients, but not yet collected any cash. This type of transaction is frequently described as providing services *on account.*

Accrual accounting requires companies to recognize revenue in the period in which the work is done regardless of when cash is collected. In this case, revenue is recognized in 2012 even though cash has not been realized (collected). Recall that revenue represents the economic benefit that results in an increase in assets from providing goods and services to customers. The specific asset that increases is called **Accounts Receivable.** The balance in Accounts Receivable represents the amount of cash the company expects to collect in the future. Since the revenue recognition causes assets (accounts receivable) to increase, it is classified as an asset source transaction. Its effect on the financial statements follows.

Assets			=	Liab.	+	Stockholders' Equity			Rev.	−	Exp.	=	Net Inc.	Cash Flow
Cash	+	Accts. Rec.	=			Com. Stk.	+	Ret. Earn.	Rev.	−	Exp.	=	Net Inc.	Cash Flow
NA	+	84,000	=	NA	+	NA	+	84,000	84,000	−	NA	=	84,000	NA

Notice that the event affects the income statement but not the statement of cash flows. The statement of cash flows will be affected in the future when cash is collected.

EVENT 3   Cato collected $60,000 cash from customers in partial settlement of its accounts receivable.

The collection of an account receivable is an **asset exchange transaction.** One asset account (Cash) increases and another asset account (Accounts Receivable) decreases. The amount of total assets is unchanged. The effect of the $60,000 collection of receivables on the financial statements is as follows.

Assets			=	Liab.	+	Stockholders' Equity			Rev.	−	Exp.	=	Net Inc.	Cash Flow
Cash	+	Accts. Rec.	=			Com. Stk.	+	Ret. Earn.	Rev.	−	Exp.	=	Net Inc.	Cash Flow
60,000	+	(60,000)	=	NA	+	NA	+	NA	NA	−	NA	=	NA	60,000 OA

Notice that collecting the cash did not affect the income statement. The revenue was recognized when the work was done (see Event 2). Revenue would be double counted if it were recognized again when the cash is collected. The statement of cash flows reflects a cash inflow from operating activities.

Other Events

EVENT 4   Cato paid the instructor $10,000 for teaching training courses (salary expense).

Cash payment for salary expense is an **asset use transaction.** Both the asset account Cash and the equity account Retained Earnings decrease by $10,000. Recognizing the expense decreases net income on the income statement. Since Cato paid cash for the expense, the statement of cash flows reflects a cash outflow from operating activities. These effects on the financial statements follow.

Assets		=	Liab.	+	Stockholders' Equity							
Cash	+	Accts. Rec.	=		Com. Stk.	+	Ret. Earn.	Rev.	−	Exp.	=	Net Inc.	Cash Flow
(10,000)	+	NA	=	NA	+	NA	+	(10,000)	NA	−	10,000	=	(10,000)	(10,000) OA

EVENT 5   Cato paid $2,000 cash for advertising costs. The advertisements appeared in 2012.

Cash payments for advertising expenses are asset use transactions. Both the asset account Cash and the equity account Retained Earnings decrease by $2,000. Recognizing the expense decreases net income on the income statement. Since the expense was paid with cash, the statement of cash flows reflects a cash outflow from operating activities. These effects on the financial statements follow.

Assets		=	Liab.	+	Stockholders' Equity							
Cash	+	Accts. Rec.	=		Com. Stk.	+	Ret. Earn.	Rev.	−	Exp.	=	Net Inc.	Cash Flow
(2,000)	+	NA	=	NA	+	NA	+	(2,000)	NA	−	2,000	=	(2,000)	(2,000) OA

EVENT 6   Cato signed contracts for $42,000 of consulting services to be performed in 2013.

The $42,000 for consulting services to be performed in 2013 is not recognized in the 2012 financial statements. Revenue is recognized for work actually completed, *not* work expected to be completed. This event does not affect any of the financial statements.

Assets		=	Liab.	+	Stockholders' Equity							
Cash	+	Accts. Rec.	=		Com. Stk.	+	Ret. Earn.	Rev.	−	Exp.	=	Net Inc.	Cash Flow
NA	+	NA	=	NA	+	NA	+	NA	NA	−	NA	=	NA	NA

Accounting for Accrued Salary Expense (Adjusting Entry)

It is impractical to record many business events as they occur. For example, Cato incurs salary expense continually as the instructor teaches courses. Imagine the impossibility of trying to record salary expense second by second! Companies normally record transactions when it is most convenient. The most convenient time to record many expenses is when they are paid. Often, however, a single business transaction pertains to more than one accounting period. To provide accurate financial reports in such cases, companies may need to recognize some expenses before paying cash for them. Expenses that are recognized before cash is paid are called **accrued expenses.** The accounting for Event 7 illustrates the effect of recognizing accrued salary expense.

EVENT 7   At the end of 2012. Cato recorded accrued salary expense of $6,000 (the salary expense is for courses the instructor taught in 2012 that Cato will pay cash for in 2013).

Accrual accounting requires that companies recognize expenses in the period in which they are incurred regardless of when cash is paid. Cato must recognize all salary expense in the period in which the instructor worked (2012) even though Cato will not pay the instructor again until 2013. Cato must also recognize the obligation (liability) it has to pay the instructor. To accurately report all 2012 salary expense and year-end obligations, Cato must record the unpaid salary expense and salary liability before preparing its financial statements. The entry to recognize the accrued salary expense is called an **adjusting entry.** Like all adjusting entries, it is only to update the accounting records; it does not affect cash.

This adjusting entry decreases stockholders' equity (retained earnings) and increases a liability account called **Salaries Payable.** The balance in the Salaries Payable account represents the amount of cash the company is obligated to pay the instructor in the future. The effect of the expense recognition on the financial statements follows.

Assets			=	Liab.	+	Stockholders' Equity								
Cash	+	Accts. Rec.	=	Sal. Pay.	+	Com. Stk.	+	Ret. Earn.	Rev.	−	Exp.	=	Net Inc.	Cash Flow
NA	+	NA	=	6,000	+	NA	+	(6,000)	NA	−	6,000	=	(6,000)	NA

This event is a **claims exchange transaction.** The claims of creditors (liabilities) increase and the claims of stockholders (retained earnings) decrease. Total claims remain unchanged. The salary expense is reported on the income statement. The statement of cash flows is not affected.

Be careful not to confuse liabilities with expenses. Although liabilities may increase when a company recognizes expenses, liabilities are not expenses. Liabilities are obligations. They can arise from acquiring assets as well as recognizing expenses. For example, when a business borrows money from a bank, it recognizes an increase in assets (cash) and liabilities (notes payable). The borrowing transaction does not affect expenses.

✓ CHECK YOURSELF 2.1

During 2012, Anwar Company earned $345,000 of revenue on account and collected $320,000 cash from accounts receivable. Anwar paid cash expenses of $300,000 and cash dividends of $12,000. Determine the amount of net income Anwar should report on the 2012 income statement and the amount of cash flow from operating activities Anwar should report on the 2012 statement of cash flows.

Answer   Net income is $45,000 ($345,000 revenue − $300,000 expenses). The cash flow from operating activities is $20,000, the amount of revenue collected in cash from customers (accounts receivable) minus the cash paid for expenses ($320,000 − $300,000). Dividend payments are classified as financing activities and do not affect the determination of either net income or cash flow from operating activities.

EXHIBIT 2.1

Transaction Data for 2012 Recorded in General Ledger Accounts

1	Cato Consultants acquired $5,000 cash by issuing common stock.
2	Cato provided $84,000 of consulting services on account.
3	Cato collected $60,000 cash from customers in partial settlement of its accounts receivable.
4	Cato paid $10,000 cash for salary expense.
5	Cato paid $2,000 cash for 2012 advertising costs.
6	Cato signed contracts for $42,000 of consulting services to be performed in 2013.
7	Cato recognized $6,000 of accrued salary expense.

	Assets			=	Liabilities	+	Stockholders' Equity				
Event No.	Cash	+	Accounts Receivable	=	Salaries Payable	+	Common Stock	+	Retained Earnings		Other Account Titles
Beg. bal.	0		0		0		0		0		
1	5,000						5,000				
2			84,000						84,000		Consulting revenue
3	60,000		(60,000)								
4	(10,000)								(10,000)		Salary expense
5	(2,000)								(2,000)		Advertising expense
6											
7					6,000				(6,000)		Salary Expense
End bal.	53,000	+	24,000	=	6,000	+	5,000	+	66,000		

Summary of Events and General Ledger

The previous section of this chapter described seven events Cato Consultants experienced during the 2012 accounting period. These events are summarized in Exhibit 2.1. The associated general ledger accounts are also shown in the exhibit. The information in these accounts is used to prepare the financial statements. The revenue and expense items appear in the Retained Earnings column with their account titles immediately to the right of the dollar amounts. The amounts are color coded to help you trace the data to the financial statements. Data in red appear on the balance sheet, data in blue on the income statement, and data in green on the statement of cash flows.

Organize general ledger accounts under an accounting equation.

Vertical Statements Model

The financial statements for Cato Consultants' 2012 accounting period are represented in a vertical statements model in Exhibit 2.2. A vertical statements model arranges a set of financial statement information vertically on a single page. Like horizontal statements models, vertical statements models are learning tools. They illustrate interrelationships among financial statements. The models do not, however, portray the full, formal presentation formats companies use in published financial statements. For example, statements models may use summarized formats with abbreviated titles and dates. As you read the following explanations of each financial statement, trace the color coded financial data from Exhibit 2.1 to Exhibit 2.2.

Prepare financial statements based on accrual accounting.

EXHIBIT 2.2	Vertical Statements Model

CATO CONSULTANTS
Financial Statements*
Income Statement
For the Year Ended December 31, 2012

Consulting revenue	$84,000
Salary expense	(16,000)
Advertising expense	(2,000)
Net income	$66,000

Statement of Changes in Stockholders' Equity
For the Year Ended December 31, 2012

Beginning common stock	$ 0	
Plus: Common stock issued	5,000	
Ending common stock		$ 5,000
Beginning retained earnings	0	
Plus: Net income	66,000	
Less: Dividends	0	
Ending retained earnings		66,000
Total stockholders' equity		$71,000

Balance Sheet
As of December 31, 2012

Assets		
Cash	$53,000	
Accounts receivable	24,000	
Total assets		$77,000
Liabilities		
Salaries payable		$ 6,000
Stockholders' equity		
Common stock	$ 5,000	
Retained earnings	66,000	
Total stockholders' equity		71,000
Total liabilities and stockholders' equity		$77,000

Statement of Cash Flows
For the Year Ended December 31, 2012

Cash flows from operating activities		
Cash receipts from customers	$60,000	
Cash payments for salary expense	(10,000)	
Cash payments for advertising expenses	(2,000)	
Net cash flow from operating activities		$48,000
Cash flow from investing activities		0
Cash flows from financing activities		
Cash receipt from issuing common stock	5,000	
Net cash flow from financing activities		5,000
Net change in cash		53,000
Plus: Beginning cash balance		0
Ending cash balance		$53,000

*In real-world annual reports, financial statements are normally presented separately with appropriate descriptions of the date to indicate whether the statement applies to the entire accounting period or a specific point in time.

Income Statement

The income statement reflects accrual accounting. Consulting revenue represents the price Cato charged for all the services it performed in 2012, even though Cato had not by the end of the year received cash for some of the services performed. Expenses include all costs incurred to produce revenue, whether paid for by year-end or not. We can now expand the definition of expenses introduced in Chapter 1. Expenses were previously defined as assets consumed in the process of generating revenue. Cato's adjusting entry to recognize accrued salaries expense did not reflect consuming assets. Instead of a decrease in assets, Cato recorded an increase in liabilities (salaries payable). An **expense** can therefore be more precisely defined as *a decrease in assets or an increase in liabilities resulting from operating activities undertaken to generate revenue.*

Statement of Changes in Stockholders' Equity

The statement of changes in stockholders' equity reports the effects on equity of issuing common stock, earning net income, and paying dividends to stockholders. It identifies how an entity's equity increased and decreased during the period as a result of transactions with stockholders and operating the business. In the Cato case, the statement shows that equity increased when the business acquired $5,000 cash by issuing common stock. The statement also reports that equity increased by $66,000 from earning income and that none of the $66,000 of net earnings was distributed to owners (no dividends were paid). Equity at the end of the year is $71,000 ($5,000 + $66,000).

Balance Sheet

The balance sheet discloses an entity's assets, liabilities, and stockholders' equity at a particular point in time. Cato Consultants had two assets at the end of the 2012 accounting period: cash of $53,000 and accounts receivable of $24,000. These assets are listed on the balance sheet in order of liquidity. Of the $77,000 in total assets, creditors have a $6,000 claim, leaving stockholders with a $71,000 claim.

Statement of Cash Flows

The statement of cash flows explains the change in cash from the beginning to the end of the accounting period. It can be prepared by analyzing the Cash account. Since Cato Consultants was established in 2012, its beginning cash balance was zero. By the end of the year, the cash balance was $53,000. The statement of cash flows explains this increase. The Cash account increased because Cato collected $60,000 from customers and decreased because Cato paid $12,000 for expenses. As a result, Cato's net cash inflow from operating activities was $48,000. Also, the business acquired $5,000 cash through the financing activity of issuing common stock, for a cumulative cash increase of $53,000 ($48,000 + $5,000) during 2012.

Comparing Cash Flow from Operating Activities with Net Income

The amount of net income measured using accrual accounting differs from the amount of cash flow from operating activities. For Cato Consulting in 2012, the differences are summarized below.

	Accrual Accounting	Cash Flow
Consulting revenue	$84,000	$60,000
Salary expense	(16,000)	(10,000)
Advertising expense	(2,000)	(2,000)
Net income	$66,000	$48,000

Many students begin their first accounting class with the misconception that revenue and expense items are cash equivalents. The Cato illustration demonstrates that

LO 4

Describe the closing process, the accounting cycle, and the matching concept.

a company may recognize a revenue or expense without a corresponding cash collection or payment in the same accounting period.

The Closing Process

Recall that the temporary accounts (revenue, expense, and dividend) are closed prior to the start of the next accounting cycle. The closing process transfers the amount in each of these accounts to the Retained Earnings account, leaving each temporary account with a zero balance.

Exhibit 2.3 shows the general ledger accounts for Cato Consultants after the revenue and expense accounts have been closed to retained earnings. The closing entry labeled Cl.1 transfers the balance in the Consulting Revenue account to the Retained Earnings account. Closing entries Cl.2 and Cl.3 transfer the balances in the expense accounts to retained earnings.

EXHIBIT 2.3

General Ledger Accounts for Cato Consultants

Assets		=	Liabilities		+	Stockholders' Equity	
Cash			**Salaries Payable**			**Common Stock**	
(1)	5,000		(7)	6,000		(1)	5,000
(3)	60,000		Bal.	6,000			
(4)	(10,000)					**Retained Earnings**	
(5)	(2,000)						
Bal.	53,000					Cl.1	84,000
						Cl.2	(16,000)
						Cl.3	(2,000)
Accounts Receivable						Bal.	66,000
(2)	84,000						
(3)	(60,000)					**Consulting Revenue**	
Bal.	24,000						
						(2)	84,000
						Cl.1	(84,000)
						Bal.	0
						Salary Expense	
						(4)	(10,000)
						(7)	(6,000)
						Cl.2	16,000
						Bal.	0
						Advertising Expense	
						(5)	(2,000)
						Cl.3	2,000
						Bal.	0

Steps in an Accounting Cycle

An accounting cycle, which is represented graphically in Exhibit 2.4, involves several steps. The four steps identified to this point are (1) recording transactions; (2) adjusting the accounts; (3) preparing financial statements; and (4) closing the temporary accounts. The first step occurs continually throughout the accounting period. Steps 2, 3, and 4 normally occur at the end of the accounting period.

The Matching Concept

Cash basis accounting can distort reported net income because it sometimes fails to match expenses with the revenues they produce. To illustrate, consider the $6,000 of accrued salary expense that Cato Consultants recognized at the end of 2012. The instructor's teaching produced revenue in 2012. If Cato waited until 2013 (when it paid the instructor) to recognize $6,000 of the total $16,000 salary expense, then $6,000 of the expense would not be matched with the revenue it generated. By using accrual accounting, Cato recognized all the salary expense in the same accounting period in which the consulting revenue was recognized. A primary goal of accrual accounting is to appropriately match expenses with revenues, the **matching concept.**

Appropriately matching expenses with revenues can be difficult even when using accrual accounting. For example, consider Cato's advertising expense. Money spent on advertising may generate revenue in future accounting periods as well as in the current period. A prospective customer could save an advertising brochure for several years before calling Cato for training services. It is difficult to know when and to what extent advertising produces revenue. When the connection between an expense and the corresponding revenue is vague, accountants commonly match the expense with the period in which it is incurred. Cato matched (recognized) the entire $2,000 of advertising cost with the 2012 accounting period even though some of that cost might generate revenue in future accounting periods. Expenses that are matched with the period in which they are incurred are frequently called **period costs.**

Matching is not perfect. Although it would be more accurate to match expenses with revenues than with periods, there is sometimes no obvious direct connection between expenses and revenue. Accountants must exercise judgment to select the accounting period in which to recognize revenues and expenses. The concept of conservatism influences such judgment calls.

The Conservatism Principle

When faced with a recognition dilemma, **conservatism** guides accountants to select the alternative that produces the lowest amount of net income. In uncertain circumstances, accountants tend to delay revenue recognition and accelerate expense recognition. The conservatism principle holds that it is better to understate net income than to overstate it. If subsequent developments suggest that net income should have been higher, investors will respond more favorably than if they learn it was really lower. This practice explains why Cato recognized all of the advertising cost as expense in 2012 even though some of that cost may generate revenue in future accounting periods.

SECOND ACCOUNTING CYCLE

The effects of Cato Consultants' 2013 events are as follows:

EVENT 1 Cato paid $6,000 to the intructor to settle the salaries payable obligation.

Cash payments to creditors are *asset use transactions.* When Cato pays the instructor, both the asset account Cash and the liability account Salaries Payable decrease. The

Explain how business events affect financial statements over multiple accounting cycles.

cash payment does not affect the income statement. The salary expense was recognized in 2012 when the instructor taught the classes. The statement of cash flows reflects a cash outflow from operating activities. The effects of this transaction on the financial statements are shown here.

Assets	=	Liab.	+	Stk. Equity		Rev.	−	Exp.	=	Net Inc.	Cash Flow
Cash	=	Sal. Pay.				Rev.	−	Exp.	=	Net Inc.	Cash Flow
(6,000)	=	(6,000)	+	NA		NA	−	NA	=	NA	(6,000) OA

Prepaid Items (Cost versus Expense)

EVENT 2   On March 1, 2013, Cato signed a one-year lease agreement and paid $12,000 cash in advance to rent office space. The one-year lease term began on March 1.

Accrual accounting draws a distinction between the terms *cost* and *expense*. A **cost** *might be either an asset or an expense*. If a company has already consumed a purchased resource in the process of earning revenue, the cost of the resource is an *expense*. For example, companies normally pay for electricity the month after using it. The cost of electric utilities is therefore usually recorded as an expense. In contrast, if a company purchases a resource it will use in the future to generate revenue, the cost of the resource represents an *asset*. Accountants record such a cost in an asset account and **defer** recognizing an expense until the resource is used to produce revenue. Deferring the expense recognition provides more accurate **matching** of revenues and expenses.

The cost of the office space Cato leased in Event 2 is an asset. It is recorded in the asset account *Prepaid Rent*. Cato expects to benefit from incurring this cost for the next twelve months. Expense recognition is deferred until Cato uses the office space to help generate revenue. Other common deferred expenses include *prepaid insurance* and *prepaid taxes*. As these titles imply, deferred expenses are frequently called **prepaid items**. Exhibit 2.5 illustrates the relationship between costs, assets, and expenses.

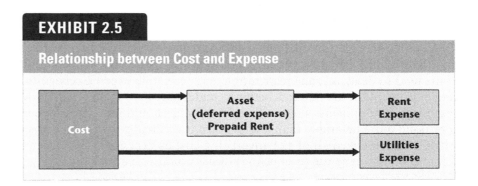

EXHIBIT 2.5

Relationship between Cost and Expense

Cost → Asset (deferred expense) Prepaid Rent → Rent Expense

Cost → Utilities Expense

Purchasing prepaid rent is an asset exchange transaction. The asset account Cash decreases and the asset account Prepaid Rent increases. The amount of total assets is unaffected. The income statement is unaffected. Expense recognition is deferred until the office space is used. The statement of cash flows reflects a cash outflow from operating activities. The effects of this transaction on the financial statements are shown here.

Assets		= Liab. + Stk. Equity			Rev.	–	Exp.	=	Net Inc.	Cash Flow
Cash	+ Prep. Rent									
(12,000)	+ 12,000	= NA	+	NA	NA	–	NA	=	NA	(12,000) OA

Accounting for Receipt of Unearned Revenue

EVENT 3   Cato received $18,000 cash in advance from Westberry Company for consulting services Cato agreed to perform over a one-year period beginning June 1, 2013.

Cato must defer (delay) recognizing any revenue until it performs (does the work) the consulting services for Westberry. From Cato's point of view, the deferred revenue is a liability because Cato is obligated to perform services in the future. The liability is called **unearned revenue.** The cash receipt is an *asset source transaction.* The asset account Cash and the liability account Unearned Revenue both increase. Collecting the cash has no effect on the income statement. The revenue will be reported on the income statement after Cato performs the services. The statement of cash flows reflects a cash inflow from operating activities. The effects of this transaction on the financial statements are shown here.

Assets	=	Liab.	+	Stk. Equity	Rev.	–	Exp.	=	Net Inc.	Cash Flow
Cash	=	Unearn. Rev.								
18,000	=	18,000	+	NA	NA	–	NA	=	NA	18,000 OA

Accounting for Supplies Purchase

EVENT 4   Cato purchased $800 of supplies on account.

The purchase of supplies on account is an *asset source transaction.* The asset account Supplies and the liability account Accounts Payable increase. The income statement is unaffected. Expense recognition is deferred until the supplies are used. The statement of cash flows is not affected. The effects of this transaction on the financial statements are shown here.

Assets	=	Liab.	+	Stk. Equity	Rev.	–	Exp.	=	Net Inc.	Cash Flow
Supplies	=	Accts. Pay.								
800	=	800	+	NA	NA	–	NA	=	NA	NA

Other 2013 Events

EVENT 5   Cato provided $96,400 of consulting services on account.

Providing services on account is an *asset source transaction.* The asset account Accounts Receivable and the stockholders' equity account Retained Earnings increase.

Revenue and net income increase. The statement of cash flows is not affected. The effects of this transaction on the financial statements are shown here.

Assets	=	Liab.	+	Stk. Equity						
Accts. Rec.	=			Ret. Earn.	Rev.	−	Exp.	=	Net Inc.	Cash Flow
96,400	=	NA	+	96,400	96,400	−	NA	=	96,400	NA

EVENT 6   Cato collected $105,000 cash from customers as partial settlement of accounts receivable.

Collecting money from customers who are paying accounts receivable is an *asset exchange transaction.* One asset account (Cash) increases and another asset account (Accounts Receivable) decreases. The amount of total assets is unchanged. The income statement is not affected. The statement of cash flows reports a cash inflow from operating activities. The effects of this transaction on the financial statements are shown here.

Assets			=	Liab.	+	Stk. Equity				
Cash	+	Accts. Rec.					Rev.	−	Exp.	=	Net Inc.	Cash Flow
105,000	+	(105,000)	=	NA	+	NA	NA	−	NA	=	NA	105,000 OA

EVENT 7   Cato paid $32,000 cash for salary expense.

Cash payments for salary expense are *asset use transactions.* Both the asset account Cash and the equity account Retained Earnings decrease by $32,000. Recognizing the expense decreases net income on the income statement. The statement of cash flows reflects a cash outflow from operating activities. The effects of this transaction on the financial statements are shown here.

Assets	=	Liab.	+	Stk. Equity						
Cash	=			Ret. Earn.	Rev.	−	Exp.	=	Net Inc.	Cash Flow
(32,000)	=	NA	+	(32,000)	NA	−	32,000	=	(32,000)	(32,000) OA

EVENT 8   Cato incurred $21,000 of other operating expenses on account.

Recognizing expenses incurred on account are *claims exchange transactions.* One claims account (Accounts Payable) increases and another claims account (Retained Earnings) decreases. The amount of total claims is not affected. Recognizing the expenses decreases net income. The statement of cash flows is not affected. The effects of this transaction on the financial statements are shown here.

Assets	=	Liab.	+	Stk. Equity						
		Accts. Pay.	+	Ret. Earn.	Rev.	−	Exp.	=	Net Inc.	Cash Flow
NA	=	21,000	+	(21,000)	NA	−	21,000	=	(21,000)	NA

EVENT 9   Cato paid $18,200 in partial settlement of accounts payable.

Paying accounts payable is an *asset use transaction.* The asset account Cash and the liability account Accounts Payable decrease. The statement of cash flows reports a cash outflow for operating activities. The income statement is not affected. The effects of this transaction on the financial statements are shown here.

Assets	=	Liab.	+	Stk. Equity	Rev.	−	Exp.	=	Net Inc.	Cash Flow
Cash	=	Accts. Pay.			Rev.	−	Exp.	=	Net Inc.	Cash Flow
(18,200)	=	(18,200)	+	NA	NA	−	NA	=	NA	(18,200) OA

EVENT 10   Cato paid $79,500 to purchase land it planned to use in the future as a building site for its home office.

Purchasing land with cash is an *asset exchange transaction.* One asset account, Cash, decreases and another asset account, Land, increases. The amount of total assets is unchanged. The income statement is not affected. The statement of cash flows reports a cash outflow for investing activities. The effects of this transaction on the financial statements are shown here.

Assets			=	Liab.	+	Stk. Equity	Rev.	−	Exp.	=	Net Inc.	Cash Flow
Cash	+	Land					Rev.	−	Exp.	=	Net Inc.	Cash Flow
(79,500)	+	79,500	=	NA	+	NA	NA	−	NA	=	NA	(79,500) IA

EVENT 11   Cato paid $21,000 in cash dividends to its stockholders.

Cash payments for dividends are *asset use transactions.* Both the asset account Cash and the equity account Retained Earnings decrease. Recall that dividends are wealth transfers from the business to the stockholders, not expenses. They are not incurred in the process of generating revenue. They do not affect the income statement. The statement of cash flows reflects a cash outflow from financing activities. The effects of this transaction on the financial statements are shown here.

Assets	=	Liab.	+	Stk. Equity	Rev.	−	Exp.	=	Net Inc.	Cash Flow
Cash	=			Ret. Earn.	Rev.	−	Exp.	=	Net Inc.	Cash Flow
(21,000)	=	NA	+	(21,000)	NA	−	NA	=	NA	(21,000) FA

EVENT 12   Cato acquired $2,000 cash from issuing additional shares of common stock.

Issuing common stock is an *asset source transaction.* The asset account Cash and the stockholders' equity account Common Stock increase. The income statement is unaffected. The statement of cash flows reports a cash inflow from financing activities. The effects of this transaction on the financial statements are shown here.

Assets	=	Liab.	+	Stk. Equity	Rev.	−	Exp.	=	Net Inc.	Cash Flow
Cash	=			Com. Stk.	Rev.	−	Exp.	=	Net Inc.	Cash Flow
2,000	=	NA	+	2,000	NA	−	NA	=	NA	2,000 FA

Adjusting Entries

Recall that companies make adjusting entries at the end of an accounting period to update the account balances before preparing the financial statements. Adjusting entries ensure that companies report revenues and expenses in the appropriate accounting period; adjusting entries never affect the Cash account.

Accounting for Supplies (Adjusting Entry)

EVENT 13   After determining through a physical count that it had $150 of unused supplies on hand as of December 31, Cato recognized supplies expense.

Companies would find the cost of recording supplies expense each time a pencil, piece of paper, envelope, or other supply item is used to far outweigh the benefit derived from such tedious recordkeeping. Instead, accountants transfer to expense the total cost of all supplies used during the entire accounting period in a single year-end adjusting entry. The cost of supplies used is determined as follows.

Beginning supplies balance + Supplies purchased = Supplies available for use

Supplies available for use − Ending supplies balance = Supplies used

Companies determine the ending supplies balance by physically counting the supplies on hand at the end of the period. Cato used $650 of supplies during the year (zero beginning balance + $800 supplies purchase = $800 available for use; $800 available for use − $150 ending balance = $650). Recognizing Cato's supplies expense is an *asset use transaction.* The asset account Supplies and the stockholders' equity account Retained Earnings decrease. Recognizing supplies expense reduces net income. The statement of cash flows is not affected. The effects of this transaction on the financial statements are shown here.

Assets	=	Liab.	+	Stk. Equity						
Supplies	=			Ret. Earn.	Rev.	−	Exp.	=	Net Inc.	Cash Flow
(650)	=	NA	+	(650)	NA	−	650	=	(650)	NA

Accounting for Prepaid Rent (Adjusting Entry)

EVENT 14   Cato recognized rent expense for the office space used during the accounting period.

Recall that Cato paid $12,000 on March 1, 2013, to rent office space for one year (see Event 2). The portion of the lease cost that represents using office space from March 1 through December 31 is computed as follows.

$12,000 Cost of annual lease ÷ 12 Months = $1,000 Cost per month

$1,000 Cost per month × 10 Months used = $10,000 Rent expense

Recognizing the rent expense decreases the asset account Prepaid Rent and the stockholders' equity account Retained Earnings. Recognizing rent expense reduces net income. The statement of cash flows is not affected. The cash flow effect was recorded in the March 1 event. These effects on the financial statements follow.

Assets	=	Liab.	+	Stk. Equity						
Prep. Rent	=			Ret. Earn.	Rev.	−	Exp.	=	Net Inc.	Cash Flow
(10,000)	=	NA	+	(10,000)	NA	−	10,000	=	(10,000)	NA

✓ CHECK YOURSELF 2.2

Rujoub Inc. paid $18,000 cash for one year of insurance coverage that began on November 1, 2012. Based on this information alone, determine the cash flow from operating activities that Rujoub would report on the 2012 and 2013 statements of cash flows. Also, determine the amount of insurance expense Rujoub would report on the 2012 income statement and the amount of prepaid insurance (an asset) that Rujoub would report on the December 31, 2012, balance sheet.

Answer   Since Rujoub paid all of the cash in 2012, the 2012 statement of cash flows would report an $18,000 cash outflow from operating activities. The 2013 statement of cash flows would report zero cash flow from operating activities. The expense would be recognized in the periods in which the insurance is used. In this case, insurance expense is recognized at the rate of $1,500 per month ($18,000 ÷ 12 months). Rujoub used two months of insurance coverage in 2012 and therefore would report $3,000 (2 months × $1,500) of insurance expense on the 2012 income statement. Rujoub would report a $15,000 (10 months × $1,500) asset, prepaid insurance, on the December 31, 2012, balance sheet. The $15,000 of prepaid insurance would be recognized as insurance expese in 2013 when the insurance coverage is used.

Accounting for Unearned Revenue (Adjusting Entry)

EVENT 15   Cato recognized the portion of the unearned revenue it earned during the accounting period.

Recall that Cato received an $18,000 cash advance from Westberry Company to provide consulting services from June 1, 2013, to May 31, 2014 (see Event 3). By December 31, Cato had earned 7 months (June 1 through December 31) of the revenue related to this contract. Rather than recording the revenue continuously as it performed the consulting services, Cato can simply recognize the amount earned in a single adjustment to the accounting records at the end of the accounting period. The amount of the adjustment is computed as follows.

$18,000 ÷ 12 \text{ months} = $1,500 \text{ revenue earned per month}

$1,500 × 7 \text{ months} = $10,500 \text{ revenue to be recognized in } 2013

The adjusting entry moves $10,500 from the Unearned Revenue account to the Consulting Revenue account. This entry is a *claims exchange transaction.* The liability account Unearned Revenue decreases and the equity account Retained Earnings increases. The effects of this transaction on the financial statements are shown here.

Assets	=	Liab.	+	Stk. Equity						
		Unearn. Rev.	+	Ret. Earn.	Rev.	−	Exp.	=	Net Inc.	Cash Flow
NA	=	(10,500)	+	10,500	10,500	−	NA	=	10,500	NA

Recall that revenue was previously defined as an economic benefit a company obtains by providing customers with goods and services. In this case the economic benefit is a decrease in the liability account Unearned Revenue. **Revenue** can therefore be more precisely defined as *an increase in assets or a decrease in liabilities that a company obtains by providing customers with goods or services.*

✓ CHECK YOURSELF 2.3

Sanderson & Associates received a $24,000 cash advance as a retainer to provide legal services to a client. The contract called for Sanderson to render services during a one-year period beginning October 1, 2012. Based on this information alone, determine the cash flow from operating activities Sanderson would report on the 2012 and 2013 statements of cash flows. Also determine the amount of revenue Sanderson would report on the 2012 and 2013 income statements.

Answer Since Sanderson collected all of the cash in 2012, the 2012 statement of cash flows would report a $24,000 cash inflow from operating activities. The 2013 statement of cash flows would report zero cash flow from operating activities. Revenue is recognized in the period in which it is earned. In this case revenue is earned at the rate of $2,000 per month ($24,000 ÷ 12 months = $2,000 per month). Sanderson rendered services for three months in 2012 and nine months in 2013. Sanderson would report $6,000 (3 months × $2,000) of revenue on the 2012 income statement and $18,000 (9 months × $2,000) of revenue on the 2013 income statement.

Answers to The Curious Accountant

Because the Meredith Corporation receives cash from customers before actually providing any magazines to them, the company has not earned any revenue when it receives the cash. Thus, Meredith has a liability called *unearned revenue.* If it closed its books on December 31, then $3 of Arno's subscription would be recognized as revenue in 2012. The remaining $9 would appear on the balance sheet as a liability.

Meredith Corporation actually ends its accounting year on June 30 each year. A copy of the 2009 balance sheet for the company is presented in Exhibit 2.6. The liability for unearned subscription revenue was $319.1 ($170.7 + $148.4) million—which represented about 30.1 percent of Meredith's total liabilities!

Will Meredith need cash to pay these subscription liabilities? Not exactly. The liabilities will not be paid directly with cash. Instead, they will be satisfied by providing magazines to the subscribers. However, Meredith will need cash to pay for producing and distributing the magazines supplied to the customers. Even so, the amount of cash required to provide magazines will probably differ significantly from the amount of unearned revenues. In most cases, subscription fees do not cover the cost of producing and distributing magazines. By collecting significant amounts of advertising revenue, publishers can provide magazines to customers at prices well below the cost of publication. The amount of unearned revenue is not likely to coincide with the amount of cash needed to cover the cost of satisfying the company's obligation to produce and distribute magazines. Even though the association between unearned revenues and the cost of providing magazines to customers is not direct, a knowledgeable financial analyst can use the information to make estimates of future cash flows and revenue recognition.

| **EXHIBIT 2.6** | Balance Sheet for Meredith Corporation |

CONSOLIDATED BALANCE SHEETS
Meredith Corporation and Subsidiaries
As of June 30 (amounts in thousands)

	2009	2008
Assets		
Current assets		
Cash and cash equivalents	$ 27,910	$ 37,644
Accounts receivable		
(net of allowances of $13,810 in 2009 and $23,944 in 2008)	192,367	230,978
Inventories	28,151	44,085
Current portion of subscription acquisition costs	60,017	59,939
Current portion of broadcast rights	8,297	10,779
Deferred income taxes	—	2,118
Other current assets	23,398	17,547
Total current assets	340,140	403,090
Property, plant, and equipment		
Land	19,500	20,027
Buildings and improvements	125,779	122,977
Machinery and equipment	276,376	273,633
Leasehold improvements	14,208	12,840
Construction in progress	9,041	17,458
Total property, plant, and equipment	444,904	446,935
Less accumulated depreciation	(253,597)	(247,147)
Net property, plant, and equipment	191,307	199,788
Subscription acquisition costs	63,444	60,958
Broadcast rights	4,545	7,826
Other assets	45,907	74,472
Intangible assets, net	561,581	781,154
Goodwill	462,379	532,332
Total assets	$1,669,303	$2,059,620
Liabilities and Shareholders' Equity		
Current liabilities		
Current portion of long-term debt	$ —	$ 75,000
Current portion of long-term broadcast rights payable	10,560	11,141
Accounts payable	86,381	79,028
Accrued expenses		
Compensation and benefits	42,667	40,894
Distribution expenses	12,224	13,890
Other taxes and expenses	26,653	47,923
Total accrued expenses	81,544	102,707
Current portion of unearned subscription revenues	170,731	175,261
Total current liabilities	349,216	443,137
Long-term debt	380,000	410,000
Long-term broadcast rights payable	11,851	17,186
Unearned subscription revenues	148,393	157,872
Deferred income taxes	64,322	139,598
Other noncurrent liabilities	106,138	103,972
Total liabilities	1,059,920	1,271,765
Shareholders' equity		
Series preferred stock, par value $1 per share	—	—
Common stock, par value $1 per share	35,934	36,295
Class B stock, par value $1 per share, convertible to common stock	9,133	9,181
Additional paid-in capital	53,938	52,693
Retained earnings	542,006	701,205
Accumulated other comprehensive income (loss)	(31,628)	(11,519)
Total shareholders' equity	609,383	787,855
Total liabilities and shareholder' equity	$1,669,303	$2,059,620

Accounting for Accrued Salary Expense (Adjusting Entry)

EVENT 16   Cato recognized $4,000 of accrued salary expense.

The adjusting entry to recognize the accrued salary expense is a *claims exchange transaction.* One claims account, Retained Earnings, decreases and another claims account, Salaries Payable, increases. The expense recognition reduces net income. The statement of cash flows is not affected. The effects of this transaction on the financial statements are shown here.

Assets	=	Liab.	+	Stk. Equity						
		Sal. Pay.	+	Ret. Earn.	Rev.	−	Exp.	=	Net Inc.	Cash Flow
NA	=	4,000	+	(4,000)	NA	−	4,000	=	(4,000)	NA

Summary of Events and General Ledger

The previous section of this chapter described sixteen events Cato Consultants experienced the during the 2013 accounting period. These events are summarized in Exhibit 2.7 on page 63. The associated general ledger accounts are also shown in the exhibit. The account balances at the end of 2012; shown in Exhibit 2.3, become the beginning balances for the 2013 accounting period. The 2013 transaction data are referenced to the accounting events with numbers in parentheses. The information in the ledger accounts is the basis for the financial statements in Exhibit 2.8 on pages 64 and 65. Before reading further, trace each event in the summary of events into Exhibit 2.7.

Vertical Statements Model

Financial statement users obtain helpful insights by analyzing company trends over multiple accounting cycles. Exhibit 2.8 presents for Cato Consultants a multicycle **vertical statements model** of 2012 and 2013 accounting data. To conserve space, we have combined all the expenses for each year into single amounts labeled "Operating Expenses," determined as follows.

	2012	2013
Other operating expenses	$ 0	$21,000
Salary expense	16,000	36,000
Rent expense	0	10,000
Advertising expense	2,000	0
Supplies expense	0	650
Total operating expenses	$18,000	$67,650

Similarly, we combined the cash payments for operating expenses on the statement of cash flows as follows.

	2012	2013
Supplies and other operating expenses	$ 0	$18,200*
Salary expense	10,000	38,000
Rent expense	0	12,000
Advertising expense	2,000	0
Total cash payments for operating expenses	$12,000	$68,200

*Amount paid in partial settlement of accounts payable

EXHIBIT 2.7

Ledger Accounts with 2013 Trnsaction Data

1. Cato paid $6,000 to the instructor to settle the salaries payable obligation.
2. On March 1, Cato paid $12,000 cash to lease office space for one year.
3. Cato received $18,000 cash in advance from Westberry Company for consulting services to be performed for one year beginning June 1.
4. Cato purchased $800 of supplies on account.
5. Cato provided $96,400 of consulting services on account.
6. Cato collected $105,000 cash from customers as partial settlement of accounts receivable.
7. Cato paid $32,000 cash for salary expense.
8. Cato incurred $21,000 of other operating expenses on account.
9. Cato paid $18,200 in partial settlement of accounts payable.
10. Cato paid $79,500 to purchase land it planned to use in the future as a building site for its home office.
11. Cato paid $21,000 in cash dividends to its stockholders.
12. Cato acquired $2,000 cash from issuing additional shares of common stock.

The year-end adjustments are:

13. After determining through a physical count that it had $150 of unused supplies on hand as of December 31, Cato recognized supplies expense.
14. Cato recognized rent expense for the office space used during the accounting period.
15. Cato recognized the portion of the unearned revenue it earned during the accounting period.
16. Cato recognized $4,000 of accrued salary expense.

Assets						=	Liabilities		+		Stockholders' Equity	

Assets

Cash		Prepaid Rent	
Bal.	53,000	Bal.	0
(1)	(6,000)	(2)	12,000
(2)	(12,000)	(14)	(10,000)
(3)	18,000	Bal.	2,000
(6)	105,000		
(7)	(32,000)	**Land**	
(9)	(18,200)	Bal.	0
(10)	(79,500)	(10)	79,500
(11)	(21,000)	Bal.	79,500
(12)	2,000		
Bal.	9,300		

Accounts Receivable	
Bal.	24,000
(5)	96,400
(6)	(105,000)
Bal.	15,400

Supplies	
Bal.	0
(4)	800
(13)	(650)
Bal.	150

Liabilities

Accounts Payable	
Bal.	0
(4)	800
(8)	21,000
(9)	(18,200)
Bal.	3,600

Unearned Revenue	
Bal.	0
(3)	18,000
(15)	(10,500)
Bal.	7,500

Salaries Payable	
Bal.	6,000
(1)	(6,000)
(16)	4,000
Bal.	4,000

Stockholders' Equity

Common Stock	
Bal.	5,000
(12)	2,000
Bal.	7,000

Retained Earnings	
Bal.	66,000

Dividends	
Bal.	0
(11)	(21,000)
Bal.	(21,000)

Consulting Revenue	
Bal.	0
(5)	96,400
(15)	10,500
Bal.	106,900

Other Operating Expenses	
Bal.	0
(8)	(21,000)
Bal.	(21,000)

Salary Expense	
Bal.	0
(7)	(32,000)
(16)	(4,000)
Bal.	(36,000)

Rent Expense	
Bal.	0
(14)	(10,000)
Bal.	(10,000)

Supplies Expense	
Bal.	0
(13)	(650)
Bal.	(650)

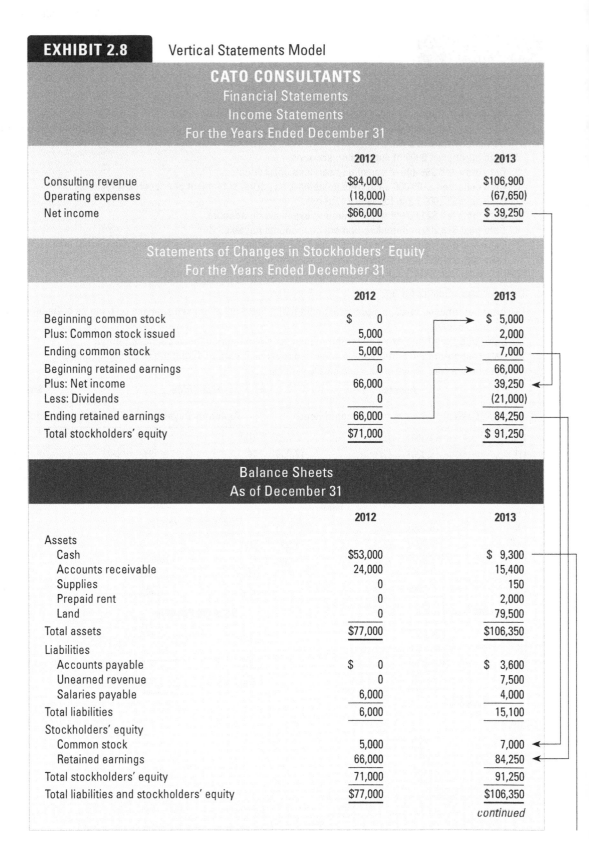

EXHIBIT 2.8   Vertical Statements Model

CATO CONSULTANTS
Financial Statements
Income Statements
For the Years Ended December 31

	2012	2013
Consulting revenue	$84,000	$106,900
Operating expenses	(18,000)	(67,650)
Net income	$66,000	$ 39,250

Statements of Changes in Stockholders' Equity
For the Years Ended December 31

	2012	2013
Beginning common stock	$ 0	$ 5,000
Plus: Common stock issued	5,000	2,000
Ending common stock	5,000	7,000
Beginning retained earnings	0	66,000
Plus: Net income	66,000	39,250
Less: Dividends	0	(21,000)
Ending retained earnings	66,000	84,250
Total stockholders' equity	$71,000	$ 91,250

Balance Sheets
As of December 31

	2012	2013
Assets		
Cash	$53,000	$ 9,300
Accounts receivable	24,000	15,400
Supplies	0	150
Prepaid rent	0	2,000
Land	0	79,500
Total assets	$77,000	$106,350
Liabilities		
Accounts payable	$ 0	$ 3,600
Unearned revenue	0	7,500
Salaries payable	6,000	4,000
Total liabilities	6,000	15,100
Stockholders' equity		
Common stock	5,000	7,000
Retained earnings	66,000	84,250
Total stockholders' equity	71,000	91,250
Total liabilities and stockholders' equity	$77,000	$106,350

continued

EXHIBIT 2.8   *Concluded*

Statements of Cash Flows
For the Years Ended December 31

	2012	2013
Cash Flows from Operating Activities		
Cash receipts from customers	$60,000	$123,000
Cash payments for operating expenses	(12,000)	(68,200)
Net cash flow from operating activities	48,000	54,800
Cash Flows from Investing Activities		
Cash payment to purchase land	0	(79,500)
Cash Flows from Financing Activities		
Cash receipts from issuing common stock	5,000	2,000
Cash payments for dividends	0	(21,000)
Net cash flow from financing activities	5,000	(19,000)
Net change in cash	53,000	(43,700)
Plus: Beginning cash balance	0	53,000
Ending cash balance	$53,000	$ 9,300

Recall that the level of detail reported in financial statements depends on user information needs. Most real-world companies combine many account balances together to report highly summarized totals under each financial statement caption. Before reading further, trace the remaining financial statement items from the ledger accounts in Exhibit 2.7 to where they are reported in Exhibit 2.8.

The vertical statements model in Exhibit 2.8 shows significant interrelationships among the financial statements. For each year, trace the amount of net income from the income statement to the statement of changes in stockholders' equity. Next, trace the ending balances of common stock and retained earnings reported on the statement of changes in stockholders' equity to the stockholders' equity section of the balance sheet. Also, confirm that the amount of cash reported on the balance sheet equals the ending cash balance on the statement of cash flows.

Other relationships connect the two accounting periods. For example, trace the ending retained earnings balance from the 2012 statement of stockholders' equity to the beginning retained earnings balance on the 2013 statement of stockholders' equity. Also, trace the ending cash balance on the 2012 statement of cash flows to the beginning cash balance on the 2013 statement of cash flows. Finally, confirm that the change in cash between the 2012 and 2013 balance sheets ($53,000 − $9,300 = $43,700 decrease) agrees with the net change in cash reported on the 2013 statement of cash flows.

✓ **CHECK YOURSELF 2.4**

Treadmore Company started the 2012 accounting period with $580 of supplies on hand. During 2012 the company paid cash to purchase $2,200 of supplies. A physical count of supplies indicated that there was $420 of supplies on hand at the end of 2012. Treadmore pays cash for supplies at the time they are purchased. Based on this information alone, determine the amount of supplies expense to be recognized on the income statement and the amount of cash flow to be shown in the operating activities section of the statement of cash flows.

Answer   The amount of supplies expense recognized on the income statement is the amount of supplies that were used during the accounting period. This amount is computed below.

$580 Beginning balance + $2,200 Supplies purchases = $2,780 Supplies available for use

$2,780 Supplies available for use − $420 Ending supplies balance = $2,360 supplies used

The cash flow from operating activities is the amount of cash paid for supplies during the accounting period. In this case, Treadmore paid $2,200 cash to purchase supplies. This amount would be shown as a cash outflow.

TRANSACTION CLASSIFICATION

Classify accounting events into one of four categories:

a. asset source transactions.
b. asset use transactions.
c. asset exchange transactions.
d. claims exchange transactions.

Chapters 1 and 2 introduced four types of transactions. Although businesses engage in an infinite number of different transactions, all transactions fall into one of four types. By learning to identify transactions by type, you can understand how unfamiliar events affect financial statements. The four types of transactions are

1. *Asset source transactions:* An asset account increases, and a corresponding claims account increases.

2. *Asset use transactions:* An asset account decreases, and a corresponding claims account decreases.

3. *Asset exchange transactions:* One asset account increases, and another asset account decreases.

4. *Claims exchange transactions:* One claims account increases, and another claims account decreases.

Also, the definitions of revenue and expense have been expanded. The complete definitions of these two elements are as follows.

1. **Revenue:** Revenue is the *economic benefit* derived from operating the business. Its recognition is accompanied by an increase in assets or a decrease in liabilities resulting from providing products or services to customers.

2. **Expense:** An expense is an *economic sacrifice* incurred in the process of generating revenue. Its recognition is accompanied by a decrease in assets or an increase in liabilities resulting from consuming assets and services in an effort to produce revenue.

≪ A Look Back

This chapter introduced accrual accounting. Accrual accounting distinguishes between *recognition* and *realization*. Recognition means reporting an economic item or event in the financial statements. In contrast, realization refers to collecting cash from the sale of assets or services. Recognition and realization can occur in different accounting periods. In addition, cash payments for expenses often occur in different accounting periods from when a company recognizes the expenses. Accrual accounting uses both *accruals* and *deferrals*.

■ The term *accrual* applies to a revenue or an expense event that are recognized before cash is exchanged. Recognizing revenue on account or accrued salaries expense are examples of accruals.

■ The term *deferral* applies to a revenue or an expense event that are recognized after cash has been exchanged. Supplies, prepaid items, and unearned revenue are examples of deferrals.

Virtually all major companies operating in the United States use accrual accounting.

A Look Forward

Chapters 1 and 2 focused on businesses that generate revenue by providing services to their customers. Examples of these types of businesses include consulting, real estate sales, medical services, and legal services. The next chapter introduces accounting practices for businesses that generate revenue by selling goods. Examples of these companies include Wal-Mart, Circuit City, Office Depot, and Lowes.

A step-by-step audio-narrated series of slides is provided on the text website at www.mhhe.com/edmondssurvey3e

 ### SELF-STUDY REVIEW PROBLEM

Gifford Company experienced the following accounting events during 2012.

1. Started operations on January 1 when it acquired $20,000 cash by issuing common stock.
2. Earned $18,000 of revenue on account.
3. On March 1 collected $36,000 cash as an advance for services to be performed in the future.
4. Paid cash operating expenses of $17,000.
5. Paid a $2,700 cash dividend to stockholders.
6. On December 31, 2012, adjusted the books to recognize the revenue earned by providing services related to the advance described in Event 3. The contract required Gifford to provide services for a one-year period starting March 1.
7. Collected $15,000 cash from accounts receivable.

Gifford Company experienced the following accounting events during 2013.

1. Earned $38,000 of cash revenue.
2. On April 1 paid $12,000 cash for an insurance policy that provides coverage for one year beginning immediately.
3. Collected $2,000 cash from accounts receivable.
4. Paid cash operating expenses of $21,000.
5. Paid a $5,000 cash dividend to stockholders.
6. On December 31, 2013, adjusted the books to recognize the remaining revenue earned by providing services related to the advance described in Event 3 of 2012.
7. On December 31, 2013, Gifford adjusted the books to recognize the amount of the insurance policy used during 2013.

Required

a. Record the events in a financial statements model like the following one. The first event is recorded as an example.

Event No.	Assets			=	Liab.	+	Stockholders' Equity							Cash Flow
	Cash + Accts. Rec. − Prep. Ins.			=	Unearn. Rev.	+	Com. Stk. + Ret. Earn.			Rev. − Exp. = Net Inc.				
1	20,000 +	NA	− NA	=	NA	+	20,000 +	NA		NA − NA =	NA			20,000 FA

b. What amount of revenue would Gifford report on the 2012 income statement?
c. What amount of cash flow from customers would Gifford report on the 2012 statement of cash flows?
d. What amount of unearned revenue would Gifford report on the 2012 and 2013 year-end balance sheets?
e. What are the 2013 opening balances for the revenue and expense accounts?

f. What amount of total assets would Gifford report on the December 31, 2012, balance sheet?

g. What claims on assets would Gifford report on the December 31, 2013, balance sheet?

Solution to Requirement a

The financial statements model follows.

Event No.	Cash	+	Accts. Rec.	+	Prep. Ins.	=	Unearn. Rev.	+	Com. Stk.	+	Ret. Earn.	Rev.	−	Exp.	=	Net Inc.	Cash Flow
2012																	
1	20,000	+	NA	+	NA	=	NA	+	20,000	+	NA	NA	−	NA	=	NA	20,000 FA
2	NA	+	18,000	+	NA	=	NA	+	NA	+	18,000	18,000	−	NA	=	18,000	NA
3	36,000	+	NA	+	NA	=	36,000	+	NA	+	NA	NA	−	NA	=	NA	36,000 OA
4	(17,000)	+	NA	+	NA	=	NA	+	NA	+	(17,000)	NA	−	17,000	=	(17,000)	(17,000) OA
5	(2,700)	+	NA	+	NA	=	NA	+	NA	+	(2,700)	NA	−	NA	=	NA	(2,700) FA
6*	NA	+	NA	+	NA	=	(30,000)	+	NA	+	30,000	30,000	−	NA	=	30,000	NA
7	15,000	+	(15,000)	+	NA	=	NA	+	NA	+	NA	NA	−	NA	=	NA	15,000 OA
Bal.	51,300	+	3,000	+	NA	=	6,000	+	20,000	+	28,300	48,000	−	17,000	=	31,000	51,300 NC

Asset, liability, and equity account balances carry forward · Rev. & exp. accts. are closed

Event No.	Cash	+	Accts. Rec.	+	Prep. Ins.	=	Unearn. Rev.	+	Com. Stk.	+	Ret. Earn.	Rev.	−	Exp.	=	Net Inc.	Cash Flow
2013																	
Bal.	51,300	+	3,000	+	NA	=	6,000	+	20,000	+	28,300	NA	−	NA	=	NA	NA
1	38,000	+	NA	+	NA	=	NA	+	NA	+	38,000	38,000	−	NA	=	38,000	38,000 OA
2	(12,000)	+	NA	+	12,000	=	NA	+	NA	+	NA	NA	−	NA	=	NA	(12,000) OA
3	2,000	+	(2,000)	+	NA	=	NA	+	NA	+	NA	NA	−	NA	=	NA	2,000 OA
4	(21,000)	+	NA	+	NA	=	NA	+	NA	+	(21,000)	NA	−	21,000	=	(21,000)	(21,000) OA
5	(5,000)	+	NA	+	NA	=	NA	+	NA	+	(5,000)	NA	−	NA	=	NA	(5,000) FA
6*	NA	+	NA	+	NA	=	(6,000)	+	NA	+	6,000	6,000	−	NA	=	6,000	NA
7†	NA	+	NA	+	(9,000)	=	NA	+	NA	+	(9,000)	NA	−	9,000	=	(9,000)	NA
Bal.	53,300	+	1,000	+	3,000	=	0	+	20,000	+	37,300	44,000	−	30,000	=	14,000	2,000 NC

*Revenue is earned at the rate of $3,000 ($36,000 ÷ 12 months) per month. Revenue recognized in 2012 is $30,000 ($3,000 × 10 months). Revenue recognized in 2013 is $6,000 ($3,000 × 2 months).

†Insurance expense is incurred at the rate of $1,000 ($12,000 ÷ 12 months) per month. Insurance expense recognized in 2013 is $9,000 ($1,000 × 9 months).

Solutions to Requirements b–g

b. Gifford would report $48,000 of revenue in 2012 ($18,000 revenue on account plus $30,000 of the $36,000 of unearned revenue).

c. The cash inflow from customers is $51,000 ($36,000 when the unearned revenue was received plus $15,000 collection of accounts receivable).

d. The December 31, 2012, balance sheet will report $6,000 of unearned revenue, which is the amount of the cash advance less the amount of revenue recognized in 2012 ($36,000 − $30,000). The December 31, 2013, unearned revenue balance is zero.

e. Since revenue and expense accounts are closed at the end of each accounting period, the beginning balances in these accounts are always zero.

f. Assets on the December 31, 2012, balance sheet are $54,300 [Gifford's cash at year end plus the balance in accounts receivable ($51,300 + $3,000)].

g. Since all unearned revenue would be recognized before the financial statements were prepared at the end of 2013, there would be no liabilities on the 2013 balance sheet. Common stock and retained earnings would be the only claims as of December 31, 2013, for a claims total of $57,300 ($20,000 + $37,300).

KEY TERMS

Accounts Receivable 46	Accrued expenses 48	Asset source
Accrual 45	Adjusting entry 48	transaction 46
Accrual accounting 45	Asset exchange transaction 46	Asset use transaction 47

QUESTIONS

1. What does accrual accounting attempt to accomplish?

2. Define *recognition.* How is it independent of collecting or paying cash?

3. What does the term *deferral* mean?

4. If cash is collected in advance of performing services, when is the associated revenue recognized?

5. What does the term *asset source transaction* mean?

6. What effect does the issue of common stock have on the accounting equation?

7. How does the recognition of revenue on account (accounts receivable) affect the income statement compared to its effect on the statement of cash flows?

8. Give an example of an asset source transaction. What is the effect of this transaction on the accounting equation?

9. When is revenue recognized under accrual accounting?

10. Give an example of an asset exchange transaction. What is the effect of this transaction on the accounting equation?

11. What is the effect on the claims side of the accounting equation when cash is collected in advance of performing services?

12. What does the term *unearned revenue* mean?

13. What effect does expense recognition have on the accounting equation?

14. What does the term *claims exchange transaction* mean?

15. What type of transaction is a cash payment to creditors? How does this type of transaction affect the accounting equation?

16. When are expenses recognized under accrual accounting?

17. Why may net cash flow from operating activities on the cash flow statement be different from the amount of net income reported on the income statement?

18. What is the relationship between the income statement and changes in assets and liabilities?

19. How does net income affect the stockholders' claims on the business's assets?

20. What is the difference between a cost and an expense?

21. When does a cost become an expense? Do all costs become expenses?

22. How and when is the cost of the *supplies used* recognized in an accounting period?

23. What does the term *expense* mean?

24. What does the term *revenue* mean?

25. What is the purpose of the statement of changes in stockholders' equity?

26. What is the main purpose of the balance sheet?

27. Why is the balance sheet dated *as of* a specific date when the income statement, statement of changes in stockholders' equity, and statement of cash flows are dated with the phrase *for the period ended?*

28. In what order are assets listed on the balance sheet?

29. What does the statement of cash flows explain?

30. What does the term *adjusting entry* mean? Give an example.

31. What types of accounts are closed at the end of the accounting period? Why is it necessary to close these accounts?

32. Give several examples of period costs.

33. Give an example of a cost that can be directly matched with the revenue produced by an accounting firm from preparing a tax return.

34. List and describe the four stages of the accounting cycle discussed in Chapter 2.

MULTIPLE-CHOICE QUESTIONS

**Multiple-choice questions are provided on the text website at
www.mhhe.com/edmondssurvey3e.**

EXERCISES

All applicable Exercises are available with McGraw-Hill's
Connect Accounting.

Where applicable in all exercises, round computations to the nearest dollar.

LO 2, 3

Exercise 2-1   *Effect of accruals on the financial statements*

Valmont, Inc., experienced the following events in 2012, in its first year of operation.

1. Received $20,000 cash from the issue of common stock.
2. Performed services on account for $50,000.
3. Paid the utility expense of $12,500.
4. Collected $39,000 of the accounts receivable.
5. Recorded $9,000 of accrued salaries at the end of the year.
6. Paid a $5,000 cash dividend to the shareholders.

Required

a. Record the events in general ledger accounts under an accounting equation. In the last column of the table, provide appropriate account titles for the Retained Earnings amounts. The first transaction has been recorded as an example.

	VALMONT, INC.						
	General Ledger Accounts						
Event	Assets		=	Liabilities	+	Stockholders' Equity		Acct. Titles for RE
	Cash	Accounts Receivable		Salaries Payable		Common Stock	Retained Earnings	
1.	20,000					20,000		

b. Prepare the income statement, statement of changes in stockholders' equity, balance sheet, and statement of cash flows for the 2012 accounting period.

c. Why is the amount of net income different from the amount of net cash flow from operating activities?

LO 2, 3

Exercise 2-2   *Effect of collecting accounts receivable on the accounting equation and financial statements*

Schroder Company earned $14,000 of service revenue on account during 2012. The company collected $11,500 cash from accounts receivable during 2012.

Required

Based on this information alone, determine the following. (*Hint:* Record the events in general ledger accounts under an accounting equation before satisfying the requirements.)

a. The balance of the accounts receivable that Schroder would report on the December 31, 2012, balance sheet.

b. The amount of net income that Schroder would report on the 2012 income statement.

c. The amount of net cash flow from operating activities that Schroder would report on the 2012 statement of cash flows.

d. The amount of retained earnings that Schroder would report on the 2012 balance sheet.

e. Why are the answers to Requirements *b* and *c* different?

LO 2, 3

Exercise 2-3   *Effect of prepaid rent on the accounting equation and financial statements*

The following events apply to 2012, the first year of operations of Sentry Services.

1. Acquired $45,000 cash from the issue of common stock.
2. Paid $18,000 cash in advance for one-year rental contract for office space.

3. Provided services for $36,000 cash.
4. Adjusted the records to recognize the use of the office space. The one-year contract started on May 1, 2012. The adjustment was made as of December 31, 2012.

Required

a. Write an accounting equation and record the effects of each accounting event under the appropriate general ledger account headings.
b. Prepare an income statement and statement of cash flows for the 2012 accounting period.
c. Explain the difference between the amount of net income and amount of net cash flow from operating activities.

Exercise 2-4 *Effect of supplies on the financial statements*

LO 1, 3

Green Copy Service, Inc., started the 2012 accounting period with $16,000 cash, $10,000 of common stock, and $6,000 of retained earnings. Green Copy Service was affected by the following accounting events during 2012.

1. Purchased $9,600 of paper and other supplies on account.
2. Earned and collected $39,000 of cash revenue.
3. Paid $7,000 cash on accounts payable.
4. Adjusted the records to reflect the use of supplies. A physical count indicated that $2,200 of supplies was still on hand on December 31, 2012.

Required

a. Show the effects of the events on the financial statements using a horizontal statements model like the following one. In the Cash Flows column, use OA to designate operating activity, IA for investing activity, FA for financing activity, and NC for net change in cash. Use NA to indicate accounts not affected by the event. The beginning balances are entered in the following example.

Event No.	Assets			=	Liab.	+	Stockholders' Equity			Rev.	−	Exp.	=	Net Inc.	Cash Flows
	Cash	+	Supplies	=	Accts. Pay	+	C. Stock	+	Ret. Earn.						
Beg. Bal.	16,000	+	0	=	0	+	10,000	+	6,000	0	−	0	=	0	0

b. Explain the difference between the amount of net income and amount of net cash flow from operating activities.

Exercise 2-5 *Effect of unearned revenue on financial statements*

LO 1, 3, 5

Michael Stone started a personal financial planning business when he accepted $120,000 cash as advance payment for managing the financial assets of a large estate. Stone agreed to manage the estate for a one-year period, beginning April 1, 2012.

Required

a. Show the effects of the advance payment and revenue recognition on the 2012 financial statements using a horizontal statements model like the following one. In the Cash Flows column, use OA to designate operating activity, IA for investing activity, FA for financing activity, and NC for net change in cash. Use NA if the account is not affected.

Event No.	Assets	=	Liab.	+	Stockholders' Equity	Rev.	−	Exp.	=	Net Inc.	Cash Flows
	Cash	=	Unearn. Rev.	+	Ret. Earn.						

b. How much revenue would Stone recognize on the 2013 income statement?
c. What is the amount of cash flow from operating activities in 2013?

Exercise 2-6 *Unearned revenue defined as a liability*

LO 3

Harry Baldwin received $500 in advance for tutoring fees when he agreed to help Joseph Jones with his introductory accounting course. Upon receiving the cash, Harry mentioned that he would have to record the transaction as a liability on his books. Jones asked, "Why a liability? You don't owe me any money, do you?"

Required

Respond to Jones' question regarding Baldwin's liability.

LO 3

Exercise 2-7 *Distinguishing between an expense and a cost*

Eddie Kirn tells you that the accountants where he works are real hair splitters. For example, they make a big issue over the difference between a cost and an expense. He says the two terms mean the same thing to him.

Required

a. Explain to Eddie the difference between a cost and an expense from an accountant's perspective.

b. Indicate whether each of the following events produces an asset or an expense.

(1) Recognized accrued salaries.

(2) Paid in advance for insurance on the building.

(3) Used supplies on hand to produce revenue.

(4) Purchased supplies on account.

(5) Purchased a building for cash.

LO 3

Exercise 2-8 *Revenue and expense recognition*

Required

a. Describe an expense recognition event that results in a decrease in assets.

b. Describe an expense recognition event that results in an increase in liabilities.

c. Describe a revenue recognition event that results in an increase in assets.

d. Describe a revenue recognition event that results in a decrease in liabilities.

LO 3

Exercise 2-9 *Transactions that affect the elements of financial statements*

Required

Give an example of a transaction that will

a. Increase a liability and decrease equity (claims exchange event).

b. Increase an asset and increase equity (asset source event).

c. Decrease a liability and increase equity (claims exchange event).

d. Increase an asset and decrease another asset (asset exchange event).

e. Increase an asset and increase a liability (asset source event).

f. Decrease an asset and decrease a liability (asset use event).

g. Decrease an asset and decrease equity (asset use event).

LO 3

Exercise 2-10 *Identifying deferral and accrual events*

Required

Identify each of the following events as an accrual, deferral, or neither.

a. Provided services on account.

b. Collected accounts receivable.

c. Paid one year's rent in advance.

d. Paid cash for utilities expense.

e. Collected $2,400 in advance for services to be performed over the next 12 months.

f. Incurred other operating expenses on account.

g. Recorded expense for salaries owed to employees at the end of the accounting period.

h. Paid a cash dividend to the stockholders.

i. Paid cash to purchase supplies to be used over the next several months.

j. Purchased land with cash.

Exercise 2-11 *Prepaid and unearned rent*

LO 2

On August 1, 2012, Woodworks paid Warehouse Rentals $54,000 for a 12-month lease on warehouse space.

Required

a. Record the deferral and the related December 31, 2012, adjustment for Woodworks in the accounting equation.

b. Record the deferral and the related December 31, 2012, adjustment for Warehouse Rentals in the accounting equation.

Exercise 2-12 *Classifying events on the statement of cash flows*

LO 3

The following transactions pertain to the operations of Fleming Company for 2012.

1. Acquired $40,000 cash from the issue of common stock.
2. Performed services for $12,000 cash.
3. Provided $55,000 of services on account.
4. Received $36,000 cash in advance for services to be performed over the next two years.
5. Incurred $30,000 of other operating expenses on account.
6. Collected $45,000 cash from accounts receivable.
7. Paid $4,000 cash for rent expense.
8. Paid $12,000 for one year's prepaid insurance.
9. Paid a $5,000 cash dividend to the stockholders.
10. Paid $22,000 cash on accounts payable.

Required

a. Classify the cash flows from these transactions as operating activities (OA), investing activities (IA), or financing activities (FA). Use NA for transactions that do not affect the statement of cash flows.

b. Prepare a statement of cash flows. (There is no beginning cash balance.)

Exercise 2-13 *Effect of accounting events on the income statement and statement of cash flows*

LO 3

Required

Explain how each of the following events and the related adjusting entry will affect the amount of *net income* and the amount of *cash flow from operating activities* reported on the year-end financial statements. Identify the direction of change (increase, decrease, or NA) and the amount of the change. Organize your answers according to the following table. The first event is recorded as an example. If an event does not have a related adjusting entry, record only the effects of the event. All adjustments are made on December 31.

	Net Income		Cash Flows from Operating Activities	
Event No.	Direction of Change	Amount of Change	Direction of Change	Amount of Change
a	NA	NA	NA	NA

a. Acquired $50,000 cash from the issue of common stock.
b. Paid $4,800 cash on October 1 to purchase a one-year insurance policy.
c. Collected $18,000 in advance for services to be performed in the future. The contract called for services to start on September 1 and to continue for one year.
d. Earned $22,000 of revenue on account. Collected $18,000 cash from accounts receivable.
e. Sold land that had cost $10,000 for $10,000.
f. Accrued salaries amounting to $8,000.

g. Provided services for $12,000 cash.

h. Paid cash for other operating expenses of $3,500.

i. Purchased $1,800 of supplies on account. Paid $1,500 cash on accounts payable. The ending balance in the Supplies account, after adjustment, was $600.

LO 1, 6

Exercise 2-14 *Identifying transaction type and effect on the financial statements*

Required

Identify whether each of the following transactions is an asset source (AS), asset use (AU), asset exchange (AE), or claims exchange (CE). Also show the effects of the events on the financial statements using the horizontal statements model. Indicate whether the event increases (I), decreases (D), or does not affect (NA) each element of the financial statements. In the Cash Flows column, designate the cash flows as operating activities (OA), investing activities (IA), or financing activities (FA). The first two transactions have been recorded as examples.

Event No.	Type of Event	Assets	=	Liabilities	+	Stockholders' Equity Common Stock	+	Stockholders' Equity Retained Earnings	Rev.	−	Exp.	=	Net Inc.	Cash Flows	
a	AS	I		NA		I		NA	NA		NA		NA	I	FA
b	AE	I/D		NA		NA		NA	NA		NA		NA	D	IA

a. Acquired cash from the issue of common stock.

b. Purchased land for cash.

c. Paid cash advance for rent on office space.

d. Collected cash from accounts receivable.

e. Performed services for cash.

f. Purchased a building with part cash *and* issued a note payable for the balance.

g. Paid cash for operating expenses.

h. Paid cash for supplies.

i. Paid a cash dividend to the stockholders.

j. Incurred operating expenses on account.

k. Paid cash on accounts payable.

l. Received cash advance for services to be provided in the future.

m. Recorded accrued salaries.

n. Performed services on account.

o. Adjusted books to reflect the amount of prepaid rent expired during the period.

p. Paid cash for salaries accrued at the end of a prior period.

LO 1

Exercise 2-15 *Effect of accruals and deferrals on financial statements: the horizontal statements model*

K. Little, Attorney at Law, experienced the following transactions in 2012, the first year of operations.

1. Purchased $2,800 of office supplies on account.

2. Accepted $30,000 on February 1, 2012, as a retainer for services to be performed evenly over the next 12 months.

3. Performed legal services for cash of $87,000.

4. Paid cash for salaries expense of $38,500.

5. Paid a cash dividend of $10,000 to the stockholders.

6. Paid $1,800 of the amount due on accounts payable.
7. Determined that at the end of the accounting period, $300 of office supplies remained on hand.
8. On December 31, 2012, recognized the revenue that had been earned for services performed in accordance with Transaction 2.

Required

Show the effects of the events on the financial statements using a horizontal statements model like the following one. In the Cash Flow column, use the initials OA to designate operating activity, IA for investing activity, FA for financing activity, and NC for net change in cash. Use NA to indicate accounts not affected by the event. The first event has been recorded as an example.

Event No.	Assets		=	Liabilities			+	Stk. Equity	Rev.	–	Exp.	=	Net Inc.	Cash Flow
	Cash	+ Supp.	=	Accts. Pay.	+	Unearn. Rev.	+	Ret. Earn.						
1	NA	+ 2,800	=	2,800	+	NA	+	NA	NA	–	NA	=	NA	NA

Exercise 2-16 *Effect of an error on financial statements*   **LO 2, 3**

On May 1, 2012, Virginia Corporation paid $18,000 cash in advance for a one-year lease on an office building. Assume that Virginia records the prepaid rent and that the books are closed on December 31.

Required

a. Show the payment for the one-year lease and the related adjusting entry to rent expense in the accounting equation.
b. Assume that Virginia Corporation failed to record the adjusting entry to reflect using the office building. How would the error affect the company's 2012 income statement and balance sheet?

Exercise 2-17 *Net income versus changes in cash*   **LO 2, 3**

In 2012, Cherry Design billed its customers $58,000 for services performed. The company collected $46,000 of the amount billed. Cherry Design incurred $41,000 of other operating expenses on acount. Cherry Design paid $30,000 of the accounts payable. Cherry Design acquired $40,000 cash from the issue of common stock. The company invested $20,000 cash in the purchase of land.

Required

Use the preceding information to answer the following questions. (*Hint:* Identify the six events described in the paragraph and record them in general ledger accounts under an accounting equation before attempting to answer the questions.)

a. What amount of revenue will Cherry Design report on the 2012 income statement?
b. What amount of cash flow from revenue will Cherry Design report on the statement of cash flows?
c. What is the net income for the period?
d. What is the net cash flow from operating activities for the period?
e. Why is the amount of net income different from the net cash flow from operating activities for the period?
f. What is the amount of net cash flow from investing activities?
g. What is the amount of net cash flow from financing activities?
h. What amounts of total assets, liabilities, and equity will Cherry Design report on the year-end balance sheet?

LO 3

Exercise 2-18 *Adjusting the accounts*

Keystore Systems experienced the following accounting events during its 2012 accounting period.

1. Paid cash to purchase land.
2. Recognized revenue on account.
3. Issued common stock.
4. Paid cash to purchase supplies.
5. Collected a cash advance for services that will be provided during the coming year.
6. Paid a cash dividend to the stockholders.
7. Paid cash for an insurance policy that provides coverage during the next year.
8. Collected cash from accounts receivable.
9. Paid cash for operating expenses.
10. Paid cash to settle an account payable.

Required

a. Identify the events that would require a year-end adjusting entry.
b. Explain why adjusting entries are made at the end of the accounting period.

LO 4, 5

Exercise 2-19 *Closing the accounts*

The following information was drawn from the accounting records of Kwon Company as of December 31, 2012, before the temporary accounts had been closed. The Cash balance was $4,000, and Notes Payable amounted to $2,000. The company had revenues of $6,000 and expenses of $3,500. The company's Land account had a $9,000 balance. Dividends amounted to $500. There was $6,000 of common stock issued.

Required

a. Identify which accounts would be classified as permanent and which accounts would be classified as temporary.
b. Assuming that Kwon's beginning balance (as of January 1, 2012) in the Retained Earnings account was $2,600, determine its balance after the nominal accounts were closed at the end of 2012.
c. What amount of net income would Kwon Company report on its 2012 income statement?
d. Explain why the amount of net income differs from the amount of the ending Retained Earnings balance.
e. What are the balances in the revenue, expense, and dividend accounts on January 1, 2013?

LO 4

Exercise 2-20 *Closing accounts and the accounting cycle*

Required

a. Identify which of the following accounts are temporary (will be closed to Retained Earnings at the end of the year) and which are permanent.
   (1) Land
   (2) Salaries Expense
   (3) Retained Earnings
   (4) Prepaid Rent
   (5) Supplies Expense
   (6) Common Stock
   (7) Notes Payable
   (8) Cash
   (9) Service Revenue
   (10) Dividends
b. List and explain the four stages of the accounting cycle. Which stage must be first? Which stage is last?

Exercise 2-21 *Closing entries*   LO 4

Required

Which of the following accounts are closed at the end of the accounting period?

a. Accounts Payable
b. Unearned Revenue
c. Prepaid Rent
d. Rent Expense
e. Service Revenue
f. Advertising Expense
g. Dividends
h. Retained Earnings
i. Utilities Expense
j. Salaries Payable
k. Salaries Expense
l. Operating Expenses

Exercise 2-22 *Matching concept*   LO 4

Companies make sacrifices known as *expenses* to obtain benefits called *revenues*. The accurate measurement of net income requires that expenses be matched with revenues. In some circumstances matching a particular expense directly with revenue is difficult or impossible. In these circumstances, the expense is matched with the period in which it is incurred.

Required

Distinguish the following items that could be matched directly with revenues from the items that would be classified as period expenses.

a. Sales commissions paid to employees.
b. Utilities expense.
c. Rent expense.
d. The cost of land that has been sold.

Exercise 2-23 *Identifying source, use, and exchange transactions*   LO 6

Required

Indicate whether each of the following transactions is an asset source (AS), asset use (AU), asset exchange (AE), or claims exchange (CE) transaction.

a. Acquired cash from the issue of stock.
b. Paid a cash dividend to the stockholders.
c. Paid cash on accounts payable.
d. Incurred other operating expenses on account.
e. Paid cash for rent expense.
f. Performed services for cash.
g. Performed services for clients on account.
h. Collected cash from accounts receivable.
i. Invested cash in a certificate of deposit.
j. Purchased land with cash.

Exercise 2-24 *Identifying asset source, use, and exchange transactions*   LO 6

Required

a. Name an asset exchange transaction that will *not* affect the statement of cash flows.
b. Name an asset exchange transaction that will affect the statement of cash flows.
c. Name an asset source transaction that will *not* affect the income statement.
d. Name an asset use transaction that will affect the income statement.
e. Name an asset use transaction that will *not* affect the income statement.

LO 3

Exercise 2-25   *Relation of elements to financial statements*

Required

Identify whether each of the following items would appear on the income statement (IS), statement of changes in stockholders' equity (SE), balance sheet (BS), or statement of cash flows (CF). Some items may appear on more than one statement; if so, identify all applicable statements. If an item would not appear on any financial statement, label it NA.

a. Prepaid rent

b. Net income

c. Utilities expense

d. Supplies

e. Cash flow from operating activities

f. Service revenue

g. Auditor's opinion

h. Accounts receivable

i. Accounts payable

j. Unearned revenue

k. Dividends

l. Beginning cash balance

m. Ending retained earnings

n. Rent expense

o. Ending cash balance

Exercise 2-26   *Analyzing the cash flow effects of different types of expenses*

The following income statements are available for Hopi, Inc., and Zuni, Inc., for 2012.

	Hopi, Inc.	Zuni, Inc.
Revenue	$100,000	$100,000
Wages expense	70,000	55,000
Depreciation expense	10,000	25,000
Net earnings	$ 20,000	$ 20,000

Required

Assume that neither company had beginning or ending balances in its Accounts Receivable or wages Payable accounts. Explain which company would have the lowest *net cash flows from operating activities* for 2012.

PROBLEMS

All applicable Problems are available with McGraw-Hill's *Connect Accounting.*

LO 1

Problem 2-27   *Recording events in a horizontal statements model*

The following events pertain to King Company.

1. Acquired $25,000 cash from the issue of common stock.

2. Provided services for $5,000

3. Provided $18,000 of services on account.

4. Collected $11,000 cash from the account receivable created in Event 3.

5. Paid $1,400 cash to purchase supplies.

6. Had $300 of supplies on hand at the end of the accounting period.

7. Received $3,600 cash in advance for services to be performed in the future.

8. Performed one-half of the services agreed to in Event 7.

9. Paid $6,000 for salaries expense.

10. Incurred $2,400 of other operating expenses on account.

11. Paid $2,000 cash on the account payable created in Event 10.

12. Paid a $2,000 cash dividend to the stockholders.

Required

Show the effects of the events on the financial statements using a horizontal statements model like the following one. In the Cash Flows column, use the letters OA to designate operating activity, IA for investing activity, FA for financing activity, and NC for net change in cash. Use NA to indicate accounts not affected by the event. The first event is recorded as an example.

	Assets			=	Liabilities			+	Stockholders' Equity			Rev.	−	Exp.	=	Net Inc.		Cash Flows
Event No.	Cash	+	Accts. Rec.	+ Supp. =	Accts. Pay.	+	Unearn. Rev.	+	Com. Stk.	+	Ret. Earn.							
1	25,000	+	NA	+ NA =	NA	+	NA	+	25,000	+	NA	NA	−	NA	=	NA		25,000 FA

Problem 2-28 *Effect of deferrals on financial statements: three separate single-cycle examples*

Required

a. On February 1, 2012, Heider, Inc., was formed when it received $80,000 cash from the issue of common stock. On May 1, 2012, the company paid $60,000 cash in advance to rent office space for the coming year. The office space was used as a place to consult with clients. The consulting activity generated $120,000 of cash revenue during 2012. Based on this information alone, record the events and related adjusting entry in the general ledger accounts under the accounting equation. Determine the amount of net income and cash flows from operating activities for 2012.

b. On January 1, 2012, the accounting firm of Bonds & Associates was formed. On August 1, 2012, the company received a retainer fee (was paid in advance) of $30,000 for services to be performed monthly during the next 12 months. Assuming that this was the only transaction completed in 2012, prepare an income statement, statement of changes in stockholders' equity, balance sheet, and statement of cash flows for 2012.

c. Edge Company had $2,200 of supplies on hand on January 1, 2012. Edge purchased $7,200 of supplies on account during 2012. A physical count of supplies revealed that $900 of supplies was on hand as of December 31, 2012. Determine the amount of supplies expense that should be recognized in the December 31, 2012 adjusting entry. Use a financial statements model to show how the adjusting entry would affect the balance sheet, income statement, and statement of cash flows.

CHECK FIGURES

a. Net Income: $80,000

b. Net Income: $12,500

Problem 2-29 *Effect of adjusting entries on the accounting equation*

LO 2

Required

Each of the following independent events requires a year-end adjusting entry. Show how each event and its related adjusting entry affect the accounting equation. Assume a December 31 closing date. The first event is recorded as an example.

CHECK FIGURE

b. adjustment amount: $1,250

	Total Assets						Stockholders' Equity		
Event/ Adjustment	Cash	+	Other Assets	=	Liabilities	+	Common Stock	+	Retained Earnings
a	−7,200		+7,200		NA		NA		NA
Adj.	NA		−5,400		NA		NA		−5,400

a. Paid $7,200 cash in advance on April 1 for a one-year insurance policy.
b. Purchased $1,400 of supplies on account. At year's end, $150 of supplies remained on hand.
c. Paid $8,400 cash in advance on March 1 for a one-year lease on office space.
d. Received a $18,000 cash advance for a contract to provide services in the future. The contract required a one-year commitment starting September 1 to be provided evenly over the year.
e. Paid $24,000 cash in advance on October 1 for a one-year lease on office space.

LO 3, 5, 6

eXcel

CHECK FIGURES
b. Net Income, 2012: $19,300
b. Net Income, 2013: $84,650

Problem 2-30 *Events for two complete accounting cycles*

Energy Consulting Company was formed on Junuary 1, 2012.

Events Affecting the 2012 Accounting Period

1. Acquired cash of $80,000 from the issue of common stock.
2. Purchased $4,200 of suplies on account.
3. Purchased land that cost $30,000 cash.
4. Paid $4,200 cash to settle accounts payable created in Event 2.
5. Recognized revenue on account of $75,000.
6. Paid $46,000 cash for other operating expenses.
7. Collected $68,000 cash from accounts receivable.

Information for 2012 Adjusting Entries

8. Recognized accrued salaries of $5,800 on December 31, 2012.
9. Had $300 of supplies on hand at the end of the accounting period.

Events Affecting the 2013 Accounting Period

1. Acquired an additional $10,000 cash from the issue of common stock.
2. Paid $5,800 cash to settle the salaries payable obligation.
3. Paid $6,000 cash in advance for a lease on office facilities.
4. Sold land that had cost $25,000 for $25,000 cash.
5. Received $8,400 cash in advance for services to be performed in the future.
6. Purchased $1,800 of supplies on account during the year.
7. Provided services on account of $90,000.
8. Collected $92,000 cash from accounts receivable.
9. Paid a cash dividend of $10,000 to the stockholders.

Information for 2013 Adjusting Entries

10. The advance payment for rental of the office facilities (see Event 3) was made on September 1 for a one-year lease term.
11. The cash advance for services to be provided in the future was collected on June 1 (see Event 5). The one-year contract started June 1.
12. Had $350 of supplies on hand at the end of the period.
13. Recognized accrued salaries of $6,500 at the end of the accounting period.

Required

a. Identify each event affecting the 2012 and 2013 accounting periods as asset source (AS), asset use (AU), asset exchange (AE), or claims exchange (CE). Record the effects of each event under the appropriate general ledger account headings of the accounting equation.
b. Prepare an income statement, statement of changes in stockholders' equity, balance sheet, and statement of cash flows for 2012 and 2013, using the vertical statements model.

LO 2, 3

CHECK FIGURES
b. $33,000
h. ($3,000)

Problem 2-31 *Effect of events on financial statements*

Reed Company had the following balances in its accounting records as of December 31, 2012.

Assets		Claims	
Cash	$ 75,000	Accounts Payable	$ 32,000
Accounts Receivable	45,000	Common Stock	90,000
Land	30,000	Retained Earnings	28,000
Totals	$150,000		$150,000

The following accounting events apply to Reed's 2012 fiscal year:

Jan.   1   Acquired an additional $50,000 cash from the issue of common stock.

April 1   Paid $8,400 cash in advance for a one-year lease for office space.

June   1   Paid a $4,000 cash dividend to the stockholders.

July   1   Purchased additional land that cost $15,000 cash.

Aug.   1   Made a cash payment on accounts payable of $28,000.

Sept. 1   Received $9,600 cash in advance as a retainer for services to be performed monthly during the next eight months.

Sept. 30   Sold land for $12,000 cash that had originally cost $12,000.

Oct.   1   Purchased $1,500 of supplies on account.

Dec. 31   Earned $75,000 of service revenue on account during the year.

       31   Received $70,000 cash collections from accounts receivable.

       31   Incurred $24,000 other operating expenses on account during the year.

       31   Recognized accrued salaries expense of $8,000.

       31   Had $400 of supplies on hand at the end of the period.

       31   The land purchased on July 1 had a market value of $21,000.

Required

Based on the preceding information, answer the following questions. All questions pertain to the 2012 financial statements. (*Hint:* Record the events in general ledger accounts under an accounting equation before answering the questions.)

a. What two transactions need additional adjusting entries at the end of the year?

b. What amount would be reported for land on the balance sheet?

c. What amount of net cash flow from operating activities would Reed report on the statement of cash flows?

d. What amount of rent expense would be reported in the income statement?

e. What amount of total liabilities would be reported on the balance sheet?

f. What amount of supplies expense would be reported on the income statement?

g. What amount of unearned revenue would be reported on the balance sheet?

h. What amount of net cash flow from investing activities would be reported on the statement of cash flows?

i. What amount of total expenses would be reported on the income statement?

j. What total amount of service revenues would be reported on the income statement?

k. What amount of cash flows from financing activities would be reported on the statement of cash flows?

l. What amount of net income would be reported on the income statement?

m. What amount of retained earnings would be reported on the balance sheet?

Problem 2-32 *Identifying and arranging elements on financial statements*

The following information was drawn from the records of Paso & Associates at December 31, 2012.

Supplies	$ 2,500	Unearned revenue	$ 5,400
Consulting revenue	120,000	Notes payable	40,000
Land	70,000	Salaries payable	9,000
Dividends	10,000	Salary expense	58,000
Cash flow from fin. activities	30,000	Common stock issued	30,000
Interest revenue	6,000	Beginning common stock	40,000
Ending retained earnings	50,100	Accounts receivable	32,000
Cash	66,000	Cash flow from inv. activities	(21,000)
Interest payable	4,000	Cash flow from oper. activities	18,000
Interest expense	9,000	Prepaid rent	8,000

LO 3

CHECK FIGURES
2012 Net Income: $59,000
2012 Total Assets: $178,500

Required

Use the preceding information to construct an income statement, statement of changes in stockholders' equity, balance sheet, and statement of cash flows. (Show only totals for each activity on the statement of cash flows.)

Problem 2-33 *Relationship of accounts to financial statements*

Required

Identify whether each of the following items would appear on the income statement (IS), statement of changes in stockholders' equity (SE), balance sheet (BS), or statement of cash flows (CF). Some items may appear on more than one statement; if so, identify all applicable statements. If an item would not appear on any financial statement, label it NA.

a. Accumulated depreciation
b. Salary expense
c. Prepaid insurance
d. Beginning common stock
e. Beginning retained earnings
f. Supplies expense
g. Operating expenses
h. Cash flow from operating activities
i. Debt to assets ratio
j. Total liabilities
k. Ending common stock
l. Interest expense
m. Consulting revenue
n. Cash flow from investing activities
o. Service revenue
p. Unearned revenue
q. Certificate of deposit
r. Interest receivable
s. Depreciation expense

t. Accounts receivable
u. Notes payable
v. Insurance expense
w. Salaries payable
x. Total assets
y. Accounts payable
z. Notes receivable
aa. Cash
bb. Supplies
cc. Cash flow from financing activities
dd. Interest revenue
ee. Ending retained earnings
ff. Net income
gg. Dividends
hh. Office equipment
ii. Debt to equity ratio
jj. Land
kk. Interest payable
ll. Rent expense

Problem 2-34 *Missing information in financial statements*

Required

Fill in the blank (as indicated by the alphabetic letters in parentheses) in the following financial statements. Assume the company started operations January 1, 2010, and that all transactions involve cash.

	For the Years		
	2010	2011	2012
Income Statements			
Revenue	$ 700	$ 1,300	$ 2,000
Expense	(a)	(700)	(1,300)
Net income	$ 200	$ (m)	$ 700
Statement of Changes in Stockholders' Equity			
Beginning common stock	$ 0	$ (n)	$ 6,000
Plus: Common stock issued	5,000	1,000	2,000
Ending common stock	5,000	6,000	(t)
Beginning retained earnings	0	100	200
Plus: Net income	(b)	(o)	700
Less: Dividends	(c)	(500)	(300)
Ending retained earnings	100	(p)	600
Total stockholders' equity	$ (d)	$ 6,200	$ 8,600

continued

Balance Sheets			
Assets			
Cash	$ (e)	$ (q)	$ (u)
Land	0	(r)	8,000
Total assets	$ (f)	$11,200	$10,600
Liabilities	$ (g)	$ 5,000	$ 2,000
Stockholders' equity			
Common stock	(h)	(s)	8,000
Retained earnings	(i)	200	600
Total stockholders' equity	(j)	6,200	8,600
Total liabilities and stockholders' equity	$8,100	$11,200	$10,600

Statements of Cash Flows			
Cash flows from operating activities			
Cash receipts from revenue	$ (k)	$ 1,300	$ (v)
Cash payments for expenses	(l)	(700)	(w)
Net cash flows from operating activities	200	600	700
Cash flows from investing activities			
Cash payments for land	0	(8,000)	0
Cash flows from financing activities			
Cash receipts from loan	3,000	3,000	0
Cash payments to reduce debt	0	(1,000)	(x)
Cash receipts from stock issue	5,000	1,000	(y)
Cash payments for dividends	(100)	(500)	(z)
Net cash flows from financing activities	7,900	2,500	(1,300)
Net change in cash	8,100	(4,900)	(600)
Plus: Beginning cash balance	0	8,100	3,200
Ending cash balance	$8,100	$ 3,200	$ 2,600

ANALYZE, THINK, COMMUNICATE

ATC 2-1   Business Applications Case   *Understanding real-world annual reports*

Required

Use the Target Corporation's annual report in Appendix B to answer the following questions. Note that net income and net earnings are synonymous terms.

a. Which accounts on Target's balance sheet are accural type accounts?

b. Which accounts on Target's balance sheet are deferral type accounts?

c. Compare Target's 2009 *net earnings* to its 2009 *cash provided by operating activities*. Which is larger?

d. First, compare Target's 2008 net earnings to its 2009 net earnings. Next, compare Target's 2008 cash provided by operating activities to its 2009 cash provided by operating activities. Which changed the most from 2008 to 2009, net earnings or cash provided by operating activities?

ATC 2-2   Group Assignment   *Financial reporting and market valuation*

The following financial highlights were drawn from the 2009 annual reports of Microsoft Corporation and Apple Inc.

	Microsoft	Apple
Revenue	$58.4 Billion	$42.9 Billion
Net income	$14.6 Billion	$ 5.7 Billion
Cash and short-term investments	$39.7 Billion	$23.1 Billion

Even so, as of May 26, 2010, Wall Street valued Microsoft at $219.19 billion and Apple at $222.12.

Divide the class into groups of four or five students.

Required

Have the members of each group reach a consensus response for each of the following tasks. Each group should elect a spokes person to represent the group.

Group Tasks

(1) Determine the amount of expenses incurred by each company.

(2) Comment on how the concept of conservatism applies to the financial information presented in this case.

(3) Speculate as to why investors would be willing to pay more for Apple than Microsoft.

Class Discussion

Randomly call on the spokes persons to compare their responses for each of the group tasks.

ATC 2-3   Research Assignment   *Investigating nonfinancial information in Nike's annual report*

Although most of this course is concerned with the financial statements themselves, all sections of a company's annual report are important. A company must file various reports with the SEC, and one of these, Form 10-K, is essentially the company's annual report. The requirements below ask you to investigate sections of Nike's annual report that explain various nonfinancial aspects of its business operations.

To obtain the Form 10-K you can use either the EDGAR system following the instructions in Appendix A or the company's website.

Required

a. In what year did Nike begin operations?

b. Other than athletic shoes, what products does Nike sell?

c. Does Nike operate businesses under names other than Nike? If so, what are they?

d. How many employees does Nike have?

e. In how many countries other than the United States does Nike sell its products?

ATC 2-4   Writing Assignment   *Conservatism and Matching*

Glenn's Cleaning Services Company is experiencing cash flow problems and needs a loan. Glenn has a friend who is willing to lend him the money he needs provided she can be convinced that he will be able to repay the debt. Glenn has assured his friend that his business is viable, but his friend has asked to see the company's financial statements. Glenn's accountant produced the following financial statements.

Income Statement		Balance Sheet	
Service Revenue	$ 38,000	Assets	$85,000
Operating Expenses	(70,000)	Liabilities	$35,000
Net Loss	$(32,000)	Stockholders' Equity	
		Common Stock	82,000
		Retained Earnings	(32,000)
		Total Liabilities and Stockholders' Equity	$85,000

Glenn made the following adjustments to these statements before showing them to his friend. He recorded $82,000 of revenue on account from Barrymore Manufacturing Company for a contract to clean its headquarters office building that was still being negotiated for the next month. Barrymore had scheduled a meeting to sign a contract the following week, so Glenn was sure that he would get the job. Barrymore was a reputable company, and Glenn was confident that he could ultimately collect the $82,000. Also, he subtracted $30,000 of accrued salaries expense and the corresponding liability. He reasoned that since he had not paid the employees, he had not incurred any expense.

Required

a. Reconstruct the income statement and balance sheet as they would appear after Glenn's adjustments.

b. Write a brief memo explaining how Glenn's treatment of the expected revenue from Barrymore violated the conservatism concept.

c. Write a brief memo explaining how Glenn's treatment of the accrued salaries expense violates the matching concept.

CHAPTER 3

Accounting for Merchandising Businesses

LEARNING OBJECTIVES

After you have mastered the material in this chapter, you will be able to:

1 Identify and explain the primary features of the perpetual inventory system.

2 Show the effects of inventory transactions on financial statements.

3 Explain the meaning of terms used to describe transportation costs, cash discounts, returns or allowances, and financing costs.

4 Explain how gains and losses differ from revenues and expenses.

5 Compare and contrast single and multistep income statements.

6 Show the effect of lost, damaged, or stolen inventory on financial statements.

7 Use common size financial statements to evaluate managerial performance.

8 Identify the primary features of the periodic inventory system. (Appendix)

CHAPTER OPENING

Previous chapters have discussed accounting for service businesses. These businesses obtain revenue by providing some kind of service such as medical or legal advice to their customers. Other examples of service companies include dry cleaning companies, maid service companies, and car washes. This chapter introduces accounting practices for merchandising businesses. **Merchandising businesses** generate revenue by selling goods. They buy the merchandise they sell from companies called suppliers. The goods purchased for resale are called **merchandise inventory.** Merchandising businesses include **retail companies** (companies that sell goods to the final consumer) and **wholesale companies** (companies that sell to other businesses). Sears, JCPenney, Target, and Sam's Club are real-world merchandising businesses.

The Curious Accountant

Janice recently purchased a gold necklace for $250 from her local Zales jewelry store. The next day she learned that Zoe bought the same necklace on-line from Blue Nile for only $200. Janice questioned how Blue Nile could sell the necklace for so much less than Zales. Zoe suggested that even though both jewelry sellers purchase their products from the same producers at about the same price, Blue Nile can charge lower prices because it does not have to operate expensive bricks-and-mortar stores, and thus has lower operating costs. Janice disagrees. She thinks the cost of operating large distribution centers and Internet server centers will offset any cost savings Blue Nile enjoys from not owning retail jewelry stores.

Exhibit 3.1 presents the income statements for Zales and Blue Nile. Based on these income statements, do you think Janice or Zoe is correct? (Answer on page 104.)

EXHIBIT 3.1   Comparative Income Statements

BLUE NILE, INC.
Consolidated Statements of Operations
(in thousands, except per share data)

	Year Ended	
	January 3, 2010	January 4, 2009
Net sales	$302,134	$295,329
Cost of sales	236,790	235,333
Gross profit	65,344	59,996
Selling, general and administrative expenses	45,997	44,005
Operating income	19,347	15,991
Other income, net:		
Interest income, net	122	1,420
Other income, net	209	445
Total other income, net	331	1,865
Income before income taxes	19,678	17,856
Income tax expense	6,878	6,226
Net income	$ 12,800	$ 11,630

ZALE CORPORATION AND SUBSIDIARIES
Consolidated Statements of Operations
(in thousands, except per share amounts)

	Year Ended July 31,	
	2009	2008 As Restated
Revenues	$1,779,744	$2,138,041
Cost and expenses:		
Cost of sales	948,572	1,089,553
Selling, general and administrative	927,249	985,028
Cost of insurance operations	7,000	6,744
Depreciation and amortization	58,947	60,244
Other charges and gains	70,095	(10,700)
Operating (loss) earnings	(232,119)	7,172
Interest expense	10,399	12,364
Other income	—	(3,500)
Loss before income taxes	(242,518)	(1,692)
Income tax (benefit) expense	(53,015)	4,761
Loss from continuing operations	(189,503)	(6,453)
Earnings from discontinued operations, net of taxes	—	7,084
Net (loss) earnings	$ (189,503)	$ 631

PRODUCT COSTS VERSUS SELLING AND ADMINISTRATIVE COSTS

Identify and explain the primary features of the perpetual inventory system.

Companies report inventory costs on the balance sheet in the asset account Merchandise Inventory. All costs incurred to acquire merchandise and ready it for sale are included in the inventory account. Examples of inventory costs include the price of goods purchased, shipping and handling costs, transit insurance, and storage costs.

Since inventory items are referred to as products, inventory costs are frequently called **product costs.**

Costs that are not included in inventory are usually called **selling and administrative costs.** Examples of selling and administrative costs include advertising, administrative salaries, sales commissions, insurance, and interest. Since selling and administrative costs are usually recognized as expenses *in the period* in which they are incurred, they are sometimes called **period costs.** In contrast, product costs are expensed when inventory is sold regardless of when it was purchased. In other words, product costs are matched directly with sales revenue, while selling and administrative costs are matched with the period in which they are incurred.

ALLOCATING INVENTORY COST BETWEEN ASSET AND EXPENSE ACCOUNTS

The cost of inventory that is available for sale during a specific accounting period is determined as follows.

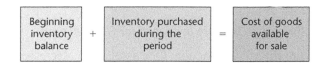

The **cost of goods available for sale** is allocated between the asset account Merchandise Inventory and an expense account called **Cost of Goods Sold.** The cost of inventory items that have not been sold (Merchandise Inventory) is reported as an asset on the balance sheet, and the cost of the items sold (Cost of Goods Sold) is expensed on the income statement. This allocation is depicted graphically as follows.

The difference between the sales revenue and the cost of goods sold is called **gross margin** or **gross profit.** The selling and administrative expenses (period costs) are subtracted from gross margin to obtain the net income.

Exhibit 3.1 displays income statements from the annual reports of Blue Nile and Zales. For each company, review the most current income statement and determine the amount of gross margin. You should find a gross profit of $65,344 for Blue Nile and a gross margin of $831,172 ($1,779,744 − $948,572) for Zales.

PERPETUAL INVENTORY SYSTEM

Most modern companies maintain their inventory records using the **perpetual inventory system,** so-called because the inventory account is adjusted perpetually (continually) throughout the accounting period. Each time merchandise is purchased, the inventory account is increased; each time it is sold, the inventory account is decreased. The following illustration demonstrates the basic features of the perpetual inventory system.

Show the effects of inventory transactions on financial statements.

June Gardener loved plants and grew them with such remarkable success that she decided to open a small retail plant store. She started June's Plant Shop (JPS) on January 1, 2012. The following discussion explains and illustrates the effects of the five events the company experienced during its first year of operation.

Effects of 2012 Events on Financial Statements

EVENT 1   JPS acquired $15,000 cash by issuing common stock.

This event is an asset source transaction. It increases both assets (cash) and stockholders' equity (common stock). The income statement is not affected. The statement of cash flows reflects an inflow from financing activities. These effects are shown here.

Assets				=	Liab.	+	Stockholders' Equity								
Cash	+	Inventory	+	Land	=	Accts. Pay.	+	Com. Stk.	+	Ret. Earn.	Rev.	−	Exp.	=	Net Inc.	Cash Flow
15,000	+	NA	+	NA	=	NA	+	15,000	+	NA	NA	−	NA	=	NA	15,000 FA

EVENT 2   JPS purchased merchandise inventory for $14,000 cash.

This event is an asset exchange transaction. One asset, cash, decreases and another asset, merchandise inventory, increases; total assets remain unchanged. Because product costs are expensed when inventory is sold, not when it is purchased, the event does not affect the income statement. The cash outflow, however, is reported in the operating activities section of the statement of cash flows. These effects are illustrated below.

Assets				=	Liab.	+	Stockholders' Equity								
Cash	+	Inventory	+	Land	=	Accts. Pay.	+	Com. Stk.	+	Ret. Earn.	Rev.	−	Exp.	=	Net Inc.	Cash Flow
(14,000)	+	14,000	+	NA	=	NA	+	NA	+	NA	NA	−	NA	=	NA	(14,000) OA

EVENT 3A   JPS recognized sales revenue from selling inventory for $12,000 cash.

The revenue recognition is the first part of a two-part transaction. The *sales part* represents a source of assets (cash increases from earning sales revenue). Both assets (cash) and stockholders' equity (retained earnings) increase. Sales revenue on the income statement increases. The $12,000 cash inflow is reported in the operating activities section of the statement of cash flows. These effects are shown in the following financial statements model.

Assets				=	Liab.	+	Stockholders' Equity								
Cash	+	Inventory	+	Land	=	Accts. Pay.	+	Com. Stk.	+	Ret. Earn.	Rev.	−	Exp.	=	Net Inc.	Cash Flow
12,000	+	NA	+	NA	=	NA	+	NA	+	12,000	12,000	−	NA	=	12,000	12,000 OA

EVENT 3B   JPS recognized $8,000 of cost of goods sold.

The expense recognition is the second part of the two-part transaction. The *expense part* represents a use of assets. Both assets (merchandise inventory) and stockholders' equity (retained earnings) decrease. An expense account, Cost of Goods Sold, is reported on the income statement. This part of the transaction does not affect the statement of cash flows. A cash outflow occurred when the goods were bought, not when they were sold. These effects are shown here.

	Assets			=	Liab.	+	Stockholders' Equity						
Cash	+ Inventory	+ Land	=	Accts. Pay.	+	Com. Stk.	+ Ret. Earn.	Rev.	− Exp.	= Net Inc.	Cash Flow
NA	+ (8,000)	+ NA	=	NA	+	NA	+ (8,000)	NA	− 8,000	= (8,000)	NA

EVENT 4   JPS paid $1,000 cash for selling and administrative expenses.

This event is an asset use transaction. The payment decreases both assets (cash) and stockholders' equity (retained earnings). The increase in selling and administrative expenses decreases net income. The $1,000 cash payment is reported in the operating activities section of the statement of cash flows. These effects are illustrated below.

	Assets			=	Liab.	+	Stockholders' Equity						
Cash	+ Inventory	+ Land	=	Accts. Pay.	+	Com. Stk.	+ Ret. Earn.	Rev.	− Exp.	= Net Inc.	Cash Flow
(1,000)	+ NA	+ NA	=	NA	+	NA	+ (1,000)	NA	− 1,000	= (1,000)	(1,000) OA

EVENT 5   JPS paid $5,500 cash to purchase land for a place to locate a future store.

Buying the land increases the Land account and decreases the Cash account on the balance sheet. The income statement is not affected. The statement of cash flow shows a cash outflow to purchase land in the investing activities section of the statement of cash flows. These effects are shown below.

	Assets			=	Liab.	+	Stockholders' Equity						
Cash	+ Inventory	+ Land	=	Accts. Pay.	+	Com. Stk.	+ Ret. Earn.	Rev.	− Exp.	= Net Inc.	Cash Flow
(5,500)	+ NA	+ 5,500	=	NA	+	NA	+ NA	NA	− NA	= NA	(5,500) IA

Financial Statements for 2012

JPS's financial statements for 2012 are shown in Exhibit 3.2. JPS had no beginning inventory in its first year, so the cost of merchandise inventory available for sale was $14,000 (the amount of inventory purchased during the period). Recall that JPS must allocate the *Cost of Goods (Inventory) Available for Sale* between the *Cost of Goods Sold* ($8,000) and the ending balance ($6,000) in the *Merchandise Inventory* account. The cost of goods sold is reported as an expense on the income statement and the ending balance of merchandise inventory is reported as an asset on the balance sheet. The difference between the sales revenue ($12,000) and the cost of goods sold ($8,000) is labeled *gross margin* ($4,000) on the income statement.

EXHIBIT 3.2

Financial Statements

2012 Income Statement		12/31/12 Balance Sheet			2012 Statement of Cash Flows		
Sales revenue	$12,000	Assets			Operating activities		
Cost of goods sold	(8,000)	Cash	$ 6,500		Inflow from customers	$12,000	
Gross margin	4,000	Merchandise inventory	6,000		Outflow for inventory	(14,000)	
Less: Operating exp.		Land	5,500		Outflow for selling		
Selling and		Total assets		$18,000	& admin. exp.	(1,000)	
admin. exp.	(1,000)	Liabilities		$ 0	Net cash outflow for		
Net income	$ 3,000	Stockholders' equity			operating activities		$ (3,000)
		Common stock	$15,000		Investing activities		
		Retained earnings	3,000		Outflow to purchase land		(5,500)
		Total stockholders' equity		18,000	Financing activities		
		Total liab. and stk. equity		$18,000	Inflow from stock issue		15,000
					Net change in cash		6,500
					Plus: Beginning cash balance		0
					Ending cash balance		$ 6,500

✓ CHECK YOURSELF 3.1

Phambroom Company began 2012 with $35,600 in its Inventory account. During the year, it purchased inventory costing $356,800 and sold inventory that had cost $360,000 for $520,000. Based on this information alone, determine (1) the inventory balance as of December 31, 2012, and (2) the amount of gross margin Phambroom would report on its 2012 income statement.

Answer

1. $35,600 Beginning inventory + $356,800 Purchases = $392,400 Goods available for sale

   $392,400 Goods available for sale − $360,000 Cost of goods sold = $32,400 Ending inventory

2. Sales revenue − Cost of goods sold = Gross margin

   $520,000 − $360,000 = $160,000

Transportation Cost, Purchase Returns and Allowances, and Cash Discounts Related to Inventory Purchases

Explain the meaning of terms used to describe transportation costs, cash discounts, returns or allowances, and financing costs.

Purchasing inventory often involves: (1) incurring transportation costs, (2) returning inventory or receiving purchase allowances (cost reductions), and (3) taking cash discounts (also cost reductions). During its second accounting cycle, JPS encountered these kinds of events. The final account balances at the end of the 2012 fiscal year become the beginning balances for 2013: Cash, $6,500; Merchandise Inventory, $6,000; Land, 5,500; Common Stock, $15,000; and Retained Earnings, $3,000.

Effects of 2013 Events on Financial Statements

JPS experienced the following events during its 2013 accounting period. The effects of each of these events are explained and illustrated in the following discussion.

EVENT 1   JPS borrowed $4,000 cash by issuing a note payable.

JPS borrowed the money to enable it to purchase a plot of land for a site for a store it planned to build in the near future. Borrowing the money increases the Cash account and the Note Payable account on the balance sheet. The income statement is not affected. The statement of cash flow shows a cash flow from financing activities. These effects are shown below.

| Assets | | | | = | Liab. | | + | Stockholders' Equity | | | | | |
Cash +	Accts. Rec. +	Inventory +	Land =		Accts. Pay. +	Notes Pay. +		Com. Stk. +	Ret. Earn.	Rev. −	Exp. =	Net Inc.	Cash Flow
4,000 +	NA +	NA +	NA =		NA +	4,000 +		NA +	NA	NA −	NA =	NA	4,000 FA

EVENT 2   JPS purchased on account merchandise inventory with a list price of $11,000.

The inventory purchase increases both assets (merchandise inventory) and liabilities (accounts payable) on the balance sheet. The income statement is not affected until later, when inventory is sold. Since the inventory was purchased on account, there was no cash outflow. These effects are shown here.

| Assets | | | | = | Liab. | | + | Stockholders' Equity | | | | | |
Cash +	Accts. Rec. +	Inventory +	Land =		Accts. Pay. +	Notes Pay. +		Com. Stk. +	Ret. Earn.	Rev. −	Exp. =	Net Inc.	Cash Flow
NA +	NA +	11,000 +	NA =		11,000 +	NA +		NA +	NA	NA −	NA =	NA	NA

Accounting for Purchase Returns and Allowances

EVENT 3   JPS returned some of the inventory purchased in Event 2. The list price of the returned merchandise was $1,000.

To promote customer satisfaction, many businesses allow customers to return goods for reasons such as wrong size, wrong color, wrong design, or even simply because the purchaser changed his mind. The effect of a purchase return is the *opposite* of the original purchase. For JPS the **purchase return** decreases both assets (merchandise inventory) and liabilities (accounts payable). There is no effect on either the income statement or the statement of cash flows. These effects are shown below.

| Assets | | | | = | Liab. | | + | Stockholders' Equity | | | | | |
Cash +	Accts. Rec. +	Inventory +	Land =		Accts. Pay. +	Notes Pay. +		Com. Stk. +	Ret. Earn.	Rev. −	Exp. =	Net Inc.	Cash Flow
NA +	NA +	(1,000) +	NA =		(1,000) +	NA +		NA +	NA	NA −	NA =	NA	NA

Sometimes dissatisfied buyers will agree to keep goods instead of returning them if the seller offers to reduce the price. Such reductions are called allowances. **Purchase allowances** affect the financial statements the same way purchase returns do.

Purchase Discounts

EVENT 4   **JPS received a cash discount on goods purchased in Event 2. The credit terms were 2/10, n/30.**

To encourage buyers to pay promptly, sellers sometimes offer **cash discounts.** To illustrate, assume JPS purchased the inventory in Event 2 under terms **2/10, n/30** (two-ten, net thirty). These terms mean the seller will allow a 2 percent cash discount if the purchaser pays cash within 10 days from the date of purchase. The amount not paid within the first 10 days is due at the end of 30 days from date of purchase. Recall that JPS returned $1,000 of the inventory purchased in Event 1 leaving a $10,000 balance ($11,000 list price − $1,000 purchase return). If JPS pays for the inventory within 10 days, the amount of the discount is $200 ($10,000 × .02).

When cash discounts are applied to purchases they are called **purchases discounts.** When they are applied to sales, they are called sales discounts. Sales discounts will be discussed later in the chapter. A *purchase discount* reduces the cost of the inventory and the associated account payable on the balance sheet. A purchase discount does not directly affect the income statement or the statement of cash flow. These effects are shown here.

Assets				=	Liab.		+	Stockholders' Equity						
Cash	+	Accts. Rec.	+	Inventory	+	Land	=	Accts. Pay.	+	Notes Pay.	+	Com. Stk.	+	Ret. Earn.	Rev.	−	Exp.	=	Net Inc.	Cash Flow
NA	+	NA	+	(200)	+	NA	=	(200)	+	NA	+	NA	+	NA	NA	−	NA	=	NA	NA

If JPS paid the account payable after 10 days, there would be no purchase discount. In this case the balances in the Inventory and Account Payable accounts would remain at $10,000.

EVENT 5   **JPS paid the $9,800 balance due on the account payable.**

The remaining balance in the accounts payable is $9,800 ($10,000 list price − $200 purchase discount). Paying cash to settle the liability reduces cash and accounts payable on the balance sheet. The income statement is not affected. The cash outflow is shown in the operating section of the statement of cash flows. These effects are shown below.

Assets				=	Liab.		+	Stockholders' Equity						
Cash	+	Accts. Rec.	+	Inventory	+	Land	=	Accts. Pay.	+	Notes Pay.	+	Com. Stk.	+	Ret. Earn.	Rev.	−	Exp.	=	Net Inc.	Cash Flow
(9,800)	+	NA	+	NA	+	NA	=	(9,800)	+	NA	+	NA	+	NA	NA	−	NA	=	NA	(9,800) OA

The Cost of Financing Inventory

Suppose you buy inventory this month and sell it next month. Where do you get the money to pay for the inventory at the time you buy it? One way to finance the purchase is to buy it on account and withhold payment until the last day of the term for the account payable. For example, suppose you buy inventory under terms 2/10, net/30. Under these circumstances you could delay payment for 30 days after the day of purchase. This way you may be able to collect enough money from the inventory you sell

REALITY BYTES

Many real-world companies have found it more effective to impose a penalty for late payment than to use a cash discount to encourage early payment. The invoice from Arley Water Works is an example of the penalty strategy. Notice that the amount due, if paid by the due date, is $18.14. A $1.88 late charge is imposed if the bill is paid after the due date. The $1.88 late charge is in fact interest. If Arley Water Works collects the payment after the due date, the utility will receive cash of $20.02. The collection will increase cash ($20.02), reduce accounts receivable ($18.14), and increase interest revenue ($1.88).

to pay for the inventory you purchased. Refusing the discount allows you the time needed to generate the cash necessary to pay off the liability (account payable). Unfortunately, this is usually a very expensive way to finance the purchase of inventory.

While the amount of a cash discount may appear small, the discount period is short. Consider the terms 2/10, net/30. Since you can pay on the tenth day and still receive the discount, you obtain financing for only 20 days (30-day full credit term − 10-day discount term). In other words, you must forgo a 2 percent discount to obtain a loan with a 20-day term. What is the size of the discount in annual terms? The answer is determined by the following formula.

Annual rate = Discount rate × (365 days ÷ term of the loan)

Annual rate = 2% × (365 ÷ 20)

Annual rate = 36.5%

This means that a 2 percent discount rate for 20 days is equivalent to a 36.5 percent annual rate of interest. So, if you do not have the money to pay the account payable, but can borrow money from a bank at less than 36.5 percent annual interest, you should borrow the money and pay off the account payable within the discount period.

Accounting for Transportation Costs

EVENT 6   The shipping terms for the inventory purchased in Event 2 were FOB shipping point. JPS paid the freight company $300 cash for delivering the merchandise.

The terms **FOB shipping point** and **FOB destination** identify whether the buyer or the seller is responsible for transportation costs. If goods are delivered FOB shipping point, the buyer is responsible for the freight cost. If goods are delivered FOB destination, the seller is responsible. When the buyer is responsible, the freight cost is called **transportation-in.** When the seller is responsible, the cost is called **transportation-out.** The following table summarizes freight cost terms.

Responsible Party	Buyer	Seller
Freight terms	FOB shipping point	FOB destination
Account title	Merchandise inventory	Transportation-out

Event 6 indicates the inventory was delivered FOB shipping point, so JPS (the buyer) is responsible for the $300 freight cost. Since incurring transportation-in costs is necessary to obtain inventory, these costs are added to the inventory account. The freight cost increases one asset account (Merchandise Inventory) and decreases another asset account (Cash). The income statement is not affected by this transaction because transportation-in costs are not expensed when they are incurred. Instead they are expensed as part of *cost of goods sold* when the inventory is sold. However, the cash paid for transportation-in costs is reported as an outflow in the operating activities section of the statement of cash flows. The effects of *transportation-in costs* are shown here.

		Assets			=	Liab.			+	Stockholders' Equity						
Cash	+	Accts. Rec.	+ Inventory	+ Land	=	Accts. Pay.	+	Notes Pay.	+	Com. Stk.	+	Ret. Earn.	Rev. − Exp. = Net Inc.			Cash Flow
(300)	+	NA	+ 300	+ NA	=	NA	+	NA	+	NA	+	NA	NA − NA = NA			(300) OA

EVENT 7A   JPS recognized $24,750 of revenue on the cash sale of merchandise that cost $11,500.

The sale increases assets (cash) and stockholders' equity (retained earnings). The revenue recognition increases net income. The $24,750 cash inflow from the sale is reported in the operating activities section of the statement of cash flows. These effects are shown below.

		Assets			=	Liab.			+	Stockholders' Equity						
Cash	+	Accts. Rec.	+ Inventory	+ Land	=	Accts. Pay.	+	Notes Pay.	+	Com. Stk.	+	Ret. Earn.	Rev. − Exp. = Net Inc.			Cash Flow
24,750	+	NA	+ NA	+ NA	=	NA	+	NA	+	NA	+	24,750	24,750 − NA = 24,750			24,750 OA

EVENT 7B   JPS recognized $11,500 of cost of goods sold.

When goods are sold, the product cost—*including a proportionate share of transportation-in and adjustments for purchase returns and allowances*—is transferred from the Merchandise Inventory account to the expense account, Cost of Goods Sold. Recognizing cost of goods sold decreases both assets (merchandise inventory) and stockholders' equity (retained earnings). The expense recognition for cost of goods sold decreases net income. Cash flow is not affected. These effects are shown here.

		Assets			=	Liab.			+	Stockholders' Equity						
Cash	+	Accts. Rec.	+ Inventory	+ Land	=	Accts. Pay.	+	Notes Pay.	+	Com. Stk.	+	Ret. Earn.	Rev. − Exp. = Net Inc.			Cash Flow
NA	+	NA	+ (11,500)	+ NA	=	NA	+	NA	+	NA	+	(11,500)	NA − 11,500 = (11,500)			NA

EVENT 8   JPS paid $450 cash for freight costs on inventory delivered to customers.

Assume the merchandise sold in Event 7A was shipped FOB destination. Also assume JPS paid the freight cost in cash. FOB destination means the seller is responsible for the freight cost, which is called transportation-out. Transportation-out is reported on the income statement as an operating expense in the section below gross margin. The cost of freight on goods shipped to customers is incurred *after* the goods are sold. It is not part of the costs to obtain goods or ready them for sale. Recognizing the expense of transportation-out reduces assets (cash) and stockholders' equity (retained earnings). Operating expenses increase and net income decreases. The cash outflow is reported in the operating activities section of the statement of cash flows. These effects are shown below.

| | | | | | | | | | | | Stockholders' | | | | | | |
| Assets | | | | | = | Liab. | | + | | Equity | | | | | | | |
Cash	+	Accts. Rec.	+	Inventory	+	Land	=	Accts. Pay.	+	Notes Pay.	+	Com. Stk.	+	Ret. Earn.	Rev.	−	Exp.	=	Net Inc.	Cash Flow
(450)	+	NA	+	NA	+	NA	=	NA	+	NA	+	NA	+	(450)	NA	−	450	=	(450)	(450) OA

If the terms had been FOB shipping point, the customer would have been responsible for the transportation cost and JPS would not have recorded an expense.

EVENT 9   JPS paid $5,000 cash for selling and administrative expenses.

The effect on the balance sheet is to decrease both assets (cash) and stockholders' equity (retained earnings). Recognizing the selling and administrative expenses decreases net income. The $5,000 cash outflow is reported in the operating activities section of the statement of cash flows. These effects are shown below.

| | | | | | | | | | | | Stockholders' | | | | | | |
| Assets | | | | | = | Liab. | | + | | Equity | | | | | | | |
Cash	+	Accts. Rec.	+	Inventory	+	Land	=	Accts. Pay.	+	Notes Pay.	+	Com. Stk.	+	Ret. Earn.	Rev.	−	Exp.	=	Net Inc.	Cash Flow
(5,000)	+	NA	+	NA	+	NA	=	NA	+	NA	+	NA	+	(5,000)	NA	−	5,000	=	(5,000)	(5,000) OA

EVENT 10   JPS paid $360 cash for interest expense on the note described in Event 1.

The effect on the balance sheet is to decrease both assets (cash) and stockholders' equity (retained earnings). Recognizing the interest expense decreases net income. The $360 cash outflow is reported in the operating activities section of the statement of cash flows. These effects are shown below.

| | | | | | | | | | | | Stockholders' | | | | | | |
| Assets | | | | | = | Liab. | | + | | Equity | | | | | | | |
Cash	+	Accts. Rec.	+	Inventory	+	Land	=	Accts. Pay.	+	Notes Pay.	+	Com. Stk.	+	Ret. Earn.	Rev.	−	Exp.	=	Net Inc.	Cash Flow
(360)	+	NA	+	NA	+	NA	=	NA	+	NA	+	NA	+	(360)	NA	−	360	=	(360)	(360) OA

RECOGNIZING GAINS AND LOSSES

EVENT 11   JPS sold the land that had cost $5,500 for $6,200 cash.

LO 4

Explain how gains and losses differ from revenues and expenses.

When JPS sells merchandise inventory for more than it cost, the difference between the sales revenue and the cost of the goods sold is called the *gross margin.* In contrast, when JPS sells land for more than it cost, the difference between the sales price and the cost of the land is called a **gain.** Why is one called *gross margin* and the other a *gain*? The terms are used to alert financial statement users to the fact that the nature of the underlying transactions is different.

JPS' primary business is selling inventory, not land. The term *gain* indicates profit resulting from transactions that are not likely to regularly recur. Similarly, had the land sold for less than cost the difference would have been labeled **loss** rather than expense. This term also indicates the underlying transaction is not from normal, recurring operating activities. Gains and losses are shown separately on the income statement to communicate the expectation that they are nonrecurring.

The presentation of gains and losses in the income statement is discussed in more detail in a later section of the chapter. At this point note that the sale increases cash, decreases land, and increases retained earnings on the balance sheet. The income statement shows a gain on the sale of land and net income increases. The $6,200 cash inflow is shown as an investing activity on the statement of cash flows. These effects are shown below:

Assets				=	Liab.		+	Stockholders' Equity						
Cash	+ Accts. Rec.	+ Inventory	+ Land	=	Accts. Pay.	+ Notes Pay.	+	Com. Stk.	+ Ret. Earn.	Gain	− Exp.	= Net Inc.	Cash Flow	
6,200	+ NA	+ NA	+ (5,500)	=	NA	+ NA	+	NA	+ 700	700	− NA	= 700	6,200	IA

✓ CHECK YOURSELF 3.2

Tsang Company purchased $32,000 of inventory on account with payment terms of 2/10, n/30 and freight terms FOB shipping point. Freight costs were $1,100. Tsang obtained a $2,000 purchase allowance because the inventory was damaged upon arrival. Tsang paid for the inventory within the discount period. Based on this information alone, determine the balance in the inventory account.

Answer

List price of inventory	$32,000
Plus: Transportation-in costs	1,100
Less: Purchase returns and allowances	(2,000)
Less: Purchase discount [($32,000 − $2,000) × .02]	(600)
Balance in inventory account	$30,500

MULTISTEP INCOME STATEMENT

JPS' 2013 income statement is shown in Exhibit 3.3. Observe the form of this statement carefully. It is more informative than one which simply subtracts expenses from revenues. First, it compares sales revenue with the cost of the goods that were sold to produce that revenue. The difference between the sales revenue and the cost of goods sold is called *gross margin*. Next, the operating expenses are subtracted from the gross margin to determine the *operating income*. **Operating income** is the amount of income that is generated from the normal recurring operations of a business. Items that are not expected to recur on a regular basis are subtracted from the operating income to determine the amount of *net income*.[1]

EXHIBIT 3.3

JUNE'S PLANT SHOP
Income Statement
For the Period Ended December 31, 2013

Sales revenue	$ 24,750
Cost of goods sold	(11,500)
Gross margin	13,250
Less: Operating expenses	
Selling and administrative expense	(5,000)
Transportation-out	(450)
Operating income	7,800
Nonoperating items	
Interest expense	(360)
Gain on the sale of land	700
Net income	$ 8,140

EXHIBIT 3.4

Income Statement Format Used by U.S. Companies

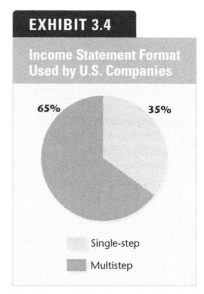

65%   35%

■ Single-step
■ Multistep

Data Source: AICPA, *Accounting Trends and Techniques*.

EXHIBIT 3.5

JUNE'S PLANT SHOP
Balance Sheet
As of December 31, 2013

Assets		
Cash	$25,540	
Merchandise inventory	4,600	
Total assets		$30,140
Liabilities		
Notes payable		$ 4,000
Stockholders' equity		
Common stock	$15,000	
Retained earnings	11,140	
Total stockholders' equity		26,140
Total liabilities and stockholders' equity		$30,140

Income statements that show these additional relationships are called **multistep income statements.** Income statements that display a single comparison of all revenues minus all expenses are called **single-step income statements.** To this point in the text we have shown only single-step income statements to promote simplicity. However, the multistep form is used more frequently in practice. Exhibit 3.4 shows the percentage of companies that use the multistep versus the single-step format. Go to Exhibit 3.1 and identify the company that presents its income statement in the multistep format. You should have identified Blue Nile as the company using the multistep format. Zale's statement is shown in the single-step format.

---

[1]Revenue and expense items with special characteristics may be classified as discontinued or extraordinary items. These items are shown separately just above net income regardless of whether a company uses a single-step or multistep format. Further discussion of these items is beyond the scope of this text.

EXHIBIT 3.6

JUNE'S PLANT SHOP
Statement of Cash Flows
For the Period Ended December 31, 2013

Operating activities		
Inflow from customers	$ 24,750	
Outflow for inventory*	(10,100)	
Outflow for transportation-out	(450)	
Outflow for selling and administrative expense	(5,000)	
Outflow for interest expense	(360)	
Net cash outflow for operating activities		$ 8,840
Investing activities		
Inflow from sale of land		6,200
Financing activities		
Inflow from issue of note payable		4,000
Net change in cash		19,040
Plus beginning cash balance		6,500
Ending cash balance		$25,540

*Net cost on inventory $9,800 + transportation-in $300 = $10,100

Note that interest is reported as a *nonoperating* item on the income statement in Exhibit 3.3. In contrast, it is shown in the *operating* activities section of the statement of cash flows in Exhibit 3.6. When the FASB issued Statement of Financial Accounting Standard (SFAS) 95, it required interest to be reported in the operating activities section of the statement of cash flows. There was no corresponding requirement for the treatment of interest on the income statement. Prior to SFAS 95, interest was considered to be a nonoperating item. Most companies continued to report interest as a nonoperating item on their income statements even though they were required to change how it was reported on the statement of cash flows. As a result, there is frequent inconsistency in the way interest is reported on the two financial statements.

Also note that while the gain on the sale of land is shown on the income statement, it is not included in the operating activities section of the statement of cash flows. Since the gain is a nonoperating item, it is included in the cash inflow from the sale of land shown in the investing activities section. In this case the full cash inflow from the sale of land ($6,200) is shown in the investing activities section of the statement of cash flows in Exhibit 3.6.

LOST, DAMAGED, OR STOLEN INVENTORY

LO 6

Show the effect of lost, damaged, or stolen inventory on financial statements.

Most merchandising companies experience some level of inventory **shrinkage,** a term that reflects decreases in inventory for reasons other than sales to customers. Inventory may be stolen by shoplifters, damaged by customers or employees, or even simply lost or misplaced. Since the *perpetual* inventory system is designed to record purchases and sales of inventory as they occur, the balance in the merchandise inventory account represents the amount of inventory that *should* be on hand at any given time. By taking a physical count of the merchandise inventory at the end of the accounting period and comparing that amount with the book balance in the Merchandise Inventory account, managers can determine the amount of any inventory shrinkage. If goods have been lost, damaged, or stolen, the book balance will be higher than the actual amount of inventory on hand and an adjusting entry is required to reduce assets and equity. The Merchandise Inventory account is reduced, and an expense for the amount of the lost, damaged, or stolen inventory is recognized.

REALITY BYTES

"Closed for Inventory Count" is a sign you frequently see on retail stores sometime during the month of January. Even if companies use a perpetual inventory system, the amount of inventory on hand may be unknown because of lost, damaged, or stolen goods. The only way to determine the amount of inventory on hand is to count it. Why count it in January? Christmas shoppers and many after-Christmas sales shoppers are satiated by mid-January, leaving the stores low on both merchandise and customers. Accordingly, stores have less merchandise to count and "lost sales" are minimized during January. Companies that do not depend on seasonal sales (e.g., a plumbing supplies wholesale business) may choose to count inventory at some other time during the year. Counting inventory is not a revenue-generating activity; it is a necessary evil that should be conducted when it least disrupts operations.

Adjustment for Lost, Damaged, or Stolen Inventory

To illustrate, assume that Midwest Merchandising Company maintains perpetual inventory records. Midwest determined, through a physical count, that it had $23,500 of merchandise inventory on hand at the end of the accounting period. The balance in the Inventory account was $24,000. Midwest must make an adjusting entry to write down the Inventory account so the amount reported on the financial statements agrees with the amount actually on hand at the end of the period. The write-down decreases both assets (inventory) and stockholders' equity (retained earnings). The write-down increases expenses and decreases net income. Cash flow is not affected. The effects on the statements are as follows.

Assets	=	Liab.	+	Equity	Rev.	−	Exp.	=	Net Inc.	Cash Flow
(500)	=	NA	+	(500)	NA	−	500	=	(500)	NA

Theoretically, inventory losses are operating expenses. However, because such losses are normally immaterial in amount, they are usually added to cost of goods sold for external reporting purposes.

EVENTS AFFECTING SALES

To this point we assumed JPS did not offer cash discounts to its customers. However, sales, as well as purchases of inventory, can be affected by returns, allowances, and discounts. **Sales discounts** are price reductions offered by sellers to encourage buyers to pay promptly. To illustrate, assume JPS engaged in the following selected events during January 2014.

EVENT 1A   JPS sold on account merchandise with a list price of $8,500. Payment terms were 1/10, n/30. The merchandise had cost JPS $4,000.

The sale increases both assets (accounts receivable) and shareholders' equity (retained earnings). Recognizing revenue increases net income. The statement of cash flows is not affected. The effects on the financial statements follow.

Assets					=	Liab.	+	Stockholders' Equity			Rev.	−	Exp.	=	Net Inc.	Cash Flow
Cash	+	Accts. Rec.	+	Inventory	=	Note Pay.	+	Com. Stk.	+	Retained Earnings						
NA	+	8,500	+	NA	=	NA	+	NA	+	8,500	8,500	−	NA	=	8,500	NA

EVENT 1B   JPS recognized $4,000 of cost of goods sold.

Recognizing the expense decreases assets (merchandise inventory) and stockholders' equity (retained earnings). Cost of goods sold increases and net income decreases. Cash flow is not affected. The effects on the financial statements follow.

Assets				=	Liab.	+	Stockholders' Equity			Rev.	−	Exp.	=	Net Inc.	Cash Flow
Cash	+	Accts. Rec.	+	Inventory	=	Note Pay.	+	Com. Stk.	+	Retained Earnings						
NA	+	NA	+	(4,000)	=	NA	+	NA	+	(4,000)	NA	−	4,000	=	(4,000)	NA

Accounting for Sales Returns and Allowances

EVENT 2A   A customer from Event 1A returned inventory with a $1,000 list price. The merchandise had cost JPS $450.

The sales return decreases both assets (accounts receivable) and stockholders' equity (retained earnings) on the balance sheet. Sales and net income decrease. Cash flow is not affected. The effects on the financial statements follow.

Assets				=	Liab.	+	Stockholders' Equity			Rev.	−	Exp.	=	Net Inc.	Cash Flow
Cash	+	Accts. Rec.	+	Inventory	=	Note Pay.	+	Com. Stk.	+	Retained Earnings						
NA	+	(1,000)	+	NA	=	NA	+	NA	+	(1,000)	(1,000)	−	NA	=	(1,000)	NA

EVENT 2B   The cost of the goods ($450) is returned to the inventory account.

Since JPS got the inventory back, the sales return increases both assets (merchandise inventory) and stockholders' equity (retained earnings). The expense (cost of goods sold) decreases and net income increases. Cash flow is not affected. The effects on the financial statements follow.

Assets				=	Liab.	+	Stockholders' Equity			Rev.	−	Exp.	=	Net Inc.	Cash Flow
Cash	+	Accts. Rec.	+	Inventory	=	Note Pay.	+	Com. Stk.	+	Retained Earnings						
NA	+	NA	+	450	=	NA	+	NA	+	450	NA	−	(450)	=	450	NA

Accounting for Sales Discounts

EVENT 3   JPS collected the balance of the accounts receivable generated in Event 1A. Recall the goods were sold under terms 1/10, net/30.

ALTERNATIVE 1   The collection occurs before the discount period has expired (within 10 days from the date of the sale).

JPS would give the buyer a 1 percent discount. Given the original sales amount of $8,500 and a sales return of $1,000, the amount of the discount is $75 [($8,500 − $1,000) × .01]. The sales discount reduces the amount of accounts receivable and retained earnings on the balance sheet. It also reduces the amount of revenue and the net income shown on the balance sheet. It does not affect the statement of cash flows. The effects on the financial statements follow.

Assets				=	Liab.	+	Stockholders' Equity			Rev.	−	Exp.	=	Net Inc.	Cash Flow
Cash	+	Accts. Rec.	+	Inventory	=	Note Pay.	+	Com. Stk.	+	Retained Earnings					
NA	+	(75)	+	NA	=	NA	+	NA	+	(75)	(75)	−	NA	=	(75)	NA

The balance due on the account receivable is $7,425 ($8,500 original sales − $1,000 sales return − $75 discount). The collection increases the Cash account and decreases the Accounts Receivable account. The income statement is not affected. The cash inflow is shown in the operating activities section of the statement of cash flows. The effects on the financial statements follow.

Assets				=	Liab.	+	Stockholders' Equity			Rev.	−	Exp.	=	Net Inc.	Cash Flow
Cash	+	Accts. Rec.	+	Inventory	=	Accts. Pay.	+	Com. Stk.	+	Retained Earnings					
7,425	+	(7,425)	+	NA	=	NA	+	NA	+	NA	NA	−	NA	=	NA	7,425 OA

Net Sales

The gross amount of sales minus **sales returns and allowance** and sales discounts is commonly called **net sales.** Companies are not required by GAAP to show sales returns and allowance and sales discount on their income statement. Indeed, most companies show only the amount of *net sales* on the income statement. In this case the net sales amount to $7,425 ($8,500 original sales − $1,000 sales return − $75 discount).

ALTERNATIVE 2   **The collection occurs after the discount period has expired (after 10 days from the date of the sale).**

Under these circumstances there is no sales discount. The amount collected is $7,500 ($8,500 original sale − $1,000 sales return). Net sales shown on the income statement would also be $7,500.

COMMON SIZE FINANCIAL STATEMENTS

How good is a $1,000,000 increase in net income? The answer is not clear because there is no indication as to the size of the company. A million dollar increase may be excellent for a small company but would be virtually meaningless for a company the size of Exxon. To enable meaningful comparisons analysts prepare **common size financial statements.** Common size statements display information in percentages as well as absolute dollar amounts.

To illustrate, we expand the income statements for JPS to include percentages. The results are shown in Exhibit 3.7. The percentage data are computed by defining net sales as the base figure, or 100 percent. The other amounts on the statements are then

LO 7

Use common sizes financial statements to evaluate managerial performance.

The income statement data show that compared to Zales, Blue Nile does save money by not operating bricks-and-mortar stores. This can be determined by comparing each company's net income to its sales. For Blue Nile this percentage is 4.2% ($12,800 ÷ $302,134), which means that while 4.2% of each dollar of revenue goes to profit, 95.8% goes to pay for expenses. For Zales this percentage is a *negative* 10.6% [($189,503) ÷ 1,779,744]. Clearly, Blue Nile did better than Zales. This result is despite the fact that compared to Blue Nile, Zales charges a higher price for the jewelry it sells. Compare each company's gross margin to its sales. Blue Nile's gross margin is 21.6% of its sales ($65,344 ÷ $302,134), which means that 78.4% of each dollar of revenue goes to pay for the product that was sold. For Zales these percentages are 46.7% for the gross margin [(1,779,744 − $948,572) ÷ 1,779,744] and 53.3% for cost of goods sold. This shows that while Blue Nile charges less for its products, it makes up for the lower gross margin with lower operating expenses.

shown as a percentage of net sales. For example, the *cost of goods sold percentage* is the dollar amount of *cost of goods sold* divided by the dollar amount of *net sales,* which produces a percentage of 66.7 percent ($8,000 ÷ $12,000) for 2012 and 46.5 percent ($11,500 ÷ $24,750) for 2013. Other income statement items are computed using the same approach.

These common size statements provide insight into the company's operating strategy. For example, assume JPS relocated its store in an upscale mall in early 2013.

EXHIBIT 3.7   Common Size Financial Statements

JUNE'S PLANT SHOP
Income Statement
For the Period Ended

	2012		2013	
Net sales*	$12,000	100.0%	$24,750	100.0%
Cost of goods sold	(8,000)	66.7	(11,500)	46.5
Gross margin	4,000	33.3	13,250	53.5
Less: Operating expenses				
Selling and administrative expense	(1,000)	8.3	(5,000)	20.2
Transportation-out			(450)	1.8
Operating income	3,000	25.0	7,800	31.5
Nonoperating items				
Interest expense			(360)	(1.5)
Gain on the sale of land			700	2.8
Net income	$3,000	25.0	$8,140	32.9

*Since JPS did not offer sales discounts or have sales returns and allowances during 2012 or 2013, the amount of sales revenue is equal to the amount of net sales. We use the term *net sales* here because it is more commonly used in business practice. Percentages do not add exactly because they have been rounded.

Management realized that the company would have to pay more for operating expenses but believed those expenses could be offset by charging significantly higher prices. The common size income statement confirms that the company's goals were accomplished. Note that the gross margin increased from 33.3 percent of sales to 53.5 percent, confirming that the company was able to increase prices. Also, note that operating expenses increased. Selling and administrative expense increased from 8.3 percent of sales to 20.2 percent. Also, the company experienced a new expense, transportation out, for delivering merchandise to its customers. These increases in expenses confirm the fact that JPS is paying more for rental space and providing additional services to its customers. The common size statements, therefore, support the conclusion that JPS's increase in net income from $3,000 to $8,140 was a result of management's new operating strategy. As a side note, the new operating strategy may also explain why JPS sold its land in late 2013. Considering the success the company experienced at the new location, there was no motive to build a store on the land.

A Look Back

Merchandising companies earn profits by selling inventory at prices that are higher than the cost paid for the goods. Merchandising companies include *retail companies* (companies that sell goods to the final consumer) and *wholesale companies* (companies that sell to other merchandising companies). The products sold by merchandising companies are called *inventory.* The costs to purchase inventory, to receive it, and to ready it for sale are *product costs,* which are first accumulated in an inventory account (balance sheet asset account) and then recognized as cost of goods sold (income statement expense account) in the period in which goods are sold. Purchases and sales of inventory can be recorded continually as goods are bought and sold (perpetual system) or at the end of the accounting period (periodic system, discussed in the chapter appendix).

Accounting for inventory includes the treatment of cash discounts, transportation costs, and returns and allowances. The cost of inventory is the list price less any purchase returns and allowances and purchase discounts, plus transportation-in costs. The cost of freight paid to acquire inventory (*transportation-in*) is considered a product cost. The cost of freight paid to deliver inventory to customers (*transportation-out*) is a selling expense. *Sales returns and allowances* and *sales discounts* are subtracted from sales revenue to determine the amount of *net sales* reported on the income statement. Purchase returns and allowances reduce product cost. Theoretically, the cost of lost, damaged, or stolen inventory is an operating expense. However, because these costs are usually immaterial in amount they are typically included as part of cost of goods sold on the income statement.

Some companies use a *multistep income statement* which reports product costs separately from selling and administrative costs. Cost of goods sold is subtracted from sales revenue to determine *gross margin.* Selling and administrative expenses are subtracted from gross margin to determine income from operations. Other companies report income using a *single-step format* in which the cost of goods sold is listed along with selling and administrative items in a single expense category that is subtracted in total from revenue to determine income from operations.

Managers of merchandising businesses operate in a highly competitive environment. They must manage company operations carefully to remain profitable. *Common size financial statements* (statements presented on a percentage basis) and ratio analysis are useful monitoring tools. Common size financial statements permit ready comparisons among different-size companies. Although a $1 million increase in sales may be good for a small company and bad for a large company, a 10 percent increase can apply to any size company.

>> A Look Forward

To this point, the text has explained the basic accounting cycle for service and merchandising businesses. Future chapters more closely address specific accounting issues. For example, in Chapter 5 you will learn how to deal with inventory items that are purchased at differing prices. Other chapters will discuss a variety of specific practices that are widely used by real-world companies.

APPENDIX

LO 8

Identify the primary features of the periodic inventory system.

Periodic Inventory System

Under certain conditions, it is impractical to record inventory sales transactions as they occur. Consider the operations of a fast-food restaurant. To maintain perpetual inventory records, the restaurant would have to transfer from the Inventory account to the Cost of Goods Sold account the *cost* of each hamburger, order of fries, soft drink, or other food items as they were sold. Obviously, recording the cost of each item at the point of sale would be impractical without using highly sophisticated computer equipment (recording the selling price the customer pays is captured by cash registers; the difficulty lies in capturing inventory cost).

The **periodic inventory system** offers a practical solution for recording inventory transactions in a low-technology, high-volume environment. Inventory costs are recorded in a Purchases account at the time of purchase. Purchase returns and allowances and transportation-in are recorded in separate accounts. No entries for the cost of merchandise purchases or sales are recorded in the Inventory account during the period. The cost of goods sold is determined at the end of the period as shown in Exhibit 3.8.

EXHIBIT 3.8

Schedule of Cost of Goods Sold for 2013	
Beginning inventory	$ 6,000
Purchases	11,000
Purchase returns and allowances	(1,000)
Purchase discounts	(200)
Transportation-in	300
Cost of goods available for sale	16,100
Ending inventory	4,600
Cost of goods sold	$11,500

The perpetual and periodic inventory systems represent alternative procedures for recording the same information. The amounts of cost of goods sold and ending inventory reported in the financial statements will be the same regardless of the method used.

The **schedule of cost of goods sold** presented in Exhibit 3.8 is used for internal reporting purposes. It is normally not shown in published financial statements. The amount of cost of goods sold is reported as a single line item on the income statement. The income statement in Exhibit 3.3 will be the same whether JPS maintains perpetual or periodic inventory records.

Advantages and Disadvantages of the Periodic System versus the Perpetual System

The chief advantage of the periodic method is recording efficiency. Recording inventory transactions occasionally (periodically) requires less effort than recording them continually (perpetually). Historically, practical limitations offered businesses like fast-food restaurants or grocery stores no alternative to using the periodic system. The sheer volume of transactions made recording individual decreases to the Inventory account balance as each item was sold impossible. Imagine the number of transactions a grocery store would have to record every business day to maintain perpetual records.

Although the periodic system provides a recordkeeping advantage over the perpetual system, perpetual inventory records provide significant control advantages over periodic records. With perpetual records, the book balance in the Inventory account should agree with the amount of inventory in stock at any given time. By comparing that book balance with the results of a physical inventory count, management can determine the amount of lost, damaged, destroyed, or stolen inventory. Perpetual records also permit more timely and accurate reorder decisions and profitability assessments.

When a company uses the *periodic* inventory system, lost, damaged, or stolen merchandise is automatically included in cost of goods sold. Because such goods are not included in the year-end physical count, they are treated as sold regardless of the reason for their absence. Since the periodic system does not separate the cost of lost, damaged, or stolen merchandise from the cost of goods sold, the amount of any inventory shrinkage is unknown. This feature is a major disadvantage of the periodic system. Without knowing the amount of inventory losses, management cannot weigh the costs of various security systems against the potential benefits.

Advances in such technology as electronic bar code scanning and increased computing power have eliminated most of the practical constraints that once prevented merchandisers with high-volume, low dollar-value inventories from recording inventory transactions on a continual basis. As a result, use of the perpetual inventory system has expanded rapidly in recent years and continued growth can be expected. This text, therefore, concentrates on the perpetual inventory system.

A step-by-step audio-narrated series of slides is provided on the text website at www.mhhe.com/edmondssurvey3e.

 SELF-STUDY REVIEW PROBLEM

Academy Sales Company (ASC) started the 2012 accounting period with the balances given in the financial statements model shown below. During 2012 ASC experienced the following business events.

1. Purchased $16,000 of merchandise inventory on account, terms 2/10, n/30.
2. The goods that were purchased in Event 1 were delivered FOB shipping point. Freight costs of $600 were paid in cash by the responsible party.
3. Returned $500 of goods purchased in Event 1.
4a. Recorded the cash discount on the goods purchased in Event 1.
4b. Paid the balance due on the account payable within the discount period.
5a. Recognized $21,000 of cash revenue from the sale of merchandise.
5b. Recognized $15,000 of cost of goods sold.
6. The merchandise in Event 5a was sold to customers FOB destination. Freight costs of $950 were paid in cash by the responsible party.
7. Paid cash of $4,000 for selling and administrative expenses.
8. Sold the land for $5,600 cash.

Required

a. Record the above transactions in a financial statements model like the one shown below.

Event No.	Cash	+	Inventory	+	Land	=	Accts. Pay.	+	Com. Stk.	+	Ret. Earn.	Rev./ Gain	−	Exp.	=	Net Inc.	Cash Flow
Bal.	25,000	+	3,000	+	5,000	=	–0–	+	18,000	+	15,000	NA	−	NA	=	NA	NA

b. Prepare a schedule of cost of goods sold. (Appendix)
c. Prepare a multistep income statement. Include common size percentages on the income statement.
d. ASC's gross margin percentage in 2011 was 22%. Based on the common size data in the income statement, did ASC raise or lower its prices in 2012? (Appendix)
e. Assuming a 10 percent rate of growth, what is the amount of net income expected for 2013?

Solution

a.

Event No.	Cash	+	Inventory	+	Land	=	Accts. Pay.	+	Com. Stk.	+	Ret. Earn.	Rev./ Gain	−	Exp.	=	Net Inc.	Cash Flow	
Bal.	25,000	+	3,000	+	5,000	=	–0–	+	18,000	+	15,000	NA	−	NA	=	NA	NA	
1		+	16,000			=	16,000	+		+			−		=			
2	(600)	+	600			=		+		+			−		=		(600)	OA
3		+	(500)			=	(500)	+		+			−		=			
4a		+	(310)			=	(310)	+		+			−		=			
4b	(15,190)	+				=	(15,190)	+		+			−		=		(15,190)	OA
5a	21,000	+				=		+		+	21,000	21,000	−		=	21,000	21,000	OA
5b		+	(15,000)			=		+		+	(15,000)		−	15,000	=	(15,000)		
6	(950)	+				=		+		+	(950)		−	950	=	(950)	(950)	OA
7	(4,000)	+				=		+		+	(4,000)		−	4,000	=	(4,000)	(4,000)	OA
8	5,600	+			(5,000)	=		+		+	600	600	−		=	600	5,600	IA
Bal.	30,860	+	3,790		–0–	=	–0–	+	18,000	+	16,650	21,600	−	19,950	=	1,650	5,860	NC

b.

ACADEMY SALES COMPANY
Schedule of Cost of Goods Sold
For the Period Ended December 31, 2012

Beginning inventory	$ 3,000
Plus purchases	16,000
Less: Purchase returns and allowances	(500)
Less: Purchases discounts	(310)
Plus: Transportation-in	600
Goods available for sale	18,790
Less: Ending inventory	3,790
Cost of goods sold	$(15,000)

c.

ACADEMY SALES COMPANY
Income Statement*
For the Period Ended December 31, 2012

Net sales	$21,000	100.0%
Cost of goods sold	(15,000)	71.4
Gross margin	6,000	28.6
Less: Operating expenses		
Selling and administrative expense	(4,000)	19.0
Transportation-out	(950)	4.5
Operating income	1,050	5.0
Nonoperating items		
Gain on the sale of land	600	2.9
Net income	$ 1,650	7.9

*Percentages do not add exactly because they have been rounded.

d. All other things being equal, the higher the gross margin percentage, the higher the sales prices. Since the gross margin percentage increased from 22% to 28.6%, the data suggest that Academy raised its sales prices.

e. $1,155 [$1,050 + (.10 × $1,050)]. Note that the gain is not expected to recur.

KEY TERMS

Cash discount 94	Merchandising businesses 86	Sales returns and
Common size financial	Multistep income	allowances 103
statements 103	statement 99	Schedule of cost of goods
Cost of goods available for	Net sales 103	sold 106
sale 89	Operating income (or loss) 99	Selling and administrative
Cost of Goods Sold 89	Period costs 89	costs 89
FOB (free on board)	Periodic inventory system 106	Shrinkage 100
destination 95	Perpetual inventory	Single-step income
FOB (free on board) shipping	system 89	statement 99
point 95	Product costs 89	Transportation-in
Gain 98	Purchase discount 94	(freight-in) 95
Gross margin 89	Purchase returns and	Transportation-out
Gross profit 89	allowances 93	(freight-out) 95
Loss 98	Retail companies 86	2/10, n/30 94
Merchandise inventory 86	Sales discounts 101	Wholesale companies 86

QUESTIONS

1. Define *merchandise inventory*. What types of costs are included in the Merchandise Inventory account?

2. What is the difference between a product cost and a selling and administrative cost?

3. How is the cost of goods available for sale determined?

4. What portion of cost of goods available for sale is shown on the balance sheet? What portion is shown on the income statement?

5. When are period costs expensed? When are product costs expensed?

6. If **PetCo** had net sales of $600,000, goods available for sale of $450,000, and cost of goods sold of $375,000, what is its gross margin? What amount of inventory will be shown on its balance sheet?

7. Describe how the perpetual inventory system works. What are some advantages of using the perpetual inventory system? Is it necessary to take a physical inventory when using the perpetual inventory system?

8. What are the effects of the following types of transactions on the accounting equation? Also identify the financial statements that are affected. (Assume that the perpetual inventory system is used.)

   a. Acquisition of cash from the issue of common stock.

   b. Contribution of inventory by an owner of a company.

   c. Purchase of inventory with cash by a company.

   d. Sale of inventory for cash.

9. Northern Merchandising Company sold inventory that cost $12,000 for $20,000 cash. How does this event affect the accounting equation? What financial statements and

accounts are affected? (Assume that the perpetual inventory system is used.)

10. If goods are shipped FOB shipping point, which party (buyer or seller) is responsible for the shipping costs?

11. Define *transportation-in*. Is it a product or a period cost?

12. Quality Cellular Co. paid $80 for freight on merchandise that it had purchased for resale to customers (transportation-in) and paid $135 for freight on merchandise delivered to customers (transportation-out). The $80 payment is added to what account? The $135 payment is added to what account?

13. Why would a seller grant an allowance to a buyer of the his merchandise?

14. Dyer Department Store purchased goods with the terms 2/10, n/30. What do these terms mean?

15. Eastern Discount Stores incurred a $5,000 cash cost. How does the accounting for this cost differ if the cash were paid for inventory versus commissions to sales personnel?

16. What is the purpose of giving a cash discount to charge customers?

17. Define *transportation-out*. Is it a product cost or a period cost for the seller?

18. **Ball Co.** purchased inventory with a list price of $4,000 with the terms 2/10, n/30. What amount will be added to the Merchandise Inventory account?

19. Explain the difference between purchase returns and sales returns. How do purchase returns affect the financial statements of both buyer and seller? How do sales returns affect the financial statements of both buyer and seller?

20. Explain the difference between gross margin and a gain.
21. What is the difference between a multistep income statement and a single-step income statement?
22. What is the advantage of using common size income statements to present financial information for several accounting periods?
23. What is the purpose of preparing a schedule of cost of goods sold?

24. Explain how the periodic inventory system works. What are some advantages of using the periodic inventory system? What are some disadvantages of using the periodic inventory system? Is it necessary to take a physical inventory when using the periodic inventory system?
25. Why does the periodic inventory system impose a major disadvantage for management in accounting for lost, stolen, or damaged goods?

 ## MULTIPLE-CHOICE QUESTIONS

Multiple-choice questions are provided on the text website at www.mhhe.com/edmondssurvey3e.

EXERCISES

All applicable Exercises are available with McGraw-Hill's *Connect Accounting*.

When the instructions for *any* exercise or problem call for the preparation of an income statement, use the *multistep format* unless otherwise indicated.

LO 1, 2

Exercise 3-1 *Comparing a merchandising company with a service company*

The following information is available for two different types of businesses for the 2012 accounting period. Eady CPAs is a service business that provides accounting services to small businesses. Campus Clothing is a merchandising business that sells sports clothing to college students.

Data for Eady CPAs

1. Borrowed $40,000 from the bank to start the business.
2. Provided $30,000 of services to customers and collected $30,000 cash.
3. Paid salary expense of $20,000.

Data for Campus Clothing

1. Borrowed $40,000 from the bank to start the business.
2. Purchased $25,000 inventory for cash.
3. Inventory costing $16,400 was sold for $30,000 cash.
4. Paid $3,600 cash for operating expenses.

Required

a. Prepare an income statement, a balance sheet, and a statement of cash flows for each of the companies.
b. Which of the two businesses would have product costs? Why?
c. Why does Eady CPAs not compute gross margin on its income statement?
d. Compare the assets of both companies. What assets do they have in common? What assets are different? Why?

LO 2

Exercise 3-2 *Effect of inventory transactions on financial statements: perpetual system*

Mark Dixon started a small merchandising business in 2012. The business experienced the following events during its first year of operation. Assume that Dixon uses the perpetual inventory system.

1. Acquired $40,000 cash from the issue of common stock.
2. Purchased inventory for $30,000 cash.
3. Sold inventory costing $20,000 for $32,000 cash.

Required

a. Record the events in a statements model like the one shown below.

Assets			=	Equity			Rev.	−	Exp.	=	Net Inc.	Cash Flow
Cash	+	Inv.	=	Com. Stk.	+	Ret. Earn.						

b. Prepare an income statement for 2012 (use the multistep format).
c. What is the amount of total assets at the end of the period?

Exercise 3-3   *Effect of inventory transactions on the income statement and statement of cash flows: Perpetual system*   **LO 2**

During 2012, Knight Merchandising Company purchased $15,000 of inventory on account. Knight sold inventory on account that cost $12,500 for $17,500. Cash payments on accounts payable were $10,000. There was $11,000 cash collected from accounts receivable. Knight also paid $3,500 cash for operating expenses. Assume that Knight started the accounting period with $14,000 in both cash and common stock.

Required

a. Identify the events described in the preceding paragraph and record them in a horizontal statements model like the following one:

Assets					=	Liab.	+	Equity			Rev.	−	Exp.	=	Net inc.	Cash Flow
Cash	+	Accts. Rec.	+	Inv.	=	Accts. Pay.	+	Com. Stk.	+	Ret. Earn.						
14,000	+	NA	+	NA	=	NA	+	14,000	+	NA	NA	−	NA	=	NA	NA

b. What is the balance of accounts receivable at the end of 2012?
c. What is the balance of accounts payable at the end of 2012?
d. What are the amounts of gross margin and net income for 2012?
e. Determine the amount of net cash flow from operating activities.
f. Explain why net income and retained earnings are the same for Knight. Normally would these amounts be the same? Why or why not?

Exercise 3-4   *Recording inventory transactions in a financial statements model*   **LO 2**

Kona Clothing experienced the following events during 2012, its first year of operation:

1. Acquired $14,000 cash from the issue of common stock.
2. Purchased inventory for $8,000 cash.
3. Sold inventory costing $6,000 for $9,000 cash.
4. Paid $800 for advertising expense.

Required

Record the events in a statements model like the one shown below.

Assets			=	Equity			Rev.	−	Exp.	=	Net Inc.	Cash Flow
Cash	+	Inv.	=	Com. Stk.	+	Ret. Earn.						

Exercise 3-5   *Understanding the freight terms FOB shipping point and FOB destination*

Required

Determine which party, buyer or seller, is responsible for freight charges in each of the following situations:

a. Sold merchandise, freight terms, FOB destination.
b. Sold merchandise, freight terms, FOB shipping point.
c. Purchased merchandise, freight terms, FOB destination.
d. Purchased merchandise, freight terms, FOB shipping point.

LO 2, 3

Exercise 3-6   *Effect of purchase returns and allowances and freight costs on the financial statements: perpetual system*

The beginning account balances for Jerry's Auto Shop as of January 1, 2012 follows:

Account Titles	Beginning Balances
Cash	$28,000
Inventory	14,000
Common stock	36,000
Retained earnings	6,000
Total	$42,000

The following events affected the company during the 2012 accounting period:

1. Purchased merchandise on account that cost $18,000.
2. The goods in Event 1 were purchased FOB shipping point with freight cost of $1,000 cash.
3. Returned $3,600 of damaged merchandise for credit on account.
4. Agreed to keep other damaged merchandise for which the company received a $1,400 allowance.
5. Sold merchandise that cost $16,000 for $34,000 cash.
6. Delivered merchandise to customers in Event 5 under terms FOB destination with freight costs amounting to $800 cash.
7. Paid $12,000 on the merchandise purchased in Event 1.

Required

a. Organize appropriate ledger accounts under an accounting equation. Record the beginning balances and the transaction data in the accounts.
b. Prepare an income statement and a statement of cash flows for 2012.
c. Explain why a difference does or does not exist between net income and net cash flow from operating activities.

LO 2, 3

Exercise 3-7   *Accounting for product costs: Perpetual inventory system*

Which of the following would be *added* to the Inventory account for a merchandising business using the perpetual inventory system?

Required

a. Transportation-out.
b. Purchase discount.
c. Transportation-in.
d. Purchase of a new computer to be used by the business.
e. Purchase of inventory.
f. Allowance received for damaged inventory.

Exercise 3-8 *Effect of product cost and period cost: horizontal statements model* LO 1, 2, 3

The Toy Store experienced the following events for the 2012 accounting period:

1. Acquired $20,000 cash from the issue of common stock.
2. Purchased $56,000 of inventory on account.
3. Received goods purchased in Event 2 FOB shipping point; freight cost of $600 paid in cash.
4. Sold inventory on account that cost $35,000 for $57,400.
5. Freight cost on the goods sold in Event 4 was $420. The goods were shipped FOB destination. Cash was paid for the freight cost.
6. Customer in Event 4 returned $4,000 worth of goods that had a cost of $2,400.
7. Collected $47,000 cash from accounts receivable.
8. Paid $44,000 cash on accounts payable.
9. Paid $1,100 for advertising expense.
10. Paid $1,000 cash for insurance expense.

Required

a. Which of these events affect period (selling and administrative) costs? Which result in product costs? If neither, label the transaction NA.

b. Record each event in a horizontal statements model like the following one. The first event is recorded as an example.

Assets			=	Liab.	+	Equity			Rev.	–	Exp.	=	Net Inc.	Cash Flow
Cash	+ Accts. Rec.	+ Inv.	=	Accts. Pay.	+	C. Stk.	+	Ret. Earn.						
20,000	+ NA	+ NA	=	NA	+	20,000	+	NA	NA	–	NA	=	NA	20,000 FA

Exercise 3-9 *Cash discounts and purchase returns* LO 3

On April 6, 2012, Taylor Furnishings purchased $12,400 of merchandise from Bergin's Imports, terms 2/10 n/45. On April 8, Taylor returned $1,200 of the merchandise to Bergin's Imports for credit. Taylor paid cash for the merchandise on April 15, 2012.

Required

a. What is the amount that Taylor must pay Bergin's Imports on April 15?

b. Record the events in a horizontal statements model like the following one.

Assets		=	Liab.	+	Equity			Rev.	–	Exp.	=	Net Inc.	Cash Flow
Cash	+ Inv.	=	Accts. Pay.	+	C. Stock.	+	Ret. Earn.						

c. How much must Taylor pay for the merchandise purchased if the payment is not made until April 20, 2012?

d. Record the payment in event (c) in a horizontal statements model like the one above.

e. Why would Taylor want to pay for the merchandise by April 15?

Exercise 3-10 *Effect of sales returns and allowances and freight costs on the financial statements: perpetual system* LO 2, 3

Stash Company began the 2012 accounting period with $10,000 cash, $38,000 inventory, $25,000 common stock, and $23,000 retained earnings. During the 2012 accounting period, Stash experienced the following events.

1. Sold merchandise costing $28,000 for $46,000 on account to Jack's Furniture Store.
2. Delivered the goods to Jack's under terms FOB destination. Freight costs were $500 cash.

3. Received returned goods from Jack's. The goods cost Stash $2,000 and were sold to Jack's for $3,000.
4. Granted Jack's $2,000 allowance for damaged goods that Jack's agreed to keep.
5. Collected partial payment of $25,000 cash from accounts receivable.

Required

a. Record the events in a statements model like the one shown below.

	Assets				=	Equity			Rev.	−	Exp.	=	Net Inc.	Cash Flow
Cash	+	Accts. Rec.	+	Inv.	=	Com. Stk.	+	Ret. Earn.						

b. Prepare an income statement, a balance sheet, and a statement of cash flows.
c. Why would Stash grant the $2,000 allowance to Jack's? Who benefits more?

LO 2, 3   **Exercise 3-11**   *Effect of cash discounts on financial statements: perpetual system*

Campus Computers was started in 2012. The company experienced the following accounting events during its first year of operation.

1. Started business when it acquired $50,000 cash from the issue of common stock.
2. Purchased merchandise with a list price of $46,000 on account, terms 2/10, n/30.
3. Paid off one-half of the accounts payable balance within the discount period.
4. Sold merchandise on account that had a list price of $48,000. Credit terms were 1/20, n/30. The merchandise had cost Campus Computers $28,000.
5. Collected cash from the account receivable within the discount period.
6. Paid $7,200 cash for operating expenses.
7. Paid the balance due on accounts payable. The payment was not made within the discount period.

Required

a. Record the events in a horizontal statements model like the following one.

	Assets				=	Liab.	+		Equity			Rev.	−	Exp.	=	Net Inc.	Cash Flow
Cash	+	Accts. Rec.	+	Inv.	=	Accts. Pay.	+	Com. Stk.	+	Ret. Earn.							

b. What is the amount of gross margin for the period? What is the net income for the period?
c. Why would Campus Computers sell merchandise with the terms 1/20, n/30?
d. What do the terms 2/10, n/30 in Event 2 mean to Campus Computers?

LO 2, 3   **Exercise 3-12**   *Comparing gross margin and gain on sale of land*

Usrey Sales Company had the following balances in its accounts on January 1, 2012.

Cash	$ 70,000
Merchandise Inventory	50,000
Land	120,000
Common Stock	100,000
Retained Earnings	140,000

Usrey experienced the following events during 2012.

1. Sold merchandise inventory that cost $40,000 for $75,000.
2. Sold land that cost $50,000 for $80,000.

Required

a. Determine the amount of gross margin recognized by Usrey.
b. Determine the amount of the gain on the sale of land recognized by Usrey.
c. Comment on how the gross margin versus the gain will be recognized on the income statement.
d. Comment on how the gross margin versus the gain will be recognized on the statement of cash flows.

Exercise 3-13 *Effect of inventory losses: perpetual system*

LO 2, 6

Reeves Design experienced the following events during 2012, its first year of operation.

1. Started the business when it acquired $40,000 cash from the issue of common stock.
2. Paid $28,000 cash to purchase inventory.
3. Sold inventory costing $21,500 for $34,200 cash.
4. Physically counted inventory showing $5,800 inventory was on hand at the end of the accounting period.

Required

a. Determine the amount of the difference between book balance and the actual amount of inventory as determined by the physical count.
b. Explain how differences between the book balance and the physical count of inventory could arise. Why is being able to determine whether differences exist useful to management?

Exercise 3-14 *Determining the effect of inventory transactions on the horizontal statements model: perpetual system*

LO 2

Causey Sales Company experienced the following events:

1. Purchased merchandise inventory for cash.
2. Purchased merchandise inventory on account.
3. Sold merchandise inventory for cash. Label the revenue recognition 3a and the expense recognition 3b.
4. Sold merchandise inventory on account. Label the revenue recognition 4a and the expense recognition 4b.
5. Returned merchandise purchased on account.
6. Paid cash for selling and administrative expenses.
7. Paid cash on accounts payable not within the discount period.
8. Paid cash for transportation-in.
9. Collected cash from accounts receivable.
10. Paid cash for transportation-out.

Required

Identify each event as asset source (AS), asset use (AU), asset exchange (AE), or claims exchange (CE). Also explain how each event affects the financial statements by placing a + for increase, − for decrease, or NA for not affected under each of the components in the following statements model. Assume the company uses the perpetual inventory system. The first event is recorded as an example.

Event No.	Event Type	Assets	=	Liab.	+	Equity	Rev.	−	Exp.	=	Net Inc.	Cash Flow
1	AE	+−	=	NA	+	NA	NA	−	NA	=	NA	−OA

LO 4

Exercise 3-15 *Single-step and multistep income statements*

The following information was taken from the accounts of Healthy Foods Market, a small grocery store at December 31, 2012. The accounts are listed in alphabetical order, and all have normal balances.

Accounts payable	$ 300
Accounts receivable	1,040
Advertising expense	200
Cash	820
Common stock	600
Cost of goods sold	900
Interest expense	140
Merchandise inventory	500
Prepaid rent	280
Retained earnings	1,050
Sales revenue	2,400
Salaries expense	260
Supplies expense	210
Gain on sale of land	75

Required

First, prepare an income statement for the year using the single-step approach. Then prepare another income statement using the multistep approach.

LO 2

Exercise 3-16 *Determining the cost of financing inventory*

On January 1, 2012, Fran started a small flower merchandising business that she named Fran's Flowers. The company experienced the following events during the first year of operation.

1. Started the business by issuing common stock for $20,000 cash.
2. Paid $28,000 cash to purchase inventory.
3. Sold merchandise that cost $16,000 for $36,000 on account.
4. Collected $30,000 cash from accounts receivable.
5. Paid $7,500 for operating expenses.

Required

a. Organize ledger accounts under an accounting equation and record the events in the accounts.
b. Prepare an income statement, a balance sheet, and a statement of cash flows.
c. Since Fran sold inventory for $36,000, she will be able to recover more than half of the $40,000 she invested in the stock. Do you agree with this statement? Why or why not?

LO 3

Exercise 3-17 *Inventory financing costs*

Joan Sweatt comes to you for advice. She has just purchased a large amount of inventory with the terms 2/10, n/30. The amount of the invoice is $540,000. She is currently short of cash but has decent credit. She can borrow the money needed to settle the account payable at an annual interest rate of 7%. Joan is sure she will have the necessary cash by the due date of the invoice but not by the last day of the discount period.

Required

a. Convert the discount rate into an annual interest rate.
b. Make a recommendation regarding whether Sweatt should borrow the money and pay off the account payable within the discount period.

LO 8

Exercise 3-18 *Effect of inventory transactions on the income statement and balance sheet: periodic system (Appendix)*

Joe Dodd owns Joe's Sporting Goods. At the beginning of the year, Joe's had $8,400 in inventory. During the year, Joe's purchased inventory that cost $42,000. At the end of the year, inventory on hand amounted to $17,600.

Required

Calculate the following:

a. Cost of goods available for sale during the year.

b. Cost of goods sold for the year.

c. Amount of inventory Joe's would report on the year-end balance sheet.

Exercise 3-19   *Determining cost of goods sold: periodic system (Appendix)*

LO 8

Lane Antiques uses the periodic inventory system to account for its inventory transactions. The following account titles and balances were drawn from Lane's records: beginning balance in inventory, $24,000; purchases, $150,000; purchase returns and allowances, $10,000; sales, $400,000; sales returns and allowances, $2,500; freight-in, $750; and operating expenses, $26,000. A physical count indicated that $18,000 of merchandise was on hand at the end of the accounting period.

Required

a. Prepare a schedule of cost of goods sold.

b. Prepare a multistep income statement.

Exercise 3-20   *Using common size statements and ratios to make comparisons*

LO 7

At the end of 2012, the following information is available for Chicago and St. Louis companies:

	Chicago	St. Louis
Sales	$3,000,000	$3,000
Cost of goods sold	1,800,000	2,100
Selling and administrative expenses	960,000	780
Total assets	3,750,000	3,750
Stockholders' equity	1,000,000	1,200

Required

a. Prepare common size income statements for each company.

b. One company is a high-end retailer, and the other operates a discount store. Which is the discounter? Support your selection by referring to the common size statements.

PROBLEMS

All applicable Problems are available with McGraw-Hill's
Connect Accounting.

Problem 3-21   *Basic transactions for three accounting cycles: perpetual system*

LO 2

Ginger's Flower Company was started in 2012 when it acquired $80,000 cash from the issue of common stock. The following data summarize the company's first three years' operating activities. Assume that all transactions were cash transactions.

CHECK FIGURES
2012 Net Income: $8,000
2014 Total Assets: $112,000

	2012	2013	2014
Purchases of inventory	$ 60,000	$ 90,000	$ 130,000
Sales	102,000	146,000	220,000
Cost of goods sold	54,000	78,000	140,000
Selling and administrative expenses	40,000	52,000	72,000

Required

Prepare an income statement (use multistep format) and balance sheet for each fiscal year. (*Hint:* Record the transaction data for each accounting period in the accounting equation before preparing the statements for that year.)

Problem 3-22 *Identifying product and period costs*

Required

Indicate whether each of the following costs is a product cost or a period (selling and administrative) cost.

a. Advertising expense.
b. Insurance on vans used to deliver goods to customers.
c. Salaries of sales supervisors.
d. Monthly maintenance expense for a copier.
e. Goods purchased for resale.
f. Cleaning supplies for the office.
g. Freight on goods purchased for resale.
h. Salary of the marketing director.
i. Freight on goods sold to customer with terms FOB destination.
j. Utilities expense incurred for office building.

Problem 3-23 *Identifying freight costs*

Required

For each of the following events, determine the amount of freight paid by The Dive Shop. Also indicate whether the freight cost would be classified as a product or period (selling and administrative) cost.

a. Purchased merchandise inventory with freight costs of $1,400. The merchandise was shipped FOB destination.
b. Shipped merchandise to customers, freight terms FOB destination. The freight costs were $300.
c. Purchased inventory with freight costs of $500. The goods were shipped FOB shipping point.
d. Sold merchandise to a customer. Freight costs were $800. The goods were shipped FOB shipping point.

Problem 3-24 *Effect of purchase returns and allowances and purchase discounts on the financial statements: perpetual system*

The following events were completed by Chan's Imports in September 2012.

Sept. 1 Acquired $60,000 cash from the issue of common stock.
　　　1 Purchased $36,000 of merchandise on account with terms 2/10, n/30.
　　　5 Paid $800 cash for freight to obtain merchandise purchased on September 1.
　　　8 Sold merchandise that cost $20,000 to customers for $38,000 on account, with terms 2/10, n/30.
　　　8 Returned $1,500 of defective merchandise from the September 1 purchase to the supplier.
　　10 Paid cash for the balance due on the merchandise purchased on September 1.
　　20 Received cash from customers of September 8 sale in settlement of the account balances, but not within the discount period.
　　30 Paid $4,900 cash for selling expenses.

Required

a. Record each event in a statements model like the following one. The first event is recorded as an example.

Assets				=	Liab.	+	Equity			Rev.	−	Exp.	=	Net Inc.	Cash Flow
Cash	+	Accts. Rec.	+ Inv.	=	Accts. Pay.	+	Com. Stk.	+	Ret. Earn.	Rev.	−	Exp.	=	Net Inc.	Cash Flow
60,000	+	NA	+ NA	=	NA	+	60,000	+	NA	NA	−	NA	=	NA	60,000 FA

b. Prepare an income statement for the month ending September 30.

c. Prepare a statement of cash flows for the month ending September 30.

d. Explain why there is a difference between net income and cash flow from operating activities.

Problem 3-25 *Comprehensive cycle problem: Perpetual system*

At the beginning of 2012, the Jeater Company had the following balances in its accounts:

Cash	$ 4,300
Inventory	9,000
Common stock	10,000
Retained earnings	3,300

During 2012, the company experienced the following events.

1. Purchased inventory that cost $2,200 on account from Blue Company under terms 1/10, n/30. The merchandise was delivered FOB shipping point. Freight costs of $110 were paid in cash.

2. Returned $200 of the inventory that it had purchased because the inventory was damaged in transit. The freight company agreed to pay the return freight cost.

3. Paid the amount due on its account payable to Blue Company within the cash discount period.

4. Sold inventory that had cost $3,000 for $5,500 on account, under terms 2/10, n/45.

5. Received merchandise returned from a customer. The merchandise originally cost $400 and was sold to the customer for $710 cash during the previous accounting period. The customer was paid $710 cash for the returned merchandise.

6. Delivered goods FOB destination in Event 4. Freight costs of $60 were paid in cash.

7. Collected the amount due on the account receivable within the discount period.

8. Took a physical count indicating that $7,970 of inventory was on hand at the end of the accounting period.

Required

a. Identify these events as asset source (AS), asset use (AU), asset exchange (AE), or claims exchange (CE).

b. Record each event in a statements model like the following one.

	Balance Sheet					Income Statement			Statement of Cash Flows
Event	Assets	=	Liab.	=	Equity	Rev. − Exp. = Net Inc.			
	Cash + Accts. Rec. + Mdse. Inv.	=	Accts. Pay.	+	Ret. Earn.				

c. Prepare an income statement, a statement of changes in stockholders' equity, a balance sheet, and a statement of cash flows.

Problem 3-26 *Using common size income statements to make comparisons*

The following income statements were drawn from the annual reports of Pierro Sales Company.

	2012*	2013*
Net sales	$520,600	$580,500
Cost of goods sold	(369,600)	(401,500)
Gross margin	151,000	179,000
Less: Operating expense		
Selling and administrative expenses	(64,800)	(81,300)
Net income	$ 86,200	$ 97,700

*All dollar amounts are reported in thousands.

The president's message in the company's annual report stated that the company had implemented a strategy to increase market share by spending more on advertising. The president indicated that prices held steady and sales grew as expected. Write a memo indicating whether you agree with the president's statements. How has the strategy affected profitability? Support your answer by measuring growth in sales and selling expenses. Also prepare common size income statements and make appropriate references to the differences between 2012 and 2013.

Problem 3-27   *Preparing a schedule of cost of goods sold and multistep and single-step income statements: Periodic system (Appendix)*

The following account titles and balances were taken from the adjusted trial balance of Brisco Farm Co. for 2012. The company uses the periodic inventory system.

Account Title	Balance
Sales returns and allowances	$ 3,250
Miscellaneous expense	400
Transportation-out	700
Sales	69,750
Advertising expense	2,750
Salaries expense	8,500
Transportation-in	1,725
Purchases	42,000
Interest expense	360
Merchandise inventory, January 1	6,200
Rent expense	5,000
Merchandise inventory, December 31	4,050
Purchase returns and allowances	1,250
Loss on sale of land	3,400
Utilities expense	710

Required

a. Prepare a schedule to determine the amount of cost of goods sold.

b. Prepare a multistep income statement.

c. Prepare a single-step income statement.

Problem 3-28   *Comprehensive cycle problem: Periodic system (Appendix)*

The following trial balance pertains to Nate's Grocery as of January 1, 2012:

Account Title	Beginning Balances
Cash	$26,000
Accounts receivable	4,000
Merchandise inventory	50,000
Accounts payable	4,000
Common stock	43,000
Retained earnings	33,000
Totals	$80,000

The following events occurred in 2012. Assume that Nate's uses the periodic inventory method.

1. Purchased land for $9,000 cash.
2. Purchased merchandise on account for $96,000, terms 1/10 n/45.
3. Paid freight of $1,000 cash on merchandise purchased FOB shipping point.
4. Returned $3,600 of defective merchandise purchased in Event 2.
5. Sold merchandise for $86,000 cash.
6. Sold merchandise on account for $90,000, terms 2/10 n/30.
7. Paid cash within the discount period on accounts payable due on merchandise purchased in Event 2.

8. Paid $11,600 cash for selling expenses.
9. Collected $50,000 of the accounts receivable from Event 6 within the discount period.
10. Collected $40,000 of the accounts receivable but not within the discount period.
11. Paid $6,400 of other operating expenses.
12. A physical count indicated that $47,600 of inventory was on hand at the end of the accounting period.

Required

a. Record the above transactions in a horizontal statements model like the following one.

Event	Balance Sheet									Income Statement				Statement of Cash Flows
	Assets				=	Equity				Rev.	−	Exp.	= Net Inc.	
	Cash +	Accts. Rec. +	Mdse. Inv. +	Land =		Accts. Pay. +	Com. Stock +	Ret. Earn.						

b. Prepare a schedule of cost of goods sold and an income statement.

ANALYZE, THINK, COMMUNICATE

ATC 3-1   Business Application Case   *Understanding real world annual reports*

Use the Target Corporation's annual report in Appendix B to answer the following questions related to Target's 2009 fiscal year.

Target Corporation

Required

a. What percentage of Target's *total revenues* end up as net earnings?
b. What percentage of Target's *sales* go to pay for the costs of the goods being sold?
c. What costs does Target include in its Cost of Sales account?
d. When does Target recognize revenue from the sale of gift cards?

ATC 3-2   Group Exercise   *Multistep income statement*

The following quarterly information is given for Raybon for the year ended 2012 (amounts shown are in millions).

	First Quarter	Second Quarter	Third Quarter	Fourth Quarter
Net Sales	$736.0	$717.4	$815.2	$620.1
Gross Margin	461.9	440.3	525.3	252.3
Net Income	37.1	24.6	38.6	31.4

Required

a. Divide the class into groups and organize the groups into four sections. Assign each section financial information for one of the quarters.

   (1) Each group should compute the cost of goods sold and operating expenses for the specific quarter assigned to its section and prepare a multistep income statement for the quarter.

   (2) Each group should compute the gross margin percentage and cost of goods sold percentage for its specific quarter.

   (3) Have a representative of each group put that quarter's sales, cost of goods sold percentage, and gross margin percentage on the board.

Class Discussion

b. Have the class discuss the change in each of these items from quarter to quarter and explain why the change might have occurred. Which was the best quarter and why?

ATC 3-3   Research Assignment   *Analyzing Amazon.com's income statement*

Complete the requirements below using the most recent financial statements available [20xx] on Amazon.com's corporate website. Obtain the statements on the internet by following the steps below. (Be aware that the formatting of the company's website may have changed since these instructions were written.)

- Go to www.amazon.com.
- At the bottom of the screen, under "Get to Know Us," click on "Investor Relations."
- Annual Reports and Proxies.
- Click on "20xx Annual Report" (the most recent year).

Read the following sections of the annual report:

- The income statement, which Amazon.com calls the "Consolidated Statement of Operations."
- In the footnotes section, "Note 1—Description of Business and Accounting Policies," read the subsections titled "*Revenues,*" "*Shipping Activities,*" and "*Cost of Sales.*"

Required

a. What percentage of Amazon's sales end up as net income?

b. What percentage of Amazon's sales go to pay for the costs of the goods being sold?

c. What specific criteria are necessary before Amazon will recognize a sale as having been completed and record the related revenue?

d. How does Amazon account for (report on its income statement) the shipping costs it incurs to ship goods to its customers?

ATC 3-4   Written Assignment, Critical Thinking   *Effect of sales returns on financial statements*

Bell Farm and Garden Equipment reported the following information for 2012:

Net Sales of Equipment	$2,450,567
Other Income	6,786
Cost of Goods Sold	1,425,990
Selling, General, and Administrative Expense	325,965
Net Operating Income	$ 705,398

Selected information from the balance sheet as of December 31, 2012, follows.

Cash and Marketable Securities	$113,545
Inventory	248,600
Accounts Receivable	82,462
Property, Plant, and Equipment—Net	335,890
Other Assets	5,410
Total Assets	$785,907

Assume that a major customer returned a large order to Bell on December 31, 2012. The amount of the sale had been $146,800 with a cost of sales of $94,623. The return was recorded in the books on January 1, 2013. The company president does not want to correct the books. He argues that it makes no difference as to whether the return is recorded in 2012 or 2013. Either way, the return has been duly recognized.

Required

a. Assume that you are the CFO for Bell Farm and Garden Equipment Co. Write a memo to the president explaining how omitting the entry on December 31, 2012, could cause the financial statements to be misleading to investors and creditors. Explain how omitting the return from the customer would affect net income and the balance sheet.

b. Why might the president want to record the return on January 1, 2013, instead of December 31, 2012?

CHAPTER 4

Internal Controls, Accounting for Cash, and Ethics

LEARNING OBJECTIVES

After you have mastered the material in this chapter, you will be able to:

1 Identify the key elements of a strong system of internal control.

2 Prepare a bank reconciliation.

3 Discuss the role of ethics in the accounting profession.

4 Describe the auditor's role in financial reporting.

CHAPTER OPENING

In the first three chapters, we covered the basics of the accounting system. By now you should understand how basic business events affect financial statements and how the accounting cycle works. Accounting is an elegant system that when implemented correctly provides meaningful information to investors and other stakeholders. However, without effective control, the accounting system can be manipulated in ways that may overstate business performance. This can lead investors to make bad decisions, which can result in huge losses when the true performance is revealed. This chapter discusses the importance of internal control systems. The chapter also discusses accounting for cash, an area where good internal controls are critical. The chapter concludes with a discussion on the importance of ethical conduct in the accounting profession.

The Curious Accountant

On December 11, 2008, Bernard Madoff was arrested on suspicion of having defrauded the clients of his investment company, Bernard L. Madoff Investments (BMI), of $50 billion. Later estimates would put the losses at over $60 billion. Although his clients believed the money they sent to BMI was being invested in the stock market, it was actually just being deposited into bank accounts.

Mr. Madoff was accused of operating the largest Ponzi scheme in history. Clients were sent monthly statements falsely showing that their investments were earning income and growing at a steady rate, even when the overall stock market was falling. When individual investors asked to withdraw their funds, they were simply given money that had been deposited by other investors.

This fraudulent system works as long as more new money is being deposited than is being withdrawn. Unfortunately for BMI, with the severe stock-market decline of 2008 too many clients got nervous and asked to withdraw their money, including the gains they believed they had earned over the years. At this point the Ponzi scheme failed.

How could such a pervasive fraud go undetected for so long? (Answer on page 136.)

KEY FEATURES OF INTERNAL CONTROL SYSTEMS

Identify the key elements of a strong system of internal control.

During the early 2000s a number of accounting related scandals cost investors billions. In 2001, Enron's share price went from $85 to $0.30 after it was revealed that the company had billions of dollars in losses that were not reported on the financial statements. Several months later, WorldCom reported an $11 billion accounting fraud, which included hundreds of millions in personal loans to then CEO, Bernie Ebbers.

The Enron and WorldCom accounting scandals had such devastating effects that they led congress to pass the Sarbanes-Oxley Act of 2002 (SOX). SOX requires public companies to evaluate their *internal control* and to publish those findings with their SEC filings. **Internal control** is the process designed to ensure reliable financial reporting, effective and efficient operations, and compliance with applicable laws and regulations. Safeguarding assets against theft and unauthorized use, acquisition, or disposal is also part of internal control.

Section 404 of Sarbanes-Oxley requires a statement of management's responsibility for establishing and maintaining adequate internal control over financial reporting by public companies. This section includes an assessment of the controls and the identification of the framework used for the assessment. The framework established by The Committee of Sponsoring Organizations of the Treadway Commission (COSO) in 1992 is the de facto standard by which SOX compliance is judged. COSO's framework titled *Internal Control—An Integrated Framework* recognizes five interrelated components including:

1. *Control Environment.* The integrity and ethical values of the company, including its code of conduct, involvement of the board of directors, and other actions that set the tone of the organization.

2. *Risk Assessment.* Management's process of identifying potential risks that could result in misstated financial statements and developing actions to address those risks.

3. *Control Activities.* These are the activities usually thought of as "the internal controls." They include such things as segregation of duties, account reconciliations, and information processing controls that are designed to safeguard assets and enable an organization to timely prepare reliable financial statements.

4. *Information and Communication.* The internal and external reporting process, and includes an assessment of the technology environment.

5. *Monitoring.* Assessing the quality of a company's internal control over time and taking actions as necessary to ensure it continues to address the risks of the organization.

In 2004 COSO updated the framework to help entities design and implement effective enterprise-wide approaches to risk management. The updated document is titled *Enterprise Risk Management (ERM)—An Integrated Framework.* The ERM framework introduces an enterprise-wide approach to risk management as well as concepts such as risk appetite, risk tolerance, and portfolio view. While SOX applies only to U.S. public companies, the ERM framework has been adopted by both public and private organizations around the world.

The ERM framework does not replace the internal control framework. Instead, it incorporates the internal control framework within it. Accordingly, companies may decide to look to the ERM framework both to satisfy their internal control needs and to move toward a fuller risk management process.

While a detailed discussion of the COSO documents is beyond the scope of this text, the following overview of the more common *control activities* of the internal control framework is insightful.

Separation of Duties

The likelihood of fraud or theft is reduced if collusion is required to accomplish it. Clear **separation of duties** is frequently used as a deterrent to corruption. When duties are separated, the work of one employee can act as a check on the work of another employee. For example, a person selling seats to a movie may be tempted to steal money received from customers who enter the theater. This temptation is reduced if the person staffing the box office is required to issue tickets that a second employee collects as people enter the theater. If ticket stubs collected by the second employee are compared with the cash receipts from ticket sales, any cash shortages would become apparent. Furthermore, friends and relatives of the ticket agent could not easily enter the theater without paying. Theft or unauthorized entry would require collusion between the ticket agent and the usher who collects the tickets. Both individuals would have to be dishonest enough to steal, yet trustworthy enough to convince each other they would keep the embezzlement secret. Whenever possible, the functions of *authorization, recording,* and *custody of assets* should be performed by separate individuals.

Quality of Employees

A business is only as good as the people it employs. Cheap labor is not a bargain if the employees are incompetent. Employees should be properly trained. In fact, they should be trained to perform a variety of tasks. The ability of employees to substitute for one another prevents disruptions when co-workers are absent because of illnesses, vacations, or other commitments. The capacity to rotate jobs also relieves boredom and increases respect for the contributions of other employees. Every business should strive to maximize the productivity of every employee. Ongoing training programs are essential to a strong system of internal control.

Bonded Employees

The best way to ensure employee honesty is to hire individuals with *high levels of personal integrity.* Employers should screen job applicants using interviews, background checks, and recommendations from prior employers or educators. Even so, screening programs may fail to identify character weaknesses. Further, unusual circumstances may cause honest employees to go astray. Therefore, employees in positions of trust should be bonded. A **fidelity bond** provides insurance that protects a company from losses caused by employee dishonesty.

Required Absences

Employees should be required to take regular vacations and their duties should be rotated periodically. Employees may be able to cover up fraudulent activities if they are always present at work. Consider the case of a parking meter collection agent who covered the same route for several years with no vacation. When the agent became sick, a substitute collected more money each day than the regular reader usually reported. Management checked past records and found that the ill meter reader had been understating the cash receipts and pocketing the difference. If management had required vacations or rotated the routes, the embezzlement would have been discovered much earlier.

Procedures Manual

Appropriate accounting procedures should be documented in a **procedures manual.** The manual should be routinely updated. Periodic reviews should be conducted to ensure that employees are following the procedures outlined in the manual.

Authority and Responsibility

Employees are motivated by clear lines of authority and responsibility. They work harder when they have the authority to use their own judgment and they exercise reasonable caution when they are held responsible for their actions. Businesses should prepare an **authority manual** that establishes a definitive *chain of command.* The authority manual should guide both specific and general authorizations. **Specific authorizations** apply to specific positions within the organization. For example, investment decisions are authorized at the division level while hiring decisions are authorized at the departmental level. In contrast, **general authority** applies across different levels of management. For example, employees at all levels may be required to fly coach or to make purchases from specific vendors.

Prenumbered Documents

How would you know if a check were stolen from your check book? If you keep a record of your check numbers, the missing number would tip you off immediately. Businesses also use prenumbered checks to avoid the unauthorized use of their bank accounts. In fact, prenumbered forms are used for all important documents such as purchase orders, receiving reports, invoices, and checks. To reduce errors, prenumbered forms should be as simple and easy to use as possible. Also, the documents should allow for authorized signatures. For example, credit sales slips should be signed by the customer to clearly establish who made the purchase, reducing the likelihood of unauthorized transactions.

Physical Control

Employees walk away with billions of dollars of business assets each year. To limit losses, companies should establish adequate physical control over valuable assets. For example, inventory should be kept in a storeroom and not released without proper authorization. Serial numbers on equipment should be recorded along with the name of the individual who is responsible for the equipment. Unannounced physical counts should be conducted randomly to verify the presence of company-owned equipment. Certificates of deposit and marketable securities should be kept in fireproof vaults. Access to these vaults should be limited to authorized personnel. These procedures protect the documents from fire and limit access to only those individuals who have the appropriate security clearance to handle the documents.

In addition to safeguarding assets, there should be physical control over the accounting records. The accounting journals, ledgers, and supporting documents should be kept in a fireproof safe. Only personnel responsible for recording transactions in the journals should have access to them. With limited access, there is less chance that someone will change the records to conceal fraud or embezzlement.

Performance Evaluations

Because few people can evaluate their own performance objectively, internal controls should include independent verification of employee performance. For example, someone other than the person who has control over inventory should take a physical count of inventory. Internal and external audits serve as independent verification of performance. Auditors should evaluate the effectiveness of the internal control system as well as verify the accuracy of the accounting records. In addition, the external auditors attest to the company's use of generally accepted accounting principles in the financial statements.

Limitations

A system of internal controls is designed to prevent or detect errors and fraud. However, no control system is foolproof. Internal controls can be circumvented by collusion among employees. Two or more employees working together can hide embezzlement by covering for each other. For example, if an embezzler goes on vacation, fraud will not be reported by a replacement who is in collusion with the embezzler. No system can prevent all fraud. However, a good system of internal controls minimizes illegal or unethical activities by reducing temptation and increasing the likelihood of early detection.

CHECK YOURSELF 4.1

What are nine features of an internal control system?

Answer
The nine features follow.

1. Separating duties so that fraud or theft requires collusion.
2. Hiring and training competent employees.
3. Bonding employees to recover losses through insurance.

4. Requiring employees to be absent from their jobs so that their replacements can discover errors or fraudulent activity that might have occurred.
5. Establishing proper procedures for processing transactions.
6. Establishing clear lines of authority and responsibility.
7. Using prenumbered documents.
8. Implementing physical controls such as locking cash in a safe.
9. Conducting performance evaluations through independent internal and external audits.

ACCOUNTING FOR CASH

For financial reporting purposes, **cash** generally includes currency and other items that are payable *on demand,* such as checks, money orders, bank drafts, and certain savings accounts. Savings accounts that impose substantial penalties for early withdrawal should be classified as *investments* rather than cash. Postdated checks or IOUs represent *receivables* and should not be included in cash. As illustrated in Exhibit 4.1, most companies combine currency and other payable on demand items in a single balance sheet account with varying titles.

Companies must maintain a sufficient amount of cash to pay employees, suppliers, and other creditors. When a company fails to pay its legal obligations, its creditors can force the company into bankruptcy. Even so, management should avoid accumulating more cash than is needed. The failure to invest excess cash in earning assets reduces profitability. Cash inflows and outflows must be managed to prevent a shortage or surplus of cash.

Controlling Cash

Controlling cash, more than any other asset, requires strict adherence to internal control procedures. Cash has universal appeal. A relatively small suitcase filled with high-denomination currency can represent significant value. Furthermore, the rightful owner of currency is difficult to prove. In most cases, possession constitutes ownership. As a result, cash is highly susceptible to theft and must be carefully protected. Cash is most susceptible to embezzlement when it is received or disbursed. The following controls should be employed to reduce the likelihood of theft.

Cash Receipts

A record of all cash collections should be prepared immediately upon receipt. The amount of cash on hand should be counted regularly. Missing amounts of money can be detected by comparing the actual cash on hand with the book balance. Employees who receive cash should give customers a copy of a written receipt. Customers usually review their receipts to ensure they have gotten credit for the amount paid and call any errors to the receipts clerk's attention. This not only reduces errors but also provides a control on the clerk's honesty. Cash receipts should be deposited in a bank on a timely basis. Cash collected late in the day should be deposited in a night depository. Every effort should be made to minimize the amount of cash on hand. Keeping large amounts of cash on hand not only increases the risk of loss from theft but also places employees in danger of being harmed by criminals who may be tempted to rob the company.

Cash Payments

To effectively control cash, a company should make all disbursements using checks, thereby providing a record of cash payments. All checks should be prenumbered, and unused checks should be locked up. Using prenumbered checks allows companies to easily identify lost or stolen checks by comparing the numbers on unused and canceled checks with the numbers used for legitimate disbursements.

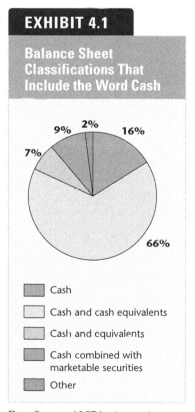

EXHIBIT 4.1

Balance Sheet Classifications That Include the Word Cash

- Cash
- Cash and cash equivalents
- Cash and equivalents
- Cash combined with marketable securities
- Other

Data Source: AICPA, *Accounting Trends and Techniques.*

REALITY BYTES

Could you afford to buy a safe like the one shown here? The vault is only one of many expensive security devices used by banks to safeguard cash. By using checking accounts, companies are able to avoid many of the costs associated with keeping cash safe. In addition to providing physical control, checking accounts enable companies to maintain a written audit trail of cash receipts and payments. Checking accounts represent the most widely used internal control device in modern society. It is difficult to imagine a business operating without the use of checking accounts.

The duties of approving disbursements, signing checks, and recording transactions should be separated. If one person is authorized to approve, sign, and record checks, he or she could falsify supporting documents, write an unauthorized check, and record a cover-up transaction in the accounting records. By separating these duties, the check signer reviews the documentation provided by the approving individual before signing the check. Likewise, the recording clerk reviews the work of both the approving person and the check signer when the disbursement is recorded in the accounting records. Thus writing unauthorized checks requires trilevel collusion.

Supporting documents with authorized approval signatures should be required when checks are presented to the check signer. For example, a warehouse receiving order should be matched with a purchase order before a check is approved to pay a bill from a supplier. Before payments are approved, invoice amounts should be checked and payees verified as valid vendors. Matching supporting documents with proper authorization discourages employees from creating phony documents for a disbursement to a friend or fictitious business. Also, the approval process serves as a check on the accuracy of the work of all employees involved.

Supporting documents should be marked *Paid* when the check is signed. If the documents are not indelibly marked, they could be retrieved from the files and resubmitted for a duplicate, unauthorized payment. A payables clerk could collude with the payee to split extra cash paid out by submitting the same supporting documents for a second payment.

All spoiled and voided checks should be defaced and retained. If defaced checks are not retained, an employee could steal a check and then claim that it was written incorrectly and thrown away. The clerk could then use the stolen check to make an unauthorized payment.

Checking Account Documents

The previous section explained the need for businesses to use checking accounts. A description of four main types of forms associated with a bank checking account follows.

Signature Card

A bank **signature card** shows the bank account number and the signatures of the people authorized to sign checks. The card is retained in the bank's files. If a bank employee is unfamiliar with the signature on a check, he or she can refer to the signature card to verify the signature before cashing the check.

Deposit Ticket

Each deposit of cash or checks is accompanied by a **deposit ticket,** which normally identifies the account number and the name of the account. The depositor lists the individual amounts of currency, coins, and checks, as well as the total deposited, on the deposit ticket.

Bank Check

A written check affects three parties: (1) the person or business writing the check (the *payer*); (2) the bank on which the check is drawn; and (3) the person or business to whom the check is payable (the *payee*). Companies often write **checks** using multicopy, prenumbered forms, with the name of the issuing business preprinted on the face of each check. A remittance notice is usually attached to the check forms. This portion of the form provides the issuer space to record what the check is for (e.g., what invoices are being paid), the amount being disbursed, and the date of payment. When signed by the person whose signature is on the signature card, the check authorizes the bank to transfer the face amount of the check from the payer's account to the payee.

Bank Statement

Periodically, the bank sends the depositor a **bank statement.** The bank statement is presented from the bank's point of view. Checking accounts are liabilities to a bank because the bank is obligated to pay back the money that customers have deposited in their accounts. Therefore, in the bank's accounting records a customer's checking account has a *credit* balance. As a result, **bank statement debit memos** describe transactions that reduce the customer's account balance (the bank's liability). **Bank statement credit memos** describe activities that increase the customer's account balance (the bank's liability). Since a checking account is an asset (cash) to the depositor, a *bank statement debit memo* requires a *credit entry* to the cash account on the depositor's books. Likewise, when a bank tells you that it has credited your account, you will debit your cash account in response.

Bank statements normally report (a) the balance of the account at the beginning of the period; (b) additions for customer deposits made during the period; (c) other additions described in credit memos (e.g., for interest earned); (d) subtractions for the payment of checks drawn on the account during the period; (e) other subtractions described in debit memos (e.g., for service charges); (f) a running balance of the account; and (g) the balance of the account at the end of the period. The sample bank statement in Exhibit 4.2 on the next page illustrates these items. Normally, the canceled checks or copies of them are enclosed with the bank statement.

RECONCILING THE BANK ACCOUNT

Usually the ending balance reported on the bank statement differs from the balance in the depositor's cash account as of the same date. The discrepancy is normally attributable to timing differences. For example, a depositor deducts the amount of a check from its cash account when it writes the check. However, the bank does not deduct the amount of the check from the depositor's account until the payee presents it for payment, which may be days, weeks, or even months after the check is written. As a result, the balance on the depositor's books is lower than the balance on the bank's books. Companies prepare a **bank reconciliation** to explain the differences between the cash balance reported on the bank statement and the cash balance recorded in the depositor's accounting records.

Prepare a bank reconciliation.

Determining True Cash Balance

A bank reconciliation normally begins with the cash balance reported by the bank which is called the **unadjusted bank balance.** The adjustments necessary to determine the amount of cash that the depositor actually owns as of the date of the bank statement are then added to and subtracted from the unadjusted bank balance. The final total is the **true cash balance.** The true cash balance is independently reached a second time by making adjustments to the **unadjusted book balance.** The bank account is reconciled when the true cash balance determined from the perspective of the unadjusted

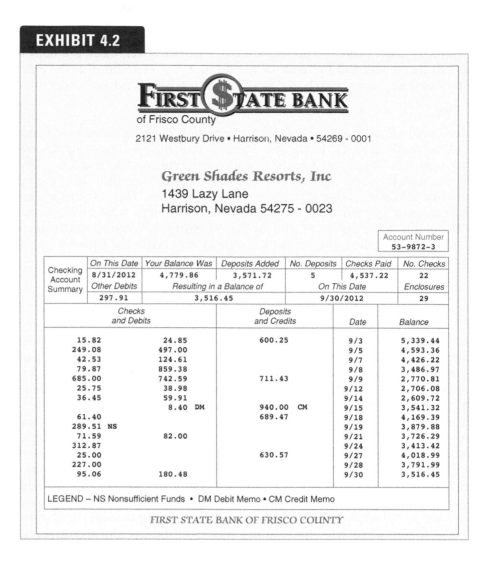

EXHIBIT 4.2

FIRST $TATE BANK
of Frisco County

2121 Westbury Drive • Harrison, Nevada • 54269 - 0001

Green Shades Resorts, Inc
1439 Lazy Lane
Harrison, Nevada 54275 - 0023

Account Number
53-9872-3

Checking Account Summary	On This Date	Your Balance Was	Deposits Added	No. Deposits	Checks Paid	No. Checks
	8/31/2012	4,779.86	3,571.72	5	4,537.22	22
	Other Debits	Resulting in a Balance of		On This Date		Enclosures
	297.91	3,516.45		9/30/2012		29

Checks and Debits			Deposits and Credits	Date	Balance
15.82	24.85		600.25	9/3	5,339.44
249.08	497.00			9/5	4,593.36
42.53	124.61			9/7	4,426.22
79.87	859.38			9/8	3,486.97
685.00	742.59		711.43	9/9	2,770.81
25.75	38.98			9/12	2,706.08
36.45	59.91			9/14	2,609.72
	8.40 DM		940.00 CM	9/15	3,541.32
61.40			689.47	9/18	4,169.39
289.51 NS				9/19	3,879.88
71.59	82.00			9/21	3,726.29
312.87				9/24	3,413.42
25.00			630.57	9/27	4,018.99
227.00				9/28	3,791.99
95.06	180.48			9/30	3,516.45

LEGEND – NS Nonsufficient Funds • DM Debit Memo • CM Credit Memo

FIRST STATE BANK OF FRISCO COUNTY

bank balance agrees with the true cash balance determined from the perspective of the unadjusted *book* balance. The procedures a company uses to determine the *true cash balance* from the two different perspectives are outlined here.

Adjustments to the Bank Balance

A typical format for determining the true cash balance beginning with the unadjusted bank balance is

> Unadjusted bank balance
> + Deposits in transit
> − Outstanding checks
> _____
> = True cash balance

Deposits in transit. Companies frequently leave deposits in the bank's night depository or make them on the day following the receipt of cash. Such deposits are called **deposits in transit.** Because these deposits have been recorded in the depositor's accounting records but have not yet been added to the depositor's account by the bank, they must be added to the unadjusted bank balance.

Outstanding checks. These are disbursements that have been properly recorded as cash deductions on the depositor's books. However, the bank has not deducted the amounts from the depositor's bank account because the checks have not yet been presented by the payee to the bank for payment; that is, the checks have not cleared the bank. **Outstanding checks** must be subtracted from the unadjusted bank balance to determine the true cash balance.

Adjustments to the Book Balance

A typical format for determining the true cash balance beginning with the unadjusted book balance is as follows.

```
Unadjusted book balance
+ Accounts receivable collections
+ Interest earned
− Bank service charges
− Non-sufficient-funds (NSF) checks
= True cash balance
```

Accounts receivable collections.   To collect cash as quickly as possible, many companies have their customers send payments directly to the bank. The bank adds the collection directly to the depositor's account and notifies the depositor about the collection through a credit memo that is included on the bank statement. The depositor adds the amount of the cash collections to the unadjusted book balance in the process of determining the true cash balance.

Interest earned.   Banks pay interest on certain checking accounts. The amount of the interest is added directly to the depositor's bank account. The bank notifies the depositor about the interest through a credit memo that is included on the bank statement. The depositor adds the amount of the interest revenue to the unadjusted book balance in the process of determining the true cash balance.

Service charges.   Banks frequently charge depositors fees for services performed. They may also charge a penalty if the depositor fails to maintain a specified minimum cash balance throughout the period. Banks deduct such fees and penalties directly from the depositor's account and advise the depositor of the deduction through a debit memo that is included on the bank statement. The depositor deducts such **service charges** from the unadjusted book balance to determine the true cash balance.

Non-sufficient-funds (NSF) checks.   **NSF checks** are checks that a company obtains from its customers and deposits in its checking account. However, when the checks are submitted to the customers' banks for payment, the banks refuse payment because there is insufficient money in the customers' accounts. When such checks are returned, the amounts of the checks are deducted from the company's bank account balance. The company is advised of NSF checks through debit memos that appear on the bank statement. The depositor deducts the amounts of the NSF checks from the unadjusted book balance in the process of determining the true cash balance.

Correction of Errors

In the course of reconciling the bank statement with the cash account, the depositor may discover errors in the bank's records, the depositor's records, or both. If an error is found on the bank statement, an adjustment for it is made to the unadjusted bank balance to determine the true cash balance, and the bank should be notified immediately to correct its records. Errors made by the depositor require adjustments to the book balance to arrive at the true cash balance.

Certified Checks

A **certified check** is guaranteed for payment by a bank. Whereas a regular check is deducted from the customer's account when it is presented for payment, a certified check is deducted from the customer's account when the bank certifies that the check is good.

Certified checks, therefore, *have* been deducted by the bank in determining the unadjusted bank balance, whether they have cleared the bank or remain outstanding as of the date of the bank statement. Since certified checks are deducted both from bank and depositor records immediately, they do not cause differences between the depositor and bank balances. As a result, certified checks are not included in a bank reconciliation.

Illustrating a Bank Reconciliation

The following example illustrates preparing the bank reconciliation for Green Shades Resorts, Inc. (GSRI). The bank statement for GSRI is displayed in Exhibit 4.2. Exhibit 4.3 illustrates the completed bank reconciliation. The items on the reconciliation are described below.

Adjustments to the Bank Balance

As of September 30, 2012, the bank statement showed an unadjusted balance of $3,516.45. A review of the bank statement disclosed three adjustments that had to be made to the unadjusted bank balance to determine GSRI's true cash balance.

1. Comparing the deposits on the bank statement with deposits recorded in GSRI's accounting records indicated there was $724.11 of deposits in transit.

2. An examination of the returned checks disclosed that the bank had erroneously deducted a $25 check written by Green Valley Resorts from GSRI's bank account. This amount must be added back to the unadjusted bank balance to determine the true cash balance.

3. The checks returned with the bank statement were sorted and compared to the cash records. Three checks with amounts totaling $235.25 were outstanding.

After these adjustment are made GSRI's true cash balance is determined to be $4,030.31.

EXHIBIT 4.3

GREEN SHADES RESORTS, INC.
Bank Reconciliation
September 30, 2012

Unadjusted bank balance, September 30, 2012			$3,516.45
Add: Deposits in transit			724.11
Bank error: Check drawn on Green Valley Resorts charged to GSRI			25.00
Less: Outstanding checks			

Check No.	Date	Amount
639	Sept. 18	$ 13.75
646	Sept. 20	29.00
672	Sept. 27	192.50

Total	(235.25)
True cash balance, September 30, 2012	$4,030.31
Unadjusted book balance, September 30, 2012	$3,361.22
Add: Receivable collected by bank	940.00
Error made by accountant (Check no. 633 recorded as $63.45 instead of $36.45)	27.00
Less: Bank service charges	(8.40)
NSF check	(289.51)
True cash balance, September 30, 2012	$4,030.31

Adjustments to the Book Balance

As indicated in Exhibit 4.3, GSRI's unadjusted book balance as of September 30, 2012, was $3,361.22. This balance differs from GSRI's true cash balance because of four unrecorded accounting events:

1. The bank collected a $940 account receivable for GSRI.
2. GSRI's accountant made a $27 recording error.
3. The bank charged GSRI an $8.40 service fee.
4. GSRI had deposited a $289.51 check from a customer who did not have sufficient funds to cover the check.

Two of these four adjustments increase the unadjusted cash balance. The other two decrease the unadjusted cash balance. After the adjustments have been recorded, the cash account reflects the true cash balance of $4,030.31 ($3,361.22 unadjusted cash balance + $940.00 receivable collection + $27.00 recording error − $8.40 service charge − $289.51 NSF check). Because the true balance determined from the perspective of the bank statement agrees with the true balance determined from the perspective of GSRI's books, the bank statement has been successfully reconciled with the accounting records.

Updating GSRI's Accounting Records

Each of the adjustments to the book balance must be recorded in GSRI's financial records. The effects of each adjustment on the financial statements are as follows.

ADJUSTMENT 1 *Recording the $940 receivable collection increases cash and reduces accounts receivable.*

The event is an asset exchange transaction. The effect of the collection on GSRI's financial statements is

Assets		=	Liab.	+	Equity	Rev.	−	Exp.	=	Net Inc.	Cash Flow
Cash +	Accts. Rec.										
940 +	(940)	=	NA	+	NA	NA	−	NA	=	NA	940 OA

ADJUSTMENT 2 *Assume the $27 recording error occurred because GSRI's accountant accidentally transposed two numbers when recording check no. 633 for utilities expense.*

The check was written to pay utilities expense of $36.45 but was recorded as a $63.45 disbursement. Since cash payments are overstated by $27.00 ($63.45 − $36.45), this amount must be added back to GSRI's cash balance and deducted from the utilities expense account, which increases net income. The effects on the financial statements are

Assets	=	Liab.	+	Equity	Rev.	−	Exp.	=	Net Inc.	Cash Flow
Cash	=			Ret. Earn.						
27	=	NA	+	27	NA	−	(27)	=	27	27 OA

ADJUSTMENT 3 *The $8.40 service charge is an expense that reduces assets, stockholders' equity, net income, and cash.*

The effects are

Assets	=	Liab.	+	Equity	Rev.	−	Exp.	=	Net Inc.	Cash Flow	
Cash	=			Ret. Earn.							
(8.40)	=	NA	+	(8.40)	NA	−	8.40	=	(8.40)	(8.40)	OA

ADJUSTMENT 4 *The $289.51 NSF check reduces GSRI's cash balance.*

When it originally accepted the customer's check, GSRI increased its cash account. Because there is not enough money in the customer's bank account to pay the check, GSRI didn't actually receive cash so GSRI must reduce its cash account. GSRI will still try to collect the money from the customer. In the meantime, it will show the amount of the NSF check as an account receivable. The adjusting entry to record the NSF check is an asset exchange transaction. Cash decreases and accounts receivable increases. The effect on GSRI's financial statements is

Assets			=	Liab.	+	Equity	Rev.	−	Exp.	=	Net Inc.	Cash Flow	
Cash	+	Accts. Rec.											
(289.51)	+	289.51	=	NA	+	NA	NA	−	NA	=	NA	(289.51)	OA

Answers to The Curious Accountant

As this chapter explains, separation of duties is one of the primary features of a good system of internal controls. However, separation of duties is not designed to detect fraud at the very top level of management. Mr. Madoff ran BMI with almost complete control; he had no boss.

Even with a good system of internal controls, there is always some level of trust required in business. Mr. Madoff had an excellent reputation in the investment community. He had even been the president of the NASDAQ. His investors trusted him and assumed they could depend on his independent auditor to detect any major problems with the way BMI was investing, or not investing, their money.

Federal prosecutors believe that BMI's auditor, David Friehling, did very little in the way of properly auditing BMI's books. In fact, on March 18, 2009, he also was arrested and charged with falsely certifying BMI's financial statements. He faces up to 105 years in prison if convicted.

On March 12, 2009, the 70-year-old Mr. Madoff pled guilty to 11 felony charges. On June 29, 2009, he was sentenced to a term of 150 years in prison.

✓ CHECK YOURSELF 4.2

The following information was drawn from Reliance Company's October bank statement. The unadjusted bank balance on October 31 was $2,300. The statement showed that the bank had collected a $200 account receivable for Reliance. The statement also included $20 of bank service charges for October and a $100 check payable to Reliance that was returned NSF. A comparison of the bank statement with company accounting records indicates that there was a $500 deposit in transit and $1,800 of checks outstanding at the end of the month. Based on this information, determine the true cash balance on October 31.

Answer   Since the unadjusted book balance is not given, start with the unadjusted bank balance to determine the true cash balance. The collection of the receivable, the bank service charges, and the NSF check are already recognized in the unadjusted bank balance, so these items are not used to determine the true cash balance. Determine the true cash balance by adding the deposit in transit to and subtracting the outstanding checks from the unadjusted bank balance. The true cash balance is $1,000 ($2,300 unadjusted bank balance + $500 deposit in transit − $1,800 outstanding checks).

IMPORTANCE OF ETHICS

The chapter began with a discussion of the importance of internal control systems in preventing accounting scandals. After the Enron and WorldCom scandals and the passage of the Sarbanes-Oxley Act, much more attention has been paid to establishing effective internal control systems. However, despite this increase in legislation and awareness, accounting scandals continue to occur. In 2008, Lehman Brothers declared bankruptcy after it was discovered that the company had kept more than $50 billion in loans off the balance sheet by classifying them as sales. Several months later, Bernie Madoff used a Ponzi scheme to leave his investors with more than $21.2 billion in cash losses. These examples illustrate that legislation alone will not prevent accounting scandals. To prevent a scandal it is necessary to develop a culture that fosters and promotes ethical conduct.

Discuss the role of ethics in the accounting profession.

The accountant's role in society requires trust and credibility. Accounting information is worthless if the accountant is not trustworthy. Similarly, tax and consulting advice is useless if it comes from an incompetent person. The high ethical standards required by the profession state "a certified public accountant assumes an obligation of self-discipline above and beyond requirements of laws and regulations." The **American Institute of Certified Public Accountants** requires its members to comply with the **Code of Professional Conduct.** Section I of the Code includes six articles that are summarized in Exhibit 4.4. The importance of ethical conduct is universally recognized across a broad spectrum of accounting organizations. The Institute of Management Accountants requires its members to follow a set of Standards of Ethical Conduct. The Institute of Internal Auditors also requires its members to subscribe to the organization's Code of Ethics.

Common Features of Criminal and Ethical Misconduct

Unfortunately, it takes more than a code of conduct to stop fraud. People frequently engage in activities that they know are unethical or even criminal. The auditing profession has identified three elements that are typically present when fraud occurs.

1. The availability of an opportunity.
2. The existence of some form of pressure leading to an incentive.
3. The capacity to rationalize.

EXHIBIT 4.4

Articles of AICPA Code of Professional Conduct

Article I Responsibilities
In carrying out their responsibilities as professionals, members should exercise sensitive professional and moral judgments in all their activities.

Article II The Public Interest
Members should accept the obligation to act in a way that will serve the public interest, honor the public trust, and demonstrate commitment to professionalism.

Article III Integrity
To maintain and broaden public confidence, members should perform all professional responsibilities with the highest sense of integrity.

Article IV Objectivity and Independence
A member should maintain objectivity and be free of conflicts of interest in discharging professional responsibilities. A member in public practice should be independent in fact and appearance when providing auditing and other attestation services.

Article V Due Care
A member should observe the profession's technical and ethical standards, strive continually to improve competence and the quality of services, and discharge professional responsibility to the best of the member's ability.

Article VI Scope and Nature of Services
A member in public practice should observe the principles of the Code of Professional Conduct in determining the scope and nature of services to be provided.

The three elements are frequently arranged in the shape of a triangle as shown in Exhibit 4.5.

Opportunity is shown at the head to the triangle because without opportunity fraud could not exist. The most effective way to reduce opportunities for ethical or criminal misconduct is to implement an effective set of internal controls. *Internal controls* are policies and procedures that a business implements to reduce opportunities

---

EXHIBIT 4.5

The Fraud Triangle

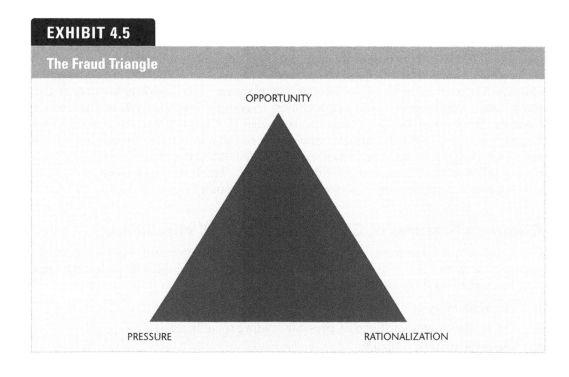

for fraud and to assure that its objectives will be accomplished. Specific controls are tailored to meet the individual needs of particular businesses. For example, banks use elaborate vaults to protect cash and safety deposit boxes, but universities have little use for this type of equipment. Even so, many of the same procedures are used by a wide variety of businesses. The internal control policies and procedures that have gained widespread acceptance are discussed in a subsequent chapter.

Only a few employees turn to the dark side even when internal control is weak and opportunities abound. So, what causes one person to commit fraud and another to remain honest? The second element of the fraud triangle recognizes **pressure** as a key ingredient of misconduct. A manager who is told "either make the numbers or you are fired" is more likely to cheat than one who is told to "tell it like it is." Pressure can come from a variety of sources.

- Personal vices such as drug addiction, gambling, and promiscuity.
- Intimidation from superiors.
- Personal debt from credit cards, consumer and mortgage loans, or poor investments.
- Family expectations to provide a standard of living that is beyond one's capabilities.
- Business failure caused by poor decision making or temporary factors such as a poor economy.
- Loyalty or trying to be agreeable.

The third and final element of the fraud triangle is **rationalization.** Few individuals think of themselves as evil. They develop rationalizations to justify their misconduct. Common rationalizations include the following.

- Everybody does it.
- They are not paying me enough. I'm only taking what I deserve.
- I'm only borrowing the money. I'll pay it back.
- The company can afford it. Look what they are paying the officers.
- I'm taking what my family needs to live like everyone else.

Most people are able to resist pressure and the tendency to rationalize ethical or legal misconduct. However, some people will yield to temptation. What can accountants do to protect themselves and their companies from unscrupulous characters? The answer lies in personal integrity. The best indicator of personal integrity is past performance. Accordingly, companies must exercise due care in performing appropriate background investigations before hiring people to fill positions of trust.

Ethical misconduct is a serious offense in the accounting profession. A single mistake can destroy an accounting career. If you commit a white-collar crime, you normally lose the opportunity to hold a white-collar job. Second chances are rarely granted; it is extremely important that you learn how to recognize and avoid the common features of ethical misconduct. To help you prepare for the real-world situations you are likely to encounter, we include ethical dilemmas in the end-of-chapter materials. When working with these dilemmas, try to identify the (1) opportunity, (2) pressure, and (3) rationalization associated with the particular ethical situation described. If you are not an ethical person, accounting is not the career for you.

ROLE OF THE INDEPENDENT AUDITOR

As previously explained, financial statements are prepared in accordance with certain rules called *generally accepted accounting principles (GAAP)*. Thus, when General Electric publishes its financial statements, it is saying, "here are our financial statements prepared according to GAAP." How can a financial analyst know that a company really did follow GAAP? Analysts and other statement users rely on **audits** conducted by **certified public accountants (CPAs).**

Describe the auditor's role in financial reporting.

The primary roles of an independent auditor (CPA) are summarized below:

1. Conducts a financial audit (a detailed examination of a company's financial statements and underlying accounting records).

2. Assumes both legal and professional responsibilities to the public as well as to the company paying the auditor.

3. Determines if financial statements are *materially* correct rather than *absolutely* correct.

4. Presents conclusions in an audit report that includes an opinion as to whether the statements are prepared in conformity with GAAP. In rare cases, the auditor issues a disclaimer.

5. Maintains professional confidentiality of client records. The auditor is not, however, exempt from legal obligations such as testifying in court.

The Financial Statement Audit

What is an audit? There are several types of audits. The type most relevant to this course is a **financial statement audit,** often referred to as simply a financial audit. The financial audit is a detailed examination of a company's financial statements and the documents that support those statements. It also tests the reliability of the accounting system used to produce the financial reports. A financial audit is conducted by an **independent auditor.**

The term *independent auditor* typically refers to a *firm* of certified public accountants. CPAs are licensed by state governments to provide services to the public. They are to be as independent of the companies they audit as is reasonably possible. To help assure independence, CPAs and members of their immediate families may not be employees of the companies they audit. Further, they cannot have investments in the companies they audit. Although CPAs are paid by the companies they audit, the audit fee may not be based on the outcome of the audit.

Although the independent auditors are chosen by, paid by, and can be fired by their client companies, the auditors are primarily responsible to *the public.* In fact, auditors have a legal responsibility to those members of the public who have a financial interest in the company being audited. If investors in a company lose money, they sometimes sue the independent auditors in an attempt to recover their losses, especially if the losses were related to financial failure. A lawsuit against auditors will succeed only if the auditors failed in their professional responsibilities when conducting the audit. Auditors are not responsible for the success or failure of a company. Instead, they are responsible for the appropriate reporting of that success or failure. While recent debacles such as Bernard Madoff Investments produce spectacular headlines, auditors are actually not sued very often, considering the number of audits they perform.

Materiality and Financial Audits

Auditors do not guarantee that financial statements are absolutely correct—only that they are free from *material* misstatements. This is where things get a little fuzzy. What is a *material misstatement?* The concept of materiality is very subjective. If ExxonMobil inadvertently overstated its sales by $1 million, would this be material? In 2009, ExxonMobil had approximately $311 billion of sales! A $1 million error in computing sales at ExxonMobil is like a $1 error in computing the pay of a person who makes $311,000 per year—not material at all! An error, or other reporting problem, is **material** if knowing about it would influence the decisions of an *average prudent investor.*

Financial audits are not directed toward the discovery of fraud. Auditors are, however, responsible for providing *reasonable assurance* that statements are free from material misstatements, whether caused by errors or fraud. Also, auditors are responsible for evaluating whether internal control procedures are in place to help prevent material misstatements due to fraud. If fraud is widespread in a company, normal audit procedures should detect it.

Accounting majors take at least one and often two or more courses in auditing to understand how to conduct an audit. An explanation of auditing techniques is beyond the scope of this course, but at least be aware that auditors do not review how the company accounted for every transaction. Along with other methods, auditors use statistics to choose representative samples of transactions to examine.

Types of Audit Opinions

Once an audit is complete, the auditors present their conclusions in a report that includes an *audit opinion.* There are three basic types of audit opinions.

An **unqualified opinion,** despite its negative-sounding name, is the most favorable opinion auditors can express. It means the auditor believes the financial statements are in compliance with GAAP without qualification, reservation, or exception. Most audits result in unqualified opinions because companies correct any reporting deficiencies the auditors find before the financial statements are released.

The most negative report an auditor can issue is an **adverse opinion.** An adverse opinion means that one or more departures from GAAP are so material that the financial statements do not present a fair picture of the company's status. The auditor's report explains the unacceptable accounting practice(s) that resulted in the adverse opinion being issued. Adverse opinions are very rare because public companies are required by law to follow GAAP.

A **qualified opinion** falls between an unqualified and an adverse opinion. A qualified opinion means that for the most part, the company's financial statements are in compliance with GAAP, but the auditors have reservations about something in the statements. The auditors' report explains why the opinion is qualified. A qualified opinion usually does not imply a serious accounting problem, but users should read the auditors' report and draw their own conclusions.

If an auditor is unable to perform the audit procedures necessary to determine whether the statements are prepared in accordance with GAAP, the auditor cannot issue an opinion on the financial statements. Instead, the auditor issues a **disclaimer of opinion.** A disclaimer means that the auditor is unable to obtain enough information to confirm compliance with GAAP.

Regardless of the type of report they issue, auditors are only expressing their judgment about whether the financial statements present a fair picture of a company. They do not provide opinions regarding the investment quality of a company.

The ultimate responsibility for financial statements rests with the executives of the reporting company. Just like auditors, managers can be sued by investors who believe they lost money due to improper financial reporting. This is one reason all business persons should understand accounting fundamentals.

Confidentiality

The **confidentiality** rules in the AICPA's code of ethics for CPAs prohibits auditors from *voluntarily disclosing* information they have acquired as a result of their accountant-client relationships. However, accountants may be required to testify in a court of law. In general, federal law does not recognize an accountant-client privilege as it does with attorneys and clergy. Some federal courts have taken exception to this position, especially as it applies to tax cases. State law varies with respect to accountant-client privilege. Furthermore, if auditors terminate a client relationship because of ethical or legal disagreements and they are subsequently contacted by a successor auditor, they are required to inform the successor of the reasons for the termination. In addition, auditors must consider the particular circumstances of a case when assessing the appropriateness of disclosing confidential information. Given the diverse legal positions governing accountant-client confidentiality, auditors should seek legal counsel prior to disclosing any information obtained in an accountant-client relationship.

To illustrate, assume that Joe Smith, CPA, discovers that his client Jane Doe is misrepresenting information reported in her financial statements. Smith tries to convince Doe to correct the misrepresentations, but she refuses to do so. Smith is required by the code of ethics to terminate his relationship with Doe. However, Smith is not permitted to disclose Doe's dishonest reporting practices unless he is called on to testify in a legal hearing or to respond to an inquiry by Doe's successor accountant.

With respect to the discovery of significant fraud, the auditor is required to inform management at least one level above the position of the employee who is engaged in the fraud and to notify the board of directors of the company. Suppose that Joe Smith, CPA, discovers that Jane Doe, employee of Western Company, is embezzling money from Western. Smith is required to inform Doe's supervisor and to notify Western's board of directors. However, Smith is prohibited from publicly disclosing the fraud.

<< A Look Back

The policies and procedures used to provide reasonable assurance that the objectives of an enterprise will be accomplished are called *internal controls*. While the mechanics of internal control systems vary from company to company, the more prevalent features include the following.

1. *Separation of duties.* Whenever possible, the functions of authorization, recording, and custody should be exercised by different individuals.

2. *Quality of employees.* Employees should be qualified to competently perform the duties that are assigned to them. Companies must establish hiring practices to screen out unqualified candidates. Furthermore, procedures should be established to ensure that employees receive appropriate training to maintain their competence.

3. *Bonded employees.* Employees in sensitive positions should be covered by a fidelity bond that provides insurance to reimburse losses due to illegal actions committed by employees.

4. *Required absences.* Employees should be required to take extended absences from their jobs so that they are not always present to hide unscrupulous or illegal activities.

5. *Procedures manual.* To promote compliance, the procedures for processing transactions should be clearly described in a manual.

6. *Authority and responsibility.* To motivate employees and promote effective control, clear lines of authority and responsibility should be established.

7. *Prenumbered documents.* Prenumbered documents minimize the likelihood of missing or duplicate documents. Prenumbered forms should be used for all important documents such as purchase orders, receiving reports, invoices, and checks.

8. *Physical control.* Locks, fences, security personnel, and other physical devices should be employed to safeguard assets.

9. *Performance evaluations.* Because few people can evaluate their own performance objectively, independent performance evaluations should be performed. Substandard performance will likely persist unless employees are encouraged to take corrective action.

Because cash is such an important business asset and because it is tempting to steal, much of the discussion of internal controls in this chapter focused on cash controls. Special procedures should be employed to control the receipts and payments of cash. One of the most common control policies is to use *checking accounts* for all payments except petty cash disbursements.

A *bank reconciliation* should be prepared each month to explain differences between the bank statement and a company's internal accounting records. A common reconciliation format determines the true cash balance based on both bank and book records. Items that typically appear on a bank reconciliation include the following:

Unadjusted bank balance	xxx	Unadjusted book balance	xxx
Add		Add	
Deposits in transit	xxx	Interest revenue	xxx
		Collection of receivables	xxx
Subtract		Subtract	
Outstanding checks	xxx	Bank service charges	xxx
		NSF checks	xxx
True cash balance	xxx	True cash balance	xxx

Agreement of the two true cash balances provides evidence that accounting for cash transactions has been accurate.

The chapter discussed the importance of ethics in the accounting profession. The *American Institute of Public Accountants* requires all of its members to comply with the *Code of Professional Conduct.* Situations where *opportunity, pressure,* and *rationalization* exist can lead employees to conduct unethical acts, which, in cases like Enron, have destroyed the organization. Finally, the chapter discussed the auditor's role in financial reporting, including the materiality concept and the types of audit opinions that may be issued.

A Look Forward

The next chapter focuses on more specific issues related to accounts receivables and inventory. Accounting for receivables and payable was introduced in Chapter 2, using relatively simple illustrations. For example, we assumed that customers who purchased services on account always paid their bills. In real business practice, some customers do not pay their bills. Among other topics, Chapter 5 examines how companies account for uncollectible accounts receivable.

Accounting for inventory was discussed in Chapter 3. However, we assumed that all inventory items were purchased at the same price. This is unrealistic given that the price of goods is constantly changing. Chapter 5 discusses how to account for inventory items that are purchased at different times and different prices.

A step-by-step audio-narrated series of slides is provided on the text website at www.mhhe.com/edmondssurvey3e.

SELF-STUDY REVIEW PROBLEM

The following information pertains to Terry's Pest Control Company (TPCC) for July:

1. The unadjusted bank balance at July 31 was $870.
2. The bank statement included the following items:
   (a) A $60 credit memo for interest earned by TPCC.
   (b) A $200 NSF check made payable to TPCC.
   (c) A $110 debit memo for bank service charges.
3. The unadjusted book balance at July 31 was $1,400.

4. A comparison of the bank statement with company accounting records disclosed the following:

(a) A $400 deposit in transit at July 31.

(b) Outstanding checks totaling $120 at the end of the month.

Required

Prepare a bank reconciliation.

Solution

TERRY'S PEST CONTROL COMPANY
Bank Reconciliation
July 31

Unadjusted bank balance	$ 870
Add: Deposits in transit	400
Less: Outstanding checks	(120)
True cash balance	$1,150
Unadjusted book balance	$1,400
Add: Interest revenue	60
Less: NSF check	(200)
Less: Bank service charges	(110)
True cash balance	$1,150

KEY TERMS

Adverse opinion 141
American Institute of Certified Public Accountants 137
Audits 139
Authority manual 127
Bank reconciliation 131
Bank statement 131
Bank statement credit memo 131
Bank statement debit memo 131
Cash 129
Certified check 133
Certified public accountants (CPAs) 139

Checks 131
Code of Professional Conduct 137
Confidentiality 141
Deposit ticket 131
Deposits in transit 132
Disclaimer of opinion 141
Fidelity bond 127
Financial statement audit 140
General authority 127
Independent auditor 140
Internal controls 126
Material 140
Non-sufficient-funds (NSF) checks 133

Opportunity 138
Outstanding checks 133
Pressure 139
Procedures manual 127
Qualified opinion 141
Rationalization 139
Separation of duties 126
Service charges 133
Signature card 130
Specific authorizations 127
True cash balance 131
Unadjusted bank balance 131
Unadjusted book balance 131
Unqualified opinion 141

QUESTIONS

1. What motivated congress to pass the Sarbanes-Oxley Act (SOX) of 2002?

2. Define the term *internal control*.

3. Explain the relationship between SOX and COSO.

4. Name and briefly define the five components of COSO's internal control framework.

5. Explain how COSO's *Enterprise Risk Management—An Integrated Framework* project relates to COSO's *Internal Control—An Integrated Framework* project.

6. List several control activities of an effective internal control system.

7. What is meant by *separation of duties?* Give an illustration.

8. What are the attributes of a high-quality employee?

9. What is a fidelity bond? Explain its purpose.

10. Why is it important that every employee periodically take a leave of absence or vacation?

11. What are the purpose and importance of a procedures manual?

12. What is the difference between specific and general authorizations?

13. Why should documents (checks, invoices, receipts) be prenumbered?

14. What procedures are important in the physical control of assets and accounting records?

15. What is the purpose of independent verification of performance?

16. What items are considered cash?

17. Why is cash more susceptible to theft or embezzlement than other assets?

18. Giving written copies of receipts to customers can help prevent what type of illegal acts?

19. What procedures can help to protect cash receipts?

20. What procedures can help protect cash disbursements?

21. What effect does a debit memo in a bank statement have on the Cash account? What effect does a credit memo in a bank statement have on the Cash account?

22. What information is normally included in a bank statement?

23. Why might a bank statement reflect a balance that is larger than the balance recorded in the depositor's books? What could cause the bank balance to be smaller than the book balance?

24. What is the purpose of a bank reconciliation?

25. What is an outstanding check?

26. What is a deposit in transit?

27. What is a certified check?

28. How is an NSF check accounted for in the accounting records?

29. Name and comment on the three elements of the fraud triangle.

30. What are the six articles of ethical conduct set out under section I of the AICPA's Code of Professional Conduct?

MULTIPLE-CHOICE QUESTIONS

Multiple-choice questions are provided on the text website at www.mhhe.com/edmondssurvey3e.

EXERCISES

All applicable Exercises are available with McGraw-Hill's *Connect Accounting.*

Exercise 4-1   *SOX and COSO's Internal Control Frameworks*   LO 1

Required

a. Explain what the acronym SOX refers to.

b. Define the acronym COSO and explain how it relates to SOX.

c. Name and briefly define the five components of COSO's internal control framework.

d. Define the acronym ERM and explain how it relates to COSO's internal control framework.

Exercise 4-2   *Control activities of a strong internal control system*   LO 1

Required

List and describe nine control activities of a strong internal control system discussed in this chapter.

Exercise 4-3   *Internal controls for small businesses*   LO 1

Required

Assume you are the owner of a small business that has only two employees.

a. Which of the internal control procedures are most important to you?

b. How can you overcome the limited opportunity to use the separation-of-duties control procedure?

Exercise 4-4   *Internal control for cash*   LO 1

Required

a. Why are special controls needed for cash?

b. What is included in the definition of *cash*?

LO 1

Exercise 4-5 *Internal control procedures to prevent deception*

Emergency Care Medical Centers (ECMC) hired a new physician, Ken Major, who was an immediate success. Everyone loved his bedside manner; he could charm the most cantankerous patient. Indeed, he was a master salesman as well as an expert physician. Unfortunately, Major misdiagnosed a case that resulted in serious consequences to the patient. The patient filed suit against ECMC. In preparation for the defense, ECMC's attorneys discovered that Major was indeed an exceptional salesman. He had worked for several years as district marketing manager for a pharmaceutical company. In fact, he was not a physician at all! He had changed professions without going to medical school. He had lied on his application form. His knowledge of medical terminology had enabled him to fool everyone. ECMC was found negligent and lost a $3 million lawsuit.

Required

Identify the relevant internal control procedures that could have prevented the company's losses. Explain how these procedures would have prevented Major's deception.

LO 1

Exercise 4-6 *Internal control procedures to prevent embezzlement*

Bell Gates was in charge of the returns department at The Software Company. She was responsible for evaluating returned merchandise. She sent merchandise that was reusable back to the warehouse, where it was restocked in inventory. Gates was also responsible for taking the merchandise that she determined to be defective to the city dump for disposal. She had agreed to buy a tax planning program for one of her friends at a discount through her contacts at work. That is when the idea came to her. She could simply classify one of the reusable returns as defective and bring it home instead of taking it to the dump. She did so and made a quick $150. She was happy, and her friend was ecstatic; he was able to buy a $400 software package for only $150. He told his friends about the deal, and soon Gates had a regular set of customers. She was caught when a retail store owner complained to the marketing manager that his pricing strategy was being undercut by The Software Company's direct sales to the public. The marketing manager was suspicious because The Software Company had no direct marketing program. When the outside sales were ultimately traced back to Gates, the company discovered that it had lost over $10,000 in sales revenue because of her criminal activity.

Required

Identify an internal control procedure that could have prevented the company's losses. Explain how the procedure would have stopped the embezzlement.

LO 2

Exercise 4-7 *Treatment of NSF check*

Rankin Stationery's bank statement contained a $250 NSF check that one of its customers had written to pay for supplies purchased.

Required

a. Show the effects of recognizing the NSF check on the financial statements by recording the appropriate amounts in a horizontal statements model like the following one:

Assets		=	Liab.	+	Equity	Rev.	−	Exp.	=	Net Inc.	Cash Flow
Cash +	Accts. Rec.										

b. Is the recognition of the NSF check on Rankin's books an asset source, use, or exchange transaction?

c. Suppose the customer redeems the check by giving Rankin $270 cash in exchange for the bad check. The additional $20 was a service fee charged by Rankin. Show the effects on the financial statements in the horizontal statements model in Requirement *a*.

d. Is the receipt of cash referenced in Requirement *c* an asset source, use, or exchange transaction?

Exercise 4-8 *Adjustments to the balance per books*   **LO 2**

Required

Identify which of the following items are added to or subtracted from the unadjusted *book balance* to arrive at the true cash balance. Distinguish the additions from the subtractions by placing a + beside the items that are added to the unadjusted book balance and a − beside those that are subtracted from it. The first item is recorded as an example.

Reconciling Items	Book Balance Adjusted?	Added or Subtracted?
Outstanding checks	No	N/A
Interest revenue earned on the account		
Deposits in transit		
Service charge		
Automatic debit for utility bill		
Charge for checks		
NSF check from customer		
ATM fee		

Exercise 4-9 *Adjustments to the balance per bank*   **LO 2**

Required

Identify which of the following items are added to or subtracted from the unadjusted *bank balance* to arrive at the true cash balance. Distinguish the additions from the subtractions by placing a + beside the items that are added to the unadjusted bank balance and a − beside those that are subtracted from it. The first item is recorded as an example.

Reconciling Items	Bank Balance Adjusted?	Added or Subtracted?
Bank service charge	No	N/A
Outstanding checks		
Deposits in transit		
Debit memo		
Credit memo		
ATM fee		
Petty cash voucher		
NSF check from customer		
Interest revenue		

Exercise 4-10 *Adjusting the cash account*   **LO 2**

As of June 30, 2012, the bank statement showed an ending balance of $13,879.85. The unadjusted Cash account balance was $13,483.75. The following information is available:

1. Deposit in transit, $1,476.30.
2. Credit memo in bank statement for interest earned in June, $35.
3. Outstanding check, $1,843.74.
4. Debit memo for service charge, $6.34.

Required

Determine the true cash balance by preparing a bank reconciliation as of June 30, 2012, using the preceding information.

LO 2

Exercise 4-11   *Determining the true cash balance, starting with the unadjusted bank balance*

The following information is available for Hamby Company for the month of June:

1. The unadjusted balance per the bank statement on June 30 was $68,714.35.
2. Deposits in transit on June 30 were $1,464.95.
3. A debit memo was included with the bank statement for a service charge of $25.38.
4. A $4,745.66 check written in June had not been paid by the bank.
5. The bank statement included a $944 credit memo for the collection of a note. The principal of the note was $859, and the interest collected amounted to $85.

Required

Determine the true cash balance as of June 30 (*Hint:* It is not necessary to use all of the preceding items to determine the true balance.)

LO 2

Exercise 4-12   *Determining the true cash balance, starting with the unadjusted book balance*

Crumbley Company had an unadjusted cash balance of $6,450 as of May 31. The company's bank statement, also dated May 31, included a $38 NSF check written by one of Crumbley's customers. There were $548.60 in outstanding checks and $143.74 in deposits in transit as of May 31. According to the bank statement, service charges were $30, and the bank collected a $450 note receivable for Crumbley. The bank statement also showed $18 of interest revenue earned by Crumbley.

Required

Determine the true cash balance as of May 31. (*Hint:* It is not necessary to use all of the preceding items to determine the true balance.)

LO 3

Exercise 4-13   *AICPA Code of Professional Conduct*

Walter Walker owns and operates Walker Enterprises. Walter's sister, Sarah, is the independent public accountant for Walker Enterprises. Sarah worked for the Walker Enterprises for five years before she started her independent CPA practice. Walter considered hiring a different accounting firm but ultimately decided that no one knew his business as well as his sister.

Required

Use the AICPA Code of Professional Conduct to evaluate the appropriateness of Sarah's client relationship with Walker Enterprises.

LO 3

Exercise 4-14   *AICPA Code of Professional Conduct*

Courtney Simmons owns the fastest growing CPA practice in her local community. She attributes her success to her marketing skills. She makes a special effort to get to know her clients personally. She attends their weddings, anniversary celebrations, and birthday parties on a regular basis. Courtney always brings lavish presents, and her clients reciprocate by showering her with expensive gifts on her special occasions. This social activity consumes a lot of time. Indeed, it has cut into the time she once spent on continuing education. Even so, her practice has grown at the rate of 25 percent per year for the last three years. Courtney could not be happier with her progress.

Required

Use the AICPA Code of Professional Conduct to evaluate the appropriateness of Courtney's marketing strategy.

LO 3

Exercise 4-15   *Fraud triangle*

Bill Perry is a CPA with a secret. His secret is that he gambles on sports. Bill knows that his profession disapproves of gambling, but considers the professional standards to be misguided in his case. Bill really doesn't consider his bets to be gambling because he spends a lot of time studying sports facts. He believes that he is simply making educated decisions based on facts. He argues that using sports, facts to place bets is no different than using accounting information to buy stock.

Required

Use the fraud triangle as a basis to comment on Bill Perry's gambling activities.

Exercise 4-16 *Confidentiality and the auditor*

LO 4

West Aston discovered a significant fraud in the accounting records of a high profile client. The story has been broadcast on national airways. Aston was unable to resolve his remaining concerns with the company's management team and ultimately resigned from the audit engagement. Aston knows that he will be asked by several interested parties, including his friends and relatives, the successor auditor, and prosecuting attorneys in a court of law to tell what he knows. He has asked you for advice.

Required

Write a memo that explains Aston's disclosure responsibilities to each of the interested parties.

Exercise 4-17 *Auditor responsibilities*

LO 4

You have probably heard it is unwise to bite the hand that feeds you. Independent auditors are chosen by, paid by, and can be fired by the companies they audit. What keeps the auditor independent? In other words, what stops an auditor from blindly following the orders of a client?

Required

Write a memo that explains the reporting responsibilities of an independent auditor.

PROBLEMS

All applicable Problems are available with McGraw-Hill's
Connect Accounting.

ACCOUNTING

Problem 4-18 *Using internal control to restrict illegal or unethical behavior*

LO 1

Required

For each of the following fraudulent acts, describe one or more internal control procedures that could have prevented (or helped prevent) the problems.

a. Everyone in the office has noticed what a dedicated employee Jennifer Reidel is. She never misses work, not even for a vacation. Reidel is in charge of the petty cash fund. She transfers funds from the company's bank account to the petty cash account on an as-needed basis. During a surprise audit, the petty cash fund was found to contain fictitious receipts. Over a three-year period, Reidel had used more than $4,000 of petty cash to pay for personal expenses.

b. Bill Bruton was hired as the vice president of the manufacturing division of a corporation. His impressive resume listed a master's degree in business administration from a large state university and numerous collegiate awards and activities, when in fact Bruton had only a high school diploma. In a short time, the company was in poor financial condition because of his inadequate knowledge and bad decisions.

c. Havolene Manufacturing has good internal control over its manufacturing materials inventory. However, office supplies are kept on open shelves in the employee break room. The office supervisor has noticed that he is having to order paper, tape, staplers, and pens with increasing frequency.

Problem 4-19 *Preparing a bank reconciliation*

LO 2

Bob Carson owns a card shop, Card Talk. The following cash information is available for the month of August, 2012.

As of August 31, the bank statement shows a balance of $17,000. The August 31 unadjusted balance in the Cash account of Card Talk is $16,000. A review of the bank statement revealed the following information:

1. A deposit of $2,260 on August 31, 2012, does not appear on the August bank statement.

2. It was discovered that a check to pay for baseball cards was correctly written and paid by the bank for $4,040 but was recorded on the books as $4,400.

CHECK FIGURE
True Cash Balance, August 31, 2012: $16,260

3. When checks written during the month were compared with those paid by the bank, three checks amounting to $3,000 were found to be outstanding.
4. A debit memo for $100 was included in the bank statement for the purchase of a new supply of checks.

Required

Prepare a bank reconciliation at the end of August showing the true cash balance.

LO 2

Problem 4-20   *Missing information in a bank reconciliation*

The following data apply to Superior Auto Supply Inc. for May 2012.

1. Balance per the bank on May 31, $8,000.
2. Deposits in transit not recorded by the bank, $975.
3. Bank error; check written by Allen Auto Supply was charged to Superior Auto Supply's account, $650.
4. The following checks written and recorded by Superior Auto Supply were not included in the bank statement:

CHECK FIGURE
Unadjusted Cash Balance,
May 31, 2012: $5,565

3013	$ 385
3054	735
3056	1,900

5. Note collected by the bank, $500.
6. Service charge for collection of note, $10.
7. The bookkeeper recorded a check written for $188 to pay for the May utilities expense as $888 in the cash disbursements journal.
8. Bank service charge in addition to the note collection fee, $25.
9. Customer checks returned by the bank as NSF, $125.

Required

Determine the amount of the unadjusted cash balance per Superior Auto Supply's books.

LO 2

eXcel

CHECK FIGURE
b. No book adjustment

Problem 4-21   *Adjustments to the cash account based on the bank reconciliation*

Required

Determine whether the following items included in Yang Company's bank reconciliation will require adjustments or corrections on Yang's books.

a. An $877 deposit was recorded by the bank as $778.
b. Four checks totaling $450 written during the month of January were not included with the January bank statement.
c. A $54 check written to Office Max for office supplies was recorded in the general journal as $45.
d. The bank statement indicated that the bank had collected a $330 note for Yang.
e. Yang recorded $500 of receipts on January 31, which were deposited in the night depository of the bank. These deposits were not included in the bank statement.
f. Service charges of $22 for the month of January were listed on the bank statement.
g. The bank charged a $297 check drawn on Cave Restaurant to Yang's account. The check was included in Yang's bank statement.
h. A check of $31 was returned by the bank because of insufficient funds and was noted on the bank statement. Yang received the check from a customer and thought that it was good when it was deposited into the account.

Problem 4-22 *Bank reconciliation and adjustments to the cash account*   **LO 2**

The following information is available for Cooters Garage for March 2012:

BANK STATEMENT
HAZARD STATE BANK
215 MAIN STREET
HAZARD, GA 30321

Cooters Garage	Account number
629 Main Street	62–00062
Hazard, GA 30321	March 31, 2012

Beginning balance 3/1/2012	$15,000.00
Total deposits and other credits	7,000.00
Total checks and other debits	6,000.00
Ending balance 3/31/2012	16,000.00

Checks and Debits		Deposits and Credits	
Check No.	Amount	Date	Amount
1462	$1,163.00	March 1	$1,000.00
1463	62.00	March 2	1,340.00
1464	1,235.00	March 6	210.00
1465	750.00	March 12	1,940.00
1466	1,111.00	March 17	855.00
1467	964.00	March 22	1,480.00
DM	15.00	CM	175.00
1468	700.00		

The following is a list of checks and deposits recorded on the books of Cooters Garage for March 2012:

Date	Check No.	Amount of Check	Date	Amount of Deposit
March 1	1463	$ 62.00	March 1	$1,340.00
March 5	1464	1,235.00	March 5	210.00
March 6	1465	750.00		
March 9	1466	1,111.00	March 10	1,940.00
March 10	1467	964.00		
March 14	1468	70.00	March 16	855.00
March 19	1469	1,500.00	March 19	1,480.00
March 28	1470	102.00	March 29	2,000.00

Other Information

1. Check no. 1462 was outstanding from February.
2. A credit memo for collection of accounts receivable was included in the bank statement.
3. All checks were paid at the correct amount.
4. The bank statement included a debit memo for service charges.
5. The February 28 bank reconciliation showed a deposit in transit of $1,000.
6. Check no. 1468 was for the purchase of equipment.
7. The unadjusted Cash account balance at March 31 was $16,868.

Required

a. Prepare the bank reconciliation for Cooters Garage at the end of March.
b. Explain how the adjustments described above affect the cash account.

LO 1, 2

CHECK FIGURE
a. True Cash Balance, Jun 30,
2012: $2,093

Problem 4-23 *Bank reconciliation and internal control*

Following is a bank reconciliation for Surf Shop for June 30, 2012:

	Cash Account	Bank Statement
Balance as of 6/30/2012	$ 1,618	$ 3,000
Deposit in transit		600
Outstanding checks		(1,507)
Note collected by bank	2,000	
Bank service charge	(25)	
NSF check	(1,500)	
Adjusted cash balance as of 6/30/2012	$ 2,093	$ 2,093

When reviewing the bank reconciliation, Surf's auditor was unable to locate any reference to the NSF check on the bank statement. Furthermore, the clerk who reconciles the bank account and records the adjusting entries could not find the actual NSF check that should have been included in the bank statement. Finally, there was no specific reference in the accounts receivable supporting records identifying a party who had written a bad check.

Required

a. Prepare a corrected bank reconciliation.

b. What is the total amount of cash missing, and how was the difference between the "true cash" per the bank and the "true cash" per the books hidden on the reconciliation prepared by the former employee?

c. What could Surf's Shop do to avoid cash theft in the future?

LO 3

Problem 4-24 *Fraud Triangle*

Pete Chalance is an accountant with a shady past. Suffice it to say that he owes some very unsavory characters a lot of money. Despite his past, Pete works hard at keeping up a strong professional image. He is a manager at Smith and Associates, a fast-growing CPA firm. Pete is highly regarded around the office because he is a strong producer of client revenue. Indeed, on several occasions he exceeded his authority in establishing prices with clients. This is typically a partner's job but who could criticize Pete, who is most certainly bringing in the business. Indeed, Pete is so good that he is able to pull off the following scheme. He bills clients at inflated rates and then reports the ordinary rate to his accounting firm. Say, for example, the normal charge for a job is $2,500. Pete will smooth talk the client, then charge him $3,000. He reports the normal charge of $2,500 to his firm and keeps the extra $500 for himself. He knows it isn't exactly right. Even so, his firm gets its regular charges and the client willingly pays for the services rendered. He thinks to himself, as he pockets his ill-gotten gains, who is getting hurt anyway?

Required

The text discusses three common features (conditions) that motivate ethical misconduct. Identify and explain each of the three features as they appear in the above scenario.

LO 4

Problem 4-25 *Materiality and the auditor*

Sharon Waters is an auditor. Her work at two companies disclosed inappropriate recognition of revenue. Both cases involved dollar amounts in the $100,000 range. In one case. Waters considered the item material and required her client to restate earnings. In the other case, Waters dismissed the misstatement as being immaterial.

Required

Write a memo that explains how a $100,000 misstatement of revenue is acceptable for one company but unacceptable for a different company.

Problem 4-26 *Types of audit reports*

Jim Morris is a partner of a regional accounting firm. Mr. Morris was hired by a client to audit the company's books. After extensive work, Mr. Morris determined that he was unable to perform the appropriate audit procedures.

Required

a. Name the type of audit report that Mr. Morris should issue with respect to the work that he did accomplish.

b. If Mr. Morris had been able to perform the necessary audit procedures, there are three types of audit reports that he could have issued depending on the outcome of the audit. Name and describe these three types of audit reports.

ANALYZE, THINK, COMMUNICATE

ATC 4-1 **Business Application Case** *Understanding real-world annual reports*

Use the Target Corporation's annual report in Appendix B to answer the following questions.

Required

a. Instead of "Cash," the company's balance sheet uses the account name "Cash and cash equivalents." How does the company define cash equivalents?

b. The annual report has two reports in which management is clearly identified as having responsibility for the company's financial reporting and internal controls. What are the names of these reports and on what pages are they located?

ATC 4-2 **Group Assignment** *Bank reconciliations*

The following cash and bank information is available for three companies at June 30, 2012.

Cash and Adjustment Information	Peach Co.	Apple Co.	Pear Co.
Unadjusted cash balance per books, 6/30	$45,620	$32,450	$23,467
Outstanding checks	1,345	2,478	2,540
Service charge	50	75	35
Balance per bank statement, 6/30	48,632	37,176	24,894
Credit memo for collection of notes receivable	4,500	5,600	3,800
NSF check	325	145	90
Deposits in transit	2,500	3,200	4,800
Credit memo for interest earned	42	68	12

Required

a. Organize the class into three sections and divide each section into groups of three to five students. Assign Peach Co. to section 1, Apple Co. to section 2, and Pear Co. to section 3.

Group Tasks

(1) Prepare a bank reconciliation for the company assigned to your group.

(2) Select a representative from a group in each section to put the bank reconciliation on the board.

Class Discussion:

b. Discuss the cause of the difference between the unadjusted cash balance and the ending balance for the bank statement. Also, discuss types of adjustment that are commonly made to the bank balance and types of adjustment that are commonly made to the unadjusted book balance.

ATC 4-3 Research Assignment *Investigating Cash and Management Issues at Smucker's*

Using the most current Form 10-K available on EDGAR, or the company's website, answer the following questions about the J. M. Smucker Company. Instructions for using EDGAR are in Appendix A. *Note: In some years the financial statements, footnotes, etc., portion of Smucker's annual report have been located at the end of the Form 10-K, in or just after "Item 15."*

Required

a. Instead of "Cash," the company's balance sheet uses the account name "Cash and cash equivalents." How does the company define cash equivalents?

b. The annual report has two reports in which management clearly acknowledges its responsibility for the company's financial reporting and internal controls. What are the names of these reports and on what pages are they located?

ATC 4-4 Writing Assignment *Internal control procedures*

Sarah Johnson was a trusted employee of Evergreen Trust Bank. She was involved in everything. She worked as a teller, she accounted for the cash at the other teller windows, and she recorded many of the transactions in the accounting records. She was so loyal that she never would take a day off, even when she was really too sick to work. She routinely worked late to see that all the day's work was posted into the accounting records. She would never take even a day's vacation because they might need her at the bank. Adam and Jammie, CPAs, were hired to perform an audit, the first complete audit that had been done in several years. Johnson seemed somewhat upset by the upcoming audit. She said that everything had been properly accounted for and that the audit was a needless expense. When Adam and Jammie examined some of the bank's internal control procedures, it discovered problems. In fact, as the audit progressed, it became apparent that a large amount of cash was missing. Numerous adjustments had been made to customer accounts with credit memorandums, and many of the transactions had been posted several days late. In addition, there were numerous cash payments for "office expenses." When the audit was complete, it was determined that more than $100,000 of funds was missing or improperly accounted for. All fingers pointed to Johnson. The bank's president, who was a close friend of Johnson, was bewildered. How could this type of thing happen at this bank?

Required

Prepare a written memo to the bank president, outlining the procedures that should be followed to prevent this type of problem in the future.

ATC 4-5 Ethical Dilemma *I need just a little extra money*

John Riley, a certified public accountant, has worked for the past eight years as a payroll clerk for Southeast Industries, a small furniture manufacturing firm in the Northeast. John recently experienced unfortunate circumstances. His teenage son required major surgery and the medical bills not covered by John's insurance have financially strained John's family.

John works hard and is a model employee. Although he received regular performance raises during his first few years with Southeast. John's wages have not increased in three years. John asked his supervisor, Bill Jameson, for a raise. Bill agreed that John deserved a raise, but told him he could not currently approve one because of sluggish sales.

A disappointed John returned to his duties while the financial pressures in his life continued. Two weeks later, Larry Tyler, an assembly worker at Southwest, quit over a dispute with management. John conceived an idea. John's duties included not only processing employee terminations but also approving time cards before paychecks were issued and then distributing the paychecks to firm personnel. John decided to delay processing Mr. Tyler's termination, to forge timecards for Larry Tyler for the next few weeks, and to cash the checks himself. Since he distributed paychecks, no one would find out, and John reasoned that he was really entitled to the extra money anyway. In fact, no one did discover his maneuver and John stopped the practice after three weeks.

Required

a. Does John's scheme affect Southeast's balance sheet? Explain your answer.

b. Review the AICPA's Articles of Professional Conduct and comment on any of the standards that have been violated.

c. Identify the three elements of unethical and criminal conduct recognized in the fraud triangle.

CHAPTER 8

Proprietorships, Partnerships, and Corporations

LEARNING OBJECTIVES

After you have mastered the material in this chapter, you will be able to:

1 Identify the primary characteristics of sole proprietorships, partnerships, and corporations.

2 Analyze financial statements to identify the different types of business organizations.

3 Explain the characteristics of major types of stock issued by corporations.

4 Explain how to account for different types of stock issued by corporations.

5 Show how treasury stock transactions affect a company's financial statements.

6 Explain the effects of declaring and paying cash dividends on a company's financial statements.

7 Explain the effects of stock dividends and stock splits on a company's financial statements.

8 Show how the appropriation of retained earnings affects financial statements.

9 Explain some uses of accounting information in making stock investment decisions.

CHAPTER OPENING

You want to start a business. How should you structure it? Should it be a sole proprietorship, partnership, or corporation? Each form of business structure presents advantages and disadvantages. For example, a sole proprietorship allows maximum independence and control while partnerships and corporations allow individuals to pool resources and talents with other people. This chapter discusses these and other features of the three primary forms of business structure.

The Curious Accountant

Imagine your rich uncle rewarded you for doing well in your first accounting course by giving you $10,000 to invest in the stock of one company. After reviewing many recent annual reports, you narrowed your choice to two companies with the following characteristics:

Mystery Company A: This company began operations in 2003, but did not begin selling its stock to the public until April 16, 2009. In its first six years of operations it had total earnings of approximately $1.6 million. By the time it went public it was already a leader in its field. At its current price of $23 you could buy approximately 435 shares. A friend told you that a globally minded person like you would be crazy not to buy this stock.

Mystery Company B: This company has been in existence since 1837 and has made a profit most years. In the most recent five years, its net earnings totaled over $51.8 *billion*, and it paid dividends of over $21 *billion*. This stock is selling for about $62 per share, so you can buy 161 shares of it. Your friend said "you would have to be goofy to buy this stock."

The names of the real-world companies described above are disclosed later. Based on the information provided, which company's stock would you buy? (Answer on page 290.)

FORMS OF BUSINESS ORGANIZATIONS

Identify the primary characteristics of sole proprietorships, partnerships, and corporations.

Sole proprietorships are owned by a single individual who is responsible for making business and profit distribution decisions. If you want to be the absolute master of your destiny, you should organize your business as a proprietorship. Establishing a sole proprietorship is usually as simple as obtaining a business license from local government authorities. Usually no legal ownership agreement is required.

Partnerships allow persons to share their talents, capital, and the risks and rewards of business ownership. Because two or more individuals share ownership, partnerships require clear agreements about how authority, risks, and profits will be shared. Prudent partners minimize misunderstandings by hiring attorneys to prepare a **partnership agreement** which defines the responsibilities of each partner and describes how income or losses will be divided. Because the measurement of income affects the distribution of profits, partnerships frequently hire accountants to ensure that records are maintained in accordance with generally accepted accounting principles (GAAP). Partnerships (and sole proprietorships) also may need professional advice to deal with tax issues.

A **corporation** is a separate legal entity created by the authority of a state government. The paperwork to start a corporation is complex. For most laypersons, engaging professional attorneys and accountants to assist with the paperwork is well worth the fees charged.

Each state has separate laws governing establishing corporations. Many states follow the standard provisions of the Model Business Corporation Act. All states require the initial application to provide **articles of incorporation** which normally include the following information: (1) the corporation's name and proposed date of incorporation; (2) the purpose of the corporation; (3) the location of the business and its expected life (which can be *perpetuity,* meaning *endless*); (4) provisions for capital stock; and (5) the names and addresses of the members of the first board of directors, the individuals with the ultimate authority for operating the business. If the articles are in order, the state establishes the legal existence of the corporation by issuing a charter of incorporation. The charter and the articles are public documents.

ADVANTAGES AND DISADVANTAGES OF DIFFERENT FORMS OF BUSINESS ORGANIZATION

Each form of business organization presents a different combination of advantages and disadvantages. Persons wanting to start a business or invest in one should consider the characteristics of each type of business structure.

Regulation

Few laws specifically affect the operations of proprietorships and partnerships. Corporations, however, are usually heavily regulated. The extent of government regulation depends on the size and distribution of a company's ownership interests. Ownership interests in corporations are normally evidenced by **stock certificates.**

Ownership of corporations can be transferred from one individual to another through exchanging stock certificates. As long as the exchanges (buying and selling of shares of stock, often called *trading*) are limited to transactions between individuals, a company is defined as a **closely held corporation.** However, once a corporation reaches a certain size, it may list its stock on a stock exchange such as the New York Stock Exchange or the American Stock Exchange. Trading on a stock exchange is limited to the stockbrokers who are members of the exchange. These brokers represent buyers and sellers who are willing to pay the brokers commissions for exchanging stock certificates on their behalf. Although closely held corporations are relatively free from government regulation, companies whose stock is publicly traded on the exchanges by brokers are subject to extensive regulation.

The extensive regulation of trading on stock exchanges began in the 1930s. The stock market crash of 1929 and the subsequent Great Depression led Congress to pass the **Securities Act of 1933** and the **Securities Exchange Act of 1934** to regulate issuing stock and to govern the exchanges. The 1934 act also created the Securities and Exchange Commission (SEC) to enforce the securities laws. Congress gave the SEC legal authority to establish accounting principles for corporations that are registered on the exchanges. However, the SEC has generally deferred its rule-making authority to private sector accounting bodies such as the Financial Accounting Standards Board (FASB), effectively allowing the accounting profession to regulate itself.

A number of high-profile business failures around the turn of the last century raised questions about the effectiveness of self-regulation and the usefulness of audits to protect the public. The Sarbanes-Oxley Act of 2002 was adopted to address these concerns. The act creates a five-member Public Company Accounting Oversight Board (PCAOB) with the authority to set and enforce auditing, attestation, quality control, and ethics standards for auditors of public companies. The PCAOB is empowered to impose disciplinary and remedial sanctions for violations of its rules, securities laws, and professional auditing and accounting standards. Public corporations operate in a complex regulatory environment that requires the services of attorneys and professional accountants.

Double Taxation

Corporations pay income taxes on their earnings and then owners pay income taxes on distributions (dividends) received from corporations. As a result, distributed corporate profits are taxed twice—first when income is reported on the corporation's income tax return and a second time when distributions are reported on individual owners' tax returns. This phenomenon is commonly called **double taxation** and is a significant disadvantage of the corporate form of business organization.

To illustrate, assume Glide Corporation earns pretax income of $100,000. Glide is in a 30 percent tax bracket. The corporation itself will pay income tax of $30,000 ($100,000 × 0.30). If the corporation distributes the after-tax income of $70,000 ($100,000 − $30,000) to individual stockholders in 15 percent tax brackets,[1] the $70,000 dividend will be reported on the individual tax returns, requiring tax payments of $10,500 ($70,000 × .15). Total income tax of $40,500 ($30,000 + $10,500) is due on $100,000 of earned income. In contrast, consider a proprietorship that is owned by an individual in a 30 percent tax bracket. If the proprietorship earns and distributes $100,000 profit, the total tax would be only $30,000 ($100,000 × .30).

Double taxation can be a burden for small companies. To reduce that burden, tax laws permit small closely held corporations to elect "S Corporation" status. S Corporations are taxed as proprietorships or partnerships. Also, many states have recently enacted laws permitting the formation of **limited liability companies (LLCs)** which offer many of the benefits of corporate ownership yet are in general taxed as partnerships. Because proprietorships and partnerships are not separate legal entities, company earnings are taxable to the owners rather than the company itself.

Limited Liability

Given the disadvantages of increased regulation and double taxation, why would anyone choose the corporate form of business structure over a partnership or proprietorship? A major reason is that the corporate form limits an investor's potential liability as an owner of a business venture. Because a corporation is legally separate from its owners, creditors cannot claim owners' personal assets as payment for the company's debts. Also, plaintiffs

[1]As a result of the Jobs and Growth Tax Relief Reconciliation Act (JGTRRA) of 2003, dividends received in tax years after 2002 are taxed at a maximum rate of 15 percent for most taxpayers. Lower income individuals pay a 5 percent tax on dividends received on December 31, 2007, or earlier. This rate falls to zero in 2008. The provisions of JGTRRA are set to expire on December 31, 2008.

Answers to The Curious Accountant

Mystery Company A is Rosetta Stone, Inc., as of July 7, 2010. The company's main products provide computer-aided learning of over 30 languages. The company has developed a visually based learning system that does not require much translation from one language to another. Therefore, the same product used by an English speaker to learn Spanish can, with only minimal changes, be used by a French speaker to learn Spanish. Some analysts believe this gives the company opportunities for large growth without a correspondingly large increase in investment.

Mystery Company B is Procter & Gamble, Inc. (as of July 7, 2010). Of course, only the future will tell which company is the better investment.

must sue the corporation, not its owners. The most that owners of a corporation can lose is the amount they have invested in the company (the value of the company's stock).

Unlike corporate stockholders, the owners of proprietorships and partnerships are *personally liable* for actions they take in the name of their companies. In fact, partners are responsible not only for their own actions but also for those taken by any other partner on behalf of the partnership. The benefit of **limited liability** is one of the most significant reasons the corporate form of business organization is so popular.

Continuity

Unlike partnerships or proprietorships, which terminate with the departure of their owners, a corporation's life continues when a shareholder dies or sells his or her stock. Because of **continuity** of existence, many corporations formed in the 1800s still thrive today.

Transferability of Ownership

The **transferability** of corporate ownership is easy. An investor simply buys or sells stock to acquire or give up an ownership interest in a corporation. Hundreds of millions of shares of stock are bought and sold on the major stock exchanges each day.

Transferring the ownership of proprietorships is much more difficult. To sell an ownership interest in a proprietorship, the proprietor must find someone willing to purchase the entire business. Because most proprietors also run their businesses, transferring ownership also requires transferring management responsibilities. Consider the difference in selling $1 million of Exxon stock versus selling a locally owned gas station. The stock could be sold on the New York Stock Exchange within minutes. In contrast, it could take years to find a buyer who is financially capable of and interested in owning and operating a gas station.

Transferring ownership in partnerships can also be difficult. As with proprietorships, ownership transfers may require a new partner to make a significant investment and accept management responsibilities in the business. Further, a new partner must accept and be accepted by the other partners. Personality conflicts and differences in management style can cause problems in transferring ownership interests in partnerships.

Management Structure

Partnerships and proprietorships are usually managed by their owners. Corporations, in contrast, have three tiers of management authority. The *owners* (**stockholders**) represent the highest level of organizational authority. The stockholders *elect* a **board of directors** to oversee company operations. The directors then *hire* professional executives to manage the company on a daily basis. Because large corporations can offer high salaries and challenging career opportunities, they can often attract superior managerial talent.

While the management structure used by corporations is generally effective, it sometimes complicates dismissing incompetent managers. The chief executive officer (CEO) is usually a member of the board of directors and is frequently influential in choosing other board members. The CEO is also in a position to reward loyal board members. As a result, board members may be reluctant to fire the CEO or other top executives even if the individuals are performing poorly. Corporations operating under such conditions are said to be experiencing **entrenched management.**

Ability to Raise Capital

Because corporations can have millions of owners (shareholders), they have the opportunity to raise huge amounts of capital. Few individuals have the financial means to build and operate a telecommunications network such as AT&T or a marketing distribution system such as Walmart. However, by pooling the resources of millions of owners through public stock and bond offerings, corporations generate the billions of dollars of capital needed for such massive investments. In contrast, the capital resources of proprietorships and partnerships are limited to a relatively small number of private owners. Although proprietorships and partnerships can also obtain resources by borrowing, the amount creditors are willing to lend them is usually limited by the size of the owners' net worth.

APPEARANCE OF CAPITAL STRUCTURE IN FINANCIAL STATEMENTS

The ownership interest (equity) in a business is composed of two elements: (1) owner/investor contributions and (2) retained earnings. The way these two elements are reported in the financial statements differs for each type of business structure (proprietorship, partnership, or corporation).

LO 2

Analyze financial statements to identify the different types of business organizations.

Presentation of Equity in Proprietorships

Owner contributions and retained earnings are combined in a single Capital account on the balance sheets of proprietorships. To illustrate, assume that Worthington Sole Proprietorship was started on January 1, 2012, when it acquired a $5,000 capital contribution from its owner, Phil Worthington. During the first year of operation, the company generated $4,000 of cash revenues, incurred $2,500 of cash expenses, and distributed $1,000 cash to the owner. Exhibit 8.1 displays 2012 financial statements for Worthington's company. Note on the *capital statement* that distributions are called **withdrawals.** Verify that the $5,500 balance in the Capital account on the balance sheet includes the $5,000 owner contribution and the retained earnings of $500 ($1,500 net income − $1,000 withdrawal).

EXHIBIT 8.1

WORTHINGTON SOLE PROPRIETORSHIP
Financial Statements
As of December 31, 2012

Income Statement		Capital Statement		Balance Sheet	
Revenue	$4,000	Beginning capital balance	$ 0	Assets	
Expenses	2,500	Plus: Investment by owner	5,000	Cash	$5,500
Net income	$1,500	Plus: Net income	1,500	Equity	
		Less: Withdrawal by owner	(1,000)	Worthington, capital	$5,500
		Ending capital balance	$5,500		

CHECK YOURSELF 8.1

Weiss Company was started on January 1, 2012, when it acquired $50,000 cash from its owner(s). During 2012 the company earned $72,000 of net income. Explain how the equity section of Weiss's December 31, 2012, balance sheet would differ if the company were a proprietorship versus a corporation.

Answer *Proprietorship* records combine capital acquisitions from the owner and earnings from operating the business in a single capital account. In contrast, *corporation* records separate capital acquisitions from the owners and earnings from operating the business. If Weiss were a proprietorship, the equity section of the year-end balance sheet would report a single capital component of $122,000. If Weiss were a corporation, the equity section would report two separate equity components, most likely common stock of $50,000 and retained earnings of $72,000.

Presentation of Equity in Partnerships

The financial statement format for reporting partnership equity is similar to that used for proprietorships. Contributed capital and retained earnings are combined. However, a separate capital account is maintained for each partner in the business to reflect each partner's ownership interest.

To illustrate, assume that Sara Slater and Jill Johnson formed a partnership on January 1, 2012. The partnership acquired $2,000 of capital from Slater and $4,000 from Johnson. The partnership agreement called for each partner to receive an annual distribution equal to 10 percent of her capital contribution. Any further earnings were to be retained in the business and divided equally between the partners. During 2012, the company earned $5,000 of cash revenue and incurred $3,000 of cash expenses, for net income of $2,000 ($5,000 − $3,000). As specified by the partnership agreement, Slater received a $200 ($2,000 × 0.10) cash withdrawal and Johnson received $400 ($4,000 × 0.10). The remaining $1,400 ($2,000 − $200 − $400) of income was retained in the business and divided equally, adding $700 to each partner's capital account.

Exhibit 8.2 displays financial statements for the Slater and Johnson partnership. Again, note that distributions are called *withdrawals*. Also find on the balance sheet a *separate capital account* for each partner. Each capital account includes the amount of the partner's contributed capital plus her proportionate share of the retained earnings.

EXHIBIT 8.2

SLATER AND JOHNSON PARTNERSHIP
Financial Statements
As of December 31, 2012

Income Statement		Capital Statement		Balance Sheet	
Revenue	$5,000	Beginning capital balance	$ 0	Assets	
Expenses	3,000	Plus: Investment by owners	6,000	Cash	$7,400
Net income	$2,000	Plus: Net income	2,000	Equity	
		Less: Withdrawal by owners	(600)	Slater, capital	$2,700
		Ending capital balance	$7,400	Johnson, capital	4,700
				Total capital	$7,400

Presentation of Equity in Corporations

Corporations have more complex capital structures than proprietorships and partnerships. Explanations of some of the more common features of corporate capital structures and transactions follow.

CHARACTERISTICS OF CAPITAL STOCK

Stock issued by corporations may have a variety of different characteristics. For example, a company may issue different classes of stock that grant owners different rights and privileges. Also, the number of shares a corporation can legally issue may differ from the number it actually has issued. Further, a corporation can even buy back its own stock. Finally, a corporation may assign different values to the stock it issues. Accounting for corporate equity transactions is discussed in the next section of the text.

Explain the characteristics of major types of stock issued by corporations.

Par Value

Many states require assigning a **par value** to stock. Historically, par value represented the maximum liability of the investors. Par value multiplied by the number of shares of stock issued represents the minimum amount of assets that must be retained in the company as protection for creditors. This amount is known as **legal capital.** To ensure that the amount of legal capital is maintained in a corporation, many states require that purchasers pay at least the par value for a share of stock initially purchased from a corporation. To minimize the amount of assets that owners must maintain in the business, many corporations issue stock with very low par values, often $1 or less. Therefore, *legal capital* as defined by par value has come to have very little relevance to investors or creditors. As a result, many states allow corporations to issue no-par stock.

Stated Value

No-par stock may have a stated value. Like par value, **stated value** is an arbitrary amount assigned by the board of directors to the stock. It also has little relevance to investors and creditors. Stock with a par value and stock with a stated value are accounted for exactly the same way. When stock has no par or stated value, accounting for it is slightly different. These accounting differences are illustrated later in this chapter.

Other Valuation Terminology

The price an investor must pay to purchase a share of stock is the **market value.** The sales price of a share of stock may be more or less than the par value. Another term analysts frequently associate with stock is *book value.* **Book value per share** is calculated by dividing total stockholders' equity (assets − liabilities) by the number of shares of stock owned by investors. Book value per share differs from market value per share because equity is measured in historical dollars and market value reflects investors' estimates of a company's current value.

Stock: Authorized, Issued, and Outstanding

As part of the regulatory function, states approve the maximum number of shares of stock corporations are legally permitted to issue. This maximum number is called **authorized stock.** Authorized stock that has been sold to the public is called **issued stock.** When a corporation buys back some of its issued stock from the public, the repurchased stock is called **treasury stock.** Treasury stock is still considered to be issued stock, but it is no longer outstanding. **Outstanding stock** (total issued stock minus treasury stock) is stock owned by investors outside the corporation. For example, assume a company that is authorized to issue 150 shares of stock issues 100 shares to investors, and then buys back 20 shares of treasury stock. There are 150 shares authorized, 100 shares issued, and 80 shares outstanding.

FOCUS ON INTERNATIONAL ISSUES

Considering the almost countless number of differences that could exist between U.S. GAAP and IFRS, it is not surprising that some of those that do exist relate to very specific issues. Consider the case of the timing of stock splits.

Assume a company that ends its fiscal year on December 31, 2011, declares a 2-for-1 stock split on January 15, 2012, before it has issued its 2011 annual report. Should the company apply the effects of the stock split retroactively to is 2011 financial statements, or begin showing the effects of the split on its 2012 statements? Under U.S. GAAP the split must be applied retroactively to the 2011 statements since they had not been issued at the time of the split. Under IFRS the 2011 statements would not show the effects of the split, but the 2012 statements would. By the way, an event that occurs between a company's fiscal year-end and the date its annual report is released is called a *subsequent event* by accountants.

Obviously no one can know every GAAP rule, much less all of the differences between GAAP and IFRS. This is why it is important to learn how to find answers to specific accounting questions as well as to develop an understanding of the basic accounting rules. Most important, if you are not sure you know the answer, do not assume you do.

Classes of Stock

The corporate charter defines the number of shares of stock authorized, the par value or stated value (if any), and the classes of stock that a corporation can issue. Most stock issued is either *common* or *preferred.*

Common Stock

All corporations issue **common stock.** Common stockholders bear the highest risk of losing their investment if a company is forced to liquidate. On the other hand, they reap the greatest rewards when a corporation prospers. Common stockholders generally enjoy several rights, including: (1) the right to buy and sell stock, (2) the right to share in the distribution of profits, (3) the right to share in the distribution of corporate assets in the case of liquidation, (4) the right to vote on significant matters that affect the corporate charter, and (5) the right to participate in the election of directors.

Preferred Stock

Many corporations issue **preferred stock** in addition to common stock. Holders of preferred stock receive certain privileges relative to holders of common stock. In exchange for special privileges in some areas, preferred stockholders give up rights in other areas. Preferred stockholders usually have no voting rights and the amount of their dividends is usually limited. Preferences granted to preferred stockholders include the following.

1. *Preference as to assets.* Preferred stock often has a liquidation value. In case of bankruptcy, preferred stockholders must be paid the liquidation value before any assets are distributed to common stockholders. However, preferred stockholder claims still fall behind creditor claims.

2. *Preference as to dividends.* Preferred shareholders are frequently guaranteed the right to receive dividends before common stockholders. The amount of the preferred dividend is normally stated on the stock certificate. It may be stated as a

dollar value (say, $5) per share or as a percentage of the par value. Most preferred stock has **cumulative dividends,** meaning that if a corporation is unable to pay the preferred dividend in any year, the dividend is not lost but begins to accumulate. Cumulative dividends that have not been paid are called **dividends in arrears.** When a company pays dividends, any preferred stock arrearages must be paid before any other dividends are paid. Noncumulative preferred stock is not often issued because preferred stock is much less attractive if missed dividends do not accumulate.

To illustrate the effects of preferred dividends, consider Dillion, Incorporated, which has the following shares of stock outstanding.

> Preferred stock, 4%, $10 par, 10,000 shares
> Common stock, $10 par, 20,000 shares

Assume the preferred stock dividend has not been paid for two years. If Dillion pays $22,000 in dividends, how much will each class of stock receive? It depends on whether the preferred stock is cumulative.

Allocation of Distribution for Cumulative Preferred Stock

	To Preferred	To Common
Dividends in arrears	$ 8,000	$ 0
Current year's dividends	4,000	10,000
Total distribution	$12,000	$10,000

Allocation of Distribution for Noncumulative Preferred Stock

	To Preferred	To Common
Dividends in arrears	$ 0	$ 0
Current year's dividends	4,000	18,000
Total distribution	$4,000	$18,000

The total annual dividend on the preferred stock is $4,000 (0.04 × $10 par × 10,000 shares). If the preferred stock is cumulative, the $8,000 in arrears must be paid first. Then $4,000 for the current year's dividend is paid next. The remaining $10,000 goes to common stockholders. If the preferred stock is noncumulative, the $8,000 of dividends from past periods is ignored. This year's $4,000 preferred dividend is paid first, with the remaining $18,000 going to common.

Other features of preferred stock may include the right to participate in distributions beyond the established amount of the preferred dividend, the right to convert preferred stock to common stock or to bonds, and the potential for having the preferred stock called (repurchased) by the corporation. Detailed discussion of these topics is left to more advanced courses. Exhibit 8.3 indicates that roughly 25 percent of U.S. companies have preferred shares outstanding.

EXHIBIT 8.3

Presence of Preferred Stock in the Capital Structure of U.S. Companies

With preferred stock
25%

Without preferred stock
75%

Data source: AICPA, Accounting Trends and Techniques, 2006.

ACCOUNTING FOR STOCK TRANSACTIONS ON THE DAY OF ISSUE

Explain how to account for different types of stock issued by corporations.

Issuing stock with a par or stated value is accounted for differently from issuing no-par stock. For stock with either a par or stated value, the total amount acquired from the owners is divided between two separate equity accounts. The amount of the par or stated value is recorded in the stock account. Any amount received above the par or stated value is recorded in an account called **Paid-in Capital in Excess of Par** (or **Stated**) **Value**.

Issuing Par Value Stock

To illustrate the issue of common stock with a par value, assume that Nelson Incorporated is authorized to issue 250 shares of common stock. During 2012, Nelson issued 100 shares of $10 par common stock for $22 per share. The event increases assets and stockholders' equity by $2,200 ($22 × 100 shares). The increase in stockholders' equity is divided into two parts, $1,000 of par value ($10 per share × 100 shares) and $1,200 ($2,200 − $1,000) received in excess of par value. The income statement is not affected. The $2,200 cash inflow is reported in the financing activities section of the statement of cash flows. The effects on the financial statements follow.

Assets	=	Liab.	+	Equity			Rev.	−	Exp.	=	Net Inc.	Cash Flow
Cash	=			Com. Stk.	+	PIC in Excess						
2,200	=	NA	+	1,000	+	1,200	NA	−	NA	=	NA	2,200 FA

The *legal capital* of the corporation is $1,000, the total par value of the issued common stock. The number of shares issued can be easily verified by dividing the total amount in the common stock account by the par value ($1,000 ÷ $10 = 100 shares).

Stock Classification

Assume Nelson Incorporated obtains authorization to issue 400 shares of Class B, $20 par value common stock. The company issues 150 shares of this stock at $25 per share. The event increases assets and stockholders' equity by $3,750 ($25 × 150 shares). The increase in stockholders' equity is divided into two parts, $3,000 of par value ($20 per share × 150 shares) and $750 ($3,750 − $3,000) received in excess of par value. The income statement is not affected. The $3,750 cash inflow is reported in the financing activities section of the statement of cash flows. The effects on the financial statements follow.

Assets	=	Liab.	+	Equity			Rev.	−	Exp.	=	Net Inc.	Cash Flow
Cash	=			Com. Stk.	+	PIC in Excess						
3,750	=	NA	+	3,000	+	750	NA	−	NA	=	NA	3,750 FA

As the preceding event suggests, companies can issue numerous classes of common stock. The specific rights and privileges for each class are described in the individual stock certificates.

Stock Issued at Stated Value

Assume Nelson is authorized to issue 300 shares of a third class of stock, 7 percent cumulative preferred stock with a stated value of $10 per share. Nelson issued 100 shares of the preferred stock at a price of $22 per share. The effects on the financial statements are identical to those described for the issue of the $10 par value common stock.

Assets	=	Liab.	+		Equity			Rev.	−	Exp.	=	Net Inc.		Cash Flow	
Cash	=			Pfd. Stk.	+	PIC in Excess									
2,200	=	NA	+	1,000	+	1,200		NA	−	NA	=	NA		2,200	FA

Stock Issued with No Par Value

Assume that Nelson Incorporated is authorized to issue 150 shares of a fourth class of stock. This stock is no-par common stock. Nelson issues 100 shares of this no-par stock at $22 per share. The entire amount received ($22 × 100 = $2,200) is recorded in the stock account. The effects on the financial statements follow.

Assets	=	Liab.	+		Equity			Rev.	−	Exp.	=	Net Inc.		Cash Flow	
Cash	=			Com. Stk.	+	PIC in Excess									
2,200	=	NA	+	2,200	+	NA		NA	−	NA	=	NA		2,200	FA

Financial Statement Presentation

Exhibit 8.4 displays Nelson Incorporated's balance sheet after the four stock issuances described above. The exhibit assumes that Nelson earned and retained $5,000 of cash income during 2012. The stock accounts are presented first, followed by the paid-in capital in excess of par (or stated) value accounts. A wide variety of reporting formats is used in practice. For example, another popular format is to group accounts by stock class, with the paid-in capital in excess accounts listed with their associated stock accounts. Alternatively, many companies combine the different classes of stock into a single amount and provide the detailed information in footnotes to the financial statements.

EXHIBIT 8.4

NELSON INCORPORATED
Balance Sheet
As of December 31, 2012

Assets	
Cash	$15,350
Stockholders' equity	
Preferred stock, $10 stated value, 7% cumulative, 300 shares authorized, 100 issued and outstanding	$ 1,000
Common stock, $10 par value, 250 shares authorized, 100 issued and outstanding	1,000
Common stock, class B, $20 par value, 400 shares authorized, 150 issued and outstanding	3,000
Common stock, no par, 150 shares authorized, 100 issued and outstanding	2,200
Paid-in capital in excess of stated value—preferred	1,200
Paid-in capital in excess of par value—common	1,200
Paid-in capital in excess of par value—class B common	750
Total paid-in capital	10,350
Retained earnings	5,000
Total stockholders' equity	$15,350

STOCKHOLDERS' EQUITY TRANSACTIONS AFTER THE DAY OF ISSUE

Treasury Stock

Show how treasury stock transactions affect a company's financial statements.

When a company buys its own stock, the stock purchased is called *treasury stock.* Why would a company buy its own stock? Common reasons include (1) to have stock available to give employees pursuant to stock option plans, (2) to accumulate stock in preparation for a merger or business combination, (3) to reduce the number of shares outstanding in order to increase earnings per share, (4) to keep the price of the stock high when it appears to be falling, and (5) to avoid a hostile takeover (removing shares from the open market reduces the opportunity for outsiders to obtain enough voting shares to gain control of the company).

Conceptually, purchasing treasury stock is the reverse of issuing stock. When a business issues stock, the assets and equity of the business increase. When a business buys treasury stock, the assets and equity of the business decrease. To illustrate, return to the Nelson Incorporated example. Assume that in 2013 Nelson paid $20 per share to buy back 50 shares of the $10 par value common stock that it originally issued at $22 per share. The purchase of treasury stock is an asset use transaction. Assets and stockholders' equity decrease by the cost of the purchase ($20 × 50 shares = $1,000). The income statement is not affected. The cash outflow is reported in the financing activities section of the statement of cash flows. The effects on the financial statements follow.

Assets	=	Liab.	+	Equity			Rev.	–	Exp.	=	Net Inc.	Cash Flow
Cash	=			Other Equity Accts.	–	Treasury Stk.						
(1,000)	=	NA	+	NA	–	1,000	NA	–	NA	=	NA	(1,000) FA

The Treasury Stock account is a contra equity account. It is deducted from the other equity accounts in determining total stockholders' equity. In this example, the Treasury Stock account contains the full amount paid ($1,000). The original issue price and the par value of the stock have no effect on the Treasury Stock account. Recognizing the full amount paid in the treasury stock account is called the **cost method of accounting for treasury stock** transactions. Although other methods could be used, the cost method is the most common.

Assume Nelson reissues 30 shares of treasury stock at a price of $25 per share. As with any other stock issue, the sale of treasury stock is an asset source transaction. In this case, assets and stockholders' equity increase by $750 ($25 × 30 shares). The income statement is not affected. The cash inflow is reported in the financing activities section of the statement of cash flows. The effects on the financial statements follow.

Assets	=	Liab.	+	Equity					Rev.	–	Exp.	=	Net Inc.	Cash Flow
Cash	=			Other Equity Accounts	–	Treasury Stock	+	PIC from Treasury Stk.						
750	=	NA	+	NA	–	(600)	+	150	NA	–	NA	=	NA	750 FA

The decrease in the Treasury Stock account increases stockholders' equity. The $150 difference between the cost of the treasury stock ($20 per share × 30 shares = $600) and the sales price ($750) is *not* reported as a gain. The sale of treasury stock is a capital acquisition, not a revenue transaction. The $150 is additional paid-in capital. *Corporations do not recognize gains or losses on the sale of treasury stock.*

After selling 30 shares of treasury stock, 20 shares remain in Nelson's possession. These shares cost $20 each, so the balance in the Treasury Stock account is now $400 ($20 × 20 shares). Treasury stock is reported on the balance sheet directly below retained earnings. Although this placement suggests that treasury stock reduces retained earnings, the reduction actually applies to the entire stockholders' equity section. Exhibit 8.5 on page 302 shows the presentation of treasury stock in the balance sheet.

✓ CHECK YOURSELF 8.2

On January 1, 2012, Janell Company's Common Stock account balance was $20,000. On April 1, 2012, Janell paid $12,000 cash to purchase some of its own stock. Janell resold this stock on October 1, 2012, for $14,500. What is the effect on the company's cash and stockholders' equity from both the April 1 purchase and the October 1 resale of the stock?

Answer   The April 1 purchase would reduce both cash and stockholders' equity by $12,000. The treasury stock transaction represents a return of invested capital to those owners who sold stock back to the company.

The sale of the treasury stock on October 1 would increase both cash and stockholders' equity by $14,500. The difference between the sales price of the treasury stock and its cost ($14,500 − $12,000) represents additional paid-in capital from treasury stock transactions. The stockholders' equity section of the balance sheet would include Common Stock, $20,000, and Additional Paid-in Capital from Treasury Stock Transactions, $2,500.

Cash Dividend

Cash dividends are affected by three significant dates: *the declaration date, the date of record,* and *the payment date.* Assume that on October 15, 2013, the board of Nelson Incorporated declared a 7% cash dividend on the 100 outstanding shares of its $10 stated value preferred stock. The dividend will be paid to stockholders of record as of November 15, 2013. The cash payment will be made on December 15, 2013.

Explain the effects of declaring and paying cash dividends on a company's financial statements.

Declaration Date

Although corporations are not required to declare dividends, they are legally obligated to pay dividends once they have been declared. They must recognize a liability on the **declaration date** (in this case, October 15, 2013). The increase in liabilities is accompanied by a decrease in retained earnings. The income statement and statement of cash flows are not affected. The effects on the financial statements of *declaring* the $70 (0.07 × $10 × 100 shares) dividend follow.

Assets	=	Liab.	+		Equity			Rev.	−	Exp.	=	Net Inc.	Cash Flow
Cash	=	Div. Pay.	+	Com. Stk.	+	Ret. Earn.							
NA	=	70	+	NA	+	(70)		NA	−	NA	=	NA	NA

Date of Record

Cash dividends are paid to investors who owned the preferred stock on the **date of record** (in this case November 15, 2013). Any stock sold after the date of record but

REALITY BYTES

As you have learned, dividends, unlike interest on bonds, do not have to be paid. In fact, a company's board of directors must vote to pay dividends before they can be paid. Even so, once a company establishes a practice of paying a dividend of a given amount each period, usually quarterly, the company is reluctant to not pay the dividend. Furthermore, it is usually a significant news event when a company decides to increase the amount of its regular dividend.

When times are bad, however, dividends are often reduced, or eliminated entirely, as a quick way to conserve the company's cash. This occurred often as a result of the economic downturn of 2008. An article in the Feburary 28, 2009, edition of *The Wall Street Journal* listed ten large companies who had recently reduced or eliminated their common stock dividend. The companies named were: Blackstone Group, CBS, Citigroup, Dow Chemical, General Electric, JP Morgan Chase, Motorola, New York Times, Pfizer, and Textron. The article also noted that for the month of January 2009, dividends paid by companies in the S&P 500 Index were 24 percent lower than they had been in January 2008.

before the payment date (in this case December 15, 2013) is traded **ex-dividend,** meaning the buyer will not receive the upcoming dividend. The date of record is merely a cutoff date. It does not affect the financial statements.

Payment Date

Nelson actually paid the cash dividend on the **payment date.** This event has the same effect as paying any other liability. Assets (cash) and liabilities (dividends payable) both decrease. The income statement is not affected. The cash outflow is reported in the financing activities section of the statement of cash flows. The effects of the cash payment on the financial statements follow.

Assets	=	Liab.	+		Equity			Rev.	−	Exp.	=	Net Inc.	Cash Flow	
Cash	=	Div. Pay.	+	Com. Stk.	+	Ret. Earn.								
(70)	=	(70)	+	NA	+	NA		NA	−	NA	=	NA	(70)	FA

Stock Dividend

LO 7

Explain the effects of stock dividends and stock splits on a company's financial statements.

Dividends are not always paid in cash. Companies sometimes choose to issue **stock dividends,** wherein they distribute additional shares of stock to the stockholders. To illustrate, assume that Nelson Incorporated decided to issue a 10 percent stock dividend on its class B, $20 par value common stock. Because dividends apply to outstanding shares only, Nelson will issue 15 (150 outstanding shares × 0.10) additional shares of class B stock.

Assume the new shares are distributed when the market value of the stock is $30 per share. As a result of the stock dividend, Nelson will transfer $450 ($30 × 15 new shares) from retained earnings to paid-in capital.[2] The stock dividend is an equity exchange

---

[2]The accounting here applies to small stock dividends. Accounting for large stock dividends is explained in a more advanced course.

transaction. The income statement and statement of cash flows are not affected. The effects of the stock dividend on the financial statements follow.

Assets	=	Liab.	+	Equity							Rev.	−	Exp.	=	Net Inc.	Cash Flow
				Com. Stk.	+	PIC in Excess	+	Ret. Earn.								
NA	=	NA	+	300	+	150	+	(450)			NA	−	NA	=	NA	NA

Stock dividends have no effect on assets. They merely increase the number of shares of stock outstanding. Because a greater number of shares represents the same ownership interest in the same amount of assets, the market value per share of a company's stock normally declines when a stock dividend is distributed. A lower market price makes the stock more affordable and may increase demand for the stock, which benefits both the company and its stockholders.

Stock Split

A corporation may also reduce the market price of its stock through a **stock split.** A stock split replaces existing shares with a greater number of new shares. Any par or stated value of the stock is proportionately reduced to reflect the new number of shares outstanding. For example, assume Nelson Incorporated declared a 2-for-1 stock split on the 165 outstanding shares (150 originally issued + 15 shares distributed in a stock dividend) of its $20 par value, class B common stock. Nelson notes in the accounting records that the 165 old $20 par shares are replaced with 330 new $10 par shares. Investors who owned the 165 shares of old common stock would now own 330 shares of the new common stock.

Stock splits have no effect on the dollar amounts of assets, liabilities, and stockholders' equity. They only affect the number of shares of stock outstanding. In Nelson's case, the ownership interest that was previously represented by 165 shares of stock is now represented by 330 shares. Because twice as many shares now represent the same ownership interest, the market value per share should be one-half as much as it was prior to the split. However, as with a stock dividend, the lower market price will probably stimulate demand for the stock. As a result, doubling the number of shares will likely reduce the market price to slightly more than one-half of the pre-split value. For example, if the stock were selling for $30 per share before the 2-for-1 split, it might sell for $15.50 after the split.

Appropriation of Retained Earnings

The board of directors may restrict the amount of retained earnings available to distribute as dividends. The restriction may be required by credit agreements, or it may be discretionary. A retained earnings restriction, often called an *appropriation,* is an equity exchange event. It transfers a portion of existing retained earnings to **Appropriated Retained Earnings.** Total retained earnings remains unchanged. To illustrate, assume that Nelson appropriates $1,000 of retained earnings for future expansion. The income statement and the statement of cash flows are not affected. The effects on the financial statements of appropriating $1,000 of retained earnings follow.

Show how the appropriation of retained earnings affects financial statements.

Assets	=	Liab.	+	Equity							Rev.	−	Exp.	=	Net Inc.	Cash Flow
				Com. Stk.	+	Ret. Earn.	+	App. Ret. Earn.								
NA	=	NA	+	NA	+	(1,000)	+	1,000			NA	−	NA	=	NA	NA

FINANCIAL STATEMENT PRESENTATION

The 2012 and 2013 events for Nelson Incorporated are summarized below. Events 1 through 8 are cash transactions. The results of the 2012 transactions (nos. 1–5) are reflected in Exhibit 8.4. The results of the 2013 transactions (nos. 6–9) are shown in Exhibit 8.5.

1. Issued 100 shares of $10 par value common stock at a market price of $22 per share.
2. Issued 150 shares of class B, $20 par value common stock at a market price of $25 per share.
3. Issued 100 shares of $10 stated value, 7 percent cumulative preferred stock at a market price of $22 per share.
4. Issued 100 shares of no-par common stock at a market price of $22 per share.
5. Earned and retained $5,000 cash from operations.
6. Purchased 50 shares of $10 par value common stock as treasury stock at a market price of $20 per share.
7. Sold 30 shares of treasury stock at a market price of $25 per share.
8. Declared and paid a $70 cash dividend on the preferred stock.
9. Issued a 10 percent stock dividend on the 150 shares of outstanding class B, $20 par value common stock (15 additional shares). The additional shares were issued when the market price of the stock was $30 per share. There are 165 (150 + 15) class B common shares outstanding after the stock dividend.
10. Issued a 2-for-1 stock split on the 165 shares of class B, $20 par value common stock. After this transaction, there are 330 shares outstanding of the class B common stock with a $10 par value.
11. Appropriated $1,000 of retained earnings.

EXHIBIT 8.5

NELSON INCORPORATED
Balance Sheet
As of December 31, 2013

Assets		
Cash		**$21,030**
Stockholders' equity		
Preferred stock, $10 stated value, 7% cumulative,		
300 shares authorized, 100 issued and outstanding	$1,000	
Common stock, $10 par value, 250 shares authorized,		
100 issued, and 80 outstanding	1,000	
Common stock, class B, $10 par, 800 shares authorized,		
330 issued and outstanding	3,300	
Common stock, no par, 150 shares authorized,		
100 issued and outstanding	2,200	
Paid-in capital in excess of stated value—preferred	1,200	
Paid-in capital in excess of par value—common	1,200	
Paid-in capital in excess of par value—class B common	900	
Paid-in capital in excess of cost of treasury stock	150	
Total paid-in capital		$10,950
Retained earnings		
Appropriated	1,000	
Unappropriated	9,480	
Total retained earnings		10,480
Less: Treasury stock, 20 shares @ $20 per share		(400)
Total stockholders' equity		**$21,030**

The illustration assumes that Nelson earned net income of $6,000 in 2013. The ending retained earnings balance is determined as follows: Beginning Balance $5,000 − $70 Cash Dividend − $450 Stock Dividend + $6,000 Net Income = $10,480.

INVESTING IN CAPITAL STOCK

Stockholders may benefit in two ways when a company generates earnings. The company may distribute the earnings directly to the stockholders in the form of dividends. Alternatively, the company may retain some or all of the earnings to finance growth and increase its potential for future earnings. If the company retains earnings, the market value of its stock should increase to reflect its greater earnings prospects. How can analysts use financial reporting to help assess the potential for dividend payments or growth in market value?

Explain some uses of accounting information in making stock investment decisions.

Receiving Dividends

Is a company likely to pay dividends in the future? The financial statements can help answer this question. They show if dividends were paid in the past. Companies with a history of paying dividends usually continue to pay dividends. Also, to pay dividends in the future, a company must have sufficient cash and retained earnings. These amounts are reported on the balance sheet and the statement of cash flows.

Increasing the Price of Stock

Is the market value (price) of a company's stock likely to increase? Increases in a company's stock price occur when investors believe the company's earnings will grow. Financial statements provide information that is useful in predicting the prospects for earnings growth. Here also, a company's earnings history is an indicator of its growth potential. However, because published financial statements report historical information, investors must recognize their limitations. Investors want to know about the future. Stock prices are therefore influenced more by forecasts than by history.

For example:

■ On April 15, 2009, Abbott Laboratories, Inc., announced that profits for the first quarter of its 2009 fiscal year were 53 percent higher than profits in the same quarter of 2008. In reaction to this news, the price of Abbott's stock *fell* by almost 5 percent. Why did the stock market respond in this way? Because company's revenues for the quarter were less than had been expected by analysts who follow the company.

■ On May 18, 2009, Lowe's Companies, Inc., announced first quarter earnings were $0.32 per share, which was 22 percent lower than for the same period of the previous year. The stock market's reaction to the news was to *increase* the price of Lowe's stock by 8 percent. The market reacted this way because the analysts were expecting earnings per share for the first quarter to be only $0.25 per share.

In each case, investors reacted to the potential for earnings growth rather than the historical earnings reports. Because investors find forecasted statements more relevant to decision making than historical financial statements, most companies provide forecasts in addition to historical financial statements.

The value of a company's stock is also influenced by nonfinancial information that financial statements cannot provide. For example, suppose ExxonMobil announced in the middle of its fiscal year that it had just discovered substantial oil reserves on property to which it held drilling rights. Consider the following questions:

■ What would happen to the price of ExxonMobil's stock on the day of the announcement?

■ What would happen to ExxonMobil's financial statements on that day?

The price of ExxonMobil's stock would almost certainly increase as soon as the discovery was made public. However, nothing would happen to its financial statements on that day. There would probably be very little effect on its financial statements for that year. Only after the company begins to develop the oil field and sell the oil will its financial statements reflect the discovery. Changes in financial statements tend to lag behind the announcements companies make regarding their earnings potential.

Stock prices are also affected by general economic conditions and consumer confidence as well as the performance measures reported in financial statements. For example, the stock prices of virtually all companies declined sharply immediately after the September 11, 2001, terrorist attacks on the World Trade Center and the Pentagon. Historically based financial statements are of little benefit in predicting general economic conditions or changes in consumer confidence.

Exercising Control through Stock Ownership

The more influence an investor has over the operations of a company, the more the investor can benefit from owning stock in the company. For example, consider a power company that needs coal to produce electricity. The power company may purchase some common stock in a coal mining company to ensure a stable supply of coal. What percentage of the mining company's stock must the power company acquire to exercise significant influence over the mining company? The answer depends on how many investors own stock in the mining company and how the number of shares is distributed among the stockholders.

The greater its number of stockholders, the more *widely held* a company is. If stock ownership is concentrated in the hands of a few persons, a company is *closely held.* Widely held companies can generally be controlled with smaller percentages of ownership than closely held companies. Consider a company in which no existing investor owns more than 1 percent of the voting stock. A new investor who acquires a 5 percent interest would immediately become, by far, the largest shareholder and would likely be able to significantly influence board decisions. In contrast, consider a closely held company in which one current shareholder owns 51 percent of the company's stock. Even if another investor acquired the remaining 49 percent of the company, that investor could not control the company.

Financial statements contain some, but not all, of the information needed to help an investor determine ownership levels necessary to permit control. For example, the financial statements disclose the total number of shares of stock outstanding, but they normally contain little information about the number of shareholders and even less information about any relationships between shareholders. Relationships between shareholders are critically important because related shareholders, whether bound by family or business interests, might exercise control by voting as a block. For publicly traded companies, information about the number of shareholders and the identity of some large shareholders is disclosed in reports filed with the Securities and Exchange Commission.

 A Look Back

Starting a business requires obtaining financing; it takes money to make money. Although some money may be borrowed, lenders are unlikely to make loans to businesses that lack some degree of owner financing. Equity financing is therefore critical to virtually all profit-oriented businesses. This chapter has examined some of the issues related to accounting for equity transactions.

The idea that a business must obtain financing from its owners was one of the first events presented in this textbook. This chapter discussed the advantages and disadvantages of organizing a business as a sole proprietorship versus a partnership versus a corporation. These advantages and disadvantages include the following.

1. *Double taxation*—Income of corporations is subject to double taxation, but that of proprietorships and partnerships is not.

2. *Regulation*—Corporations are subject to more regulation than are proprietorships and partnerships.

3. *Limited liability*—An investor's personal assets are not at risk as a result of owning corporate securities. The investor's liability is limited to the amount of the investment. In general proprietorships and partnerships do not offer limited liability. However, laws in some states permit the formation of limited liability companies which operate like proprietorships and partnerships yet place some limits on the personal liability of their owners.

4. *Continuity*—Proprietorships and partnerships dissolve when one of the owners leaves the business. Corporations are separate legal entities that continue to exist regardless of changes in ownership.

5. *Transferability*—Ownership interests in corporations are easier to transfer than those of proprietorships or partnerships.

6. *Management structure*—Corporations are more likely to have independent professional managers than are proprietorships or partnerships.

7. *Ability to raise capital*—Because they can be owned by millions of investors, corporations have the opportunity to raise more capital than proprietorships or partnerships.

Corporations issue different classes of common stock and preferred stock as evidence of ownership interests. In general, *common stock* provides the widest range of privileges including the right to vote and participate in earnings. *Preferred stockholders* usually give up the right to vote in exchange for preferences such as the right to receive dividends or assets upon liquidation before common stockholders. Stock may have a *par value* or *stated value,* which relates to legal requirements governing the amount of capital that must be maintained in the corporation. Corporations may also issue *no-par stock,* avoiding some of the legal requirements that pertain to par or stated value stock.

Stock that a company issues and then repurchases is called *treasury stock.* Purchasing treasury stock reduces total assets and stockholders' equity. Reselling treasury stock represents a capital acquisition. The difference between the reissue price and the cost of the treasury stock is recorded directly in the equity accounts. Treasury stock transactions do not result in gains or losses on the income statement.

Companies may issue *stock splits* or *stock dividends.* These transactions increase the number of shares of stock without changing the net assets of a company. The per share market value usually drops when a company issues stock splits or dividends.

A Look Forward

Financial statement analysis is so important that Chapter 9 is devoted solely to a detailed discussion of this subject. The chapter covers vertical analysis (analyzing relationships within a specific statement) and horizontal analysis (analyzing relationships across accounting periods). Finally, the chapter discusses limitations associated with financial statement analysis.

A step-by-step audio-narrated series of slides is provided on the text website at www.mhhe.com/edmondssurvey3e.

SELF-STUDY REVIEW PROBLEM

Edwards Inc. experienced the following events:

1. Issued common stock for cash.
2. Declared a cash dividend.
3. Issued noncumulative preferred stock for cash.
4. Appropriated retained earnings.
5. Distributed a stock dividend.
6. Paid cash to purchase treasury stock.
7. Distributed a 2-for-1 stock split.
8. Issued cumulative preferred stock for cash.
9. Paid a cash dividend that had previously been declared.
10. Sold treasury stock for cash at a higher amount than the cost of the treasury stock.

Required

Show the effect of each event on the elements of the financial statements using a horizontal statements model like the one shown here. Use + for increase, − for decrease, and NA for not affected. In the Cash Flow column, indicate whether the item is an operating activity (OA), investing activity (IA), or a financing activity (FA). The first transaction is entered as an example.

Event	Assets	=	Liab.	+	Equity	Rev.	−	Exp.	=	Net Inc.	Cash Flow
1	+		NA		+	NA		NA		NA	+ FA

Solution to Self-Study Review Problem

Event	Assets	=	Liab.	+	Equity	Rev.	−	Exp.	=	Net Inc.	Cash Flow
1	+		NA		+	NA		NA		NA	+ FA
2	NA		+		−	NA		NA		NA	NA
3	+		NA		+	NA		NA		NA	+ FA
4	NA		NA		− +	NA		NA		NA	NA
5	NA		NA		− +	NA		NA		NA	NA
6	−		NA		−	NA		NA		NA	− FA
7	NA		NA		NA	NA		NA		NA	NA
8	+		NA		+	NA		NA		NA	+ FA
9	−		−		NA	NA		NA		NA	− FA
10	+		NA		+	NA		NA		NA	+ FA

KEY TERMS

QUESTIONS

1. What are the three major forms of business organizations? Describe each.

2. How are sole proprietorships formed?

3. Discuss the purpose of a partnership agreement. Is such an agreement necessary for partnership formation?

4. What is meant by the phrase *separate legal entity?* To which type of business organization does it apply?

5. What is the purpose of the articles of incorporation? What information do they provide?

6. What is the function of the stock certificate?

7. What prompted Congress to pass the Securities Act of 1933 and the Securities Exchange Act of 1934? What is the purpose of these laws?

8. What are the advantages and disadvantages of the corporate form of business organization?

9. What is a limited liability company? Discuss its advantages and disadvantages.

10. How does the term *double taxation* apply to corporations? Give an example of double taxation.

11. What is the difference between contributed capital and retained earnings for a corporation?

12. What are the similarities and differences in the equity structure of a sole proprietorship, a partnership, and a corporation?

13. Why is it easier for a corporation to raise large amounts of capital than it is for a partnership?

14. What is the meaning of each of the following terms with respect to the corporate form of organization?
    (a) Legal capital
    (b) Par value of stock
    (c) Stated value of stock
    (d) Market value of stock
    (e) Book value of stock
    (f) Authorized shares of stock
    (g) Issued stock
    (h) Outstanding stock
    (i) Treasury stock
    (j) Common stock
    (k) Preferred stock
    (l) Dividends

15. What is the difference between cumulative preferred stock and noncumulative preferred stock?

16. What is no-par stock? How is it recorded in the accounting records?

17. Assume that Best Co. has issued and outstanding 1,000 shares of $100 par value, 10 percent, cumulative preferred stock. What is the dividend per share? If the preferred dividend is two years in arrears, what total amount of dividends must be paid before the common shareholders can receive any dividends?

18. If Best Co. issued 10,000 shares of $20 par value common stock for $30 per share, what amount is added to the Common Stock account? What amount of cash is received?

19. What is the difference between par value stock and stated value stock?

20. Why might a company repurchase its own stock?

21. What effect does the purchase of treasury stock have on the equity of a company?

22. Assume that Day Company repurchased 1,000 of its own shares for $30 per share and sold the shares two weeks later for $35 per share. What is the amount of gain on the sale? How is it reported on the balance sheet? What type of account is treasury stock?

23. What is the importance of the declaration date, record date, and payment date in conjunction with corporate dividends?

24. What is the difference between a stock dividend and a stock split?

25. Why would a company choose to distribute a stock dividend instead of a cash dividend?

26. What is the primary reason that a company would declare a stock split?

27. If Best Co. had 10,000 shares of $20 par value common stock outstanding and declared a 5-for-1 stock split, how many shares would then be outstanding and what would be their par value after the split?

28. When a company appropriates retained earnings, does the company set aside cash for a specific use? Explain.

29. What is the largest source of financing for most U.S. businesses?

30. What is meant by *equity financing?* What is meant by *debt financing?*

31. What is a widely held corporation? What is a closely held corporation?

32. What are some reasons that a corporation might not pay dividends?

MULTIPLE-CHOICE QUESTIONS

Multiple-choice questions are provided on the text website at www.mhhe.com/edmondssurvey3e

EXERCISES

All applicable Exercises are available with McGraw-Hill's *Connect Accounting.*

LO 1, 2

Exercise 8-1 *Effect of accounting events on the financial statements of a sole proprietorship*

A sole proprietorship was started on January 1, 2012, when it received $60,000 cash from Mark Pruitt, the owner. During 2012, the company earned $40,000 in cash revenues and paid $19,300 in cash expenses. Pruitt withdrew $5,000 cash from the business during 2012.

Required

Prepare the income statement, capital statement (statement of changes in equity), balance sheet, and statement of cash flows for Pruitt's 2012 fiscal year.

LO 1, 2

Exercise 8-2 *Effect of accounting events on the financial statements of a partnership*

Justin Harris and Paul Berryhill started the HB partnership on January 1, 2012. The business acquired $56,000 cash from Harris and $84,000 from Berryhill. During 2012, the partnership earned $65,000 in cash revenues and paid $32,000 for cash expenses. Harris withdrew $2,000 cash from the business, and Berryhill withdrew $3,000 cash. The net income was allocated to the capital accounts of the two partners in proportion to the amounts of their original investments in the business.

Required

Prepare the income statement, capital statement, balance sheet, and statement of cash flows for the HB partnership for the 2012 fiscal year.

LO 1, 2

Exercise 8-3 *Effect of accounting events on the financial statements of a corporation*

Morris Corporation was started with the issue of 5,000 shares of $10 par common stock for cash on January 1, 2012. The stock was issued at a market price of $18 per share. During 2012, the company earned $63,000 in cash revenues and paid $41,000 for cash expenses. Also, a $4,000 cash dividend was paid to the stockholders.

Required

Prepare the income statement, statement of changes in stockholders' equity, balance sheet, and statement of cash flows for Morris Corporation's 2012 fiscal year.

Exercise 8-4   *Effect of issuing common stock on the balance sheet*

Newly formed Home Medical Corporation has 100,000 shares of $5 par common stock authorized. On March 1, 2012, Home Medical issued 10,000 shares of the stock for $12 per share. On May 2 the company issued an additional 20,000 shares for $20 per share. Home Medical was not affected by other events during 2012.

Required

a. Record the transactions in a horizontal statements model like the following one. In the Cash Flow column, indicate whether the item is an operating activity (OA), investing activity (IA), or financing activity (FA). Use NA to indicate that an element was not affected by the event.

Assets	=	Liab.	+		Equity			Rev.	−	Exp.	=	Net Inc.		Cash Flow
Cash	=		+	Com. Stk.	+	Paid-in Excess								

b. Determine the amount Home Medical would report for common stock on the December 31, 2012, balance sheet.

c. Determine the amount Home Medical would report for paid-in capital in excess of par.

d. What is the total amount of capital contributed by the owners?

e. What amount of total assets would Home Medical report on the December 31, 2012, balance sheet?

Exercise 8-5   *Recording and reporting common and preferred stock transactions*

Rainoy, Inc., was organized on June 5, 2012. It was authorized to issue 400,000 shares of $10 par common stock and 50,000 shares of 4 percent cumulative class A preferred stock. The class A stock had a stated value of $25 per share. The following stock transactions pertain to Rainoy, Inc.

1. Issued 20,000 shares of common stock for $15 per share.
2. Issued 10,000 shares of the class A preferred stock for $30 per share.
3. Issued 50,000 shares of common stock for $18 per share.

Required

Prepare the stockholders' equity section of the balance sheet immediately after these transactions have been recognized.

Exercise 8-6   *Effect of no-par common and par preferred stock on the horizontal statements model*

Eaton Corporation issued 5,000 shares of no-par common stock for $20 per share. Eaton also issued 2,000 shares of $50 par, 6 percent noncumulative preferred stock at $60 per share.

Required

Record these events in a horizontal statements model like the following one. In the cash flow column, indicate whether the item is an operating activity (OA), investing activity (IA), or financing activity (FA). Use NA to indicate that an element was not affected by the event.

Assets	=		Equity				Rev.	−	Exp.	=	Net Inc.		Cash Flow
Cash	=	Pfd. Stk.	+	Com. Stk.	+	PIC in Excess							

Exercise 8-7   *Issuing stock for assets other than cash*

Kaylee Corporation was formed when it issued shares of common stock to two of its shareholders. Kaylee issued 5,000 shares of $10 par common stock to K. Breslin in exchange for $60,000 cash (the issue price was $12 per share). Kaylee also issued 2,500 shares of stock to T. Lindsay in exchange for a one-year-old delivery van on the same day. Lindsay had originally paid $35,000 for the van.

Required

a. What was the market value of the delivery van on the date of the stock issue?

b. Show the effect of the two stock issues on Kaylee's books in a horizontal statements model like the following one. In the Cash Flow column, indicate whether the item is an operating activity (OA), investing activity (IA), or financing activity (FA). Use NA to indicate that an element was not affected by the event.

Assets	=	Equity			Rev. − Exp. = Net Inc.	Cash Flow
Cash + Van	=	Com. Stk. + PIC in Excess				

LO 5

Exercise 8-8   *Treasury stock transactions*

Graves Corporation repurchased 2,000 shares of its own stock for $40 per share. The stock has a par of $10 per share. A month later Graves resold 1,200 shares of the treasury stock for $48 per share.

Required

What is the balance of the treasury stock account after these transactions are recognized?

LO 5

Exercise 8-9   *Recording and reporting treasury stock transactions*

The following information pertains to Smoot Corp. at January 1, 2012.

Common stock, $10 par, 10,000 shares authorized,	
2,000 shares issued and outstanding	$20,000
Paid-in capital in excess of par, common stock	15,000
Retained earnings	65,000

Smoot Corp. completed the following transactions during 2012:

1. Issued 1,000 shares of $10 par common stock for $28 per share.
2. Repurchased 200 shares of its own common stock for $25 per share.
3. Resold 50 shares of treasury stock for $26 per share.

Required

a. How many shares of common stock were outstanding at the end of the period?

b. How many shares of common stock had been issued at the end of the period?

c. Organize the transactions data in accounts under the accounting equation.

d. Prepare the stockholders' equity section of the balance sheet reflecting these transactions. Include the number of shares authorized, issued, and outstanding in the description of the common stock.

LO 6

Exercise 8-10   *Effect of cash dividends on financial statements*

On October 1, 2012, Smart Corporation declared a $60,000 cash dividend to be paid on December 30 to shareholders of record on November 20.

Required

Record the events occurring on October 1, November 20, and December 30 in a horizontal statements model like the following one. In the Cash Flow column, indicate whether the item is an operating activity (OA), investing activity (IA), or financing activity (FA).

Date	Assets = Liab. + Com. Stock + Ret. Earn.	Rev. − Exp. = Net Inc.	Cash Flow

Exercise 8-11 *Accounting for cumulative preferred dividends*   **LO 6**

When Polledo Corporation was organized in January 2012, it immediately issued 5,000 shares of $50 par, 5 percent, cumulative preferred stock and 10,000 shares of $10 par common stock. The company's earnings history is as follows: 2012, net loss of $15,000; 2013, net income of $60,000; 2014, net income of $95,000. The corporation did not pay a dividend in 2012.

Required

a. How much is the dividend arrearage as of January 1, 2013?

b. Assume that the board of directors declares a $40,000 cash dividend at the end of 2013 (remember that the 2012 and 2013 preferred dividends are due). How will the dividend be divided between the preferred and common stockholders?

Exercise 8-12 *Cash dividends for preferred and common shareholders*

B&S Corporation had the following stock issued and outstanding at January 1, 2012:

1. 100,000 shares of $5 par common stock.
2. 5,000 shares of $100 par, 5 percent, noncumulative preferred stock.

On May 10, B&S Corporation declared the annual cash dividend on its 5,000 shares of preferred stock and a $1 per share dividend for the common shareholders. The dividends will be paid on June 15 to the shareholders of record on May 30.

Required

Determine the total amount of dividends to be paid to the preferred shareholders and common shareholders.

Exercise 8-13 *Cash dividends: common and preferred stock*   **LO 6**

Varsity Corp. had the following stock issued and outstanding at January 1, 2012.

1. 200,000 shares of no-par common stock.
2. 10,000 shares of $100 par, 8 percent, cumulative preferred stock. (Dividends are in arrears for one year, 2011.)

On February 1, 2012, Varsity declared a $200,000 cash dividend to be paid March 31 to shareholders of record on March 10.

Required

What amount of dividends will be paid to the preferred shareholders versus the common shareholders?

Exercise 8-14 *Accounting for stock dividends*   **LO 7**

Rollins Corporation issued a 5 percent stock dividend on 10,000 shares of its $10 par common stock. At the time of the dividend, the market value of the stock was $14 per share.

Required

a. Compute the amount of the stock dividend.

b. Show the effects of the stock dividend on the financial statements using a horizontal statements model like the following one.

Assets	=	Liab.	+	Com. Stk.	+	PIC in Excess	+	Ret. Earn.	Rev.	−	Exp.	=	Net Inc.	Cash Flow

Exercise 8-15 *Determining the effects of stock splits on the accounting records*   **LO 7**

The market value of Coe Corporation's common stock had become excessively high. The stock was currently selling for $180 per share. To reduce the market price of the common stock, Coe declared a 2-for-1 stock split for the 300,000 outstanding shares of its $10 par common stock.

Required

a. How will Coe Corporation's books be affected by the stock split?
b. Determine the number of common shares outstanding and the par value after the split.
c. Explain how the market value of the stock will be affected by the stock split.

LO 9

Exercise 8-16   *Corporate announcements*

Super Drugs (one of the three largest drug makers) just reported that its 2012 third-quarter profits had increased substantially over its 2011 third-quarter profits. In addition to this announcement, the same day, Super Drugs also announced that the Food and Drug Administration had just denied approval of a new drug used to treat high blood pressure that Super Drugs developed. The FDA was concerned about potential side effects of the drug.

Required

Using the above information, answer the following questions.

a. What do you think will happen to the stock price of Super Drugs on the day these two announcements are made? Explain your answer.
b. How will the balance sheet be affected on that day by the above announcements?
c. How will the income statement be affected on that day by the above announcements?
d. How will the statement of cash flows be affected on that day by the above announcements?

PROBLEMS

All applicable Problems are available with McGraw-Hill's
Connect Accounting.

LO 1, 2

eXcel

CHECK FIGURES
a. Net Income: $5,500
b. Macy Calloway Capital: $25,400

Problem 8-17   *Effect of business structure on financial statements*

Calloway Company was started on January 1, 2012, when the owners invested $40,000 cash in the business. During 2012, the company earned cash revenues of $18,000 and incurred cash expenses of $12,500. The company also paid cash distributions of $3,000.

Required

Prepare the 2012 income statement, capital statement (statement of changes in equity), balance sheet, and statement of cash flows using each of the following assumptions. (Consider each assumption separately.)

a. Calloway is a sole proprietorship owned by Macy Calloway.
b. Calloway is a partnership with two partners, Macy Calloway and Artie Calloway. Macy Calloway invested $25,000 and Artie Calloway invested $15,000 of the $40,000 cash that was used to start the business. A. Calloway was expected to assume the vast majority of the responsibility for operating the business. The partnership agreement called for A. Calloway to receive 60 percent of the profits and M. Calloway to get the remaining 40 percent. With regard to the $3,000 distribution, A. Calloway withdrew $1,200 from the business and M. Calloway withdrew $1,800.
c. Calloway is a corporation. It issued 5,000 shares of $5 par common stock for $40,000 cash to start the business.

LO 4–6

eXcel

CHECK FIGURES
b. Preferred Stock, 2012: $50,000
c. Common Shares Outstanding, 2013: 19,500

Problem 8-18   *Recording and reporting stock transactions and cash dividends across two accounting cycles*

Davis Corporation was authorized to issue 100,000 shares of $10 par common stock and 50,000 shares of $50 par, 6 percent, cumulative preferred stock. Davis Corporation completed the following transactions during its first two years of operation.

2012

Jan. 2   Issued 5,000 shares of $10 par common stock for $28 per share.
      15   Issued 1,000 shares of $50 par preferred stock for $70 per share.

Feb. 14   Issued 15,000 shares of $10 par common stock for $30 per share.

Dec. 31   During the year, earned $170,000 of cash service revenue and paid $110,000 of cash operating expenses.

    31   Declared the cash dividend on outstanding shares of preferred stock for 2012. The dividend will be paid on January 31 to stockholders of record on January 15, 2013.

2013

Jan. 31   Paid the cash dividend declared on December 31, 2012.

Mar. 1   Issued 2,000 shares of $50 par preferred stock for $58 per share.

June 1   Purchased 500 shares of common stock as treasury stock at $43 per share.

Dec. 31   During the year, earned $210,000 of cash service revenue and paid $175,000 of cash operating expenses.

    31   Declared the dividend on the preferred stock and a $0.60 per share dividend on the common stock.

Required

a. Organize the transaction data in accounts under an accounting equation.

b. Prepare the stockholders' equity section of the balance sheet at December 31, 2012.

c. Prepare the balance sheet at December 31, 2013.

Problem 8-19   *Recording and reporting treasury stock transactions*

Midwest Corp. completed the following transactions in 2012, the first year of operation.

1. Issued 20,000 shares of $10 par common stock at par.

2. Issued 2,000 shares of $30 stated value preferred stock at $32 per share.

3. Purchased 500 shares of common stock as treasury stock for $15 per share.

4. Declared a 5 percent dividend on preferred stock.

5. Sold 300 shares of treasury stock for $18 per share.

6. Paid the cash dividend on preferred stock that was declared in Event 4.

7. Earned cash service revenue of $75,000 and incurred cash operating expenses of $42,000.

8. Appropriated $6,000 of retained earnings.

Required

a. Organize the transaction in accounts under an accounting equation.

b. Prepare the stockholders' equity section of the balance sheet as of December 31, 2012.

Problem 8-20   *Recording and reporting treasury stock transactions*

Boley Corporation reports the following information in its January 1, 2012, balance sheet:

Stockholders' equity	
Common stock, $10 par value,	
50,000 shares authorized, 30,000 shares issued and outstanding	$300,000
Paid-in capital in excess of par value	150,000
Retained earnings	100,000
Total stockholders' equity	$550,000

During 2012, Boley was affected by the following accounting events.

1. Purchased 1,000 shares of treasury stock at $18 per share.

2. Reissued 600 shares of treasury stock at $20 per share.

3. Earned $64,000 of cash service revenues.

4. Paid $38,000 of cash operating expenses.

Required

Prepare the stockholders' equity section of the year-end balance sheet.

LO 5, 6, 8

CHECK FIGURE
b. Total Paid-In Capital: $264,900

LO 5

CHECK FIGURES
Total Paid-In Capital: $451,200
Total Stockholders' Equity:
$570,000

Problem 8-21 *Recording and reporting stock dividends*

Chan Corp. completed the following transactions in 2012, the first year of operation.

1. Issued 20,000 shares of $20 par common stock for $30 per share.
2. Issued 5,000 shares of $50 par, 5 percent, preferred stock at $51 per share.
3. Paid the annual cash dividend to preferred shareholders.
4. Issued a 5 percent stock dividend on the common stock. The market value at the dividend declaration date was $40 per share.
5. Later that year, issued a 2-for-1 split on the 21,000 shares of outstanding common stock.
6. Earned $210,000 of cash service revenues and paid $140,000 of cash operating expenses.

Required

a. Record each of these events in a horizontal statements model like the following one. In the Cash Flow column, indicate whether the item is an operating activity (OA), investing activity (IA), or financing activity (FA). Use NA to indicate that an element is not affected by the event.

Assets = Liab. +	Equity						Rev. − Exp. = Net Inc.	Cash Flow
	Pfd. Stk. +	Com. Stk. +	PIC in Excess PS +	PIC in Excess CS +	Ret. Earn.			

b. Prepare the stockholders' equity section of the balance sheet at the end of 2012.

Problem 8-22 *Analyzing the stockholders' equity section of the balance sheet*

The stockholders' equity section of the balance sheet for Brawner Company at December 31, 2012, is as follows:

Stockholders' Equity		
Paid-in capital		
Preferred stock, ? par value, 6% cumulative, 50,000 shares authorized, 30,000 shares issued and outstanding	$300,000	
Common stock, $10 stated value, 150,000 shares authorized, 50,000 shares issued and ? outstanding	500,000	
Paid-in capital in excess of par—Preferred	30,000	
Paid-in capital in excess of stated value—Common	200,000	
Total paid-in capital		$1,030,000
Retained earnings		250,000
Treasury stock, 1,000 shares		(100,000)
Total stockholders' equity		$1,180,000

Note: The market value per share of the common stock is $25, and the market value per share of the preferred stock is $12.

Required

a. What is the par value per share of the preferred stock?
b. What is the dividend per share on the preferred stock?
c. What is the number of common stock shares outstanding?
d. What was the average issue price per share (price for which the stock was issued) of the common stock?
e. Explain the difference between the average issue price and the market price of the common stock.
f. If Brawner declared a 2-for-1 stock split on the common stock, how many shares would be outstanding after the split? What amount would be transferred from the retained earnings account because of the stock split? Theoretically, what would be the market price of the common stock immediately after the stock split?

Problem 8-23   *Different forms of business organization*

Shawn Bates was working to establish a business enterprise with four of his wealthy friends. Each of the five individuals would receive a 20 percent ownership interest in the company. A primary goal of establishing the enterprise was to minimize the amount of income taxes paid. Assume that the five investors are taxed at the rate of 15% on dividend income and 30% on all other income and that the corporate tax rate is 30 percent. Also assume that the new company is expected to earn $400,000 of cash income before taxes during its first year of operation. All earnings are expected to be immediately distributed to the owners.

Required

Calculate the amount of after-tax cash flow available to each investor if the business is established as a partnership versus a corporation. Write a memo explaining the advantages and disadvantages of these two forms of business organization. Explain why a limited liability company may be a better choice than either a partnership or a corporation.

Problem 8-24   *Effects of equity transactions on financial statements*

The following events were experienced by Abbot Inc.:

1. Issued cumulative preferred stock for cash.
2. Issued common stock for cash.
3. Distributed a 2-for-1 stock split on the common stock.
4. Issued noncumulative preferred stock for cash.
5. Appropriated retained earnings.
6. Sold treasury stock for an amount of cash that was more than the cost of the treasury stock.
7. Distributed a stock dividend.
8. Paid cash to purchase treasury stock.
9. Declared a cash dividend.
10. Paid the cash dividend declared in Event 9.

Required

Show the effect of each event on the elements of the financial statements using a horizontal statements model like the following one. Use + for increase, − for decrease, and NA for not affected. In the Cash Flow column, indicate whether the item is an operating activity (OA), investing activity (IA), or financing activity (FA). The first transaction is entered as an example.

Event No.	Assets	=	Liab.	+	Equity	Rev.	−	Exp.	=	Net Inc.	Cash Flow
1	+		NA		+	NA		NA		NA	+ FA

ANALYZE, THINK, COMMUNICATE

ATC 8-1   Business Applications Case   *Understanding real-world annual reports*

Use the **Target Corporation**'s annual report in Appendix B to answer the following questions.

Required

a. What is the par value per share of Target's stock?

b. How many shares of Target's common stock were *outstanding* as of January 31, 2010?

c. Target's annual report provides some details about the company's executive officers. How many are identified? What is their minimum, maximum, and average age? How many are females?

d. Target's balance sheet does not show a balance for treasury stock. Does this mean the company has not repurchased any of its own stock? Explain.

ATC 8-2   Group Assignment   *Missing information*

Listed here are the stockholders' equity sections of three public companies for years ending in 2008 and 2007:

	2008	2007
Wendy's (in thousands) (merger with Triare in 2008)		
Stockholders' equity		
Common stock, ?? stated value per share, authorized:		
1,500,000; 470,424 in 2008 and 93,576 in		
2007 shares issued, respectively	$ 47,042	$ 9,357
Capital in excess of stated value	2,752,987	291,122
Retained earnings	(357,541)	167,267
Acc. other comp. income (loss)	(43,253)	(2,098)
Treasury stock, at cost: 1,220 in 2008 and 841 in 2007	(15,944)	(16,774)
Coca-Cola (in millions)		
Stockholders' equity		
Common stock, ?? par value per share, authorized:		
5,600; issued: 3,519 shares in 2008 and 3,519 shares in 2007	880	880
Capital surplus	7,966	7,378
Reinvested earnings	38,513	36,235
Acc. other comp. inc. (loss)	(2,674)	(626)
Treasury stock, at cost: (1,207 shares in 2008; 1,201 shares in 2007)	(24,213)	(23,375)
Harley-Davidson (dollar amounts are presented in thousands)		
Stockholders' equity		
Common stock, ?? par value per share, authorized: 800,000,000, issued:		
335,653,577 in 2008 and 335,211,201 shares in 2007	3,357	3,352
Additional paid-in capital	846,796	812,224
Retained earnings	6,458,778	6,117,567
Acc. other comp. inc. (loss)	(522,526)	(137,258)
Treasury stock, at cost: 102,889,370 for 2008 and 96,725,399 for 2007	(4,670,802)	(4,420,394)

Required

a.   Divide the class in three sections and divide each section into groups of three to five students. Assign each section one of the companies.

Group Tasks

Based on the company assigned to your group, answer the following questions.

b.   What is the per share par or stated value of the common stock in 2008?

c.   What was the average issue price of the common stock for each year?

d.   How many shares of stock are outstanding at the end of each year?

e.   What is the average cost per share of the treasury stock for 2008?

f.   Do the data suggest that your company was profitable in 2008?

g.   Can you determine the amount of net income from the information given? What is missing?

h.   What is the total stockholders' equity of your company for each year?

Class Discussion

i.   Have each group select a representative to present the information about its company. Compare the share issue price and the par or stated value of the companies.

j.   Compare the average issue price to the current market price for each of the companies. Speculate about what might cause the difference.

ATC 8-3   Research Assignment   *Analyzing PepsiCo's equity structure*

Using either Big Lots, Inc. most current Form 10-K or the company's annual report, answer the questions below. To obtain the Form 10-K use either the EDGAR system following the instructions in Appendix A or the company's website. The company's annual report is available on its website.

Required

a.   What is the *book value* of Big Lots' stockholders' equity that is shown on the company's balance sheet?

b. What is the par value of Big Lots' common stock?

c. Does Big Lots have any treasury stock? If so, how many shares of treasury stock does the company hold?

d. Why does the stock of a company such as a Big Lots have a market value that is higher than its book value?

ATC 8-4   Writing Assignment   *Comparison of organizational forms*

Jim Baku and Scott Hanson are thinking about opening a new restaurant. Baku has extensive marketing experience but does not know that much about food preparation. However, Hanson is an excellent chef. Both will work in the business, but Baku will provide most of the funds necessary to start the business. At this time, they cannot decide whether to operate the business as a partnership or a corporation.

Required

Prepare a written memo to Baku and Hanson describing the advantages and disadvantages of each organizational form. Also, from the limited information provided, recommend the organizational form you think they should use.

ATC 8-5   Ethical Dilemma   *Bad news versus very bad news*

Louise Stinson, the chief financial officer of Bostonian Corporation, was on her way to the president's office. She was carrying the latest round of bad news. There would be no executive bonuses this year. Corporate profits were down. Indeed, if the latest projections held true, the company would report a small loss on the year-end income statement. Executive bonuses were tied to corporate profits. The executive compensation plan provided for 10 percent of net earnings to be set aside for bonuses. No profits meant no bonuses. While things looked bleak, Stinson had a plan that might help soften the blow.

After informing the company president of the earnings forecast, Stinson made the following suggestion: Because the company was going to report a loss anyway, why not report a big loss? She reasoned that the directors and stockholders would not be much more angry if the company reported a large loss than if it reported a small one. There were several questionable assets that could be written down in the current year. This would increase the current year's loss but would reduce expenses in subsequent accounting periods. For example, the company was carrying damaged inventory that was estimated to have a value of $2,500,000. If this estimate were revised to $500,000, the company would have to recognize a $2,000,000 loss in the current year. However, next year when the goods were sold, the expense for cost of goods sold would be $2,000,000 less and profits would be higher by that amount. Although the directors would be angry this year, they would certainly be happy next year. The strategy would also have the benefit of adding $200,000 to next year's executive bonus pool ($2,000,000 × 0.10). Furthermore, it could not hurt this year's bonus pool because there would be no pool this year because the company is going to report a loss.

Some of the other items that Stinson is considering include (1) converting from straight-line to accelerated depreciation, (2) increasing the percentage of receivables estimated to be uncollectible in the current year and lowering the percentage in the following year, and (3) raising the percentage of estimated warranty claims in the current period and lowering it in the following period. Finally, Stinson notes that two of the company's department stores have been experiencing losses. The company could sell these stores this year and thereby improve earnings next year. Stinson admits that the sale would result in significant losses this year, but she smiles as she thinks of next year's bonus check.

Required

a. Explain how each of the three numbered strategies for increasing the amount of the current year's loss would affect the stockholders' equity section of the balance sheet in the current year. How would the other elements of the balance sheet be affected?

b. If Stinson's strategy were effectively implemented, how would it affect the stockholders' equity in subsequent accounting periods?

c. Comment on the ethical implications of running the company for the sake of management (maximization of bonuses) versus the maximization of return to stockholders.

d. Formulate a bonus plan that will motivate managers to maximize the value of the firm instead of motivating them to manipulate the reporting process.

e. How would Stinson's strategy of overstating the amount of the reported loss in the current year affect the company's current P/E ratio?

CHAPTER 10

An Introduction to Managerial Accounting

LEARNING OBJECTIVES

After you have mastered the material in this chapter, you will be able to:

1 Distinguish between managerial and financial accounting.

2 Identify the cost components of a product made by a manufacturing company: the cost of materials, labor, and overhead.

3 Explain the effects on financial statements of product costs versus general, selling, and administrative costs.

4 Prepare a schedule of cost of goods manufactured and sold.

5 Distinguish product costs from upstream and downstream costs.

6 Explain how product costing differs in service, merchandising, and manufacturing companies.

7 Show how just-in-time inventory can increase profitability.

8 Identify and explain the standards contained in IMA's Statement of Ethical Professional Practice.

9 Identify emerging trends in accounting (Appendix A).

CHAPTER OPENING

Andy Grove, Senior Advisor to Executive Management of Intel Corporation, is credited with the motto "Only the paranoid survive." Mr. Grove describes a wide variety of concerns that make him paranoid. Specifically, he declares:

> I worry about products getting screwed up, and I worry about products getting introduced prematurely.
> I worry about factories not performing well, and I worry about having too many factories. I worry about

hiring the right people, and I worry about morale slacking off. And, of course, I worry about competitors. I worry about other people figuring out how to do what we do better or cheaper, and displacing us with our customers.

Do Intel's historically based financial statements contain the information Mr. Grove needs? No. **Financial accounting** is not designed to satisfy all the information needs of business managers. Its scope is limited to the needs of external users such as investors and creditors. The field of accounting designed to meet the needs of internal users is called **managerial accounting.**

The Curious Accountant

In the first course of accounting, you learned how retailers, such as Sears, account for the cost of equipment that lasts more than one year. Recall that the equipment was recorded as an asset when purchased, and then it was depreciated over its expected useful life. The depreciation charge reduced the company's assets and increased its expenses. This approach was justified under the matching principle, which seeks to recognize costs as expenses in the same period that the cost (resource) is used to generate revenue.

Is depreciation always shown as an expense on the income statement? The answer may surprise you. Consider the following scenario. Schwinn manufactures the bicycles that it sells to Sears. In order to produce the bicycles, Schwinn had to purchase a robotic machine that it expects can be used to produce 50,000 bicycles.

Do you think Schwinn should account for depreciation on its manufacturing equipment the same way Sears accounts for depreciation on its registers at the checkout counters? If not, how should Schwinn account for its depreciation? Remember the matching principle when thinking of your answer. (Answer on page 368.)

DIFFERENCES BETWEEN MANAGERIAL AND FINANCIAL ACCOUNTING

Distinguish between managerial and financial accounting.

While the information needs of internal and external users overlap, the needs of managers generally differ from those of investors or creditors. Some distinguishing characteristics are discussed in the following section.

Users and Types of Information

Financial accounting provides information used primarily by investors, creditors, and others *outside* a business. In contrast, managerial accounting focuses on information used by executives, managers, and employees who work *inside* the business. These two user groups need different types of information.

Internal users need information to *plan, direct,* and *control* business operations. The nature of information needed is related to an employee's job level. Lower level employees use nonfinancial information such as work schedules, store hours, and customer service policies. Moving up the organizational ladder, financial information becomes increasingly important. Middle managers use a blend of financial and nonfinancial information, while senior executives concentrate on financial data. To a lesser degree, senior executives also use general economic data and nonfinancial operating information. For example, an executive may consider the growth rate of the economy before deciding to expand the company's workforce.

External users (investors and creditors) have greater needs for general economic information than do internal users. For example, an investor debating whether to purchase stock versus bond securities might be more interested in government tax policy than financial statement data. Exhibit 10.1 summarizes the information needs of different user groups.

Level of Aggregation

External users generally desire *global information* that reflects the performance of a company as a whole. For example, an investor is not so much interested in the performance of a particular Sears store as she is in the performance of Sears Roebuck Company versus that of JC Penney Company. In contrast, internal users focus on detailed information about specific subunits of the company. To meet the needs of the different user groups, financial accounting data are more aggregated than managerial accounting data.

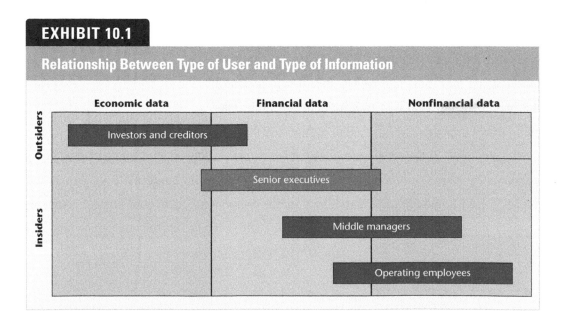

EXHIBIT 10.1

Relationship Between Type of User and Type of Information

Regulation

As previously discussed, the information in financial statements is highly regulated to protect the public interest.

Beyond financial statement data, much of the information generated by management accounting systems is proprietary information not available to the public. Because this information is not distributed to the public, it need not be regulated to protect the public interest. Management accounting is restricted only by the **value-added principle.** Management accountants are free to engage in any information gathering and reporting activity so long as the activity adds value in excess of its cost. For example, management accountants are free to provide forecasted information to internal users. In contrast, financial accounting as prescribed by GAAP does not permit forecasting.

Information Characteristics

While financial accounting is characterized by its objectivity, reliability, consistency, and historical nature, managerial accounting is more concerned with relevance and timeliness. Managerial accounting uses more estimates and fewer facts than financial accounting. Financial accounting reports what happened yesterday; managerial accounting reports what is expected to happen tomorrow.

Time Horizon and Reporting Frequency

Financial accounting information is reported periodically, normally at the end of a year. Management cannot wait until the end of the year to discover problems. Planning, controlling, and directing require immediate attention. Managerial accounting information is delivered on a continuous basis.

FOCUS ON **INTERNATIONAL** ISSUES

FINANCIAL ACCOUNTING VERSUS MANAGERIAL ACCOUNTING—AN INTERNATIONAL PERSPECTIVE

This chapter has already explained some of the conceptual differences between financial and managerial accounting, but these differences have implications for international businesses as well. With respect to financial accounting, publicly traded companies in most countries must follow the generally accepted accounting principles (GAAP) for their country, but these rules can vary from country to country. Generally, companies that are audited under the auditing standards of the United States follow the standards established by the Financial Accounting Standards Board. Most companies located outside of the United States follow the standards established by the International Accounting Standards Board. For example, the United States is one of very few countries whose GAAP allow the use of the LIFO inventory cost flow assumption.

Conversely, most of the managerial accounting concepts introduced in this course can be used by businesses in any country. For example, *activity-based management (ABM)* is a topic addressed in the appendix to this chapter and is used by many companies in the United States. Meanwhile, a study published in *Accountancy Ireland** found that approximately one-third of the companies surveyed in Ireland, the United Kingdom, and New Zealand were also either using ABM, or were considering adopting it.

*Bernard Pierce, "Activity-Based Costing; the Irish Experience: True Innovation or Passing Fad?" *Accountancy Ireland,* October 2004, pp. 28–31.

Comparative Features of Managerial versus Financial Accounting Information

Features	Managerial Accounting	Financial Accounting
Users	Insiders including executives, managers, and operators	Outsiders including investors, creditors, government agencies, analysts, and reporters
Information type	Economic and physical data as well as financial data	Financial data
Level of aggregation	Local information on subunits of the organization	Global information on the company as a whole
Regulation	No regulation, limited only by the value-added principle	Regulation by SEC, FASB, and other determiners of GAAP
Information characteristics	Estimates that promote relevance and enable timeliness	Factual information that is characterized by objectivity, reliability, consistency, and accuracy
Time horizon	Past, present, and future	Past only, historically based
Reporting frequency	Continuous reporting	Delayed with emphasis on annual reports

Exhibit 10.2 summarizes significant differences between financial and managerial accounting.

PRODUCT COSTING IN MANUFACTURING COMPANIES

Identify the cost components of a product made by a manufacturing company: the cost of materials, labor, and overhead.

A major focus for managerial accountants is determining **product cost.**[1] Managers need to know the cost of their products for a variety of reasons. For example, **cost-plus pricing** is a common business practice.[2] **Product costing** is also used to control business operations. It is useful in answering questions such as: Are costs higher or lower than expected? Who is responsible for the variances between expected and actual costs? What actions can be taken to control the variances?

The cost of making products includes the cost of materials, labor, and other resources (usually called **overhead**). To understand how these costs affect financial statements, consider the example of Tabor Manufacturing Company.

Tabor Manufacturing Company

Tabor Manufacturing Company makes wooden tables. The company spent $1,000 cash to build four tables: $390 for materials, $470 for a carpenter's labor, and $140 for tools used in making the tables. How much is Tabor's expense? The answer is zero. The $1,000 cash has been converted into products (four tables). The cash payments for materials, labor, and tools (overhead) were *asset exchange* transactions. One asset (cash) decreased while another asset (tables) increased. Tabor will not recognize any expense until the tables are sold; in the meantime, the cost of the tables is held in an asset account called **Finished Goods Inventory.** Exhibit 10.3 illustrates how cash is transformed into inventory.

Average Cost per Unit

How much did each table made by Tabor cost? The *actual* cost of each of the four tables likely differs. The carpenter probably spent a little more time on some of the tables than

---

[1]This text uses the term *product* in a generic sense to mean both goods and services.
[2]Other pricing strategies will be introduced in subsequent chapters.

EXHIBIT 10.3

Transforming the Asset Cash Into the Asset Finished Goods Inventory

Financial assets	Manufacturing process	Physical assets
$1,000 of cash	$390 materials / $470 labor / $140 overhead	$1,000 of finished goods

others. Material and tool usage probably varied from table to table. Determining the exact cost of each table is virtually impossible. Minute details such as a second of labor time cannot be effectively measured. Even if Tabor could determine the exact cost of each table, the information would be of little use. Minor differences in the cost per table would make no difference in pricing or other decisions management needs to make. Accountants therefore normally calculate cost per unit as an *average*. In the case of Tabor Manufacturing, the **average cost** per table is $250 ($1,000 ÷ 4 units). Unless otherwise stated, assume *cost per unit* means *average cost per unit*.

✓ CHECK YOURSELF 10.1

All boxes of General Mills' Total Raisin Bran cereal are priced at exactly the same amount in your local grocery store. Does this mean that the actual cost of making each box of cereal was exactly the same?

Answer   No, making each box would not cost exactly the same amount. For example, some boxes contain slightly more or less cereal than other boxes. Accordingly, some boxes cost slightly more or less to make than others do. General Mills uses average cost rather than actual cost to develop its pricing strategy.

Costs Can Be Assets or Expenses

It might seem odd that wages earned by production workers are recorded as inventory instead of being expensed. Remember, however, that expenses are assets used in the process of *earning revenue*. The cash paid to production workers is not used to produce revenue. Instead, the cash is used to produce inventory. Revenue will be earned when the inventory is used (sold). So long as the inventory remains on hand, all product costs (materials, labor, and overhead) remain in an inventory account.

When a table is sold, the average cost of the table is transferred from the Inventory account to the Cost of Goods Sold (expense) account. If some tables remain unsold at the end of the accounting period, part of the *product costs* is reported as an asset (inventory) on the balance sheet while the other part is reported as an expense (cost of goods sold) on the income statement.

Costs that are not classified as product costs are normally expensed in the period in which they are incurred. These costs include *general operating costs, selling and administrative costs, interest costs,* and the *cost of income taxes.*

To illustrate, return to the Tabor Manufacturing example. Recall that Tabor made four tables at an average cost per unit of $250. Assume Tabor pays an employee who sells three of the tables at a $200 sales commission. The sales commission is expensed immediately. The total product cost for the three tables (3 tables × $250 each = $750) is expensed on the income statement as cost of goods sold. The portion of the total product cost remaining in inventory is $250 (1 table × $250). Exhibit 10.4 shows the relationship between the costs incurred and the expenses recognized for Tabor Manufacturing Company.

EXHIBIT 10.4

Cost Classification for Tabor Manufacturing Company

EFFECT OF PRODUCT COSTS ON FINANCIAL STATEMENTS

Explain the effects on financial statements of product costs versus general, selling, and administrative costs.

We illustrate accounting for product costs in manufacturing companies with Patillo Manufacturing Company, a producer of ceramic pottery. Patillo, started on January 1, 2012, experienced the following accounting events during its first year of operations.[3] *Assume that all transactions except 6, 8, and 10 are cash transactions.*

1. Acquired $15,000 cash by issuing common stock.
2. Paid $2,000 for materials that were used to make products. All products started were completed during the period.
3. Paid $1,200 for salaries of selling and administrative employees.
4. Paid $3,000 for wages of production workers.
5. Paid $2,800 for furniture used in selling and administrative offices.

---

[3]This illustration assumes that all inventory started during the period was completed during the period. Patillo therefore uses only one inventory account, Finished Goods Inventory. Many manufacturing companies normally have three categories of inventory on hand at the end of an accounting period: Raw Materials Inventory, Work in Process Inventory (inventory of partially completed units), and Finished Goods Inventory.

6. Recognized depreciation on the office furniture purchased in Event 5. The furniture was acquired on January 1, had a $400 estimated salvage value, and a four-year useful life. The annual depreciation charge is $600 [($2,800 − $400) ÷ 4].

7. Paid $4,500 for manufacturing equipment.

8. Recognized depreciation on the equipment purchased in Event 7. The equipment was acquired on January 1, had a $1,500 estimated salvage value, and a three-year useful life. The annual depreciation charge is $1,000 [($4,500 − $1,500) ÷ 3].

9. Sold inventory to customers for $7,500 cash.

10. The inventory sold in Event 9 cost $4,000 to make.

The effects of these transactions on the balance sheet, income statement, and statement of cash flows are shown in Exhibit 10.5. Study each row in this exhibit, paying particular attention to how similar costs such as salaries for selling and administrative personnel and wages for production workers have radically different effects on the financial statements. The example illustrates the three elements of product costs, materials (Event 2), labor (Event 4), and overhead (Event 8). These events are discussed in more detail below.

EXHIBIT 10.5

Effect of Product versus Selling and Administrative Costs on Financial Statements

Event No.	Cash	+	Inventory	+	Office Furn.*	+	Manuf. Equip.*	=	Com. Stk.	+	Ret. Earn.	Rev.	−	Exp.	=	Net Inc.	Cash Flow	
						Assets					**Equity**							
1	15,000							=	15,000								15,000	FA
2	(2,000)	+	2,000														(2,000)	OA
3	(1,200)							=			(1,200)		−	1,200	=	(1,200)	(1,200)	OA
4	(3,000)	+	3,000														(3,000)	OA
5	(2,800)	+			2,800												(2,800)	IA
6					(600)			=			(600)		−	600	=	(600)		
7	(4,500)	+					4,500										(4,500)	IA
8			1,000	+			(1,000)											
9	7,500							=			7,500	7,500			=	7,500	7,500	OA
10			(4,000)					=			(4,000)		−	4,000	=	(4,000)		
Totals	9,000	+	2,000	+	2,200	+	3,500	=	15,000	+	1,700	7,500	−	5,800	=	1,700	9,000	NC

*Negative amounts in these columns represent accumulated depreciation.

Materials Costs (Event 2)

Materials used to make products are usually called **raw materials.** The cost of raw materials is first recorded in an asset account (Inventory). The cost is then transferred from the Inventory account to the Cost of Goods Sold account at the time the goods are sold. Remember that materials cost is only one component of total manufacturing costs. When inventory is sold, the combined cost of materials, labor, and overhead is expensed as *cost of goods sold*. The costs of materials that can be easily and conveniently traced to products are called **direct raw materials** costs.

Labor Costs (Event 4)

The salaries paid to selling and administrative employees (Event 3) and the wages paid to production workers (Event 4) are accounted for differently. Salaries paid to selling and administrative employees are expensed immediately, but the cost of production wages is added to inventory. Production wages are expensed as part of cost of goods sold at the time the inventory is sold. Labor costs that can be easily and conveniently traced to products are called **direct labor** costs. The cost flow of wages for production employees versus salaries for selling and administrative personnel is shown in Exhibit 10.6.

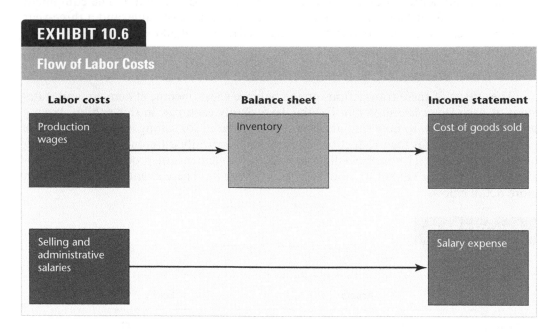

EXHIBIT 10.6

Flow of Labor Costs

Overhead Costs (Event 8)

Although depreciation cost totaled $1,600 ($600 on office furniture and $1,000 on manufacturing equipment), only the $600 of depreciation on the office furniture is expensed directly on the income statement. The depreciation on the manufacturing equipment is split between the income statement (cost of goods sold) and the balance sheet (inventory). The depreciation cost flow for the manufacturing equipment versus the office furniture is shown in Exhibit 10.7.

EXHIBIT 10.7

Flow of Depreciation Costs

Total Product Cost

A summary of Patillo Manufacturing's total product cost is shown in Exhibit 10.8.

EXHIBIT 10.8

Schedule of Inventory Costs

Materials	$2,000
Labor	3,000
Manufacturing overhead*	1,000
Total product costs	6,000
Less: Cost of goods sold	(4,000)
Ending inventory balance	$2,000

*Depreciation ([$4,500 − $1,500] ÷ 3)

EXHIBIT 10.9

PATILLO MANUFACTURING COMPANY
Financial Statements

Income Statement for 2012

Sales revenue		$ 7,500
Cost of goods sold		(4,000)
Gross margin		3,500
G, S, & A expenses		
Salaries expense		(1,200)
Depreciation expense—office furniture		(600)
Net income		$ 1,700

Balance Sheet as of December 31, 2012

Cash		$ 9,000
Finished goods inventory		2,000
Office furniture	$2,800	
Accumulated depreciation	(600)	
Book value		2,200
Manufacturing equipment	4,500	
Accumulated depreciation	(1,000)	
Book value		3,500
Total assets		$16,700
Stockholders' equity		
Common stock		$15,000
Retained earnings		1,700
Total stockholders' equity		$16,700

Statement of Cash Flows for 2012

Operating Activities	
Inflow from revenue	$ 7,500
Outflow for inventory	(5,000)
Outflow for S&A salaries	(1,200)
Net inflow from operating activities	1,300
Investing Activities	
Outflow for equipment and furniture	(7,300)
Financing Activities	
Inflow from stock issue	15,000
Net change in cash	9,000
Beginning cash balance	-0-
Ending cash balance	$ 9,000

General, Selling, and Administrative Costs

General, selling, and administrative costs (G,S,&A) are normally expensed *in the period* in which they are incurred. Because of this recognition pattern, nonproduct expenses are sometimes called **period costs.** In Patillo's case, the salaries expense for selling and administrative employees and the depreciation on office furniture are period costs reported directly on the income statement.

The income statement, balance sheet, and statement of cash flows for Patillo Manufacturing are displayed in Exhibit 10.9.

The $4,000 cost of goods sold reported on the income statement includes a portion of the materials, labor, and overhead costs incurred by Patillo during the year. Similarly, the $2,000 of finished goods inventory on the balance sheet includes materials, labor, and overhead costs. These product costs will be recognized as expense in the next accounting period when the goods are sold. Initially classifying a cost as a product cost delays, but does not eliminate, its recognition as an expense. All product costs are ultimately recognized as expense (cost of goods sold). Cost classification does not affect cash flow. Cash inflows and outflows are recognized in the period that cash is collected or paid regardless of whether the cost is recorded as an asset or expensed on the income statement.

Overhead Costs: A Closer Look

Costs such as depreciation on manufacturing equipment cannot be easily traced to products. Suppose that Patillo Manufacturing makes both tables and chairs. What part of the depreciation is caused by manufacturing tables versus manufacturing chairs? Similarly, suppose a production supervisor oversees employees who work on both tables and chairs. How much of the supervisor's salary relates to tables and how much to chairs? Likewise, the cost of glue used in the production department would be difficult to trace to tables versus chairs. You could count the drops of glue used on each product, but the information would not be useful enough to merit the time and money spent collecting the data.

EXHIBIT 10.10

Cost Allocation

Allocation rate
$120 ÷ 8 = $15
per labor hour

$15 × 2 hours → $30

$15 × 6 hours → $90

Costs that cannot be traced to products and services in a *cost-effective* manner are called **indirect costs.** The indirect costs incurred to make products are called **manufacturing overhead.** Some of the items commonly included in manufacturing overhead are indirect materials, indirect labor, factory utilities, rent of manufacturing facilities, and depreciation on manufacturing assets.

Because indirect costs cannot be effectively traced to products, they are normally assigned to products using **cost allocation,** a process of dividing a total cost into parts and assigning the parts to relevant cost objects. To illustrate, suppose that production workers spend an eight-hour day making a chair and a table. The chair requires two hours to complete and the table requires six hours. Now suppose that $120 of utilities cost is consumed during the day. How much of the $120 should be assigned to each piece of furniture? The utility cost cannot be directly traced to each specific piece of furniture, but the piece of furniture that required more labor also likely consumed more of the utility cost. Using this line of reasoning, it is rational to allocate the utility cost to the two pieces of furniture based on *direct labor hours* at a rate of $15 per hour ($120 ÷ 8 hours). The chair would be assigned $30 ($15 per hour × 2 hours) of the utility cost and the table would be assigned the remaining $90 ($15 × 6 hours) of utility cost. The allocation of the utility cost is shown in Exhibit 10.10.

We discuss the details of cost allocation in a later chapter. For now, recognize that overhead costs are normally allocated to products rather than traced directly to them.

Answers to The Curious Accountant

As you have seen, accounting for depreciation related to manufacturing assets is different from accounting for depreciation for nonmanufacturing assets. Depreciation on the checkout equipment at Sears is recorded as depreciation expense. Depreciation on manufacturing equipment at Schwinn is considered a product cost. It is included first as a part of the cost of inventory and eventually as a part of the expense, cost of goods sold. Recording depreciation on manufacturing equipment as an inventory cost is simply another example of the matching principle, because the cost does not become an expense until revenue from the product sale is recognized.

Manufacturing Product Cost Summary

As explained, the cost of a product made by a manufacturing company is normally composed of three categories: direct materials, direct labor, and manufacturing overhead. Relevant information about these three cost components is summarized in Exhibit 10.11.

EXHIBIT 10.11

Components of Manufacturing Product Cost

Component 1—Direct Materials
Sometimes called *raw materials*. In addition to basic resources such as wood or metals, it can include manufactured parts. For example, engines, glass, and car tires can be considered as raw materials for an automotive manufacturer. If the amount of a material in a product is known, it can usually be classified as a direct material. The cost of direct materials can be easily traced to specific products.

Component 2—Direct Labor
The cost of wages paid to factory workers involved in hands-on contact with the products being manufactured. If the amount of time employees worked on a product can be determined, this cost can usually be classified as direct labor. Like direct materials, labor costs must be easily traced to a specific product in order to be classified as a direct cost.

Component 3—Manufacturing Overhead
Costs that cannot be easily traced to specific products. Accordingly, these costs are called indirect costs. They can include but are not limited to the following:

1. Indirect materials such as glue, nails, paper, and oil. Indeed, note that indirect materials used in the production process may not appear in the finished product. An example is a chemical solvent used to clean products during the production process but not a component material found in the final product.
2. Indirect labor such as the cost of salaries paid to production supervisors, inspectors, and maintenance personnel.
3. Rental cost for manufacturing facilities and equipment.
4. Utility costs.
5. Depreciation.
6. Security.
7. The cost of preparing equipment for the manufacturing process (i.e., setup costs).
8. Maintenance cost for the manufacturing facility and equipment.

✓ CHECK YOURSELF 10.2

Lawson Manufacturing Company paid production workers wages of $100,000. It incurred materials costs of $120,000 and manufacturing overhead costs of $160,000. Selling and administrative salaries were $80,000. Lawson started and completed 1,000 units of product and sold 800 of these units. The company sets sales prices at $220 above the average per unit production cost. Based on this information alone, determine the amount of gross margin and net income. What is Lawson's pricing strategy called?

Answer   Total product cost is $380,000 ($100,000 labor + $120,000 materials + $160,000 overhead). Cost per unit is $380 ($380,000 ÷ 1,000 units). The sales price per unit is $600 ($380 + $220). Cost of goods sold is $304,000 ($380 × 800 units). Sales revenue is $480,000 ($600 × 800 units). Gross margin is $176,000 ($480,000 revenue − $304,000 cost of goods sold). Net income is $96,000 ($176,000 gross margin − $80,000 selling and administrative salaries). Lawson's pricing strategy is called *cost-plus* pricing.

SCHEDULE OF COST OF GOODS MANUFACTURED AND SOLD

To this point, we assumed all inventory started during an accounting period was also completed during that accounting period. All product costs (materials, labor, and manufacturing overhead) were either in inventory or expensed as cost of goods sold. At the end of an accounting period, however, most real-world companies have raw materials on hand, and manufacturing companies are likely to have in inventory items that have been started but are not completed. Most manufacturing companies accumulate product costs in three distinct inventory accounts: (1) **Raw Materials Inventory,** which includes lumber, metals, paints, and chemicals that will be used to make the company's products; (2) **Work in Process Inventory,** which includes partially completed products; and (3) **Finished Goods Inventory,** which includes completed products that are ready for sale.

The cost of materials is first recorded in the Raw Materials Inventory account. The cost of materials placed in production is then transferred from the Raw Materials Inventory account to the Work in Process Inventory account. The costs of labor and overhead are added to the Work in Process Inventory account. The cost of the goods completed during the period is transferred from the Work in Process Inventory account to the Finished Goods Inventory account. The cost of the goods that are sold during the accounting period is transferred from the Finished Goods Inventory account to the Cost of Goods Sold account. The balances that remain in the Raw Materials, Work in Process, and Finished Goods Inventory accounts are reported on the balance sheet. The amount of product cost transferred to the Cost of Goods Sold account is expensed on the income statement. Exhibit 10.12 shows the flow of manufacturing costs through the accounting records.

To help managers analyze manufacturing costs, companies frequently summarize product cost information is a report called a **schedule of cost of goods manufactured and sold.** To illustrate, assume that in 2013 Patillo Manufacturing Company purchased $37,950 of raw materials inventory. During 2013 Patillo used $37,000 of raw materials, incurred $34,600 of labor costs, and $26,700 of overhead costs in the process of making inventory. Also, during 2013 the company completed work on products that cost $94,600. Recall that Patillo had zero balances in its Raw Materials and Work in Process Inventory accounts at the end of 2012. It had a $2,000 balance in its Finished Goods Inventory account at the end of 2012. The 2012 ending balance becomes the

EXHIBIT 10.12

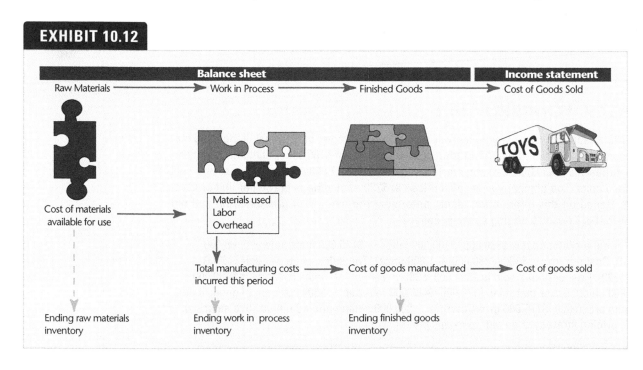

EXHIBIT 10.13

PATILLO MANUFACTURING COMPANY
Schedule of Cost of Goods Manufactured and Sold
For the Year Ended December 31, 2013

Beginning raw materials Inventory	$ 0
Plus: Raw materials purchases	37,950
Less: Ending raw materials inventory	(950)
Raw materials used	37,000
Labor	34,600
Overhead	26,700
Total manufacturing costs	98,300
Plus: Beginning work in process inventory	0
Total work in process inventory	98,300
Less: Ending work in process inventory	(3,700)
Cost of goods manufactured	94,600
Plus: Beginning finished goods inventory	2,000
Cost of goods available for sale	96,600
Less: Ending finished goods inventory	(3,200)
Cost of goods sold	$93,400

2013 beginning balance for finished goods. The 2013 ending balances for the inventory accounts were as follows: Raw Materials Inventory, $950; Work in Process Inventory, $3,700; Finished Goods Inventory, $3,200. Finally, during 2013 Patillo had sales revenue of $153,000. Patillo's schedule of cost of goods manufactured and sold for 2013 is shown in Exhibit 10.13

The $93,400 of cost of goods sold would appear on Patillo's 2013 income statement. A partial income statement for Patillo is shown in Exhibit 10.14

EXHIBIT 10.14

PATILLO MANUFACTURING COMPANY
Income Statement
For the Year Ended December 31, 2013

Sales revenue	$153,000
Cost of goods sold	(93,400)
Gross margin	$ 59,600

UPSTREAM AND DOWNSTREAM COSTS

Most companies incur product-related costs before and after, as well as during, the manufacturing process. For example, Ford Motor Company incurs significant research and development costs prior to mass producing a new car model. These **upstream costs** occur before the manufacturing process begins. Similarly, companies normally incur significant costs after the manufacturing process is complete. Examples of **downstream costs** include transportation, advertising, sales commissions, and bad debts. While upstream and downstream costs are not considered to be product costs for financial reporting purposes, profitability analysis requires that they be considered in cost-plus pricing decisions. To be profitable, a company must recover the total cost of developing, producing, and delivering its products to customers.

LO 5

Distinguish product costs from upstream and downstream costs.

PRODUCT COSTING IN SERVICE AND MERCHANDISING COMPANIES

Companies are frequently classified as being service, merchandising, or manufacturing businesses. As the name implies, service organizations provide services, rather than physical products, to consumers. For example, St. Jude Children's Hospital provides treatment programs aimed at healing patient diseases. Other common service providers include

LO 6

Explain how product costing differs in service, merchandising, and manufacturing companies.

public accountants, lawyers, restaurants, dry cleaning establishments, and lawn care companies. Merchandising businesses are sometimes called retail or wholesale companies; they sell goods other companies make. The Home Depot, Inc., Costco Wholesale Corporation, and Best Buy Co., Inc., are merchandising companies. Manufacturing companies make the goods they sell to their customers. Toyota Motor Corporation, Texaco, Inc., and American Standard Companies, Inc., are manufacturing businesses.

How do manufacturing companies differ from service and merchandising businesses? Do service and merchandising companies incur materials, labor, and overhead costs? Yes. For example, Ernst & Young, a large accounting firm, must pay employees (labor costs), use office supplies (material costs), and incur utilities, depreciation, and so on (overhead costs) in the process of conducting audits. *The primary difference between manufacturing entities and service companies is that the products provided by service companies are consumed immediately.* In contrast, products made by manufacturing companies can be held in the form of inventory until they are sold to consumers. Similarly, most labor and overhead costs incurred by merchandising companies result from providing assistance to customers. These costs are normally treated as general, selling, and administrative expenses rather than accumulated in inventory accounts. Indeed, merchandising companies are often viewed as service companies rather than considered a separate business category.

The important point to remember is that all business managers are expected to control costs, improve quality, and increase productivity. Like managers of manufacturing companies, managers of service and merchandising businesses can benefit from the analysis of the cost of satisfying their customers. For example, Wendy's, a service company, can benefit from knowing how much a hamburger costs in the same manner that Bayer Corporation, a manufacturing company, benefits from knowing the cost of a bottle of aspirin.

✓ CHECK YOURSELF 10.3

The cost of making a Burger King hamburger includes the cost of materials, labor, and overhead. Does this mean that Burger King is a manufacturing company?

Answer   No, Burger King is not a manufacturing company. It is a service company because its products are consumed immediately. In contrast, there may be a considerable delay between the time the product of a manufacturing company is made and the time it is consumed. For example, it could be several months between the time Ford Motor Company makes an Explorer and the time the Explorer is ultimately sold to a customer. The primary difference between service and manufacturing companies is that manufacturing companies have inventories of products and service companies do not.

JUST-IN-TIME INVENTORY

Show how just-in-time inventory can increase profitability.

Companies attempt to minimize the amount of inventory they maintain because of the high cost of holding it. Many **inventory holding costs** are obvious: financing, warehouse space, supervision, theft, damage, and obsolescence. Other costs are hidden: diminished motivation, sloppy work, inattentive attitudes, and increased production time.

Many businesses have been able to simultaneously reduce their inventory holding costs and increase customer satisfaction by making products available **just in time (JIT)** for customer consumption. For example, hamburgers that are cooked to order are fresher and more individualized than those that are prepared in advance and stored until a customer orders one. Many fast-food restaurants have discovered that JIT systems lead not only to greater customer satisfaction but also to lower costs through reduced waste.

Just-in-Time Illustration

To illustrate the benefits of a JIT system, consider Paula Elliot, a student at a large urban university. She helps support herself by selling flowers. Three days each week, Paula drives to a florist, purchases 25 single-stem roses, returns to the school, and sells the flowers to individuals from a location on a local street corner. She pays $2 per rose and sells each one for $3. Some days she does not have enough flowers to meet customer demand. Other days, she must discard one or two unsold flowers; she believes quality is important and refuses to sell flowers that are not fresh. During May, she purchased 300 roses and sold 280. She calculated her driving cost to be $45. Exhibit 10.15 displays Paula's May income statement.

After studying just-in-time inventory systems in her managerial accounting class, Paula decided to apply the concepts to her small business. She *reengineered* her distribution system by purchasing her flowers from a florist within walking distance of her sales location. She had considered purchasing from this florist earlier but had rejected the idea because the florist's regular selling price of $2.25 per rose was too high. After learning about *most-favored customer status,* she developed a strategy to get a price reduction. By guaranteeing that she would buy at least 30 roses per week, she was able to convince the local florist to match her current cost of $2.00 per rose. The local florist agreed that she could make purchases in batches of any size so long as the total amounted to at least 30 per week. Under this arrangement, Paula was able to buy roses *just in time* to meet customer demand. Each day she purchased a small number of flowers. When she ran out, she simply returned to the florist for additional ones.

The JIT system also enabled Paula to eliminate the cost of the *nonvalue-added activity* of driving to her former florist. Customer satisfaction actually improved because no one was ever turned away because of the lack of inventory. In June, Paula was able to buy and sell 310 roses with no waste and no driving expense. The June income statement is shown in Exhibit 10.16.

Paula was ecstatic about her $115 increase in profitability ($310 in June − $195 in May = $115 increase), but she was puzzled about the exact reasons for the change. She had saved $40 (20 flowers × $2 each) by avoiding waste and eliminated $45 of driving expenses. These two factors explained only $85 ($40 waste + $45 driving expense) of the $115 increase. What had caused the remaining $30 ($115 − $85) increase in profitability? Paula asked her accounting professor to help her identify the remaining $30 difference.

The professor explained that May sales had suffered from *lost opportunities*. Recall that under the earlier inventory system, Paula had to turn away some prospective customers because she sold out of flowers before all customers were served. Sales increased from 280 roses in May to 310 roses in June. A likely explanation for the 30 unit difference (310 − 280) is that customers who would have purchased flowers in May were unable to do so because of a lack of availability. May's sales suffered from the lost opportunity to earn a gross margin of $1 per flower on 30 roses, a $30 **opportunity cost.** This opportunity cost is the missing link in explaining the profitability difference between May and June. The total $115 difference consists of (1) $40 savings from waste elimination, (2) $45 savings from eliminating driving expense, and (3) opportunity cost of $30. The subject of opportunity cost has widespread application and is discussed in more depth in subsequent chapters of the text.

EXHIBIT 10.15

Income Statement for May

Sales revenue (280 units × $3 per unit)	$840
Cost of goods sold (280 units × $2 per unit)	(560)
Gross margin	280
Driving expense	(45)
Waste (20 units × $2 per unit)	(40)
Net income	$195

EXHIBIT 10.16

Income Statement for June

Sales revenue (310 units × $3 per unit)	$930
Cost of goods sold (310 units × $2 per unit)	(620)
Gross margin	310
Driving expense	0
Net income	$310

✓ CHECK YOURSELF 10.4

A strike at a General Motors brake plant caused an almost immediate shutdown of many of the company's assembly plants. What could have caused such a rapid and widespread shutdown?

Answer A rapid and widespread shutdown could have occurred because General Motors uses a just-in-time inventory system. With a just-in-time inventory system, there is no stockpile of inventory to draw on when strikes or other forces disrupt inventory deliveries. This illustrates a potential negative effect of using a just-in-time inventory system.

STATEMENT OF ETHICAL PROFESSIONAL PRACTICE

Identify and explain the standards contained in IMA's Statement of Ethical Professional Practice.

Management accountants must be prepared not only to make difficult choices between legitimate alternatives but also to face conflicts of a more troubling nature, such as pressure to

1. Undertake duties they have not been trained to perform competently.
2. Disclose confidential information.
3. Compromise their integrity through falsification, embezzlement, bribery, and so on.
4. Issue biased, misleading, or incomplete reports.

In Chapter 4 we explained how the American Institute of Certified Public Accountants' Code of Professional Conduct provides guidance for CPAs to avoid unethical behavior. To provide Certified Management Accountants (CMAs) with guidance for ethical conduct the Institute of Management Accountants (IMA) issued a *Statement of Ethical Professional Practice,* which is shown in Exhibit 10.17. Management accountants are also frequently required to abide by organizational codes of ethics. Failure to adhere to professional and organizational ethical standards can lead to personal disgrace, loss of employment, or imprisonment.

EXHIBIT 10.17

Statement of Ethical Professional Practice

Members of IMA shall behave ethically. A commitment to ethical professional practice includes overarching principles that express our values, and standards that guide our conduct. IMA's overarching ethical principles include: Honesty, Fairness, Objectivity, and Responsibility. Members shall act in accordance with these principles and shall encourage others within their organizations to adhere to them. A member's failure to comply with the following standards may result in disciplinary action.

Competence Each member has a responsibility to
- Maintain an appropriate level of professional expertise by continually developing knowledge and skills.
- Perform professional duties in accordance with relevant laws, regulations, and technical standards.
- Provide decision support information and recommendations that are accurate, clear, concise, and timely.
- Recognize and communicate professional limitations or other constraints that would preclude responsible judgment or successful performance of an activity.

Confidentiality Each member has a responsibility to
- Keep information confidential except when disclosure is authorized or legally required.
- Inform all relevant parties regarding appropriate use of confidential information. Monitor subordinates' activities to ensure compliance.
- Refrain from using confidential information for unethical or illegal advantage.

Integrity Each member has a responsibility to
- Mitigate actual conflicts of interest and avoid apparent conflicts of interest. Advise all parties of any potential conflicts.
- Refrain from engaging in any conduct that would prejudice carrying out duties ethically.
- Abstain from engaging in or supporting any activity that might discredit the profession.

Credibility Each member has a responsibility to
- Communicate information fairly and objectively.
- Disclose all relevant information that could reasonably be expected to influence an intended user's understanding of the reports, analyses, or recommendations.
- Disclose delays or deficiencies in information, timeliness, processing, or internal controls in conformance with organization policy and/or applicable law.

Resolution of Ethical Conflict In applying these standards, you may encounter problems identifying unethical behavior or resolving an ethical conflict. When faced with ethical issues, follow your organization's established policies on the resolution of such conflict. If these policies do not resolve the ethical conflict, consider the following courses of action.
- Discuss the issue with your immediate supervisor except when it appears that the supervisor is involved. In that case, present the issue to the next level. If you cannot achieve a satisfactory resolution, submit the issue to the next management level. Communication of such problems to authorities or individuals not employed or engaged by the organization is not considered appropriate, unless you believe there is a clear violation of the law.
- Clarify relevant ethical issues by initiating a confidential discussion with an IMA Ethics Counselor or other impartial advisor to obtain a better understanding of possible courses of action.
- Consult your own attorney as to legal obligations and rights concerning the ethical conflict.

REALITY BYTES

Unethical behavior occurs in all types of organizations. In its *2007 National Government Ethics Survey,* the Ethics Resource Center reported its findings on the occurrences and reporting of unethical behavior in local, state, and federal governments.

Fifty-seven percent of those surveyed reported having observed unethical conduct during the past year. Unethical conduct was reported most often by those in local governments (63%) and least often at the federal level (52%). The definition of ethical misconduct used in the study was quite broad, ranging from behavior such as an individual putting his or her personal interest ahead of the interest of the organization, to sexual harassment, to taking bribes. The more egregious offences, such as discrimination or taking bribes, were reported much less often than activities such as lying to customers, vendors, or the public.

Once observed, unethical behavior often was not reported. For example, only 25 percent of observed incidents of the alteration of financial records were reported to supervisors or whistleblower hotlines, and only 54 percent of observed bribes were reported.

The survey also found that only 18 percent of government entities have ethics and compliance programs in place that could be considered well-implemented. However, where well-implemented programs do exist, observed unethical misconduct is less likely to occur and more likely to be reported. In these entities only 36 percent of respondents said they had observed misconduct (compared to 57 percent overall), and when they did observe misconduct, 75 percent said they reported it.

For the complete *2007 National Government Ethics Survey,* go to www.ethics.org.

A Look Back

Managerial accounting focuses on the information needs of *internal* users, while *financial accounting* focuses on the information needs of *external* users. Managerial accounting uses economic, operating, and nonfinancial, as well as financial, data. Managerial accounting information is local (pertains to the company's subunits), is limited by cost/benefit considerations, is more concerned with relevance and timeliness, and is future oriented. Financial accounting information, on the other hand, is more global than managerial accounting information. It supplies information that applies to the whole company. Financial accounting is regulated by numerous authorities, is characterized by objectivity, is focused on reliability and accuracy, and is historical in nature.

Both managerial and financial accounting are concerned with product costing. Financial accountants need product cost information to determine the amount of inventory reported on the balance sheet and the amount of cost of goods sold reported on the income statement. Managerial accountants need to know the cost of products for pricing decisions and for control and evaluation purposes. When determining unit product costs, managers use the average cost per unit. Determining the actual cost of each product requires an unreasonable amount of time and record keeping and it makes no difference in product pricing and product cost control decisions.

Product costs are the costs incurred to make products: the costs of direct materials, direct labor, and overhead. *Overhead costs* are product costs that cannot be cost effectively traced to a product; therefore, they are assigned to products using *cost allocation.* Overhead costs include indirect materials, indirect labor, depreciation, rent, and utilities for manufacturing facilities. Product costs are first accumulated in an asset account (Inventory). They are expensed as cost of goods sold in the period the inventory is sold. The difference between sales revenue and cost of goods sold is called *gross margin.*

General, selling, and administrative costs are classified separately from product costs. They are subtracted from gross margin to determine net income. General, selling, and administrative costs can be divided into two categories. Costs incurred before the manufacturing process begins (research and development costs) are *upstream costs.* Costs incurred after manufacturing is complete (transportation) are *downstream costs.* Service companies, like manufacturing companies, incur materials, labor, and overhead costs, but the products provided by service companies are consumed immediately. Therefore, service company product costs are not accumulated in an Inventory account.

A code of ethical conduct is needed in the accounting profession because accountants hold positions of trust and face conflicts of interest. In recognition of the temptations that accountants face, the IMA has issued a *Statement of Ethical Professional Practice,* which provides accountants guidance in resisting temptations and in making difficult decisions.

Emerging trends such as *just-in-time inventory* and *activity-based management* are methods that many companies have used to reengineer their production and delivery systems to eliminate waste, reduce errors, and minimize costs. Activity-based management seeks to eliminate or reduce *nonvalue-added activities* and to create new *value-added activities.* Just-in-time inventory seeks to reduce inventory holding costs and to lower prices for customers by making inventory available just in time for customer consumption.

 ## A Look Forward

In addition to distinguishing costs by product versus G, S, & A classification, other classifications can be used to facilitate managerial decision making. In the next chapter, costs are classified according to the *behavior* they exhibit when the number of units of product increases or decreases (volume of activity changes). You will learn to distinguish between costs that vary with activity volume changes versus costs that remain fixed with activity volume changes. You will learn not only to recognize *cost behavior* but also how to use such recognition to evaluate business risk and opportunity.

APPENDIX A

Identify emerging trends in accounting.

Emerging Trends in Managerial Accounting

Global competition has forced many companies to reengineer their production and delivery systems to eliminate waste, reduce errors, and minimize costs. A key ingredient of successful **reengineering** is benchmarking. **Benchmarking** involves identifying the **best practices** used by world-class competitors. By studying and mimicking these practices, a company uses benchmarking to implement highly effective and efficient operating methods. Best practices employed by world-class companies include total quality management (TQM), activity-based management (ABM), and value-added assessment.

Total Quality Management

To promote effective and efficient operations, many companies practice **total quality management (TQM).** TQM is a two-dimensional management philosophy using (1) a systematic problem-solving philosophy that encourages frontline workers to achieve *zero defects* and (2) an organizational commitment to achieving *customer satisfaction.* A key component of TQM is **continuous improvement,** an ongoing process through which employees strive to eliminate waste, reduce response time, minimize defects, and simplify the design and delivery of products and services to customers.

Activity-Based Management

Simple changes in perspective can have dramatic results. For example, imagine how realizing the world is round instead of flat changed the nature of travel. A recent change in perspective developing in management accounting is the realization that an organization cannot manage *costs*. Instead, it manages the *activities* that cause costs to be incurred. **Activities** represent the measures an organization takes to accomplish its goals.

The primary goal of all organizations is to provide products (goods and services) their customers *value*. The sequence of activities used to provide products is called a **value chain. Activity-based management** assesses the value chain to create new or refine existing **value-added activities** and to eliminate or reduce *nonvalue-added activities*. A value-added activity is any unit of work that contributes to a product's ability to satisfy customer needs. For example, cooking is an activity that adds value to food served to a hungry customer. **Nonvalue-added activities** are tasks undertaken that do not contribute to a product's ability to satisfy customer needs. Waiting for the oven to preheat so that food can be cooked does not add value. Most customers value cooked food, but they do not value waiting for it.

To illustrate, consider the value-added activities undertaken by a pizza restaurant. Begin with a customer who is hungry for pizza; certain activities must occur to satisfy that hunger. These activities are pictured in Exhibit 10.18. At a minimum, the restaurant must conduct research and development (devise a recipe), obtain raw materials (acquire the ingredients), manufacture the product (combine and bake the ingredients), market the product (advertise its availability), and deliver the product (transfer the pizza to the customer).

EXHIBIT 10.18

Value Chain

| Conducting research and development | Obtaining materials | Manufacturing | Marketing | Delivering |

Businesses gain competitive advantages by adding activities that satisfy customer needs. For example, Domino's Pizza grew briskly by recognizing the value customers placed on the convenience of home pizza delivery. Alternatively, Little Caesar's has been highly successful by satisfying customers who value low prices. Other restaurants capitalize on customer values pertaining to taste, ambience, or location. Businesses can also gain competitive advantages by identifying and eliminating nonvalue-added activities, providing products of comparable quality at lower cost than competitors.

Value Chain Analysis Across Companies

Comprehensive value chain analysis extends from obtaining raw materials to the ultimate disposition of finished products. It encompasses the activities performed not only by a particular organization but also by that organization's suppliers and those who service its finished products. For example, PepsiCo must be concerned with the activities of the company that supplies the containers for its soft drinks as well as the retail companies that sell its products. If cans of Pepsi fail to open properly, the customer is more likely to blame PepsiCo than the supplier of the cans. Comprehensive value chain analysis can lead to identifying and eliminating nonvalue-added activities that occur between companies. For example, container producers could be encouraged to build manufacturing facilities near Pepsi's bottling factories, eliminating the nonvalue-added activity of transporting empty containers from the manufacturer to the bottling facility. The resulting cost savings benefits customers by reducing costs without affecting quality.

A step-by-step audio-narrated series of slides is provided on the text website at www.mhhe.com/edmondssurvey3e.

SELF-STUDY REVIEW PROBLEM

Tuscan Manufacturing Company makes a unique headset for use with mobile phones. The company had the following amounts in its accounts at the beginning of 2012: Cash, $795,000; Raw Materials Inventory, $5,000; Work in process Inventory, $11,000; Finished Goods Inventory, $39,000; Common Stock, $650,000; and Retained Earnings, $200,000. Tuscan experienced the following accounting events during 2012. Other than the adjusting entries for depreciation, assume that all transactions are cash transactions.

1. Paid $50,000 of research and development costs to create the headset.
2. Paid $139,000 for raw materials will be used to make headsets.
3. Placed $141,000 of the raw materials cost into the process of manufacturing headsets.
4. Paid $82,200 for salaries of selling and administrative employees.
5. Paid $224,000 for wages of production workers.
6. Paid $48,000 to purchase furniture used in selling and administrative offices.
7. Recognized depreciation on the office furniture. The furniture was acquired January 1, 2012. It has an $8,000 salvage value and a four-year useful life. The amount of depreciation is computed as [(cost − salvage) ÷ useful life]. Specifically, ($48,000 − $8,000) ÷ 4 = $10,000.
8. Paid $65,000 to purchase manufacturing equipment.
9. Recognized depreciation on the manufacturing equipment. The equipment was acquired January 1, 2012. It has a $5,000 salvage value and a three-year useful life. The amount of depreciation is computed as [(cost − salvage) ÷ useful life]. Specifically, ($65,000 − $5,000) ÷ 3 = $20,000.
10. Paid $136,000 for rent and utility costs on the manufacturing facility.
11. Paid $41,000 for inventory holding expenses for completed headsets (rental of warehouse space, salaries of warehouse personnel, and other general storage costs.)
12. Completed and transferred headsets that had a total cost of $520,000 from work in process inventory to finished goods.
13. Sold headsets for $738,200.
14. It cost Tuscan $517,400 to make the headsets sold in Event 13.

Required

a. Show how these events affect the balance sheet, income statement, and statement of cash flows by recording them in a horizontal financial statement model.
b. Explain why Tuscan's recognition of cost of goods sold expense had no impact on cash flow.
c. Prepare a schedule of costs of goods manufactured and sold, an income statement, and a balance sheet.
d. Distinguish between the product costs and the upstream and downstream costs that Tuscan incurred.

Solution to Requirement *a*

Event No.	Cash	+	Raw Mat. Inv.	+	WIP Inv.	+	Finished Goods Inv.	+	Office Furn.*	+	Manuf. Equip.*	=	Com. Stk.	+	Ret. Earn.		Rev.	−	Exp.	=	Net Inc.	Cash Flow
	795,000		5,000		11,000		39,000					=	650,000		200,000					=		
1	(50,000)											=			(50,000)			−	50,000	=	(50,000)	(50,000) OA
2	(139,000)		139,000									=								=		(139,000) OA
3			(141,000)		141,000							=								=		
4	(82,200)											=			(82,200)			−	82,200	=	(82,200)	(82,200) OA
5	(224,000)				224,000							=								=		(224,000) OA
6	(48,000)						48,000					=								=		(48,000) IA
7							(10,000)					=			(10,000)			−	10,000	=	(10,000)	
8	(65,000)										65,000	=								=		(65,000) IA
9					20,000						(20,000)	=								=		
10	(136,000)		136,000									=								=		(136,000) OA
11	(41,000)											=			(41,000)			−	41,000	=	(41,000)	(41,000) OA
12					(520,000)		520,000					=								=		
13	738,200											=			738,200		738,200			=	738,200	738,200 OA
14							(517,400)					=			(517,400)			−	517,400	=	(517,400)	
Totals	748,000	+	3,000	+	12,000	+	41,600	+	38,000	+	45,000	=	650,000	+	237,600		738,200	−	700,600	=	37,600	(47,000) NC

*Negative amounts in these columns represent accumulated depreciation.

Solution to Requirement *b*

Tuscan does not recognize a cash outflow at the time the goods are sold because the cash is paid when the materials, labor, and overhead are acquired.

Solution to Requirement *c*

TUSCAN MANUFACTURING COMPANY
Schedule of Cost of Goods Manufactured and Sold
For the Year Ended December 31, 2012

Beginning raw materials Inventory	$ 5,000
Plus: Raw materials purchases	139,000
Less: Ending raw materials inventory	(3,000)
Raw materials used	141,000
Labor	224,000
Overhead	156,000
Total manufacturing costs	521,000
Plus: Beginning work in process inventory	11,000
Total work in process inventory	532,000
Less: Ending work in process inventory	(12,000)
Cost of goods manufactured	520,000
Plus: Beginning finished goods inventory	39,000
Cost of goods available for sale	559,000
Less: Ending finished goods inventory	(41,600)
Cost of goods sold	$517,400

TUSCAN MANUFACTURING COMPANY
Income Statement
For the Year Ended December 31, 2012

Sales revenue	$738,200
Cost of goods sold	(517,400)
Gross margin	220,800
Research and development expenses	(50,000)
Selling and administrative salary expense	(82,200)
Selling and administrative depreciation expense	(10,000)
Inventory holding expenses	(41,000)
Net Income	$ 37,600

TUSCAN MANUFACTURING COMPANY
Balance Sheet
As of December 31, 2012

Assets	
Cash	$748,000
Raw materials inventory	3,000
Work in process inventory	12,000
Finished goods inventory	41,600
Manufacturing equipment less accumulated depreciation	45,000
Office furniture less accumulated depreciation	38,000
Total assets	$887,600
Equity	
Common stock	$650,000
Retained earnings	237,600
Total stockholders' equity	$887,600

Solution to Requirement *d*

Inventory product costs for manufacturing companies focus on the costs necessary to make the product. The cost of research and development (Event 1) occurs before the inventory is made and is therefore an upstream cost, not an inventory (product) cost. The inventory holding costs (Event 11) are incurred after the inventory has been made and are therefore downstream costs, not product costs. Selling costs (included in Events 4 and 7) are normally incurred after products have been made and are therefore usually classified as downstream costs. Administrative costs (also included in Events 4 and 7) are not related to making products and are therefore not classified as product costs. Administrative costs may be incurred before, during, or after products are made, so they may be classified as either upstream or downstream costs. Only the costs of materials, labor, and overhead that are actually incurred for the purpose of making goods (Events 3, 5, 9, and 10) are classified as product costs.

KEY TERMS

QUESTIONS

1. What are some differences between financial and managerial accounting?

2. What does the value-added principle mean as it applies to managerial accounting information? Give an example of value-added information that may be included in managerial accounting reports but is not shown in publicly reported financial statements.

3. How does product costing used in financial accounting differ from product costing used in managerial accounting?

4. What does the statement "costs can be assets or expenses" mean?

5. Why are the salaries of production workers accumulated in an inventory account instead of being directly expensed on the income statement?

6. How do product costs affect the financial statements? How does the classification of product cost (as an asset vs. an expense) affect net income?

7. What is an indirect cost? Provide examples of product costs that would be classified as indirect.

8. How does a product cost differ from a general, selling, and administrative cost? Give examples of each.

9. Why is cost classification important to managers?

10. What is cost allocation? Give an example of a cost that needs to be allocated.

11. What are some of the common ethical conflicts that accountants encounter?

12. What costs should be considered in determining the sales price of a product?

13. What is a just-in-time (JIT) inventory system? Name some inventory costs that can be eliminated or reduced by its use.

14. What are the two dimensions of a total quality management (TQM) program? Why is TQM being used in business practice? (Appendix)

15. What does the term *reengineering* mean? Name some reengineering practices. (Appendix)

16. How has the Institute of Management Accountants responded to the need for high standards of ethical conduct in the accounting profession? (Appendix)

17. What does the term *activity-based management* mean? (Appendix)

18. What is a value chain? (Appendix)

19. What do the terms *value-added activity* and *nonvalue-added activity* mean? Provide an example of each type of activity. (Appendix)

MULTIPLE-CHOICE QUESTIONS

**Multiple-choice questions are provided on the text website at
www.mhhe.com/edmondssurvey3e.**

EXERCISES

**All applicable Exercises are available with McGraw-Hill's
Connect Accounting.**

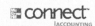

Exercise 10-1   *Identifying financial versus managerial accounting characteristics*   **LO 1**

Required

Indicate whether each of the following is representative of managerial or of financial accounting.

a. Information is factual and is characterized by objectivity, reliability, consistency, and accuracy.

b. Information is reported continuously and has a current or future orientation.

c. Information is provided to outsiders including investors, creditors, government agencies, analysts, and reporters.
d. Information is regulated by the SEC, FASB, and other sources of GAAP.
e. Information is based on estimates that are bounded by relevance and timeliness.
f. Information is historically based and usually reported annually.
g. Information is local and pertains to subunits of the organization.
h. Information includes economic and nonfinancial data as well as financial data.
i. Information is global and pertains to the company as a whole.
j. Information is provided to insiders including executives, managers, and operators.

LO 2

Exercise 10-2   *Identifying product versus general, selling, and administrative costs*

Required

Indicate whether each of the following costs should be classified as a product cost or as a general, selling, and administrative cost.

a. Direct materials used in a manufacturing company.
b. Indirect materials used in a manufacturing company.
c. Salaries of employees working in the accounting department.
d. Commissions paid to sales staff.
e. Interest on the mortgage for the company's corporate headquarters.
f. Indirect labor used to manufacture inventory.
g. Attorney's fees paid to protect the company from frivolous lawsuits.
h. Research and development costs incurred to create new drugs for a pharmaceutical company.
i. The cost of secretarial supplies used in a doctor's office.
j. Depreciation on the office furniture of the company president.

LO 2

Exercise 10-3   *Classifying costs: product or G, S, & A/asset or expense*

Required

Use the following format to classify each cost as a product cost or a general, selling, and administrative (G, S, & A) cost. Also indicate whether the cost would be recorded as an asset or an expense. The first item is shown as an example.

Cost Category	Product/ G, S, & A	Asset/ Expense
Research and development costs	G, S, & A	Expense
Cost to set up manufacturing facility		
Utilities used in factory		
Cars for sales staff		
Distributions to stockholders		
General office supplies		
Raw materials used in the manufacturing process		
Cost to rent office equipment		
Wages of production workers		
Advertising costs		
Promotion costs		
Production supplies		
Depreciation on administration building		
Depreciation on manufacturing equipment		

Exercise 10-4   *Identifying effect of product versus general, selling, and*   **LO 2, 3**
administrative costs on financial statements

Required

Nailry Industries recognized accrued compensation cost. Use the following model to show how this event would affect the company's financial statement under the following two assumptions: (1) the compensation is for office personnel and (2) the compensation is for production workers. Use pluses or minuses to show the effect on each element. If an element is not affected, indicate so by placing the letters NA under the appropriate heading.

	Assets	=	Liab.	+	Equity	Rev.	−	Exp.	=	Net Inc.	Cash Flow
1.											
2.											

Exercise 10-5   *Identify effect of product versus general, selling, and administrative*   **LO 2, 3**
costs on financial statements

Required

Milby Industries recognized the annual cost of depreciation on its December 31 financial statement. Using the following horizontal financial statements model, indicate how this event affected the company's financial statements under the following two assumptions: (1) the depreciation was on office furniture and (2) the depreciation was on manufacturing equipment. Indicate whether the event increases (I), decreases (D), or has no affect (NA) on each element of the financial statements. Also, in the Cash Flow column, indicate whether the cash flow is for operating activities (OA), investing activities (IA), or financing activities (FA). (Note: Show accumulated depreciation as a decrease in the book value of the appropriate asset account.)

Event No.	Cash	+	Inventory	+	Manuf. Equip.	+	Office Furn.	=	Com. Stk.	+	Ret. Earn.	Rev.	−	Exp.	=	Net Inc.	Cash Flow
1.																	
2.																	

with headers **Assets** spanning Cash through Office Furn., and **Equity** spanning Com. Stk. and Ret. Earn.

Exercise 10-6   *Identifying product costs in a manufacturing company*   **LO 2**

Tiffany Crissler was talking to another accounting student, Bill Tyrone. Upon discovering that the accounting department offered an upper-level course in cost measurement, Tiffany remarked to Bill, "How difficult can it be? My parents own a toy store. All you have to do to figure out how much something costs is look at the invoice. Surely you don't need an entire course to teach you how to read an invoice."

Required

a. Identify the three main components of product cost for a manufacturing entity.

b. Explain why measuring product cost for a manufacturing entity is more complex than measuring product cost for a retail toy store.

c. Assume that Tiffany's parents rent a store for $7,500 per month. Different types of toys use different amounts of store space. For example, displaying a bicycle requires more store space than displaying a deck of cards. Also, some toys remain on the shelf longer than others. Fad toys sell quickly, but traditional toys sell more slowly. Under these circumstances, how would you determine the amount of rental cost required to display each type of toy? Identify two other costs incurred by a toy store that may be difficult to allocate to individual toys.

LO 2, 3

Exercise 10-7   *Identifying product versus general, selling, and administrative costs*

A review of the accounting records of Rayford Manufacturing indicated that the company incurred the following payroll costs during the month of August.

1. Salary of the company president—$32,000.
2. Salary of the vice president of manufacturing—$16,000.
3. Salary of the chief financial officer—$18,800.
4. Salary of the vice president of marketing—$15,600.
5. Salaries of middle managers (department heads, production supervisors) in manufacturing plant—$196,000.
6. Wages of production workers—$938,000.
7. Salaries of administrative secretaries—$112,000.
8. Salaries of engineers and other personnel responsible for maintaining production equipment—$178,000.
9. Commissions paid to sales staff—$252,000.

Required

a. What amount of payroll cost would be classified as general, selling, and administrative expense?
b. Assuming that Rayford made 4,000 units of product and sold 3,600 of them during the month of August, determine the amount of payroll cost that would be included in cost of goods sold.

LO 2, 3

Exercise 10-8   *Recording product versus general, selling, and administrative costs in a financial statements model*

Pappas Manufacturing experienced the following events during its first accounting period.

1. Recognized depreciation on manufacturing equipment.
2. Recognized depreciation on office furniture.
3. Recognized revenue from cash sale of products.
4. Recognized cost of goods sold from sale referenced in Event 3.
5. Acquired cash by issuing common stock.
6. Paid cash to purchase raw materials that were used to make products.
7. Paid wages to production workers.
8. Paid salaries to administrative staff.

Required

Use the following horizontal financial statements model to show how each event affects the balance sheet, income statement, and statement of cash flows. Indicate whether the event increases (I), decreases (D), or has no effect (NA) on each element of the financial statements. In the Cash Flow column, indicate whether the cash flow is for operating activities (OA), investing activities (IA), or financing activities (FA). The first transaction has been recorded as an example. (*Note:* Show accumulated depreciation as decrease in the book value of the appropriate asset account.)

		Assets				Equity				
Event No.	Cash	+ Inventory	+ Manuf. Equip.	+ Office Furn.	= Com. Stk.	+ Ret. Earn.	Rev.	− Exp.	= Net Inc.	Cash Flow
1.	NA	I	D	NA	NA	NA	NA	NA	NA	NA

LO 2, 3

Exercise 10-9   *Allocating product costs between ending inventory and cost of goods sold*

Howle Manufacturing Company began operations on January 1. During the year, it started and completed 1,700 units of product. The company incurred the following costs.

1. Raw materials purchased and used—$3,150.
2. Wages of production workers—$3,530.

3. Salaries of administrative and sales personnel—$1,995.
4. Depreciation on manufacturing equipment—$4,370.
5. Depreciation on administrative equipment—$1,835.

Howle sold 1,020 units of product.

Required

a. Determine the total product cost for the year.
b. Determine the total cost of the ending inventory.
c. Determine the total of cost of goods sold.

Exercise 10-10 *Financial statement effects for manufacturing versus service*   **LO 6**
organizations

The following financial statements model shows the effects of recognizing depreciation in two
different circumstances. One circumstance represents recognizing depreciation on a machine
used in a factory. The other circumstance recognizes depreciation on computers used in a consulting firm. The effects of each event have been recorded using the letter (I) to represent increase, (D) for decrease, and (NA) for no effect.

Event No.	Assets				Equity							
	Cash	+	Inventory	+	Equip.	=	Com. Stk.	+	Ret. Earn.	Rev.	−	Exp.	=	Net Inc.	Cash Flow
1.	NA		NA		D		NA		D	NA		I		D	NA
2.	NA		I		D		NA		NA	NA		NA		NA	NA

Required

a. Identify the event that represents depreciation on the computers.
b. Explain why recognizing depreciation on equipment used in a manufacturing company affects financial statements differently from recognizing depreciation on equipment used in a
service organization.

Exercise 10-11 *Identifying the effect of product versus general, selling, and*   **LO 3**
administrative cost on the income statement and statement of
cash flows

Each of the following events describes acquiring an asset that requires a year-end adjusting entry.
December 31st is the end of year.

1. Paid $14,000 cash on January 1 to purchase printers to be used for administrative purposes.
   The printers had an estimated useful life of four years and a $2,000 salvage value.
2. Paid $14,000 cash on January 1 to purchase manufacturing equipment. The equipment had
   an estimated useful life of four years and a $2,000 salvage value.
3. Paid $12,000 cash in advance on May 1 for a one-year rental contract on administrative
   offices.
4. Paid $12,000 cash in advance on May 1 for a one-year rental contract on manufacturing
   facilities.
5. Paid $2,000 cash to purchase supplies to be used by the marketing department. At the end of
   the year, $400 of supplies were still on hand.
6. Paid $2,000 cash to purchase supplies to be used in the manufacturing process. At the end of
   the year, $400 of supplies were still on hand.

Required

Explain how acquiring the asset and making the adjusting entry affect the amount of net income
and the cash flow reported on the year-end financial statements. Also, in the Cash Flow column,
indicate whether the cash flow is for operating activities (OA), investing activities (IA), or
financing activities (FA). Use (NA) for no effect. Assume a December 31 annual closing date.

The first event has been recorded as an example. Assume that any products that have been made have not been sold.

	Net Income	Cash Flow
Event No.	**Amount of Change**	**Amount of Change**
1. Purchase of printers	NA	(14,000) IA
1. Make adjusting entry	(3,000)	NA

LO 4

Exercise 10-12   *Missing information in a schedule of cost of goods manufactured*

Required

Supply the missing information on the following schedule of cost of goods manufactured.

DEWBERRY CORPORATION
Schedule of Cost of Goods Manufactured
For the Year Ended December 31, 2011

Raw materials		
Beginning inventory	$?	
Plus: Purchases	120,000	
Raw materials available for use	$148,000	
Minus: Ending raw materials inventory	?	
Cost of direct raw materials used		$124,000
Direct labor		?
Manufacturing overhead		24,000
Total manufacturing costs		310,000
Plus: Beginning work in process inventory		?
Total work in process		?
Minus: Ending work in process inventory		46,000
Cost of goods manufactured		$306,000

LO 4

Exercise 10-13   *Cost of goods manufactured and sold*

The following information pertains to Pandey Manufacturing Company for March 2012. Assume actual overhead equaled applied overhead.

March 1

Inventory balances	
Raw materials	$125,000
Work in process	120,000
Finished goods	78,000

March 31

Inventory balances	
Raw materials	$ 85,000
Work in process	145,000
Finished goods	80,000

During March

Costs of raw materials purchased	$120,000
Costs of direct labor	100,000
Costs of manufacturing overhead	63,000
Sales revenues	350,000

Required

a. Prepare a schedule of cost of goods manufactured and sold.

b. Calculate the amount of gross margin on the income statement.

Exercise 10-14   *Upstream and downstream costs*

During 2011, Gallo Manufacturing Company incurred $90,000,000 of research and development (R&D) costs to create a long-life battery to use in computers. In accordance with FASB standards, the entire R&D cost was recognized as an expense in 2011. Manufacturing costs (direct materials, direct labor, and overhead) were expected to be $260 per unit. Packaging, shipping, and sales commissions were expected to be $50 per unit. Gallo expected to sell 2,000,000 batteries before new research renders the battery design technologically obsolete. During 2011, Gallo made 440,000 batteries and sold 400,000 of them.

Required

a. Identify the upstream and downstream costs.

b. Determine the 2011 amount of cost of goods sold and the ending inventory balance.

c. Determine the sales price assuming that Gallo desired to earn a profit margin equal to 25 percent of the *total cost* of developing, making, and distributing the batteries.

d. Prepare an income statement for 2011. Use the sales price determined in Requirement *c*.

e. Why would Gallo price the batteries at a level that would generate a loss for the 2011 accounting period?

Exercise 10-15   *Statement of Ethical Professional Practice*

In February 2006 former senator Warren Rudman of New Hampshire completed a 17-month investigation of an $11 billion accounting scandal at Fannie Mae (a major enterprise involved in home mortgage financing). The Rudman investigation concluded that Fannie Mae's CFO and controller used an accounting gimmick to manipulate financial statements in order to meet earnings-per-share (EPS) targets. Meeting the EPS targets triggered bonus payments for the executives. Fannie Mae's problems continued after 2006, and on September 8, 2008, it went into conservatorship under the control of the Federal Housing Financing Agency. The primary executives at the time of the Rudman investigation were replaced, and the enterprise reported a $59.8 billion loss in 2008.

Required

Review the principles of ethical professional practice shown in Exhibit 10.17. Identify and comment on which of the ethical principles the CFO and controller violated.

Exercise 10-16   *Using JIT to minimize waste and lost opportunity*

Ann Kyser, a teacher at Hewitt Middle School, is in charge of ordering the T-shirts to be sold for the school's annual fund-raising project. The T-shirts are printed with a special Hewitt School logo. In some years, the supply of T-shirts has been insufficient to satisfy the number of sales orders. In other years, T-shirts have been left over. Excess T-shirts are normally donated to some charitable organization. T-shirts cost the school $8 each and are normally sold for $14 each. Ms. Kyser has decided to order 800 shirts.

Required

a. If the school receives actual sales orders for 725 shirts, what amount of profit will the school earn? What is the cost of waste due to excess inventory?

b. If the school receives actual sales orders for 825 shirts, what amount of profit will the school earn? What amount of opportunity cost will the school incur?

c. Explain how a JIT inventory system could maximize profitability by eliminating waste and opportunity cost.

Exercise 10-17   *Using JIT to minimize holding costs*

Lee Pet Supplies purchases its inventory from a variety of suppliers, some of which require a six-week lead time before delivery. To ensure that she has a sufficient supply of goods on hand, Ms. Polk, the owner, must maintain a large supply of inventory. The cost of this inventory averages $21,000. She usually finances the purchase of inventory and pays a 9 percent annual finance charge. Ms. Polk's accountant has suggested that she should establish a relationship with a single large distributor who can satisfy all of her orders within a two-week time period. Given this quick turnaround time, she will be able to reduce her average inventory balance to $4,000.

Ms. Polk also believes that she could save $2,500 per year by reducing phone bills, insurance, and warehouse rental space costs associated with ordering and maintaining the larger level of inventory.

Required

a. Is the new inventory system available to Ms. Polk a pure or approximate just-in-time system?

b. Based on the information provided, how much of Ms. Polk's inventory holding cost could be eliminated by taking the accountant's advice?

LO 9

Exercise 10-18 *Value chain analysis (Appendix)*

Sonic Company manufactures and sells high-quality audio speakers. The speakers are encased in solid walnut cabinets supplied by Moore Cabinet Inc. Moore packages the speakers in durable moisture-proof boxes and ships them by truck to Sonic's manufacturing facility, which is located 50 miles from the cabinet factory.

Required

Identify the nonvalue-added activities that occur between the companies described in the above scenario. Explain how these nonvalue-added activities could be eliminated.

PROBLEMS

All applicable Problems are available with McGraw-Hill's
Connect Accounting.

LO 2, 3

CHECK FIGURES
a. Average Cost per Unit: $8.40
f. $90,400

Problem 10-19 *Product versus general, selling, and administrative costs*

Jolly Manufacturing Company was started on January 1, 2011, when it acquired $90,000 cash by issuing common stock. Jolly immediately purchased office furniture and manufacturing equipment costing $10,000 and $28,000, respectively. The office furniture had a five-year useful life and a zero salvage value. The manufacturing equipment had a $4,000 salvage value and an expected useful life of three years. The company paid $12,000 for salaries of administrative personnel and $16,000 for wages to production personnel. Finally, the company paid $18,000 for raw materials that were used to make inventory. All inventory was started and completed during the year. Jolly completed production on 5,000 units of product and sold 4,000 units at a price of $12 each in 2011. (Assume all transactions are cash transactions.)

Required

a. Determine the total product cost and the average cost per unit of the inventory produced in 2011.

b. Determine the amount of cost of goods sold that would appear on the 2011 income statement.

c. Determine the amount of the ending inventory balance that would appear on the December 31, 2011, balance sheet.

d. Determine the amount of net income that would appear on the 2011 income statement.

e. Determine the amount of retained earnings that would appear on the December 31, 2011, balance sheet.

f. Determine the amount of total assets that would appear on the December 31, 2011, balance sheet.

g. Determine the amount of net cash flow from operating activities that would appear on the 2011 statement of cash flows.

h. Determine the amount of net cash flow from investing activities that would appear on the 2011 statement of cash flows.

LO 3

eXcel

CHECK FIGURES
Cash balance: $33,000
Net income: $4,600

Problem 10-20 *Effect of product versus period costs on financial statements*

Hoen Manufacturing Company experienced the following accounting events during its first year of operation. With the exception of the adjusting entries for depreciation, all transactions are cash transactions.

1. Acquired $50,000 cash by issuing common stock.

2. Paid $8,000 for the materials used to make products, all of which were started and completed during the year.

3. Paid salaries of $4,400 to selling and administrative employees.
4. Paid wages of $7,000 to production workers.
5. Paid $9,600 for furniture used in selling and administrative offices. The furniture was acquired on January 1. It had a $1,600 estimated salvage value and a four-year useful life.
6. Paid $13,000 for manufacturing equipment. The equipment was acquired on January 1. It had a $1,000 estimated salvage value and a three-year useful life.
7. Sold inventory to customers for $25,000 that had cost $14,000 to make.

Required

Explain how these events would affect the balance sheet, income statement, and statement of cash flows by recording them in a horizontal financial statements model as indicated here. The first event is recorded as an example. In the Cash Flow column, indicate whether the amounts represent financing activities (FA), investing activities (IA), or operating activities (OA).

| Event No. | Assets | | | | Equity | | | | | | |
	Cash	+ Inventory	+ Manuf. Equip.*	+ Office Furn.*	= Com. Stk.	+ Ret. Earn.	Rev.	− Exp.	= Net Inc.	Cash Flow	
1	50,000				50,000					50,000	FA

*Record accumulated depreciation as negative amounts in these columns.

Problem 10-21 *Product versus general, selling, and administrative costs*

LO 3

The following transactions pertain to 2012, the first year operations of Hall Company. All inventory was started and completed during 2012. Assume that all transactions are cash transactions.

1. Acquired $4,000 cash by issuing common stock.
2. Paid $720 for materials used to produce inventory.
3. Paid $1,800 to production workers.
4. Paid $540 rental fee for production equipment.
5. Paid $180 to administrative employees.
6. Paid $144 rental fee for administrative office equipment.
7. Produced 300 units of inventory of which 200 units were sold at a price of $12 each.

Required

Prepare an income statement, balance sheet, and statement of cash flows.

CHECK FIGURES
Net income: $36
Total assets: $4,036

Problem 10-22 *Schedule of cost of goods manufactured and sold*

LO 4

Kirsoff Company makes eBook readers. The company had the following amounts at the beginning of 2011: Cash, $660,000; Raw Materials Inventory, $51,000; Work in Process Inventory, $18,000; Finished Goods Inventory, $43,000; Common Stock, $583,000; and Retained Earnings, $189,000. Kirsoff experienced the following accounting events during 2011. Other than the adjusting entries for depreciation, assume that all transactions are cash transactions.

1. Paid $23,000 of research and development costs.
2. Paid $47,000 for raw materials that will be used to make eBook readers.
3. Placed $83,000 of the raw materials cost into the process of manufacturing eBook readers.
4. Paid $60,000 for salaries of selling and administrative employees.
5. Paid $91,000 for wages of production workers.
6. Paid $90,000 to purchase equipment used in selling and administrative offices.
7. Recognized depreciation on the office equipment. The equipment was acquired on January, 1, 2011. It has a $10,000 salvage value and a five-year life. The amount of depreciation is computed as [(Cost − salvage) ÷ useful life]. Specifically, ($90,000 − $10,000) ÷ 5 = $16,000.

8. Paid $165,000 to purchase manufacturing equipment.

9. Recognized depreciation on the manufacturing equipment. The equipment was acquired on January 1, 2011. It has a $25,000 salvage value and a seven-year life. The amount of depreciation is computed as [(Cost − salvage) ÷ useful life]. Specifically, ($165,000 − $25,000) ÷ 7 = $20,000.

10. Paid $45,000 for rent and utility costs on the manufacturing facility.

11. Paid $70,000 for inventory holding expenses for completed eBook readers (rental of warehouse space, salaries of warehouse personnel, and other general storage cost).

12. Completed and transferred eBook readers that had total cost of $240,000 from work in process inventory to finished goods.

13. Sold 1,000 eBook readers for $420,000.

14. It cost Kirsoff $220,000 to make the eBook readers sold in Event 13.

Required

a. Show how these events affect the balance sheet, income statement, and statement of cash flows by recording them in a horizontal financial statements model.

b. Explain why Kirsoff's recognition of cost of goods sold had no impact on cash flow.

c. Prepare a schedule of cost of goods manufactured and sold, a formal income statement, and a balance sheet for the year.

d. Distinguish between the product costs and the upstream costs that Kirsoff incurred.

e. The company president believes that Kirsoff could save money by buying the inventory that it currently makes. The warehouse manager said that would not be a good idea because the purchase price of $230 per unit was above the $220 average cost per unit of making the product. Assuming the purchased inventory would be available on demand, explain how the company could be correct and why the production manager could be biased in his assessment of the option to buy the inventory.

CHECK FIGURES
a. Net loss: $20,000
b. Total assets: $55,000
c. Net income: $11,000

LO 3, 6

Problem 10-23   *Service versus manufacturing companies*

Goree Company began operations on January 1, 2011, by issuing common stock for $30,000 cash. During 2011, Goree received $40,000 cash from revenue and incurred costs that required $60,000 of cash payments.

Required

Prepare an income statement, balance sheet, and statement of cash flows for Goree Company for 2011, under each of the following independent scenarios.

a. Goree is a promoter of rock concerts. The $60,000 was paid to provide a rock concert that produced the revenue.

b. Goree is in the car rental business. The $60,000 was paid to purchase automobiles. The automobiles were purchased on January 1, 2011, had four-year useful lives and no expected salvage value. Goree uses straight-line depreciation. The revenue was generated by leasing the automobiles.

c. Goree is a manufacturing company. The $60,000 was paid to purchase the following items.

   (1) Paid $8,000 cash to purchase materials that were used to make products during the year.

   (2) Paid $20,000 cash for wages of factory workers who made products during the year.

   (3) Paid $2,000 cash for salaries of sales and administrative employees.

   (4) Paid $30,000 cash to purchase manufacturing equipment. The equipment was used solely to make products. It had a three-year life and a $6,000 salvage value. The company uses straight-line depreciation.

   (5) During 2011, Goree started and completed 2,000 units of product. The revenue was earned when Goree sold 1,500 units of product to its customers.

d. Refer to Requirement c. Could Goree determine the actual cost of making the 90th unit of product? How likely is it that the actual cost of the 90th unit of product was exactly the same as the cost of producing the 408th unit of product? Explain why management may be more interested in average cost than in actual cost.

Problem 10-24   *Importance of cost classification and ethics*

Cooke Manufacturing Company (CMC) was started when it acquired $40,000 by issuing common stock. During the first year of operations, the company incurred specifically identifiable product costs (materials, labor, and overhead) amounting to $24,000. CMC also incurred $16,000 of engineering design and planning costs. There was a debate regarding how the design and planning costs should be classified. Advocates of Option 1 believe that the costs should be classified as upstream general, selling, and administrative costs. Advocates of Option 2 believe it is more appropriate to classify the design and planning costs as product costs. During the year, CMC made 4,000 units of product and sold 3,000 units at a price of $24 each. All transactions were cash transactions.

Required

a. Prepare an income statement, balance sheet, and statement of cash flows under each of the two options.

b. Identify the option that results in financial statements that are more likely to leave a favorable impression on investors and creditors.

c. Assume that CMC provides an incentive bonus to the CFO who is a CMA. The bonus is equal to 13 percent of net income. Compute the amount of the bonus under each of the two options. Identify the option that provides the CFO with the higher bonus.

d. Assume the CFO knows that the design and planning costs are upstream costs that must be recognized as general, selling, and administrative expenses (Option 1). Even so, the CFO convinces management to classify the upstream costs as product cost in order to increase his bonus. Identify two principles in the Statement of Ethical Professional Practice that are violated by the CFO's behavior.

e. Comment on the conflict of interest between the company president as determined in Requirement *c* and owners of the company as indicated in Requirement *d*. Describe an incentive compensation plan that would avoid a conflict of interest between the president and the owners.

Problem 10-25   *Using JIT to reduce inventory holding costs*

Burt Manufacturing Company obtains its raw materials from a variety of suppliers. Burt's strategy is to obtain the best price by letting the suppliers know that it buys from the lowest bidder. Approximately four years ago, unexpected increase in demand resulted in materials shortages. Burt was unable to find the materials it needed even though it was willing to pay premium prices. Because of the lack of raw materials, Burt was forced to close its manufacturing facility for two weeks. Its president vowed that her company would never again be at the mercy of its suppliers. She immediately ordered her purchasing agent to perpetually maintain a one-month supply of raw materials. Compliance with the president's orders resulted in a raw materials inventory amounting to approximately $1,600,000. Warehouse rental and personnel costs to maintain the inventory amounted to $8,000 per month. Burt has a line of credit with a local bank that calls for a 12 percent annual rate of interest. Assume that Burt finances the raw materials inventory with the line of credit.

Required

a. Based on the information provided, determine the annual holding cost of the raw materials inventory.

b. Explain how a JIT system could reduce Burt's inventory holding cost.

c. Explain how most-favored customer status could enable Burt to establish a JIT inventory system without risking the raw materials shortages experienced in the past.

Problem 10-26   *Using JIT to minimize waste and lost opportunity*

CMA Review Inc. provides review courses for students studying to take the CMA exam. The cost of textbooks is included in the registration fee. Text material requires constant updating and is useful for only one course. To minimize printing costs and ensure availability of books on the first day of class, CMA Review has books printed and delivered to its offices two weeks in advance of the first class. To ensure that enough books are available, CMA Review normally orders 10 percent more than expected enrollment. Usually there is an oversupply of books that is thrown away. However, demand occasionally exceeds expectations by more than 10 percent and there are too few books available for student use. CMA Review had been forced to turn away students because of lack of textbooks. CMA Review expects to enroll approximately 100 students per course. The tuition fee is $800 per student. The cost of teachers is $25,000 per course, textbooks cost $60 each, and other operating expenses are estimated to be $35,000 per course.

Required

a. Prepare an income statement, assuming that 95 students enroll in a course. Determine the cost of waste associated with unused books.

b. Prepare an income statement, assuming that 115 students attempt to enroll in the course. Note that five students are turned away because of too few textbooks. Determine the amount of lost profit resulting from the inability to serve the five additional students.

c. Suppose that textbooks can be produced through a high-speed copying process that permits delivery *just in time* for class to start. The cost of books made using this process, however, is $65 each. Assume that all books must be made using the same production process. In other words, CMA Review cannot order some of the books using the regular copy process and the rest using the high-speed process. Prepare an income statement under the JIT system assuming that 95 students enroll in a course. Compare the income statement under JIT with the income statement prepared in Requirement *a*. Comment on how the JIT system would affect profitability.

d. Assume the same facts as in Requirement *c* with respect to a JIT system that enables immediate delivery of books at a cost of $65 each. Prepare an income statement under the JIT system, assuming that 115 students enroll in a course. Compare the income statement under JIT with the income statement prepared in Requirement *b*. Comment on how the JIT system would affect profitability.

e. Discuss the possible effect of the JIT system on the level of customer satisfaction.

LO 9

Problem 10-27 *Value chain analysis (Appendix)*

Jensen Company invented a new process for manufacturing ice cream. The ingredients are mixed in high-tech machinery that forms the product into small round beads. Like a bag of balls, the ice cream beads are surrounded by air pockets in packages. This design has numerous advantages. First, each bite of ice cream melts quickly in a person's mouth, creating a more flavorful sensation when compared to ordinary ice cream. Also, the air pockets mean that a typical serving includes a smaller amount of ice cream. This not only reduces materials cost but also provides the consumer with a low-calorie snack. A cup appears full of ice cream, but it is really half full of air. The consumer eats only half the ingredients that are contained in a typical cup of blended ice cream. Finally, the texture of the ice cream makes scooping it out of a large container easy. The frustration of trying to get a spoon into a rock-solid package of blended ice cream has been eliminated. Jensen Company named the new product Sonic Cream.

Like many other ice cream producers, Jensen Company purchases its raw materials from a food wholesaler. The ingredients are mixed in Jensen's manufacturing plant. The packages of finished product are distributed to privately owned franchise ice cream shops that sell Sonic Cream directly to the public.

Jensen provides national advertising and is responsible for all research and development costs associated with making new flavors of Sonic Cream.

Required

a. Based on the information provided, draw a comprehensive value chain for Jensen Company that includes its suppliers and customers.

b. Identify the place in the chain where Jensen Company is exercising its opportunity to create added value beyond that currently being provided by its competitors.

ANALYZE, THINK, COMMUNICATE

ATC 10-1   Business Applications Case   *Financial versus managerial accounting*

The following information was taken from the 2008 and 2009 Form 10-Ks for Dell, Inc.

	Fiscal Year Ended	
	January 30, 2009	**February 1, 2008**
Number of regular employees	76,500	82,700
Number of temporary employees	2,400	5,500
Revenues (in millions)	$61,101	$61,133
Properties owned or leased in the U.S.	7.4 million square feet	8.2 million square feet
Properties owned or leased outside the U.S.	9.4 million square feet	9.7 million square feet
Total assets (in millions)	$26,500	$27,561
Gross margin (in millions)	$10,957	$11,671

Required

a. Explain whether each line of information in the table above would best be described as being primarily financial accounting or managerial accounting in nature.

b. Provide some additional examples of managerial and financial accounting information that could apply to Dell.

c. If you analyze only the data you identified as financial in nature, does it appear that Dell's 2009 fiscal year was better or worse than its 2008 fiscal year? Explain.

d. If you analyze only the data you identified as managerial in nature, does it appear that Dell's 2009 fiscal year was better or worse than its 2008 fiscal year? Explain.

ATC 10-2   Group Assignment   *Product versus upstream and downstream costs*

Victor Holt, the accounting manager of Sexton Inc., gathered the following information for 2011. Some of it can be used to construct an income statement for 2011. Ignore items that do not appear on an income statement. Some computations may be required. For example, the cost of manufacturing equipment would not appear on the income statement. However, the cost of manufacturing equipment is needed to compute the amount of depreciation. All units of product were started and completed in 2011.

1. Issued $864,000 of common stock.
2. Paid engineers in the product design department $10,000 for salaries that were accrued at the end of the previous year.
3. Incurred advertising expenses of $70,000.
4. Paid $720,000 for materials used to manufacture the company's product.
5. Incurred utility costs of $160,000. These costs were allocated to different departments on the basis of square footage of floor space. Mr. Holt identified three departments and determined the square footage of floor space for each department to be as shown in the table below.

Department	Square Footage
Research and development	10,000
Manufacturing	60,000
Selling and administrative	30,000
Total	100,000

6. Paid $880,000 for wages of production workers.
7. Paid cash of $658,000 for salaries of administrative personnel. There was $16,000 of accrued salaries owed to administrative personnel at the end of 2011. There was no beginning balance in the Salaries Payable account for administrative personnel.
8. Purchased manufacturing equipment two years ago at a cost of $10,000,000. The equipment had an eight-year useful life and a $2,000,000 salvage value.

9. Paid $390,000 cash to engineers in the product design department.
10. Paid a $258,000 cash dividend to owners.
11. Paid $80,000 to set up manufacturing equipment for production.
12. Paid a one-time $186,000 restructuring cost to redesign the production process to implement a just-in-time inventory system.
13. Prepaid the premium on a new insurance policy covering nonmanufacturing employees. The policy cost $72,000 and had a one-year term with an effective starting date of May 1. Four employees work in the research and development department and eight employees in the selling and administrative department. Assume a December 31 closing date.
14. Made 69,400 units of product and sold 60,000 units at a price of $70 each.

Required

a. Divide the class into groups of four or five students per group, and then organize the groups into three sections. Assign Task 1 to the first section of groups, Task 2 to the second section of groups, and Task 3 to the third section of groups.

Group Tasks

(1) Identify the items that are classified as product costs and determine the amount of cost of goods sold reported on the 2011 income statement.
(2) Identify the items that are classified as upstream costs and determine the amount of upstream cost expensed on the 2011 income statement.
(3) Identify the items that are classified as downstream costs and determine the amount of downstream cost expensed on the 2011 income statement.

b. Have the class construct an income statement in the following manner. Select a member of one of the groups assigned the first group task identifying the product costs. Have that person go to the board and list the costs included in the determination of cost of goods sold. Anyone in the other groups who disagrees with one of the classifications provided by the person at the board should voice an objection and explain why the item should be classified differently. The instructor should lead the class to a consensus on the disputed items. After the amount of cost of goods sold is determined, the student at the board constructs the part of the income statement showing the determination of gross margin. The exercise continues in a similar fashion with representatives from the other sections explaining the composition of the upstream and downstream costs. These items are added to the income statement started by the first group representative. The final result is a completed income statement.

ATC 10-3   **Research Assignment**   *Identifying product costs at Snap-on, Inc.*

Use the 2008 Form 10-K for Snap-on, Inc., to complete the requirements below. To obtain the Form 10-K you can use the EDGAR system following the instructions in Appendix A, or it can be found under "Corporate Information" on the company's corporate website: www.snapon.com. Read carefully the following portions of the document.

- "Products and Services" on page 5.
- "Consolidated Statement of Earnings" on page 55.
- The following parts of Note 1 on page 60:
  - "Shipping and handling"
  - "Advertising and promotion"
- "Note 4: Inventories" on page 66.

Required

a. Does the level of detail that Snap-on provides regarding costs incurred to manufacture its products suggest the company's financial statements are designed primarily to meet the needs of external or internal users?
b. Does Snap-on treat shipping and handling costs as product or nonproduct costs?
c. Does Snap-on treat advertising and promotion costs as product or nonproduct costs?
d. In Chapter 3 you learned about a class of inventory called merchandise inventory. What categories of inventory does Snap-on report in its annual report?

ATC 10-4   Writing Assignment   *Emerging practices in managerial accounting*

An annual report of the Maytag Corporation contained the following excerpt:

> *The Company announced the restructuring of its major appliance operations in an effort to strengthen its position in the industry and to deliver improved performance to both customers and shareowners. This included the consolidation of two separate organizational units into a single operation responsible for all activities associated with the manufacture and distribution of the Company's brands of major appliances and the closing of a cooking products plant in Indianapolis, Indiana, with transfer of that production to an existing plant in Cleveland, Tennessee.*

The restructuring cost Maytag $40 million and disrupted the lives of many of the company's employees.

Required

Assume that you are Maytag's vice president of human relations. Write a letter to the employees who are affected by the restructuring. The letter should explain why it was necessary for the company to undertake the restructuring. Your explanation should refer to the ideas discussed in the section "Emerging Trends in Managerial Accounting" of this chapter (see Appendix A).

ATC 10-5   Ethical Dilemma   *Product cost versus selling and administrative expense*

Emma Emerson is a proud woman with a problem. Her daughter has been accepted into a prestigious law school. While Ms. Emerson beams with pride, she is worried sick about how to pay for the school; she is a single parent who has to support herself and her three children. She had to go heavily into debt to finance her own education. Even though she now has a good job, family needs have continued to outpace her income and her debt burden is staggering. She knows she will be unable to borrow the money needed for her daughter's law school.

Ms. Emerson is the chief financial officer (CFO) of a small manufacturing company. She has just accepted a new job offer. She has not yet told her employer that she will be leaving in a month. She is concerned that her year-end incentive bonus may be affected if her boss learns of her plans to leave. She plans to inform the company immediately after receiving the bonus. She knows her behavior is less than honorable, but she believes that she has been underpaid for a long time. Her boss, a relative of the company's owner, makes twice what she makes and does half the work. Why should she care about leaving with a little extra cash? Indeed, she is considering an opportunity to boost the bonus.

Ms. Emerson's bonus is based on a percentage of net income. Her company recently introduced a new product line that required substantial production start-up costs. Ms. Emerson is fully aware that GAAP requires these costs to be expensed in the current accounting period, but no one else in the company has the technical expertise to know exactly how the costs should be treated. She is considering misclassifying the start-up costs as product costs. If the costs are misclassified, net income will be significantly higher, resulting in a nice boost in her incentive bonus. By the time the auditors discover the misclassification, Ms. Emerson will have moved on to her new job. If the matter is brought to the attention of her new employer, she will simply plead ignorance. Considering her daughter's needs, Ms. Emerson decides to classify the start-up costs as product costs.

Required

a. Based on this information, indicate whether Ms. Emerson believes the number of units of product sold will be equal to, less than, or greater than the number of units made. Write a brief paragraph explaining the logic that supports your answer.

b. Explain how the misclassification could mislead an investor or creditor regarding the company's financial condition.

c. Explain how the misclassification could affect income taxes.

d. Identify the specific components of the fraud triangle the were present in this case.

e. Review the Statement of Ethical Professional Practice shown in Exhibit 10.14 and identify at least two principles that Ms. Emerson's misclassification of the start-up costs violated.

f. Describe the maximum penalty that could be imposed under the Sarbanes-Oxley Act for the actions Ms. Emerson has taken.

CHAPTER 11

Cost Behavior, Operating Leverage, and Profitability Analysis

LEARNING OBJECTIVES

After you have mastered the material in this chapter, you will be able to:

1 Identify and describe fixed, variable, and mixed cost behavior.

2 Demonstrate the effects of operating leverage on profitability.

3 Prepare an income statement using the contribution margin approach.

4 Calculate the magnitude of operating leverage.

5 Demonstrate how the relevant range and decision context affect cost behavior.

6 Calculate the break-even point.

7 Calculate the sales volume required to attain a target profit.

8 Calculate the margin of safety in units, dollars, and percentage.

CHAPTER OPENING

Three college students are planning a vacation. One of them suggests inviting a fourth person along, remarking that four can travel for the same cost as three. Certainly, some costs will be the same whether three or four people go on the trip. For example, the hotel room costs $800 per week, regardless of whether three or four people stay in the room. In accounting terms the cost of the hotel room is a fixed cost. The total amount of a fixed cost does not change when volume changes. The total hotel room cost is $800 whether 1, 2, 3, or 4 people use the room. In contrast, some costs vary in direct proportion with changes in volume. When volume increases, total variable cost increases; when volume decreases, total variable cost decreases. For example, the cost of tickets to a theme park is a **variable cost**. The total cost of tickets increases proportionately with each vacationer who goes to the theme park. Cost behavior (fixed versus variable) can significantly impact profitability. This chapter explains cost behavior and ways it can be used to increase profitability.

The Curious Accountant

News flash! On April 29, 2009, Eastman Kodak, Inc., announced that its first quarter's revenues decreased 29 percent compared to the same quarter in 2008, yet its earnings had decreased by 213 percent. On May 4, 2009, Walt Disney announced that a decrease in revenue of 7 percent for the just-ended quarter would cause its earnings to decrease 46 percent compared to the same quarter in 2008. On April 12, 2009, Apple computer reported that its revenue for the quarter had increased by 9 percent compared to the previous year, but its earnings increased by 15 percent.

Can you explain why such relatively small changes in these companies' revenues resulted in such relatively large changes in their earnings or losses? In other words, if a company's sales increase 10 percent, why do its earnings not also increase 10 percent? (Answer on page 402.)

FIXED COST BEHAVIOR

How much more will it cost to send one additional employee to a sales meeting? If more people buy our products, can we charge less? If sales increase by 10 percent, how will profits be affected? Managers seeking answers to such questions must consider **cost behavior.** Knowing how costs behave relative to the level of business activity enables managers to more effectively plan and control costs. To illustrate, consider the entertainment company Star Productions, Inc. (SPI).

SPI specializes in promoting rock concerts. It is considering paying a band $48,000 to play a concert. Obviously, SPI must sell enough tickets to cover this cost. In this example, the relevant activity base is the number of tickets sold. The cost of the band is a **fixed cost** because it does not change regardless of the number of tickets sold. Exhibit 11.1 illustrates the fixed cost behavior pattern, showing the *total cost* and the *cost per unit* at three different levels of activity.

Total versus *per-unit* fixed costs behave differently. The total cost for the band remains constant (fixed) at $48,000. In contrast, fixed cost per unit decreases as volume (number of tickets sold) increases. The term *fixed cost* is consistent with the behavior of *total cost*. Total fixed cost remains constant (fixed) when activity changes. However, there is a contradiction between the term *fixed cost per unit* and the *per-unit behavior pattern of a fixed cost.* Fixed cost per unit is *not* fixed. It changes with the number of tickets sold. This contradiction in terminology can cause untold confusion. Study carefully the fixed cost behavior patterns in Exhibit 11.2.

EXHIBIT 11.1

Fixed Cost Behavior

Number of tickets sold (a)	2,700	3,000	3,300
Total cost of band (b)	$48,000	$48,000	$48,000
Cost per ticket sold (b ÷ a)	$17.78	$16.00	$14.55

EXHIBIT 11.2

Fixed Cost Behavior

	When Activity Increases	When Activity Decreases
Total fixed cost	Remains constant	Remains constant
Fixed cost **per unit**	Decreases	Increases

The fixed cost data in Exhibit 11.1 help SPI's management decide whether to sponsor the concert. For example, the information influences potential pricing choices. The per-unit costs represent the minimum ticket prices required to cover the fixed cost at various levels of activity. SPI could compare these per-unit costs to the prices of competing entertainment events (such as the prices of movies, sporting events, or theater tickets). If the price is not competitive, tickets will not sell and the concert will lose money. Management must also consider the number of tickets to be sold. The volume data in Exhibit 11.1 can be compared to the band's track record of ticket sales at previous concerts. A proper analysis of these data can reduce the risk of undertaking an unprofitable venture.

OPERATING LEVERAGE

Heavy objects can be moved with little effort using *physical* leverage. Business managers apply **operating leverage** to magnify small changes in revenue into dramatic changes in profitability. The *lever* managers use to achieve disproportionate changes between revenue and profitability is fixed costs. The leverage relationships between revenue, fixed costs, and profitability are displayed in Exhibit 11.3.

When all costs are fixed, every sales dollar contributes one dollar toward the potential profitability of a project. Once sales dollars cover fixed costs, each

EXHIBIT 11.3

Operating Leverage

Small percentage change in revenue

Dramatic percentage change in profitability

Fixed costs

FOCUS ON INTERNATIONAL ISSUES

COST-VOLUME-PROFIT ANALYSIS AT A GERMAN CHEMICAL COMPANY

The greater the percentage of a company's total costs that are fixed, the more sensitive the company's earnings are to changes in revenue or volume. Operating leverage, the relationship between the changes in revenue and changes in earnings, introduced earlier, applies to companies throughout the world, large or small.

Large chemical manufacturers have significant fixed costs. It takes a lot of buildings and equipment to produce chemicals. BASF claims to be the largest chemical company in the world. It has its headquarters in Ludwigshafen, Germany. From 2004 through 2006 BASF's revenues increased 40.2 percent, but its earnings increased 60.4 percent. In other words, its earnings grew one and one-half times faster than its revenues.

Studying BASF offers insight into a true global enterprise. Though headquartered in Germany, it has manufacturing facilities at 150 locations throughout the world. Only 21 percent of its 2006 revenue came from sales within Germany, which was 1 percent less than the revenue it earned in the United States. Although its financial statements are presented in euros and prepared in accordance with international financial accounting standards, its stock is traded on the New York Stock Exchange as well as on the Frankfurt Stock Exchange.

additional sales dollar represents pure profit. As a result, a small change in sales volume can significantly affect profitability. To illustrate, assume SPI estimates it will sell 3,000 tickets for $18 each. A 10 percent difference in actual sales volume will produce a 90 percent difference in profitability. Examine the data in Exhibit 11.4 to verify this result.[1]

EXHIBIT 11.4

Effect of Operating Leverage on Profitability

Number of tickets sold	2,700	⇐ −10% ⇐	3,000	⇒ +10% ⇒	3,300
Sales revenue ($18 per ticket)	$48,600		$54,000		$59,400
Cost of band (fixed cost)	(48,000)		(48,000)		(48,000)
Gross margin	$ 600	⇐ −90% ⇐	$ 6,000	⇒ +90% ⇒	$11,400

Calculating Percentage Change

The percentages in Exhibit 11.4 are computed as follows.

$$\text{(Alternative measure − Base measure)} \div \text{Base measure} = \% \text{ change}$$

The base measure is the starting point. To illustrate, compute the percentage change in gross margin when moving from 3,000 units (base measure) to 3,300 units (the alternative measure).

$$\text{(Alternative measure − Base measure)} \div \text{Base measure} = \% \text{ change}$$

$$(\$11,400 − \$6,000) \div \$6,000 = 90\%$$

---

[1]Do not confuse operating leverage with financial leverage. Companies employ *financial leverage* when they use debt to profit from investing money at a higher rate of return than the rate they pay on borrowed money. Companies employ *operating leverage* when they use proportionately more fixed costs than variable costs to magnify the effect on earnings of changes in revenues.

The percentage *decline* in profitability is similarly computed:

(Alternative measure − Base measure) ÷ Base measure = % change

($600 − $6,000) ÷ $6,000 = (90%)

Risk and Reward Assessment

Risk refers to the possibility that sacrifices may exceed benefits. A fixed cost represents a commitment to an economic sacrifice. It represents the ultimate risk of undertaking a particular business project. If SPI pays the band but nobody buys a ticket, the company will lose $48,000. SPI can avoid this risk by substituting *variable costs* for the *fixed cost.*

REALITY BYTES

The relationship among the costs to produce goods, the volume of goods produced, the price charged for those goods, and the profit earned is relevant to all industries, but perhaps no industry demonstrates the effects of these relationships more dramatically than automobile manufacturing. First, the automobile industry is characterized by having a lot of fixed production-costs for things such as buildings, equipment, research, and development, but also financing costs associated with borrowed funds, such as the interest expense on bonds. Second, the industry is globally competitive, and companies in the United States are often at a cost disadvantage. Some of this cost disadvantage comes from obvious sources, such as having to pay higher wages than do companies in countries such as South Korea. Finally, for many customers, price and quality are more important than brand loyalty.

Over the past decades, domestic auto makers, and in particular General Motors (GM), have used different strategies to try to deal with the issues mentioned above. Early on, it had a dominant market share. As long as it produced more cars than its competitors, its fixed cost per car was lower, resulting in better profits. In the 1980s, however, foreign manufactures began increasing their market share and decreasing GM's. As its relative levels of production fell, its fixed cost per unit increased. In response, GM and others tried to regain market share by lowering prices, largely through rebates. Unfortunately this did not work, so the lower prices, combined with the higher relative fixed costs, seriously eroded profits.

These problems reached a crisis in 2008 and 2009 when GM and Chrysler sought financial help from the government and entered expedited bankruptcy proceedings.

What did GM and Chrysler hope to achieve? Primarily they needed to lower their costs, especially their fixed costs. As a result of bankruptcy proceedings, they were able to greatly reduce interest and principal payments on their outstanding bonds (fixed costs), reduce the number of brands (fixed costs), shut down some plants (fixed costs), reduce health care costs to retirees (fixed costs), and reduce the number of dealers. While reducing the number of dealers did reduce some cost to the companies, it also reduced price competition among the dealers, which had the potential of allowing the companies to charge more for their cars. All of these changes, it was hoped, would allow the companies to return to profitability.

However, before a company can be profitable, it must break even. At one time GM's break-even point was estimated at around 16 million vehicles per year. GM's CEO until 2000, Rick Wagoner, had implemented changes that reduced the company's break-even point to 12 million units. On March 29, 2009, as a condition of receiving government support, the administration of President Barack Obama asked Mr. Wagoner to resign as GM's CEO. Perhaps lost by many in the news coverage of Mr. Wagoner's resignation were reports by several news organizations that officials at the U.S. Treasury Department would ask the new leadership at GM to take steps to reduce the company's break-even point to 10 million units.

It would be a major achievement if GM can reduce its break even from 16 million units to 10 million units in the span of a few years. This may not be enough, however. In 2008 GM sold only 8.8 million units, and its sales in the first quarter of 2009 were even lower than the same quarter of 2008. Furthermore, it should be remembered that the objective of businesses is not simply to break even, but to make a profit.

VARIABLE COST BEHAVIOR

To illustrate variable cost behavior, assume SPI arranges to pay the band $16 per ticket sold instead of a fixed $48,000. Exhibit 11.5 shows the total cost of the band and the cost per ticket sold at three different levels of activity.

LO 1

Identify and describe fixed, variable, and mixed cost behavior.

EXHIBIT 11.5

Variable Cost Behavior

Number of tickets sold (a)	2,700	3,000	3,300
Total cost of band (b)	$43,200	$48,000	$52,800
Cost per ticket sold (b ÷ a)	$16	$16	$16

Because SPI will pay the band $16 for each ticket sold, the *total* variable cost increases in direct proportion to the number of tickets sold. If SPI sells one ticket, total band cost will be $16 (1 × $16); if SPI sells two tickets, total band cost will be $32 (2 × $16); and so on. The total cost of the band increases proportionately as ticket sales move from 2,700 to 3,000 to 3,300. The variable cost *per ticket* remains $16, however, regardless of whether the number of tickets sold is 1, 2, 3, or 3,000. The behavior of variable cost *per unit* is contradictory to the word *variable*. Variable cost per unit remains *constant* regardless of how many tickets are sold. Study carefully the variable cost behavior patterns in Exhibit 11.6.

EXHIBIT 11.6

Variable Cost Behavior

	When Activity Increases	When Activity Decreases
Total variable cost	Increases proportionately	Decreases proportionately
Variable cost **per unit**	Remains constant	Remains constant

Risk and Reward Assessment

Shifting the cost structure from fixed to variable enables SPI to avoid the fixed cost risk. If no one buys a ticket, SPI loses nothing because it incurs no cost. If only one person buys a ticket at an $18 ticket price, SPI earns a $2 profit ($18 sales revenue − $16 cost of band). Should managers therefore avoid fixed costs whenever possible? Not necessarily.

Shifting the cost structure from fixed to variable reduces not only the level of risk but also the potential for profits. Managers cannot avoid the risk of fixed costs without also sacrificing the benefits. Variable costs do not offer operating leverage. Exhibit 11.7 shows that a variable cost structure produces a proportional relationship between sales and profitability. A 10 percent increase or decrease in sales results in a corresponding 10 percent increase or decrease in profitability.

LO 2

Demonstrate the effects of operating leverage on profitability.

EXHIBIT 11.7

Variable Cost Eliminates Operating Leverage

Number of tickets sold	2,700	⇐ −10% ⇐	3,000	⇒ +10% ⇒	3,300
Sales revenue ($18 per ticket)	$48,600		$54,000		$59,400
Cost of band ($16 variable cost)	(43,200)		(48,000)		(52,800)
Gross margin	$ 5,400	⇐ −10% ⇐	$ 6,000	⇒ +10% ⇒	$ 6,600

✓ CHECK YOURSELF 11.1

Suppose that you are sponsoring a political rally at which Ralph Nader will speak. You estimate that approximately 2,000 people will buy tickets to hear Mr. Nader's speech. The tickets are expected to be priced at $12 each. Would you prefer a contract that agrees to pay Mr. Nader $10,000 or one that agrees to pay him $5 per ticket purchased?

Answer   Your answer would depend on how certain you are that 2,000 people will purchase tickets. If it were likely that many more than 2,000 tickets would be sold, you would be better off with a fixed cost structure, agreeing to pay Mr. Nader a flat fee of $10,000. If attendance numbers are highly uncertain, you would be better off with a variable cost structure thereby guaranteeing a lower cost if fewer people buy tickets.

Answers to The Curious Accountant

The explanation for how a company's earnings can rise faster, as a percentage, than its revenue rises is operating leverage, and operating leverage is due entirely to fixed costs. As the chapter explains, when a company's output goes up, its fixed cost per unit goes down. As long as it can keep prices about the same, this lower unit cost will result in higher profit per unit sold. In real-world companies, the relationship between changing sales levels and changing earnings levels can be very complex, but the existence of fixed costs helps to explain why a 9 percent rise in revenue can cause a 15 percent rise in net earnings.

✓ CHECK YOURSELF 11.2

If both Kroger Food Stores and Delta Airlines were to experience a 5 percent increase in revenues, which company would be more likely to experience a higher percentage increase in net income?

Answer   Delta would be more likely to experience a higher percentage increase in net income because a large portion of its cost (e.g., employee salaries and depreciation) is fixed, while a large portion of Kroger's cost is variable (e.g., cost of goods sold).

AN INCOME STATEMENT UNDER THE CONTRIBUTION MARGIN APPROACH

LO 3

Prepare an income statement using the contribution margin approach.

The impact of cost structure on profitability is so significant that managerial accountants frequently construct income statements that classify costs according to their behavior patterns. Such income statements first subtract variable costs from revenue; the resulting subtotal is called the **contribution margin.** The contribution margin represents the amount available to cover fixed expenses and thereafter to provide company profits. Net income is computed by subtracting the fixed costs from the contribution margin. A contribution margin style income statement cannot be used for public reporting (GAAP prohibits its use in external financial reports), but it is widely used for internal reporting purposes. Exhibit 11.8 illustrates income statements prepared using the contribution margin approach.

EXHIBIT 11.8

Income Statements

	Company Name	
	Bragg	**Biltmore**
Variable cost per unit (a)	$ 6	$ 12
Sales revenue (10 units × $20)	$200	$200
Variable cost (10 units × a)	(60)	(120)
Contribution margin	140	80
Fixed cost	(120)	(60)
Net income	$ 20	$ 20

MEASURING OPERATING LEVERAGE USING CONTRIBUTION MARGIN

A contribution margin income statement allows managers to easily measure operating leverage. The magnitude of operating leverage can be determined as follows.

$$\text{Magnitude of operating leverage} = \frac{\text{Contribution margin}}{\text{Net income}}$$

Calculate the magnitude of operating leverage.

Applying this formula to the income statement data reported for Bragg Company and Biltmore Company in Exhibit 11.8 produces the following measures.

Bragg Company:

$$\text{Magnitude of operating leverage} = \frac{140}{20} = 7$$

Biltmore Company:

$$\text{Magnitude of operating leverage} = \frac{80}{20} = 4$$

The computations show that Bragg is more highly leveraged than Biltmore. Bragg's change in profitability will be seven times greater than a given percentage change in revenue. In contrast, Biltmore's profits change by only four times the percentage change in revenue. For example, a 10 percent increase in revenue produces a 70 percent increase (10 percent × 7) in profitability for Bragg Company and a 40 percent increase (10 percent × 4) in profitability for Biltmore Company. The income statements in Exhibits 11.9 and 11.10 confirm these expectations.

EXHIBIT 11.9

Comparative Income Statements for Bragg Company

Units (a)	10		11
Sales revenue ($20 × a)	$200	⇒ +10% ⇒	$220
Variable cost ($6 × a)	(60)		(66)
Contribution margin	140		154
Fixed cost	(120)		(120)
Net income	$ 20	⇒ +70% ⇒	$ 34

EXHIBIT 11.10

Comparative Income Statements for Biltmore Company

Units (a)	10		11
Sales revenue ($20 × a)	$200	⇒ +10% ⇒	$220
Variable cost ($12 × a)	(120)		(132)
Contribution margin	80		88
Fixed cost	(60)		(60)
Net income	$ 20	⇒ +40% ⇒	$ 28

Operating leverage itself is neither good nor bad; it represents a strategy that can work to a company's advantage or disadvantage, depending on how it is used. The next section explains how managers can use operating leverage to create a competitive business advantage.

✓ CHECK YOURSELF 11.3

Boeing Company's 2001 10K annual report filed with the Securities and Exchange Commission refers to "higher commercial airlines segment margins." Is Boeing referring to gross margins or contribution margins?

Answer   Because the data come from the company's external annual report, the reference must be to gross margins (revenue − cost of goods sold), a product cost measure. The contribution margin (revenue − variable cost) is a measure used in internal reporting.

COST BEHAVIOR SUMMARIZED

Identify and describe fixed, variable, and mixed cost behavior.

The term *fixed* refers to the behavior of *total* fixed cost. The cost *per unit* of a fixed cost *varies inversely* with changes in the level of activity. As activity increases, fixed cost per unit decreases. As activity decreases, fixed cost per unit increases. These relationships are graphed in Exhibit 11.11.

The term *variable* refers to the behavior of *total* variable cost. Total variable cost increases or decreases proportionately with changes in the volume of activity. In contrast, variable cost *per unit* remains *fixed* at all levels of activity. These relationships are graphed in Exhibit 11.12.

The relationships between fixed and variable costs are summarized in the chart in Exhibit 11.13. Study these relationships thoroughly.

EXHIBIT 11.11

Graphical Presentation of Fixed Cost Behavior

EXHIBIT 11.12

Graphical Presentation of Variable Cost Behavior

EXHIBIT 11.13

Fixed and Variable Cost Behavior

When Activity Level Changes	Total Cost	Cost per Unit
Fixed costs	Remains constant	Changes *inversely*
Variable costs	Changes in direct proportion	Remains constant

Mixed Costs (Semivariable Costs)

Mixed costs (semivariable costs) include both fixed and variable components. For example, Star Productions, Inc., frequently arranges backstage parties at which VIP guests meet members of the band. Party costs typically include a room rental fee and the costs of refreshments. The room rental fee is fixed; it remains unchanged regardless of the number of party guests. In contrast, the refreshments costs are variable; they depend on the number of people attending the party. The total party cost is a mixed cost.

Assuming a room rental fee of $1,000 and refreshments costs of $20 per person, the total mixed cost at any volume of activity can be computed as follows.

Total cost = Fixed cost + (Variable cost per party guest × Number of guests)

If 60 people attend the backstage party the total mixed cost is

Total cost = $1,000 + ($20 × 60) = $2,200

If 90 people attend the backstage party the total mixed cost is

Total cost = $1,000 + ($20 × 90) = $2,800

Exhibit 11.14 illustrates a variety of mixed costs businesses commonly encounter.

EXHIBIT 11.14

Examples of Mixed Costs

Type of Cost	Fixed Cost Component(s)	Variable Cost Component(s)
Cost of sales staff	Monthly salary	Bonus based on sales volume
Truck rental	Monthly rental fee	Cost of gas, tires, and maintenance
Legal fees	Monthly retainer	Reimbursements to attorney for out-of-pocket costs (copying, postage, travel, filing fees)
Outpatient service cost	Salaries of doctors and nurses, depreciation of facility, utilities	Medical supplies such as bandages, sterilization solution, and paper products
Phone services	Monthly connection fee	Per-minute usage fee
LP gas utility cost	Container rental fee	Cost of gas consumed
Cable TV services	Monthly fee	Pay-per-view charges
Training cost	Instructor salary, facility cost	Textbooks, supplies
Shipping and handling	Salaries of employees who process packages	Boxes, packing supplies, tape, and other shipping supplies, postage
Inventory holding cost	Depreciation on inventory warehouse, salaries of employees managing inventory	Delivery costs, interest on funds borrowed to finance inventory, cost of supplies

The Relevant Range

Suppose SPI, the rock concert promoter mentioned earlier, must pay $5,000 to rent a concert hall with a seating capacity of 4,000 people. Is the cost of the concert hall fixed or variable? Because total cost remains unchanged regardless of whether one ticket, 4,000 tickets, or any number in between is sold, the cost is fixed relative to ticket sales. However, what if demand for tickets is significantly more than 4,000? In that case, SPI might rent a larger concert hall at a higher cost. In other words, *the cost is fixed only for a designated range of activity (1 to 4,000).*

A similar circumstance affects many variable costs. For example, a supplier may offer a volume discount to buyers who purchase more than a specified number of products. The point is that descriptions of cost behavior pertain to a specified range of activity. The range of activity over which the definitions of fixed and variable costs are valid is commonly called the **relevant range.**

Demonstrate how the relevant range and decision context affect cost behavior.

Context-Sensitive Definitions of Fixed and Variable

The behavior pattern of a particular cost may be either fixed or variable, depending on the context. For example, the cost of the band was fixed at $48,000 when SPI was considering hiring it to play a single concert. Regardless of how many tickets SPI sold, the total band cost was $48,000. However, the band cost becomes variable if SPI decides to hire it to perform at a series of concerts. The total cost and the cost per concert for one, two, three, four, or five concerts are shown in Exhibit 11.15.

In this context, the total cost of hiring the band increases proportionately with the number of concerts while cost per concert remains constant. The band cost is therefore variable. The same cost can behave as either a fixed cost or a variable cost, depending on the **activity base.** When identifying a cost as fixed or variable, first ask, fixed or variable *relative to what activity base?* The cost of the band is fixed relative to *the number of tickets sold for a specific concert;* it is variable relative to *the number of concerts produced.*

EXHIBIT 11.15

Cost Behavior Relative to Number of Concerts

Number of concerts (a)	1	2	3	4	5
Cost per concert (b)	$48,000	$48,000	$ 48,000	$ 48,000	$ 48,000
Total cost (a × b)	$48,000	$96,000	$144,000	$192,000	$240,000

✓ CHECK YOURSELF 11.4

Is the compensation cost for managers of Pizza Hut Restaurants a fixed cost or a variable cost?

Answer   The answer depends on the context. For example, because a store manager's salary remains unchanged regardless of how many customers enter a particular restaurant, it can be classified as a fixed cost relative to the number of customers at a particular restaurant. However, the more restaurants that Pizza Hut operates, the higher the total managers' compensation cost will be. Accordingly, managers' salary cost would be classified as a variable cost relative to the number of restaurants opened.

DETERMINING THE BREAK-EVEN POINT

Calculate the break-even point.

Bright Day Distributors sells nonprescription health food supplements including vitamins, herbs, and natural hormones in the northwestern United States. Bright Day recently obtained the rights to distribute the new herb mixture Delatine. Recent scientific research found that Delatine delayed aging in laboratory animals. The researchers hypothesized that the substance would have a similar effect on humans. Their theory could not be confirmed because of the relatively long human life span. The news media reported the research findings; as stories turned up on television and radio news, talk shows, and in magazines, demand for Delatine increased.

Bright Day plans to sell the Delatine at a price of $36 per bottle. Delatine costs $24 per bottle. Bright Day's management team suspects that enthusiasm for Delatine will abate quickly as the news media shift to other subjects. To attract customers immediately, the product managers consider television advertising. The marketing manager suggests running a campaign of several hundred cable channel ads at an estimated cost of $60,000.

Bright Day's first concern is whether it can sell enough units to cover its costs. The president made this position clear when he said, "We don't want to lose money on this product. We have to sell at least enough units to break even." In accounting terms, the **break-even point** is where profit (income) equals zero. So how many bottles of Delatine must be sold to produce a profit of zero? The break-even point is commonly computed using either the *equation method,* or the *contribution margin per unit method.* Both of these approaches produce the same result. They are merely different ways to arrive at the same conclusion.

Equation Method

The **equation method** begins by expressing the income statement as follows.

$$\text{Sales} - \text{Variable costs} - \text{Fixed costs} = \text{Profit (Net income)}$$

As previously stated, profit at the break-even point is zero. Therefore, the break-even point for Delatine is computed as follows.

$$\text{Sales} - \text{Variable costs} - \text{Fixed costs} = \text{Profit}$$
$$\$36N - \$24N - \$60{,}000 = \$0$$
$$\$12N = \$60{,}000$$
$$N = \$60{,}000 \div \$12$$
$$N = 5{,}000 \text{ Units}$$

Where:

N = Number of units
$36 = Sales price per unit
$24 = Variable cost per unit
$60,000 = Fixed costs

✓ CHECK YOURSELF 11.5

B-Shoc is an independent musician who is considering whether to independently produce and sell a CD. B-Shoc estimates fixed costs of $5,400 and variable costs of $2.00 per unit. The expected selling price is $8.00 per CD. Use the equation method to determine B-Shoc's break-even point.

Answer

$$\text{Sales} - \text{Variable costs} - \text{Fixed costs} = \text{Profit}$$
$$\$8N - \$2N - \$5{,}400 = \$0$$
$$\$6N = \$5{,}400$$
$$N = \$5{,}400 \div \$6$$
$$N = 900 \text{ Units (CDs)}$$

Where:

N = Number of units
$8 = Sales price per unit
$2 = Variable cost per unit
$5,400 = Fixed costs

Contribution Margin Per Unit Method

Recall that the *total contribution margin* is the amount of sales minus total variable cost. The **contribution margin per unit** is the sales price per unit minus the variable cost per unit. Therefore, the contribution margin per unit for Delatine is

Sales price per unit	$36
Less: Variable cost per unit	(24)
Contribution margin per unit	$12

For every bottle of Delatine it sells, Bright Day earns a $12 contribution margin. In other words, every time Bright Day sells a bottle of Delatine, it receives enough money to pay $24 to cover the variable cost of the bottle of Delatine and still has $12 left to go toward paying the fixed cost. Bright Day will reach the break-even point when it sells enough bottles of Delatine to cover its fixed costs. Therefore the break-even point can be determined as follows.

$$\text{Break-even point in units} = \frac{\text{Fixed costs}}{\text{Contribution margin per unit}}$$

$$\text{Break-even point in units} = \frac{\$60,000}{\$12}$$

$$\text{Break-even point in units} = 5,000 \text{ Units}$$

This result is the same as that determined under the equation method. Indeed, the contribution margin per unit method formula is an abbreviated version of the income statement formula used in the equation method. The proof is provided in the footnote below.[2]

Both the *equation method* and the *contribution margin per unit method* yield the amount of break-even sales measured *in units*. To determine the amount of break-even sales measured *in dollars*, multiply the number of units times the sales price per unit. For Delatine the break-even point measured in dollars is $180,000 (5,000 units × $36 per unit). The following income statement confirms this result.

Sales revenue (5,000 units × $36)	$180,000
Total variable expenses (5,000 units × $24)	(120,000)
Total contribution margin (5,000 units × $12)	60,000
Fixed expenses	(60,000)
Net income	$ 0

[2]The formula for the *contribution margin per unit method* is (where N is the number of units at the break-even point).

N = Fixed costs ÷ Contribution margin per unit

The income statement formula for the *equation method* produces the same result as shown below (where N is the number of units at the break-even point).

Sales − Variable costs − Fixed costs = Profit
Sales price per unit (N) − Variable cost per unit (N) − Fixed costs = Profit
Contribution margin per unit (N) − Fixed costs = Profit
Contribution margin per unit (N) − Fixed costs = 0
Contribution margin per unit (N) = Fixed costs
N = Fixed costs ÷ Contribution margin per unit

DETERMINING THE SALES VOLUME NECESSARY TO REACH A DESIRED PROFIT

Bright Day's president decides the ad campaign should produce a $40,000 profit. He asks the accountant to determine the sales volume that is required to achieve this level of profitability. Using the *equation method,* the sales volume in units required to attain the desired profit is computed as follows.

Calculate the sales volume required to attain a target profit.

$$\text{Sales} - \text{Variable costs} - \text{Fixed costs} = \text{Profit}$$
$$\$36N - \$24N - \$60{,}000 = \$40{,}000$$
$$\$12N = \$60{,}000 + \$40{,}000$$
$$N = \$100{,}000 \div \$12$$
$$N = 8{,}333 \text{ Units}$$

Where:

N = Number of units

$36 = Sales price per unit

$24 = Variable cost per unit

$60,000 = Fixed costs

$40,000 = Desired profit

The accountant used the *contribution margin per unit method* to confirm these computations as follows.

$$\text{Sales volume in units} = \frac{\text{Fixed costs} + \text{Desired profit}}{\text{Contribution margin per unit}}$$
$$= \frac{\$60{,}000 + \$40{,}000}{\$12} = 8{,}333.33 \text{ units}$$

The required volume in sales dollars is this number of units multiplied by the sales price per unit (8,333.33 units × $36 = $300,000). The following income statement confirms this result; all amounts are rounded to the nearest whole dollar.

Sales revenue (8,333.33 units × $36)	$300,000
Total variable expenses (8,333.33 units × $24)	(200,000)
Total contribution margin (8,333.33 units × $12)	100,000
Fixed expenses	(60,000)
Net income	$ 40,000

In practice, the company will not sell partial bottles of Delatine. The accountant rounds 8,333.33 bottles to whole units. For planning and decision making, managers frequently make decisions using approximate data. Accuracy is desirable, but it is not as important as relevance. Do not be concerned when computations do not produce whole numbers. Rounding and approximation are common characteristics of managerial accounting data.

✓ CHECK YOURSELF 11.6

VolTech Company manufactures small engines that it sells for $130 each. Variable costs are $70 per unit. Fixed costs are expected to be $100,000. The management team has established a target profit of $188,000. Use the contribution margin per unit method to determine how many engines VolTech must sell to attain the target profit.

Answer

$$\text{Sales volume in units} = \frac{\text{Fixed costs} + \text{Desired profit}}{\text{Contribution margin per unit}} = \frac{100{,}000 + 188{,}000}{\$130 - \$70} = 4{,}800 \text{ Units}$$

Calculate the margin of safety in units, dollars, and percentage.

CALCULATING THE MARGIN OF SAFETY

Based on the sales records of other products, Bright Day's marketing department believes that budgeted sales of 8,333 units is an attainable goal. Even so, the company president is concerned because Delatine is a new product and no one can be certain about how the public will react to it. He is willing to take the risk of introducing a new product that fails to produce a profit, but he does not want to take a loss on the product. He therefore focuses on the gap between the budgeted sales and the sales required to break even. The amount of this gap, called the *margin of safety,* can be measured in units or in sales dollars as shown here.

	In Units	In Dollars
Budgeted sales	8,333	$300,000
Break-even sales	(5,000)	(180,000)
Margin of safety	3,333	$120,000

The **margin of safety** measures the cushion between budgeted sales and the break-even point. It quantifies the amount by which actual sales can fall short of expectations before the company will begin to incur losses.

To help compare diverse products or companies of different sizes, the margin of safety can be expressed as a percentage. Divide the margin of safety by the budgeted sales volume[3] as shown here.

$$\text{Margin of safety} = \frac{\text{Budgeted sales} - \text{Break-even sales}}{\text{Budgeted sales}}$$

$$\text{Margin of safety} = \frac{\$300,000 - \$180,000}{\$300,000} \times 100 = 40\%$$

This analysis suggests actual sales would have to fall short of expected sales by 40 percent before Bright Day would experience a loss on Delatine. The large margin of safety suggests the proposed advertising program to market Delatine has minimal risk.

✓ CHECK YOURSELF 11.7

Suppose that Bright Day is considering the possibility of selling a protein supplement that will cost Bright Day $5 per bottle. Bright Day believes that it can sell 4,000 bottles of the supplement for $25 per bottle. Fixed costs associated with selling the supplement are expected to be $42,000. Does the supplement have a wider margin of safety than Delatine?

Answer Calculate the break-even point for the protein supplement.

$$\text{Break-even volume in units} = \frac{\text{Fixed costs}}{\text{Contribution margin per unit}} = \frac{\$42,000}{\$25 - \$5} = 2,100 \text{ Units}$$

Calculate the margin of safety. Note that the margin of safety expressed as a percentage can be calculated using the number of units or sales dollars. Using either units or dollars yields the same percentage.

$$\text{Margin of safety} = \frac{\text{Budgeted sales} - \text{Break-even sales}}{\text{Budgeted sales}} = \frac{4,000 - 2,100}{4,000} = 47.5\%$$

The margin of safety for Delatine (40.0 percent) is below that for the protein supplement (47.5 percent). This suggests that Bright Day is more likely to incur losses selling Delatine than selling the supplement.

[3]The margin of safety percentage can be based on actual as well as budgeted sales. For example, an analyst could compare the margins of safety of two companies under current operating conditions by substituting actual sales for budgeted sales in the computation, as follows: ([Actual sales − Break-even sales] ÷ Actual sales).

A Look Back

To plan and control business operations effectively, managers need to understand how different costs behave in relation to changes in the volume of activity. Total *fixed cost* remains constant when activity changes. Fixed cost per unit decreases with increases in activity and increases with decreases in activity. In contrast, total *variable cost* increases proportionately with increases in activity and decreases proportionately with decreases in activity. Variable cost per unit remains constant regardless of activity levels. The definitions of fixed and variable costs have meaning only within the context of a specified range of activity (the relevant range) for a defined period of time. In addition, cost behavior depends on the relevant volume measure (a store manager's salary is fixed relative to the number of customers visiting a particular store but is variable relative to the number of stores operated). A mixed cost has both fixed and variable cost components.

Fixed costs allow companies to take advantage of *operating leverage.* With operating leverage, each additional sale decreases the cost per unit. This principle allows a small percentage change in volume of revenue to cause a significantly larger percentage change in profits. The *magnitude of operating leverage* can be determined by dividing the contribution margin by net income. When all costs are fixed and revenues have covered fixed costs, each additional dollar of revenue represents pure profit. Having a fixed cost structure (employing operating leverage) offers a company both risks and rewards. If sales volume increases, fixed costs do not increase, allowing profits to soar. Alternatively, if sales volume decreases, fixed costs do not decrease and profits decline significantly more than revenues. Companies with high variable costs in relation to fixed costs do not experience as great a level of operating leverage. Their costs increase or decrease in proportion to changes in revenue. These companies face less risk but fail to reap disproportionately higher profits when volume soars.

Under the contribution margin approach, variable costs are subtracted from revenue to determine the *contribution margin.* Fixed costs are then subtracted from the contribution margin to determine net income. The contribution margin represents the amount available to pay fixed costs and provide a profit. Although not permitted by GAAP for external reporting, many companies use the contribution margin format for internal reporting purposes.

The *break-even point* (the point where total revenue equals total cost) in units can be determined by dividing fixed costs by the contribution margin per unit. The break-even point in sales dollars can be determined by multiplying the number of break-even units by the sales price per unit. To determine sales in units to obtain a designated profit, the sum of fixed costs and desired profit is divided by the contribution margin per unit.

The *margin of safety* is the number of units or the amount of sales dollars by which actual sales can fall below expected sales before a loss is incurred. The margin of safety can also be expressed as a percentage to permit comparing different size companies. The margin of safety can be computed as a percentage by dividing the difference between budgeted sales and break-even sales by the amount of budgeted sales.

A Look Forward

The next chapter begins investigating cost measurement. Accountants seek to determine the cost of certain objects. A cost object may be a product, a service, a department, a customer, or any other thing for which the cost is being determined. Some costs can be directly traced to a cost object, while others are difficult to trace. Costs that are difficult to trace to cost objects are called *indirect costs,* or *overhead.* Indirect costs are assigned to cost objects through *cost allocation.* The next chapter introduces the basic concepts and procedures of cost allocation.

A step-by-step audio-narrated series of slides is provided on the text website at www.mhhe.com/edmondssurvey3e.

SELF-STUDY REVIEW PROBLEM 1

Mensa Mountaineering Company (MMC) provides guided mountain climbing expeditions in the Rocky Mountains. Its only major expense is guide salaries; it pays each guide $4,800 per climbing expedition. MMC charges its customers $1,500 per expedition and expects to take five climbers on each expedition.

Part 1

Base your answers on the preceding information.

Required

a. Determine the total cost of guide salaries and the cost of guide salaries per climber assuming that four, five, or six climbers are included in a trip. Relative to the number of climbers in a single expedition, is the cost of guides a fixed or a variable cost?

b. Relative to the number of expeditions, is the cost of guides a fixed or a variable cost?

c. Determine the profit of an expedition assuming that five climbers are included in the trip.

d. Determine the profit assuming a 20 percent increase (six climbers total) in expedition revenue. What is the percentage change in profitability?

e. Determine the profit assuming a 20 percent decrease (four climbers total) in expedition revenue. What is the percentage change in profitability?

f. Explain why a 20 percent shift in revenue produces more than a 20 percent shift in profitability. What term describes this phenomenon?

Part 2

Assume that the guides offer to make the climbs for a percentage of expedition fees. Specifically, MMC will pay guides $960 per climber on the expedition. Assume also that the expedition fee charged to climbers remains at $1,500 per climber.

Required

g. Determine the total cost of guide salaries and the cost of guide salaries per climber assuming that four, five, or six climbers are included in a trip. Relative to the number of climbers in a single expedition, is the cost of guides a fixed or a variable cost?

h. Relative to the number of expeditions, is the cost of guides a fixed or a variable cost?

i. Determine the profit of an expedition assuming that five climbers are included in the trip.

j. Determine the profit assuming a 20 percent increase (six climbers total) in expedition revenue. What is the percentage change in profitability?

k. Determine the profit assuming a 20 percent decrease (four climbers total) in expedition revenue. What is the percentage change in profitability?

l. Explain why a 20 percent shift in revenue does not produce more than a 20 percent shift in profitability.

Solution to Part 1, Requirement *a*

Number of climbers (a)	4	5	6
Total cost of guide salaries (b)	$4,800	$4,800	$4,800
Cost per climber (b ÷ a)	1,200	960	800

Because the total cost remains constant (fixed) regardless of the number of climbers on a particular expedition, the cost is classified as fixed. Note that the cost per climber decreases as the number of climbers increases. This is the *per unit* behavior pattern of a fixed cost.

Solution to Part 1, Requirement *b*

Because the total cost of guide salaries changes proportionately each time the number of expeditions increases or decreases, the cost of salaries is variable relative to the number of expeditions.

Solution to Part 1, Requirements *c, d*, and *e*

Number of Climbers	4	Percentage Change	5	Percentage Change	6
Revenue ($1,500 per climber)	$6,000	⇐(20%)⇐	$7,500	⇒+20%⇒	$9,000
Cost of guide salaries (fixed)	4,800		4,800		4,800
Profit	$1,200	⇐(55.6%)⇐	$2,700	⇒+55.6%⇒	$4,200

Percentage change in revenue: ±$1,500 ÷ $7,500 = ±20%
Percentage change in profit: ±$1,500 ÷ $2,700 = ±55.6%

Solution to Part 1, Requirement *f*

Because the cost of guide salaries remains fixed while volume (number of climbers) changes, the change in profit, measured in absolute dollars, exactly matches the change in revenue. More specifically, each time MMC increases the number of climbers by one, revenue and profit increase by $1,500. Because the base figure for profit ($2,700) is lower than the base figure for revenue ($7,500), the percentage change in profit ($1,500 ÷ $2,700 = 55.6%) is higher than percentage change in revenue ($1,500 ÷ $7,500). This phenomenon is called *operating leverage*.

Solution for Part 2, Requirement *g*

Number of climbers (a)	4	5	6
Per climber cost of guide salaries (b)	$ 960	$ 960	$ 960
Cost per climber (b × a)	3,840	4,800	5,760

Because the total cost changes in proportion to changes in the number of climbers, the cost is classified as variable. Note that the cost per climber remains constant (stays the same) as the number of climbers increases or decreases. This is the *per unit* behavior pattern of a variable cost.

Solution for Part 2, Requirement *h*

Because the total cost of guide salaries changes proportionately with changes in the number of expeditions, the cost of salaries is also variable relative to the number of expeditions.

Solution for Part 2, Requirements *i, j*, and *k*

Number of Climbers	4	Percentage Change	5	Percentage Change	6
Revenue ($1,500 per climber)	$6,000	⇐(20%)⇐	$7,500	⇒+20%⇒	$9,000
Cost of guide salaries (variable)	3,840		4,800		5,760
Profit	$2,160	⇐(20%)⇐	$2,700	⇒+20%⇒	$3,240

Percentage change in revenue: ±$1,500 ÷ $7,500 = ±20%
Percentage change in profit: ±$540 ÷ $2,700 = ±20%

Solution for Part 2, Requirement *l*

Because the cost of guide salaries changes when volume (number of climbers) changes, the change in net income is proportionate to the change in revenue. More specifically, each time the number of climbers increases by one, revenue increases by $1,500 and net income increases by $540 ($1,500 − $960). Accordingly, the percentage change in net income will always equal the percentage change in revenue. This means that there is no operating leverage when all costs are variable.

A step-by-step audio-narrated series of slides is provided on the text website at www.mhhe.com/edmondssurvey3e.

SELF-STUDY REVIEW PROBLEM 2

Sharp Company makes and sells pencil sharpeners. The variable cost of each sharpener is $20. The sharpeners are sold for $30 each. Fixed operating expenses amount to $40,000.

Required

a. Determine the break-even point in units and sales dollars.

b. Determine the sales volume in units and dollars that is required to attain a profit of $12,000. Verify your answer by preparing an income statement using the contribution margin format.

c. Determine the margin of safety between sales required to attain a profit of $12,000 and break-even sales.

Solution to Requirement *a*

Formula for Computing Break-even Point in Units

Sales − Variable costs − Fixed costs = Profit
Sales price per unit (N) − Variable cost per unit (N) − Fixed costs = Profit
Contribution margin per unit (N) − Fixed costs = Profit
N = (Fixed costs + Profit) ÷ Contribution Margin per unit
N = ($40,000 + 0) ÷ ($30 − $20) = 4,000 Units

Break-even Point in Sales Dollars

Sales price	$ 30
× Number of units	4,000
Sales volume in dollars	$120,000

Solution to Requirement *b*

Formula for Computing Unit Sales Required to Attain Desired Profit

Sales − Variable costs − Fixed costs = Profit
Sales price per unit (N) − Variable cost per unit (N) − Fixed costs = Profit
Contribution margin per unit (N) − Fixed costs = Profit
N = (Fixed costs + Profit) ÷ Contribution margin per unit
N = ($40,000 + 12,000) ÷ ($30 − $20) = 5,200 Units

Sales Dollars Required to Attain Desired Profit

Sales price	$ 30
× Number of units	5,200
Sales volume in dollars	$156,000

Income Statement

Sales volume in units (a)	5,200
Sales revenue (a × $30)	$156,000
Variable costs (a × $20)	(104,000)
Contribution margin	52,000
Fixed costs	(40,000)
Net income	$ 12,000

Solution to Requirement *c*

Margin of Safety Computations	Units	Dollars
Budgeted sales	5,200	$156,000
Break-even sales	(4,000)	(120,000)
Margin of safety	1,200	$ 36,000

Percentage Computation

$$\frac{\text{Margin of safety in \$}}{\text{Budgeted sales}} = \frac{\$36,000}{\$156,000} = 23.08\%$$

KEY TERMS

Activity base 406
Break-even point 407
Contribution margin 402
Contribution margin per
   unit 408

Cost behavior 398
Equation method 407
Fixed cost 398
Margin of
   safety 410

Mixed costs (semivariable
   costs) 405
Operating leverage 398
Relevant range 405
Variable cost 397

QUESTIONS

1. Define *fixed cost* and *variable cost* and give an example of each.

2. How can knowing cost behavior relative to volume fluctuations affect decision making?

3. Define the term *operating leverage* and explain how it affects profits.

4. How is operating leverage calculated?

5. Explain the limitations of using operating leverage to predict profitability.

6. If volume is increasing, would a company benefit more from a pure variable or a pure fixed cost structure? Which cost structure would be advantageous if volume is decreasing?

7. Explain the risk and rewards to a company that result from having fixed costs.

8. Are companies with predominately fixed cost structures likely to be most profitable?

9. How is the relevant range of activity related to fixed and variable cost? Give an example of how the definitions of these costs become invalid when volume is outside the relevant range.

10. Which cost structure has the greater risk? Explain.

11. The president of Bright Corporation tells you that he sees a dim future for his company. He feels that his hands are tied because fixed costs are too high. He says that fixed costs do not change and therefore the situation is hopeless. Do you agree? Explain.

12. All costs are variable because if a business ceases operations, its costs fall to zero. Do you agree with the statement? Explain.

13. Verna Salsbury tells you that she thinks the terms fixed cost and variable cost are confusing. She notes that fixed cost per unit changes when the number of units changes. Furthermore, variable cost per unit remains fixed regardless of how many units are produced. She concludes that the terminology seems to be backward. Explain why the terminology appears to be contradictory.

14. What does the term *break-even point* mean? Name the two ways it can be measured.

15. How does a contribution margin income statement differ from the income statement used in financial reporting?

16. If Company A has a projected margin of safety of 22 percent while Company B has a margin of safety of 52 percent, which company is at greater risk when actual sales are less than budgeted?

17. Mary Hartwell and Jane Jamail, college roommates, are considering the joint purchase of a computer that they can share to prepare class assignments. Ms. Hartwell wants a particular model that costs $2,000; Ms. Jamail prefers a more economical model that costs $1,500. In fact, Ms. Jamail is adamant about her position, refusing to contribute more than $750 toward the purchase. If Ms. Hartwell is also adamant about her position, should she accept Ms. Jamail's $750 offer and apply that amount toward the purchase of the more expensive computer?

MULTIPLE-CHOICE QUESTIONS

Multiple-choice questions are provided on the text website at
www.mhhe.com/edmondssurvey3e.

EXERCISES

connect
|ACCOUNTING

All applicable Exercises are available with McGraw-Hill's
Connect Accounting.

LO 1, 5

Exercise 11-1   *Identifying cost behavior*

Deer Valley Kitchen, a fast-food restaurant company, operates a chain of restaurants across the nation. Each restaurant employs eight people; one is a manager who is paid a salary plus a bonus equal to 3 percent of sales. Other employees, two cooks, one dishwasher, and four waitresses, are paid salaries. Each manager is budgeted $3,000 per month for advertising cost.

Required

Classify each of the following costs incurred by Deer Valley Kitchen as fixed, variable, or mixed.

a. Cooks' salaries at a particular location relative to the number of customers.
b. Cost of supplies (cups, plates, spoons, etc.) relative to the number of customers.
c. Manager's compensation relative to the number of customers.
d. Waitresses' salaries relative to the number of restaurants.
e. Advertising costs relative to the number of customers for a particular restaurant.
f. Rental costs relative to the number of restaurants.

LO 1

Exercise 11-2   *Identifying cost behavior*

At the various activity levels shown, Amborse Company incurred the following costs.

	Units Sold	20	40	60	80	100
a.	Depreciation cost per unit	240.00	120.00	80.00	60.00	48.00
b.	Total rent cost	3,200.00	3,200.00	3,200.00	3,200.00	3,200.00
c.	Total cost of shopping bags	2.00	4.00	6.00	8.00	10.00
d.	Cost per unit of merchandise sold	90.00	90.00	90.00	90.00	90.00
e.	Rental cost per unit of merchandise sold	36.00	18.00	12.00	9.00	7.20
f.	Total phone expense	80.00	100.00	120.00	140.00	160.00
g.	Cost per unit of supplies	1.00	1.00	1.00	1.00	1.00
h.	Total insurance cost	480.00	480.00	480.00	480.00	480.00
i.	Total salary cost	$1,200.00	$1,600.00	$2,000.00	$2,400.00	$2,800.00
j.	Total cost of goods sold	1,800.00	3,600.00	5,400.00	7,200.00	9,000.00

Required

Identify each of these costs as fixed, variable, or mixed.

LO 1

Exercise 11-3   *Determining fixed cost per unit*

Henke Corporation incurs the following annual fixed costs.

Item	Cost
Depreciation	$ 50,000
Officers' salaries	120,000
Long-term lease	51,000
Property taxes	9,000

Required

Determine the total fixed cost per unit of production, assuming that Henke produces 4,000, 4,500, or 5,000 units.

Exercise 11-4 *Determining total variable cost*

LO 1

The following variable production costs apply to goods made by Watson Manufacturing Corporation.

Item	Cost per Unit
Materials	$5.00
Labor	2.50
Variable overhead	0.25
Total	$7.75

Required

Determine the total variable production cost, assuming that Watson makes 5,000, 15,000, or 25,000 units.

Exercise 11-5 *Fixed versus variable cost behavior*

LO 1, 2

Robbins Company's cost and production data for two recent months included the following.

	January	February
Production (units)	100	250
Rent	$1,500	$1,500
Utilities	$ 450	$1,125

Required

a. Separately calculate the rental cost per unit and the utilities cost per unit for both January and February.
b. Identify which cost is variable and which is fixed. Explain your answer.

Exercise 11-6 *Fixed versus variable cost behavior*

LO 1

Lovvern Trophies makes and sells trophies it distributes to little league ballplayers. The company normally produces and sells between 8,000 and 14,000 trophies per year. The following cost data apply to various activity levels.

Number of Trophies	8,000	10,000	12,000	14,000
Total costs incurred				
Fixed	$42,000			
Variable	42,000			
Total costs	$84,000			
Cost per unit				
Fixed	$ 5.25			
Variable	5.25			
Total cost per trophy	$10.50			

Required

a. Complete the preceding table by filling in the missing amounts for the levels of activity shown in the first row of the table. Round all cost per unit figures to the nearest whole penny.

b. Explain why the total cost per trophy decreases as the number of trophies increases.

LO 1, 5

Exercise 11-7   *Fixed versus variable cost behavior*

Harrel Entertainment sponsors rock concerts. The company is considering a contract to hire a band at a cost of $75,000 per concert.

Required

a. What are the total band cost and the cost per person if concert attendance is 2,000, 2,500, 3,000, 3,500, or 4,000?

b. Is the cost of hiring the band a fixed or a variable cost?

c. Draw a graph and plot total cost and cost per unit if attendance is 2,000, 2,500, 3,000, 3,500, or 4,000.

d. Identify Harrel's major business risks and explain how they can be minimized.

LO 1

Exercise 11-8   *Fixed versus variable cost behavior*

Harrel Entertainment sells souvenir T-shirts at each rock concert that it sponsors. The shirts cost $9 each. Any excess shirts can be returned to the manufacturer for a full refund of the purchase price. The sales price is $15 per shirt.

Required

a. What are the total cost of shirts and cost per shirt if sales amount to 2,000, 2,500, 3,000, 3,500, or 4,000?

b. Is the cost of T-shirts a fixed or a variable cost?

c. Draw a graph and plot total cost and cost per shirt if sales amount to 2,000, 2,500, 3,000, 3,500, or 4,000.

d. Comment on Harrel's likelihood of incurring a loss due to its operating activities.

LO 1

Exercise 11-9   *Graphing fixed cost behavior*

The following graphs depict the dollar amount of fixed cost on the vertical axes and the level of activity on the horizontal axes.

Required

a. Draw a line that depicts the relationship between total fixed cost and the level of activity.

b. Draw a line that depicts the relationship between fixed cost per unit and the level of activity.

Exercise 11-10 *Graphing variable cost behavior*

LO 1

The following graphs depict the dollar amount of variable cost on the vertical axes and the level of activity on the horizontal axes.

Total variable cost

$

Units

Variable cost per unit

$

Units

Required

a. Draw a line that depicts the relationship between total variable cost and the level of activity.

b. Draw a line that depicts the relationship between variable cost per unit and the level of activity.

Exercise 11-11 *Mixed cost at different levels of activity*

LO 1

Omar Corporation paid one of its sales representatives $4,300 during the month of March. The rep is paid a base salary plus $15 per unit of product sold. During March, the rep sold 200 units.

Required

Calculate the total monthly cost of the sales representative's salary for each of the following months.

Month	April	May	June	July
Number of units sold	240	150	250	160
Total variable cost				
Total fixed cost				
Total salary cost				

Exercise 11-12 *Using fixed cost as a competitive business strategy*

LO 1, 2

The following income statements illustrate different cost structures for two competing companies.

Income Statements		
	Company Name	
	Hank	**Rank**
Number of customers (a)	80	80
Sales revenue (a × $250)	$20,000	$20,000
Variable cost (a × $175)	N/A	(14,000)
Variable cost (a × $0)	0	N/A
Contribution margin	20,000	6,000
Fixed cost	(14,000)	0
Net income	$ 6,000	$ 6,000

Required

a. Reconstruct Hank's income statement, assuming that it serves 160 customers when it lures 80 customers away from Rank by lowering the sales price to $150 per customer.

b. Reconstruct Rank's income statement, assuming that it serves 160 customers when it lures 80 customers away from Hank by lowering the sales price to $150 per customer.

c. Explain why the price-cutting strategy increased Hank Company's profits but caused a net loss for Rank Company.

LO 3, 4

Exercise 11-13 *Using a contribution margin format income statement to measure the magnitude of operating leverage*

The following income statement was drawn from the records of Ulrich Company, a merchandising firm.

ULRICH COMPANY Income Statement For the Year Ended December 31, 2011	
Sales revenue (4,000 units × $150)	$600,000
Cost of goods sold (4,000 units × $80)	(320,000)
Gross margin	280,000
Sales commissions (10% of sales)	(60,000)
Administrative salaries expense	(90,000)
Advertising expense	(40,000)
Depreciation expense	(50,000)
Shipping and handling expenses (4,000 units × $1)	(4,000)
Net income	$ 36,000

Required

a. Reconstruct the income statement using the contribution margin format.

b. Calculate the magnitude of operating leverage.

c. Use the measure of operating leverage to determine the amount of net income Ulrich will earn if sales increase by 10 percent.

LO 4

Exercise 11-14 *Assessing the magnitude of operating leverage*

The following income statement applies to Stuart Company for the current year.

Income Statement	
Sales revenue (400 units × $25)	$10,000
Variable cost (400 units × $10)	(4,000)
Contribution margin	6,000
Fixed costs	(3,500)
Net income	$2,500

Required

a. Use the contribution margin approach to calculate the magnitude of operating leverage.

b. Use the operating leverage measure computed in Requirement *a* to determine the amount of net income that Stuart Company will earn if it experiences a 10 percent increase in revenue. The sales price per unit is not affected.

c. Verify your answer to Requirement *b* by constructing an income statement based on a 10 percent increase in sales revenue. The sales price is not affected. Calculate the percentage change in net income for the two income statements.

Exercise 11-15 *Break-even point*   **LO 6**

Connor Corporation sells products for $25 each that have variable costs of $13 per unit. Connor's annual fixed cost is $264,000.

Required

Determine the break-even point in units and dollars.

Exercise 11-16 *Desired profit*   **LO 7**

Garcia Company incurs annual fixed costs of $60,000. Variable costs for Garcia's product are $22.75 per unit, and the sales price is $35.00 per unit. Garcia desires to earn an annual profit of $45,000.

Required

Determine the sales volume in dollars and units required to earn the desired profit.

Exercise 11-17 *Determining fixed and variable cost per unit*   **LO 1**

Landry Corporation produced and sold 12,000 units of product during October. It earned a contribution margin of $96,000 on sales of $336,000 and determined that cost per unit of product was $25.

Required

Based on this information, determine the variable and fixed cost per unit of product.

Exercise 11-18 *Determining variable cost from incomplete cost data*   **LO 1**

Laya Corporation produced 200,000 watches that it sold for $16 each during 2012. The company determined that fixed manufacturing cost per unit was $7 per watch. The company reported a $800,000 gross margin on its 2011 financial statements.

Required

Determine the total variable cost, the variable cost per unit, and the total contribution margin.

Exercise 11-19 *Margin of safety*   **LO 6, 7, 8**

Information concerning a product produced by Askew Company appears here.

Sales price per unit	$145
Variable cost per unit	$55
Total annual fixed manufacturing and operating costs	$810,000

Required

Determine the following.

a. Contribution margin per unit.
b. Number of units that Askew must sell to break even.
c. Sales level in units that Askew must reach to earn a profit of $360,000.
d. Determine the margin of safety in units, sales dollars, and as a percentage.

Exercise 11-20 *Margin of safety*   **LO 8**

Jensen Company makes a product that sells for $38 per unit. The company pays $16 per unit for the variable costs of the product and incurs annual fixed costs of $176,000. Jensen expects to sell 21,000 units of product.

Required

Determine Jensen's margin of safety in units, sales dollars, and as a percentage.

PROBLEMS

|ACCOUNTING

**All applicable Problems are available with McGraw-Hill's
*Connect Accounting.***

LO 1, 5

Problem 11-21   *Identifying cost behavior*

Required

Identify the following costs as fixed or variable.
Costs related to plane trips between Seattle, Washington, and Orlando, Florida, follow. Pilots are paid on a per trip basis.

a. Pilots' salaries relative to the number of trips flown.
b. Depreciation relative to the number of planes in service.
c. Cost of refreshments relative to the number of passengers.
d. Pilots' salaries relative to the number of passengers on a particular trip.
e. Cost of a maintenance check relative to the number of passengers on a particular trip.
f. Fuel costs relative to the number of trips.

First Federal Bank operates several branch offices in grocery stores. Each branch employs a supervisor and two tellers.

g. Tellers' salaries relative to the number of tellers in a particular district.
h. Supplies cost relative to the number of transactions processed in a particular branch.
i. Tellers' salaries relative to the number of customers served at a particular branch.
j. Supervisors' salaries relative to the number of branches operated.
k. Supervisors' salaries relative to the number of customers served in a particular branch.
l. Facility rental costs relative to the size of customer deposits.

Costs related to operating a fast-food restaurant follow.

m. Depreciation of equipment relative to the number of restaurants.
n. Building rental cost relative to the number of customers served in a particular restaurant.
o. Manager's salary of a particular restaurant relative to the number of employees.
p. Food cost relative to the number of customers.
q. Utility cost relative to the number of restaurants in operation.
r. Company president's salary relative to the number of restaurants in operation.
s. Land costs relative to the number of hamburgers sold at a particular restaurant.
t. Depreciation of equipment relative to the number of customers served at a particular restaurant.

LO 1, 6

e*X*cel

CHECK FIGURES
c. Total supplies cost for
   cleaning 30 houses: $180
d. Total cost for 20 houses: $2,370

Problem 11-22   *Cost behavior and averaging*

Carlia Weaver has decided to start Carlia Cleaning, a residential house cleaning service company. She is able to rent cleaning equipment at a cost of $750 per month. Labor costs are expected to be $75 per house cleaned and supplies are expected to cost $6 per house.

Required

a. Determine the total expected cost of equipment rental and the expected cost of equipment rental per house cleaned, assuming that Carlia Cleaning cleans 10, 20, or 30 houses during one month. Is the cost of equipment a fixed or a variable cost?
b. Determine the total expected cost of labor and the expected cost of labor per house cleaned, assuming that Carlia Cleaning cleans 10, 20, or 30 houses during one month. Is the cost of labor a fixed or a variable cost?
c. Determine the total expected cost of supplies and the expected cost of supplies per house cleaned, assuming that Carlia Cleaning cleans 10, 20, or 30 houses during one month. Is the cost of supplies a fixed or a variable cost?
d. Determine the total expected cost of cleaning houses, assuming that Carlia Cleaning cleans 10, 20, or 30 houses during one month.

e. Determine the expected cost per house, assuming that Carlia Cleaning cleans 10, 20, or 30 houses during one month. Why does the cost per unit decrease as the number of houses increases?

f. If Ms. Weaver tells you that she prices her services at 25% above cost, would you assume that she means average or actual cost? Why?

Problem 11-23   *Context-sensitive nature of cost behavior classifications*

LO 5

CHECK FIGURE
b. Average teller cost for 60,000 transactions: $1.50

Pacific Bank's start-up division establishes new branch banks. Each branch opens with three tellers. Total teller cost per branch is $90,000 per year. The three tellers combined can process up to 90,000 customer transactions per year. If a branch does not attain a volume of at least 60,000 transactions during its first year of operations, it is closed. If the demand for services exceeds 90,000 transactions, an additional teller is hired, and the branch is transferred from the start-up division to regular operations.

Required

a. What is the relevant range of activity for new branch banks?

b. Determine the amount of teller cost in total and the teller cost per transaction for a branch that processes 60,000, 70,000, 80,000, or 90,000 transactions. In this case (the activity base is the number of transactions for a specific branch), is the teller cost a fixed or a variable cost?

c. Determine the amount of teller cost in total and the teller cost per branch for Pacific Bank, assuming that the start-up division operates 10, 15, 20, or 25 branches. In this case (the activity base is the number of branches), is the teller cost a fixed or a variable cost?

Problem 11-24   *Context-sensitive nature of cost behavior classifications*

LO 5

CHECK FIGURES
a. Average cost at 400 units: $200
b. Average price at 250 units: $265

Susan Hicks operates a sales booth in computer software trade shows, selling an accounting software package, *Dollar System.* She purchases the package from a software manufacturer for $175 each. Booth space at the convention hall costs $10,000 per show.

Required

a. Sales at past trade shows have ranged between 200 and 400 software packages per show. Determine the average cost of sales per unit if Ms. Hicks sells 200, 250, 300, 350, or 400 units of *Dollar System* at a trade show. Use the following chart to organize your answer. Is the cost of booth space fixed or variable?

	Sales Volume in Units (a)				
	200	**250**	**300**	**350**	**400**
Total cost of software (a × $175)	$35,000				
Total cost of booth rental	10,000				
Total cost of sales (b)	$45,000				
Average cost per unit (b ÷ a)	$ 225				

b. If Ms. Hicks wants to earn a $50 profit on each package of software she sells at a trade show, what price must she charge at sales volumes of 200, 250, 300, 350, or 400 units?

c. Record the total cost of booth space if Ms. Hicks attends one, two, three, four, or five trade shows. Record your answers in the following chart. Is the cost of booth space fixed or variable relative to the number of shows attended?

	Number of Trade Shows Attended				
	1	**2**	**3**	**4**	**5**
Total cost of booth rental	$10,000				

d. Ms. Hicks provides decorative shopping bags to customers who purchase software packages. Some customers take the bags; others do not. Some customers stuff more than one software package into a single bag. The number of bags varies in relation to the number of units sold, but the relationship is not proportional. Assume that Ms. Hicks uses $30 of bags for every 50 software packages sold. What is the additional cost per unit sold? Is the cost fixed or variable?

Problem 11-25 *Effects of operating leverage on profitability*

Webster Training Services (WTS) provides instruction on the use of computer software for the employees of its corporate clients. It offers courses in the clients' offices on the clients' equipment. The only major expense WTS incurs is instructor salaries; it pays instructors $5,000 per course taught. WTS recently agreed to offer a course of instruction to the employees of Chambers Incorporated at a price of $400 per student. Chambers estimated that 20 students would attend the course.

Base your answer on the preceding information.

Part 1:

Required

a. Relative to the number of students in a single course, is the cost of instruction a fixed or a variable cost?

b. Determine the profit, assuming that 20 students attend the course.

c. Determine the profit, assuming a 10 percent increase in enrollment (i.e., enrollment increases to 22 students). What is the percentage change in profitability?

d. Determine the profit, assuming a 10 percent decrease in enrollment (i.e., enrollment decreases to 18 students). What is the percentage change in profitability?

e. Explain why a 10 percent shift in enrollment produces more than a 10 percent shift in profitability. Use the term that identifies this phenomenon.

Part 2:

The instructor has offered to teach the course for a percentage of tuition fees. Specifically, she wants $250 per person attending the class. Assume that the tuition fee remains at $400 per student.

Required

f. Is the cost of instruction a fixed or a variable cost?

g. Determine the profit, assuming that 20 students take the course.

h. Determine the profit, assuming a 10 percent increase in enrollment (i.e., enrollment increases to 22 students). What is the percentage change in profitability?

i. Determine the profit, assuming a 10 percent decrease in enrollment (i.e., enrollment decreases to 18 students). What is the percentage change in profitability?

j. Explain why a 10 percent shift in enrollment produces a proportional 10 percent shift in profitability.

Part 3:

WTS sells a workbook with printed material unique to each course to each student who attends the course. Any workbooks that are not sold must be destroyed. Prior to the first class, WTS printed 20 copies of the books based on the client's estimate of the number of people who would attend the course. Each workbook costs $25 and is sold to course participants for $40. This cost includes a royalty fee paid to the author and the cost of duplication.

Required

k. Calculate the workbook cost in total and per student, assuming that 18, 20, or 22 students attempt to attend the course.

l. Classify the cost of workbooks as fixed or variable relative to the number of students attending the course.

m. Discuss the risk of holding inventory as it applies to the workbooks.

n. Explain how a just-in-time inventory system can reduce the cost and risk of holding inventory.

Problem 11-26 *Effects of fixed and variable cost behavior on the risk and rewards*
of business opportunities

LO 1, 2

Eastern and Western Universities offer executive training courses to corporate clients. Eastern pays
its instructors $5,310 per course taught. Western pays its instructors $295 per student enrolled in
the class. Both universities charge executives a $340 tuition fee per course attended.

CHECK FIGURES
a. Western NI: $810
b. NI: $2,610

Required

a. Prepare income statements for Eastern and Western, assuming that 18 students attend a course.

b. Eastern University embarks on a strategy to entice students from Western University by lowering its tuition to $220 per course. Prepare an income statement for Eastern, assuming that the university is successful and enrolls 36 students in its course.

c. Western University embarks on a strategy to entice students from Eastern University by lowering its tuition to $220 per course. Prepare an income statement for Western, assuming that the university is successful and enrolls 36 students in its course.

d. Explain why the strategy described in Requirement *b* produced a profit but the same strategy described in Requirement *c* produced a loss.

e. Prepare income statements for Eastern and Western Universities, assuming that 15 students attend a course, assuming that both universities charge executives a $340 tuition fee per course attended.

f. It is always better to have fixed than variable cost. Explain why this statement is false.

g. It is always better to have variable than fixed cost. Explain why this statement is false.

Problem 11-27 *Analyzing operating leverage*

LO 3, 4

Justin Zinder is a venture capitalist facing two alternative investment opportunities. He intends
to invest $1 million in a start-up firm. He is nervous, however, about future economic volatility.
He asks you to analyze the following financial data for the past year's operations of the two firms
he is considering and give him some business advice.

CHECK FIGURES
b. % of change for Kelley: 45.16
c. % of change for Ensley: (18.06)

	Company Name	
	Ensley	**Kelley**
Variable cost per unit (a)	$21.00	$10.50
Sales revenue (8,000 units × $28)	$224,000	$224,000
Variable cost (8,000 units × a)	(168,000)	(84,000)
Contribution margin	56,000	140,000
Fixed cost	(25,000)	(109,000)
Net income	$ 31,000	$ 31,000

Required

a. Use the contribution margin approach to compute the operating leverage for each firm.

b. If the economy expands in coming years, Ensley and Kelley will both enjoy a 10 percent per year increase in sales, assuming that the selling price remains unchanged. Compute the change in net income for each firm in dollar amount and in percentage. (*Note:* Because the number of units increases, both revenue and variable cost will increase.)

c. If the economy contracts in coming years, Ensley and Kelley will both suffer a 10 percent decrease in sales volume, assuming that the selling price remains unchanged. Compute the change in net income for each firm in dollar amount and in percentage. (*Note:* Because the number of units decreases, both total revenue and total variable cost will decrease.)

d. Write a memo to Justin Zinder with your analyses and advice.

Problem 11-28 *Determining the break-even point and preparing a contribution*
margin income statement

LO 3, 6

Inman Manufacturing Company makes a product that it sells for $60 per unit. The company incurs
variable manufacturing costs of $24 per unit. Variable selling expenses are $12 per unit, annual fixed
manufacturing costs are $189,000, and fixed selling and administrative costs are $141,000 per year.

CHECK FIGURE
a. 13,750 units

Required

Determine the break-even point in units and dollars using the following approaches.

a. Equation method.

b. Contribution margin per unit.

c. Contribution margin ratio.

d. Confirm your results by preparing a contribution margin income statement for the break-even sales volume.

LO 8

Problem 11-29 *Margin of safety and operating leverage*

Santiago Company is considering the addition of a new product to its cosmetics line. The company has three distinctly different options: a skin cream, a bath oil, or a hair coloring gel. Relevant information and budgeted annual income statements for each of the products follow.

	Relevant Information		
	Skin Cream	**Bath Oil**	**Color Gel**
Budgeted sales in units (a)	50,000	90,000	30,000
Expected sales price (b)	$7.00	$4.00	$13.00
Variable costs per unit (c)	$4.00	$1.50	$ 9.00
Income Statements			
Sales revenue (a × b)	$350,000	$360,000	$390,000
Variable costs (a × c)	(200,000)	(135,000)	(270,000)
Contribution margin	150,000	225,000	120,000
Fixed costs	(120,000)	(210,000)	(104,000)
Net income	$ 30,000	$ 15,000	$ 16,000

Required

a. Determine the margin of safety as a percentage for each product.

b. Prepare revised income statements for each product, assuming a 20 percent increase in the budgeted sales volume.

c. For each product, determine the percentage change in net income that results from the 20 percent increase in sales. Which product has the highest operating leverage?

d. Assuming that management is pessimistic and risk averse, which product should the company add to its cosmetic line? Explain your answer.

e. Assuming that management is optimistic and risk aggressive, which product should the company add to its cosmetics line? Explain your answer.

ANALYZE, THINK, COMMUNICATE

ATC 11-1 Business Applications *Operating leverage*

Description of Business for Amazon.com, Inc.

Amazon.com opened its virtual doors on the World Wide Web in July 1995 and we offer Earth's Biggest Selection. We seek to be Earth's most customer-centric company for three primary customer sets: consumer customers, seller customers and developer customers. In addition, we generate revenue through co-branded credit card agreements and other marketing and promotional services, such as online advertising.

Amazon.com	2008	2007
Operating revenue	$19,166	$14,835
Operating earnings	842	655

Description of Business for CSX, Inc.

CSX Corporations ("CSX") together with its subsidiaries (the "Company"), based in Jacksonville, Florida, is one of the nation's leading transportation suppliers. The Company's rail and inter-modal businesses provide rail-based transportation services including traditional rail service and the transport of intermodal containers and trailers.

CSX, Inc.	2008	2007
Operating revenue	$11,255	$10,030
Operating earnings	2,768	2,260

Required

a. Determine which company appears to have the higher operating leverage.

b. Write a paragraph or two explaining why the company you identified in Requirement *a* might be expected to have the higher operating leverage.

c. If revenues for both companies declined, which company do you think would likely experience the greater decline in operating earnings? Explain your answer.

ATC 11-2   Group Assignment   *Operating leverage*

The Parent Teacher Association (PTA) of Meadow High School is planning a fund-raising campaign. The PTA is considering the possibility of hiring Eric Logan, a world-renowned investment counselor, to address the public. Tickets would sell for $28 each. The school has agreed to let the PTA use Harville Auditorium at no cost. Mr. Logan is willing to accept one of two compensation arrangements. He will sign an agreement to receive a fixed fee of $10,000 regardless of the number of tickets sold. Alternatively, he will accept payment of $20 per ticket sold. In communities similar to that in which Meadow is located, Mr. Logan has drawn an audience of approximately 500 people.

Required

a. In front of the class, present a statement showing the expected net income assuming 500 people buy tickets.

b. Divide the class into groups and then organize the groups into four sections. Assign one of the following tasks to each section of groups.

Group Tasks

(1) Assume the PTA pays Mr. Logan a fixed fee of $10,000. Determine the amount of net income that the PTA will earn if ticket sales are 10 percent higher than expected. Calculate the percentage change in net income.

(2) Assume that the PTA pays Mr. Logan a fixed fee of $10,000. Determine the amount of net income that the PTA will earn if ticket sales are 10 percent lower than expected. Calculate the percentage change in net income.

(3) Assume that the PTA pays Mr. Logan $20 per ticket sold. Determine the amount of net income that the PTA will earn if ticket sales are 10 percent higher than expected. Calculate the percentage change in net income.

(4) Assume that the PTA pays Mr. Logan $20 per ticket sold. Determine the amount of net income that the PTA will earn if ticket sales are 10 percent lower than expected. Calculate the percentage change in net income.

c. Have each group select a spokesperson. Have one of the spokespersons in each section of groups go to the board and present the results of the analysis conducted in Requirement *b*. Resolve any discrepancies in the computations presented at the board and those developed by the other groups.

d. Draw conclusions regarding the risks and rewards associated with operating leverage. At a minimum, answer the following questions.

(1) Which type of cost structure (fixed or variable) produces the higher growth potential in profitability for a company?

(2) Which type of cost structure (fixed or variable) produces the higher risk of declining profitability for a company?

(3) Under what circumstances should a company seek to establish a fixed cost structure?

(4) Under what circumstances should a company seek to establish a variable cost structure?

ATC 11-3   Research Assignment   *Fixed versus variable cost*

Use the 2008 Form 10-K for Black & Decker Corp. (B&D) to complete the requirements below. To obtain the Form 10-K you can use the EDGAR system following the instructions in Appendix A, or it can be found under "Investor Relations" on the company's corporate website: www.bdk.com. Be sure to read carefully the following portions of the document.

■ "General Development of the Business" on page 1.

■ "Consolidated Statement of Earnings" on page 36.

Required

a. Calculate the percentage decrease in B&D's sales and its "operating income" from 2007 to 2008.

b. Would fixed costs or variable costs be more likely to explain why B&D's operating earnings decreased by a bigger percentage than its sales?

c. On page 42 B&D reported that it incurred product development costs of $146 million in 2008. If this cost is thought of in the context of the number of units of products sold, should it be considered as primarily fixed or variable in nature?

d. If the product development costs are thought of in the context of the number of new products developed, should it be considered as primarily fixed or variable in nature?

ATC 11-4   Writing Assignment   *Operating leverage, margin of safety, and cost behavior*

In the early years of the 21st century the housing market in the United States was booming. Housing prices were increasing rapidly, new houses were being constructed at a record pace, and companies doing business in the construction and home improvement industry were enjoying rising profits. In 2006 the real estate market had slowed considerably, and the slump continued through 2007.

Home Depot was one major company in the building supplies industry that was adversely affected by the slowdown in the housing market. On August 14, 2007, it announced that its revenues for the first half of the year were 3 percent lower than revenues were for the first six months of 2006. Of even greater concern was the fact that its earnings for the first half of 2007 were 21 percent lower than for the same period in the prior year.

Required

Write a memorandum that explains how a 3 percent decline in sales could cause a 21 percent decline in profits. Your memo should address the following:

a. An identification of the accounting concept involved.

b. A discussion of how various major types of costs incurred by Home Depot were likely affected by the decline in its sales.

c. The effect of the decline in sales on Home Depot's margin of safety.

ATC 11-5   Ethical Dilemma   *Profitability versus social conscience (effects of cost behavior)*

Advances in biological technology have enabled two research companies, Bio Labs Inc. and Scientific Associates, to develop an insect-resistant corn seed. Neither company is financially strong enough to develop the distribution channels necessary to bring the product to world markets. World Agra Distributors Inc. has negotiated contracts with both companies for the exclusive right to market their seed. Bio Labs signed an agreement to receive an annual royalty of $1,000,000. In contrast, Scientific Associates chose an agreement that provides for a royalty of $0.50 per pound of seed sold. Both agreements have a 10-year term. During 2010, World Agra sold approximately 1,600,000 pounds of the Bio Labs Inc. seed and 2,400,000 pounds of the Scientific Associates seed. Both types of seed were sold for $1.25 per pound. By the end of 2010, it was apparent that the seed developed by Scientific Associates was superior. Although insect infestation was virtually nonexistent for both types of seed, the seed developed by Scientific Associates produced corn that was sweeter and had consistently higher yields.

World Agra Distributors' chief financial officer, Roger Weatherstone, recently retired. To the astonishment of the annual planning committee, Mr. Weatherstone's replacement, Ray Borrough, adamantly recommended that the marketing department develop a major advertising campaign to promote the seed developed by Bio Labs Inc. The planning committee reluctantly approved the recommendation. A $100,000 ad campaign was launched; the ads emphasized the ability of the Bio Labs seed to avoid insect infestation. The campaign was silent with respect to taste or crop yield. It did not mention the seed developed by Scientific Associates. World Agra's sales staff was instructed to push the Bio Labs seed and to sell the Scientific Associates seed only on customer demand. Although total sales remained relatively constant during 2011, sales of the Scientific Associates seed fell to approximately 1,300,000 pounds while sales of the Bio Labs Inc. seed rose to 2,700,000 pounds.

Required

a. Determine the amount of increase or decrease in profitability experienced by World Agra in 2011 as a result of promoting Bio Labs seed. Support your answer with appropriate commentary.

b. Did World Agra's customers in particular and society in general benefit or suffer from the decision to promote the Bio Labs seed?

c. Review the standards of ethical conduct in Exhibit 10.17 of Chapter 10 and comment on whether Mr. Borrough's recommendation violated any of the principles in the Statement of Ethical Professional Practice.

d. Comment on your belief regarding the adequacy of the Statement of Ethical Professional Practice for Managerial Accountants to direct the conduct of management accountants.